This [illegible] ture's
great [illegible] loped
from [illegible] ry of
Euge [illegible] f the
worl [illegible] d by
supe [illegible] thers,
it pr [illegible] and
the c [illegible] rough
the a [illegible]

Each [illegible] ersity
and [illegible] Tufts
Univ [illegible] lliam
Burt [illegible] npan-
ion v [illegible] *of the*
Earl [illegible] neral
edito [illegible]

Eight Great Tragedies

Edited by

SYLVAN BARNET
MORTON BERMAN
WILLIAM BURTO

A MERIDIAN BOOK

ork,

Z, England
stralia
to, Ontario,

Penguin Books (N.Z.) Ltd, 182-190 Wairau Road, Auckland 10, New Zealand

Penguin Books Ltd, Registered Offices: Harmondsworth, Middlesex, England

Published by Meridian, an imprint of Dutton Signet, a division of Penguin Books USA Inc. Previously published in a Mentor edition.

First Meridian Printing, July, 1996
10 9 8 7 6

REGISTERED TRADEMARK—MARCA REGISTRADA

ISBN: 0-452-01172-8
CIP data is available.

Printed in the United States of America

Grateful acknowledgment is made to the following for permission to quote from the works listed.

Beacon Press, Inc. (Boston) for Aeschylus' *Prometheus Bound*, translated by E. A. Havelock. Copyright 1950 by the Beacon Press.

Cambridge University Press (New York and London) for Sophocles' *Oedipus the King*, translated by J. T. Sheppard; and for Aristotle's *Poetics*, translated by L. J. Potts.

Jonathan Cape Ltd. (London) for August Strindberg's *Miss Julie* (Original title: *Lady Julie*), translated by C. D. Locock, from *Lucky Peter's Travels;* and for *Desire Under the Elms*, from *All God's Chillun Got Wings*, by Eugene O'Neill.

Chatto and Windus Ltd. (London) for a selection from *Shakespeare's Problem Plays*, by E. M. W. Tillyard.

J. M. Dent & Sons Ltd. (London) for Eurpides' *Hippolytus*, translated by F. L. Lucas, from *Greek Drama for Everyman.*

Harcourt Brace Jovanovich, Inc. (New York) for a selection from *Principles of Literary Criticism*, by I. A. Richards.

William Heinemann Ltd. (London) for Henrik Ibsen's *Ghosts*, translated by William Archer, from *Collected Plays of Henrik Ibsen.*

Joseph Wood Krutch for *The Tragic Fallacy*, from *The Modern Temper*. Copyright 1929 by Harcourt, Brace and Company, Inc.

The Macmillan Company of Canada Ltd. (Toronto) for *On Baile's Strand*, by William Butler Yeats, from *Collected Plays of W. B. Yeats.*

Macmillan & Co., Ltd. (London) for *On Baile's Strand*, by William Butler Yeats, from *Collected Plays of W. B. Yeats.*

The Macmillan Company (New York) for Euripides' *Hippolytus*, translated by F. L. Lucas, from *Greek Drama for Everyman;* for *On Baile's Strand*, by William Butler Yeats, from *Collected Plays of W. B. Yeats.*

Ogden Nash for lines from "The Emancipation of Mr. Poplin," originally published in *The New Yorker* magazine. Copyright © 1954 by Ogden Nash.

Random House, Inc. for *Desire Under the Elms*, by Eugene O'Neill. Copyright 1924, 1952 by Eugene O'Neill.

Routledge & Kegan Paul, Ltd. (London) for a selection from *Principles of Literary Criticism*, by I. A. Richards.

E. M. W. Tillyard for a selection from *Shakespeare's Problem Plays*, by E. M. W. Tillyard.

University of Toronto Press for a selection from *Shakespeare's Problem Plays*, by E. M. W. Tillyard.

Mrs. William Butler Yeats for *On Baile's Strand*, by William Butler Yeats, from *Collected Plays of W. B. Yeats.*

CONTENTS

GENERAL INTRODUCTION

In Greek the word "tragedy" means "goat song," but the connection between tragedy and goat song is obscure. Perhaps a goat was the prize at some sort of early singing contest in Greece, or perhaps the dancers wore goat skins. One medieval writer ingeniously suggested that tragedy is called goat song because it begins prosperously, as a goat is abundantly hairy in front, and ends wretchedly, as a goat is bare in the rear. Dante Alighieri, whose *Divine Comedy* proves him to be the greatest poet of the Middle Ages, offered the engaging idea that tragedy is so called because its story is unpleasant and smelly as a goat.

The American public does not greatly approve of goat songs. We are an independent, optimistic people and like to feel that we can do anything we please. Our movies, for example, specialize in success stories with happy endings, and Hollywood has almost banished death from the screen. If there is a death in a film, it is likely to be that of either a villain or a minor character. Deaths of villains comfort us, and the death of a minor good character, such as the hero's friend (a so-called "secondary tragedy"), allows us to indulge in sentiment and yet come through smiling. Ogden Nash has summarized the dominant American view:

> To tragedy I have no addiction;
> What I always say is there's enough trouble in real life without reading about it in fiction.
> However, I don't mind tears and smiles in a judicious blending,
> And I enjoy a stormy beginning if it leads to a halcyon ending.[1]

Most people would agree with Mr. Nash that tragedy depicts man's troubles. But this is only half the story, for tragic drama

[1]"The Emancipation of Mr. Poplin," *The New Yorker,* May 8, 1954, p. 30.

does not stop with troubles, but goes on to achieve some sort of affirmation, and thus it is optimistic rather than (as commonly thought) pessimistic.

The words "optimism" and "pessimism" are, of course, too simple to summarize anything so complex as tragic drama, but however imprecise, they are relevant because they correctly imply that tragedy makes statements about mankind and the universe in which he finds himself. Tragic drama, then, is related to philosophy, and it is not an accident that the great Greek tragedies were produced during the age of Socrates and Plato, in the middle of the fifth century B.C. Philosophers, however, tend to distrust the insights of dramatists, for philosophers usually like well-defined terms and consistent rational arguments. For example, although Plato was a literary master, he scorned the poets (including dramatists) and in the *Laws* banished them from his ideal city. Plato and Socrates believed that man is capable of rational choice and that a bad choice is the result of faulty or insufficient thinking. But according to poets (notably Homer), the gods may sometimes madden or blind a man so that his action is not the result of thought at all. The tragedian is an especially dangerous poet because he depicts not rational but emotional men, and in addition to imitating or depicting emotion rather than reason he seeks to induce in his audience sympathy, an emotional rather than a rational response. Furthermore, Plato charges, the poet not only appeals to emotion but by showing excessive and unjustified suffering suggests that the gods are partly responsible for evil and that a morally good life is not always a happy life. Plato here is not so far, then, from the man in the street who wants to see the good man amply rewarded.

Nor is Plato the only philosopher critical of the moral effect of tragedy. Jean-Jacques Rousseau, for example, in the late eighteenth century, restated Plato's idea that dramatists play on the spectators' emotions and induce pointless and unthinking tears. An ardent reformer, Rousseau further objected that at a drama the audience is urged by catchy speeches to weep but not to *do* anything to set the world's affairs in order. Now, such criticisms as those of Plato and Rousseau are sufficient indications that although drama is not philosophy, it deals with morality. When a moralist is disturbed by tragedy, his reaction suggests (even though he may fail to realize it) not that tragedy has nothing to do with morals, but that tragedy implies a different set of ethical assumptions. While one can never say with certainty why something did or did *not* happen, nevertheless we may hazard the suggestion that some cultures have never produced tragic drama because their ethical systems stifle it.

Among tragedy's basic assumptions is the value of the individual's life. Societies (such as some in the Orient) which believe in reincarnation seem to worry very little about suffering in this life, especially because suffering may merely be payment for immoral behavior during a previous existence, and, in any event, the soul goes through so many physical bodies that the conflicts of any particular incarnation are, in the long view, trivial. In India Shakespeare's tragedies seem superficial, for the dominant creeds in the East suggest that "Life is an infinite Paradise. They who write tragedies are not yet enlightened."[1] On the other hand, most Westerners feel that the Indians lack sufficient respect for the body and for human life. In their quest for purity, the Indians appear to us to be insufficiently interested in man as we know him. The *Bhagavad-Gita* (Song of God), for example, a sacred Hindu text, justifies war on the grounds that death is unimportant. The Orient, we are told, accepts death without agitation, but most Westerners can easily sympathize with Shakespeare's Claudio in *Measure for Measure:*

> The weariest and most loathed worldly life,
> That age, ache, penury, and imprisonment
> Can lay on nature is a paradise
> To what we fear of death.

Death, we ought to note, is the most common of tragic endings, though some tragic dramas conclude with spiritual rather than physical decay, and many do not end with any sort of death. Aristotle did not focus on the ending, but said merely that tragedy was an imitation of a serious action. For Shakespeare and the other Elizabethans, however, as for most of us, death is the most common tragic outcome. The Elizabethan (and modern) concept was heavily influenced by the medieval idea that tragedy described a reversal from good fortune to bad, but whereas the Middle Ages merely demanded such a reversal, and did not bother to motivate the change but allowed Fate or Fortune to bring it about, the Elizabethans sought to see something other than the workings of a fickle goddess, and to this degree Elizabethan resembles Greek tragedy. In most of the tragedies of Greece and Elizabethan England suffering and

[1]Quoted in Ranjee G. Shahani, *Shakespeare through Eastern Eyes* (London: H. Joseph, 1932), p. 113.

catastrophes are partly explained, but the explanations are not so pat as to make trivial the pain or death which the heroes experience.

The tragic hero generally passes from prosperity to woe, but this movement is not merely downhill. The pain which he undergoes is often partly self-inflicted, for he willfully violates an existing code. He insists on expressing himself, even though he must suffer for his self-assertion. Thus, Aeschylus' Prometheus boldly admits that he defied Zeus's commands, and O'Neill's Abbie glories in her violation of God's edict. Most of the acts of self-assertion are the result of pride, or what the Greeks called *hybris;* the hero sets himself up as in some way equal or superior to the cosmic powers, or at least he sees himself as an extraordinary man—and he is. He often knows that he will have to suffer for his action, yet he chooses to express his mind at the expense of his body, and even of his peace of mind. He is impious or irrational, but awesome because he is "larger" than an ordinary man. The act which undoes the tragic hero, however, is, according to Aristotle, *hamartia,* or an error. Whether Aristotle meant it was a moral flaw or simply an intellectual mistake—or both—is uncertain, but great tragedies have been written with heroes of each sort. The important point is that calamity proceeds from within: the hero is not arbitrarily struck down, but has in some way contributed to his fall. "Misfortunes," Oscar Wilde said, "one can endure—they come from outside, they are accidents. But to suffer for one's own faults—ah!—there is the sting of life." Nor need the action which produces calamity be a fault; indeed, the tragedy may result from the hero's very virtue—his overwhelming love or nobility of spirit. But for Aristotle, the heroic act is a flaw because (as his treatise on ethics reveals) he believed that the good life generally consists not in one or a few intense and heroic acts, but in the lifelong practice of moderation.

Intentions may be good, but they may produce painful results, unforeseen yet logical. Cordelia, King Lear's loving daughter, summarizes one kind of tragic plight:

> We are not the first
> Who with best meaning have incurred the worst.

When the tragic hero's actions produce not the results he anticipated but contrary results (perhaps suffering instead of joy), they are said to be ironic, and the irony is heightened if the audience and not the character is first aware of the outcome. Thus, Oedipus searches diligently for a murderer and at last finds out what we already know: that he himself is the guilty man. Dramatic irony, it should be noted, is distinct from verbal irony, wherein the speaker is *conscious* that his words mean the opposite of what they say on the surface. When an instructor says to a student who is doing badly in a course, "You are in a fine spot," the words mean the opposite of what they say, and both instructor and student are conscious of the real significance of the words. The tragic hero, however, often does *not* at first understand the implications of his own words or actions.

When he asserts himself, the tragic hero is committed, sometimes unconsciously, to consequent suffering. But when troubles come—and they usually come not as single spies but in battalions—he accepts them (never passively, and usually defiantly) and, indeed, may glory in his act and in the suffering it brings. Or he may perceive the folly of his action. But whatever his attitude toward the mistake or flaw (*hamartia*) or heroic action which precipitates his fall, the punishment or suffering is so disproportionate that it usually destroys the hero's body. The destruction of the body is, however, often accompanied by such an enlargement of spirit that, no matter how awful the consequences of the error, the hero has, we feel, in a way triumphed over them and subjugated them by his greatness of mind. He reveals the full extent of his powers only under the most tremendous of pressures, and these pressures are somewhat dwarfed by his expansion. This is man's victory.

All tragedies portray suffering, and critics have often sought to find in this suffering the special pleasure which tragedy affords. Some theorists, notably Thomas Hobbes, famous for his suggestion that man's life is nasty, brutish, and short, have suggested that our pleasure is sadistic, that we enjoy contemplating the suffering of our fellows, and that attendance at a tragedy is a dignified version of watching a public execution. Lucretius, the Roman poet, took a somewhat milder view by asserting that when we are safe on land we enjoy watching a disaster at sea, not because we delight in the pains of others but because it is pleasant to perceive vividly the evils from which we are exempt. On the other hand, some critics have claimed that we identify ourselves with the tragic sufferer and derive pleasure from feeling ourselves mistreated. But although mankind includes masochists—people who enjoy being made to suffer—masochism, like sadism, is too narrow to explain the pleasures of tragedy. Similarly, the idea that tragedy excites sympathy, and sympathy is in itself a pleasurable passion, is surely not sufficient to explain the appeal of tragic drama. If sympathy afforded such pleasure, a hospital, as David Hume, the English philosopher, wrote to Adam Smith, "would be a more entertaining place than a Ball."

Literary criticism from Aristotle to the present is filled with attempts (all more or less unsuccessful) to explain our interest in tragedy. Yet whatever the secret be, those who respond to tragedy see in it not merely rich language or a well-organized story, but a meaningful picture of life, a picture which by its truth to nature clarifies—if only darkly and for a moment—our view of man's existence. There is, of course, an opposition view. Stephen Gosson, an Elizabethan Puritan, himself a reformed playwright, rejected tragedies as idle or evil entertainments. "The argument [plot] of tragedies," he wrote, "is wrath, cruelty, incest, injury, murther, either violent by sword, or voluntary by poison. The persons [are] gods, goddesses, furies, fiends, kings, queens, and mighty men. . . . The best play you can pick out is but a mixture of good and evil; how can it then be the schoolmistress of life?" When all of Gosson's charges have been admitted, there remains the fact that so long as man is composed of good and evil, and so long as the universe retains some of its enigmas, great tragedies will afford men insight into mysteries otherwise unfathomed.

PART ONE
THE TRAGEDIES

Aeschylus: *PROMETHEUS BOUND*

A tragedy, like all other works of art, is an organized entity, and thus it suggests the possibility of organization or order in the universe. Tragedy, then, resembles philosophy in its attempt to discern a pattern in the nature of things. Out of the raw material of chaotic human experience the tragic poet forges a system wherein he shows—to a degree—the relation between facts which we might otherwise think unconnected. He does not supply easy answers to the problem of good and evil; rather, he often shows the inadequacy of simple systems of mortality. But he implies, however dimly, that man's deeds are worth something and that if the ethical systems of philosophers and theologians are not wholly satisfying, there *is* nevertheless a system, even if it is imperfectly seen and not such as we would desire.

No great dramatist was more concerned to see the pattern in things, the organization of material, than Aeschylus, and he freely reworked into a new form the ancient Greek legends. Prometheus was one of the Titans, a race of giants; he was a local Athenian patron of smiths and potters because, according to the myth, he had stolen fire from the Olympians and given it to man. Zeus, king of the Olympians, punished man by creating Pandora, the first woman, and punished Prometheus by imprisoning him in a post, or, according to another tradition, by having a vulture daily devour his liver (renewed each night) while he was chained to a pillar in the mountains. Other tales of Prometheus told how he laughed behind Zeus's back after he had deceived him into choosing the bones and fat of an animal instead of the more desirable meat. In short, the stories lacked a central meaning, though they agreed that Prometheus had tricked Zeus, benefited man by giving him fire, and suffered for his deed.

The flame which Prometheus had stolen from the fiery chariot of the sun represents, on one level, illumination, and on another, technology or skill. As Sophocles was later to proclaim in a great chorus in *Antigone,* man has acquired numerous skills—but skillful or not, he must not transgress the moral law, for there is no relation between, on the one hand, manual dexterity and the intelligence to make nature serve one's purpose, and, on the other, insight into the moral nature of the universe. Expert mechanics, doctors, and pilots are not, that is to say, necessarily good men. Aeschylus tells us that Prometheus consciously gave fire to man in an effort to improve the wretched lot of humanity. When the Titans struggled with the Olympians, Prometheus, the most intelligent of the Titans, seeing that mere brute force would not win, sided with the Olympians. Aided by Prometheus, Zeus usurped the throne from his father, Kronos, and determined to wipe out man. Prometheus thereupon deserted Zeus, aided man, and was chained to the mountain. Aeschylus' drama opens with the enchainment.

The play is difficult to interpret because it is only one of three plays which show Aeschylus' interpretation of the myth, and the other two are lost. In *Prometheus Unbound,* of which a few fragments are extant, he probably showed the reconciliation of the Titan and the King, and in *Prometheus the Firebringer* Aeschylus may have dramatized the introduction into Athens of the festival of Prometheus, the running of an annual torch race. But Aeschylus' exact solution to the conflict is unknown, though some fairly sound conjectures can be made. First, we can agree to reject Karl Marx's suggestion that the play foreshadows the working class bearing the chains of capitalism. Next we might note that despite the meaning of Prometheus' name (Forethinker), he does not know quite so much as he thinks, for he seems to believe that Zeus will necessarily be overthrown by his own son, whereas the prophecy is really conditional: *if* Zeus weds Thetis he will produce a son greater than himself and will be overthrown, even as Zeus had overthrown his father. But ultimately Prometheus revealed this secret, and Thetis, later wedded to Peleus, bore Achilles, who became, as predicted, greater than his father. Prometheus' secret, then, is not exactly what he believes it to be, and, indeed, the name "Forethinker" or "Forethought" probably refers as much to the ability of the technician to foresee how skill can be applied (as the carpenter sees the planks or even the ship in the unhewn tree) as to the deep religious prophetic gift.

We know that Aeschylus envisioned some sort of reconciliation between the protagonists, a compromise which has offended those who feel that Zeus is absolutely evil. Shelley, in his verse drama, *Prometheus Unbound,* for example, believing that Aeschylus abandoned the principle of resistance to tyrants, rejected all compromise and suggested that the only solution was for Zeus to fall. Shelley's tyrant dissolves as soon as Prometheus' heart is purged of all hate. Aeschylus believed Zeus was more enduring, though he is not depicted as omnipotent. The king of the Olympians is subject to Fate, and thus, like man, he is partly molded by forces outside of himself. If we can borrow from other Aeschylean plays, through suffering Zeus learned righteousness. Zeus learned, freed his old enemies, the Titans, spared man, and granted release to Prometheus. Prometheus, too, perhaps, learned through pain that although he had from lofty motives aided man, obedience to higher powers is a duty, and he must pay for disobeying Zeus's law.

The basic conflict in the drama is clear enough, and sufficient evidence exists for us to say that Aeschylus ultimately envisioned some sort of reconciliation between Power and Intelligence, for his gods as well as his men (Prometheus, though not a man, partly symbolizes mankind) learn, and their wisdom is painfully acquired. But the inclusion of Io, tormented because she rejected Zeus's lustful advances, in this play suggests yet another view of suffering. The speeches on the evolution of civilization are relevant not only to Prometheus' gift to man and to the concept of an evolving mortality, but to the final reconciliation, for Io will ultimately bear an Egyptian king who will reunite with Greece and whose line will at length produce Heracles' mother. The son of Zeus, Heracles, will, with his father's permission, slay with his bow the vulture tormenting Prometheus. Heracles, then, will in a way be the symbol of the union between Io and Zeus. In another of Aeschylus' plays, *The Suppliants,* we learn that Zeus had tormented Io not out of malice but because, mysteriously and pitiably, only through suffering can she arrive at a final blessedness. Perhaps, then, Zeus in our play is not solely what Prometheus thinks he is, and suffering may play a necessary role in a moral universe.

Aeschylus: Biographical Note. The first great dramatist of the Western world, Aeschylus was noted in his day not only for his ninety plays (mostly tragedies, though some were lewd burlesques) but also for his heroism in battle. He was born near Athens in 525 B.C. and died in Sicily in 456/5 B.C. He presented his first play in 499 B.C., fought the Persians in the Battle of Marathon in 490 B.C., and perhaps fought them again in the decisive victory which Athens won at Salamis. A member of the aristocracy, he must have had mixed feelings as he viewed Athens' rise through commerce and her shift to demagogic democracy. Tradition, perhaps accounting for moments of near bombast, says that Dionysus appeared to him in a dream and that he composed in an inspired—or drunken—condition. He won thirteen victories at the dramatic festivals, but only seven of his plays are extant.

Prometheus Bound

TRANSLATED BY E. A. HAVELOCK

Characters

POWER, FORCE } *demons, ministers of Zeus.*

HEPHAESTUS, *son of Hera, god of volcanic fire.*

PROMETHEUS THE FORETHINKER, *a Titan, son of Earth-the-Wise, brother of Genesis, uncle to Zeus.*

CHORUS OF THE DAUGHTERS OF GENESIS (Okeanids), *representing Stars, Winds, Seas, Coasts, Fountains, Caves.*

PRIMAL GENESIS (Okeanos), *son of Earth, elder brother of Prometheus, father of the chorus.*

THE WANDERING WOMAN, *being Io of Greece and Egypt, daughter of the River Inachus, granddaughter of Genesis, future consort of Zeus.*

HERMES, *youngest son of Zeus.*

SUGGESTED STAGE DIRECTIONS

Throughout the masque, the setting remains constant. It consists of a desolate rocky terrain strewn with boulders and backed by a precipitous cliff. As the curtain rises the whole scene is shrouded in the darkness before dawn. During the first episode the day breaks, and during the last, darkness once more shrouds the stage.

The pale light of sunrise, as it appears to the east-northeast behind the precipice, outlines its upper edge and then slowly reveals a colossal figure, rather resembling a piece of massive sculpture, which seems to emerge from the face of the stone. It is set stiffly erect upon a ledge against the cliff, in an attitude suggestive of crucifixion, with the head slightly bowed, looking down upon the stage. This is a representation of PROMETHEUS *or* THE FORETHINKER, *already placed symbolically in the position which he is doomed to occupy throughout the drama. From his elevation and in virtue of his size, he seems, despite his posture of suffering, to dominate the scene and the characters who appear before him. During the first episode he remains silent. His voice thereafter is produced by an actor concealed behind him. His style is for the most part prophetic and passionate, and the total effect might remind a Greek audience of utterances delivered from an oracular shrine where the god who speaks is visibly represented.*

Below his feet and extending toward the foreground of the stage there is laid out in bold outline a map of the world, as the first Greek geographers imagined it. It is centered on the Mediterranean, and is surrounded by a circular stream, to which from the center there radiate certain great rivers.

EPISODE ONE

POWER, FORCE, and HEPHAESTUS

(*In the morning twilight there enter to* PROMETHEUS *two allegorical figures,* POWER *and* FORCE, *ministers of Zeus.* FORCE *says nothing. They are followed reluctantly by* HEPHAESTUS, *the blacksmith of the gods, carrying tools and apparatus of his trade.*)

POWER: Sirs, we have reached the frontier of the world,
The level desert of the Russian verge,
Empty of man.
Hephaestus, now, on you
Falls the commission of almighty Zeus:
Here's one that high upon the beetling cliff
You must impale. Fetter this criminal
In tireless grip of adamantine bonds.

Your triumph of fire, the technological flame
It was that he filched away and transferred to man.
This was the sin against God, and now the iron
Of retribution he must undergo,
That so the lesson be learned: with Zeus's absolute power
To be content, and so give up the road
That leads to love of man.

HEPHAESTUS: Power and Force, you both have done right well
The work assigned, fulfilling Zeus's word.
But I—how do I lack the heart to bind
To this wintry crag my kinsman deity!
Yet must I somehow find the strength. For who
May flout the rescript and the wrath of Zeus?

(*Turning and addressing* PROMETHEUS)

O son of Her whose counsels never fail,
Intelligence superb and dangerous,
In your despite and mine, now to impale
Your helpless body on this lifeless peak,
Shunned by the human race, I shall proceed.
Here neither human voice nor human glance

Will ever cheer you. Upright, facing the sun,
Catching the full force of his searing ray,
You will decline and wither like a flower,
And plead that flaming day be hidden beneath
The starry cloak of night, and plead again
For sun to warm the icy shiver of dawn:
Exchange of agony your sole relief,
He that shall rescue you being yet unborn.
This your reward who took the road that leads
To the love of man.

Deity's jealous eye you did affront
By service to man, yourself a deity.
The privilege exceeded what was right.
So you must keep this rocky hopeless place,
Sleepless, erect, with tortured limbs unflexed.
In pain continual shall your cry be heard
Helpless. But Zeus indifferent shall remain.
Power when newly won is ever harsh.
POWER: So then, why the delay, the fruitless pity
For heaven's willful son whom heaven abhors?
Yours was the prize he cheapened when he gave
The fire away to man. Therefore I say
Hate him yourself.
HEPHAESTUS: Kinship and days together both say: No.
POWER: True. But to slight the task that Jove may show,
This rather is the guilt you should forgo.
HEPHAESTUS: Your cruelty never swerves: your heart is grim.
POWER: Where's remedy to raise the dirge for him?
The pains of sympathy yield profit slim.
HEPHAESTUS: O hated skill of my mechanical hand!
POWER: Blame not this trouble on it. Understand
These sorrows no technique had ever planned.
HEPHAESTUS: If only it belonged to someone else.
POWER: All tasks are heavy save the power supreme.
To Zeus alone true liberty belongs.
HEPHAESTUS: This now I realize, and say no more.
POWER: Quick, then, the manacles, and chain him up.
Must Zeus perceive you loitering on the job?
HEPHAESTUS: Well, here are the cuffs. I got them ready myself.
(HEPHAESTUS *climbs up on a ledge to reach head and arms of figure.*)
POWER: Then grip his wrists, and take the hammer and strike
The rivets home. Flatten him to the rock.

HEPHAESTUS: So: there's a job efficiently performed.
POWER: Strike harder: twist the links. Where other skills
Are baffled, he can still invent resource!
HEPHAESTUS: Here's one arm clamped immovably in place.
POWER: Bolt fast the other also: so shall prove
This scientist how keen the wits of Zeus.
HEPHAESTUS: No one save him can rightly blame my work.
POWER: Now take the wedge. It has a ravenous jaw.
Drive it clean through the torso straight and hard.
HEPHAESTUS: Prometheus, in your pain I groan myself.
POWER: You dare to groan, to pity those by Zeus
Hated? Beware lest you need pity too.
HEPHAESTUS: Behold and see how great his sorrow is.
POWER: Behold here's one who gets what he deserves.
Now strap the imprisoning harness round his ribs.
HEPHAESTUS: I know I have no choice: you need not drive.
POWER: Drive you I will, and with my voice give tongue
If I have to. Get below and clamp the legs.
HEPHAESTUS: So, they are done. It does not take much work.
POWER: Now to the feet. Swing hard and nail them in.
Your work a stern examiner will inspect.
HEPHAESTUS: Even as you look, so chills your spoken breath.
POWER: Sentiment's cheap, but cast not in my teeth
My implacable will, this temper harsher than death.
HEPHAESTUS: He is all fettered now, so let's depart.
POWER: Go swagger on your rock and steal and give
God's proud possession to ephemeral man.
Can man for you drain off this bitter cup?
The eternal spirits, when they fashioned you
Prometheus the Prognosticator, spoke
In irony: "Physician, heal thyself!"
Where's now the great prognostic of the mind
Shall from this science extrication find?

(*Exeunt* POWER, FORCE, and HEPHAESTUS.)

EPISODE TWO

PROMETHEUS THE FORETHINKER

(*It is now broad day.* PROMETHEUS *stands where* HEPHAESTUS *has fastened him. The sun shines in the sky above his head, and before his feet is revealed the world map.*)

PROMETHEUS: O spaces of the sky and winged airs,
Fountains of rivers, and perpetual laugh
Of ocean, and thou Earth, mother of all,
And the all-seeing circle of the sun,
Behold, what gods to me a god have done!

(*Sings*)

In sore despite my strength appears,
Committed to ten thousand years
  Of desperate contention.
The newest sovereign of the blest
These shackles on my body cast.
Present with future darkly blent
Warn of unutterable pain.
When shall the agony be spent?
When shall the ordinance attain
  Its uttermost invention?

Yet why these words? Of things that are to come
My science is exact, nor like fresh news
Will my afflictions happen. It is written
That I should suffer, and as best I may
These bonds and this dark destiny accept
In servitude to iron necessity.

But neither to speak out nor hold my peace
Is easy in the face of my estate.
Giving to man magnificent resource
Myself I serve the iron will of fate.
I am the huntsman of the mystery,
The great resource that taught technology,
The secret fount of fire put in the reed
And given to man to minister his need.
This, this the error for which night and day
Nailed up beneath the sky I still must pay.

(*Sings*)

  But hark, what sound,
  What scent of air
  Comes faintly borne,
Agent of god or man or demigod?

To this cliff at the end of the world
Who comes my grief to inspect, his sight to satisfy
Of me, the god, the prisoner who all the gods defy?

Past the gigantic doors
Of Zeus's great hall they throng,
And turn their back on him whose love
For mankind was too strong.
That beat—how I shudder to hear it!—
Of flapping wings—and the air
Is heavy and stirred with the flight of bird.
Thou presence O stay! Keep the menace away
Of the fear that afflicts and the fiend that would torture its victim.

EPISODE THREE

PROMETHEUS and CHORUS

(*Enter* CHORUS OF THE DAUGHTERS OF GENESIS. *They are a collective allegorical representation of earth's atmosphere, seas, rivers, and their subterranean sources. Hence they are mounted on flying cars, which however arrive from caverns beneath the sea. They come in two semi-choruses, which fly in from the wings on opposite sides, and descend to the "orchestra" or dancing floor, the flat space in the forefront of the stage, which can be imagined as merging into the world map just behind it. Before alighting from their vehicles, they engage responsively in antiphonal lyrics, which are constructed in symmetrical pairs. These are accompanied by appropriate music and dancing.*)

FIRST SEMI-CHORUS (*sings*): Lift up your heart; we fly to friend you,
Rank upon rank, beating the air, all to this craggy place contending;
Scarcely our sire consent extending.
We have come on the wings of the wind, for we heard the metallic hammer
Striking blow on blow, till our deep sea caverns shuddered.
My tranquil pose I shed
And ran shiftless, and sped
High through the startled airs of morning.

PROMETHEUS (*sings*): O Tethys' teeming progeny!
Children of Genesis, that stream
Encircling sleeplessly the earth,
Behold, the bonds that bind me!

Pegged to this rocky mountain steep
Desolate watch and ward I keep,
And succor none shall find me.

SECOND SEMI-CHORUS (*sings*): I look, Prometheus, and my frightened vision
Blotted with tears, darkened with terror, weeps your agony foreseeing,
Beholding this your body abused and withered
Like a corpse rotting in chains: Oh contumely appalling!
A new helmsman has power in the halls of high Olympus.
Zeus's catastrophic might.
Usurped hurls into night
The monster lords that were before him.

PROMETHEUS: If but to that dark underworld,
The mortal grave beneath the earth,
Even the infinite Tartarus,
A prisoner he had sent me;
None then my present state could mark
Wind-beaten like a stone or stock,
A laugh to all that hate me.

FIRST SEMI-CHORUS: What god in heaven has ruthlessness
In your grief to find happiness?
Who fails to make your hapless woe
His own, save only Zeus, who wrathfully does show
Resolve that at any cost
Shall master the heavenly host
Unswerving, unrelenting?
He shall satisfy his heart, or comes another
Shall grasp by desperate device the unattainable scepter.

PROMETHEUS: Of me, even me, though sore despite
These limbs in manacles detain,
Shall he, the immortal president,
Have need the dark plot to explain
That shall strip away his sceptered power;
Nor with honeyed phrases in that hour
Shall he beguile me, nor will I
Flinch, though he menace from the sky;
Nor the truth reveal, till the violence
Of my bonds be slackened, and recompense
Be paid for my sore enslavement.

SECOND SEMI-CHORUS: How bold you face your bitter wrong:
No quailing glance, no nerve unstrung.
Upon your lips sits liberty.
But a terror chills my heart, fearing you are too free.
I see the advancing storm

Of anguish, and cry alarm.
Will you ever bring ship to haven
And run your prow on the strand? For the heart of Zeus is ever
Rigorous, and his ways unswerving altogether.
PROMETHEUS: I know his malice. The just and the right
Are his bondsmen that never leave his sight.
But there comes an hour
Shall undo his temper and break his power.
He will smooth and soften his anger wild,
And offer a pact of friendship mild,
Eager with me to be reconciled,
And eager shall be my answer.

EPISODE FOUR

PROMETHEUS and CHORUS

CHORIC LEADER: Uncover all your tale, and promulgate
Upon what accusation Zeus inflicts
This torture so debasing and malign.
Explain, unless the telling be too hard.
PROMETHEUS: In telling of the tale is pain enough,
But silence too is pain. Calamity
Is all my theme.

When civil war broke out
In heaven, and passions stirred twixt god and god,
Some would lord Kronos from his seat expel
And elevate his son: the other faction
Resolved that Zeus should never rule the gods.
Whereat I offered counsels excellent
To the Titan sons of firmament and earth.
But no avail. They scorned the deviousness
Of my device. Their epic pride preferred
What seemed the easy use of simple force.
But she, my mother, who holds the judgment seat,
Even Earth, that entity with many names,
Had often told me, yea had prophesied
The way of it, how not in physical strength
But cunning guile the victory should lie.

But to my explanation of the truth
They did not deign even a moment's heed.

So I in present circumstance thought best
To take my mother and join force with Zeus,
A welcome partnership to both of us.

Therefore in Tartarus' black fundament
Kronos the ancient one and his array
Are kept, because my counsels showed the way.
Zeus's power, made absolute by my defense,
For service rendered gives this recompense.
Absolute power I ween this canker finds:
To fail of trust in those that were its friends.

But as to what you ask, what charge preferred
Makes him debase me, this will I clarify.
Directly he his father's throne assumed,
To divers of the gods he variously
Prerogatives assigned, and plotted out
The pattern of his kingdom. Man alone,
Poor suffering man, meant nothing. His intent
Was to obliterate and plant fresh stock.
No one withstood this plan except myself.
But my nerve did not fail. I rescued man
From being put away a broken thing.
Therefore in torments I am bowed, that wring
Pain from my flesh and pity from your heart.
Did I who gave man sympathy deserve
Such fate as even for me cries sympathy?
So here's the ruthless spectacle you face:
My education, and Zeus's dark disgrace.

CHORIC LEADER: Of iron the heart, rock-hewn the temperament
That cannot feel your sorrows as his own.
Myself I had no wish to see you so,
Prometheus, and in seeing I find woe.

PROMETHEUS: Mournful indeed to friends my sorrows show.

CHORIC LEADER: Did you go even further than you've said?

PROMETHEUS: I made men cease their doom to anticipate.

CHORIC LEADER: To lift this curse what cure did you invent?

PROMETHEUS: I made their hearts blind citadels of hope.

CHORIC LEADER: A brave utility on man conferred—

PROMETHEUS: And, more than that, made fire their minister.

CHORIC LEADER: Wields now ephemeral man the fervent flame?

PROMETHEUS: Yes, and 'twill teach him all technologies.

CHORIC LEADER: These then the provocations for which Zeus—

PROMETHEUS: Torments unmitigated now inflicts.

CHORIC LEADER: Shows not your ordeal some far end in sight?

PROMETHEUS: When Zeus decrees, then only will it end.

CHORIC LEADER: And how shall that word come? Cannot you see
That you have slipped? What hope have you? But why
Do I say that you have slipped? It is no pleasure
Saying it, and the pain is there for you.
This issue let us leave, and unresigned
From piteous ordeal extrication find.

PROMETHEUS: Easy it is for one whose foot is clear
Of trouble to address advice to those
That flounder. I had skill to see it all.
I knew what I was doing, yes, I knew,
The time I slipped: I do acknowledge it.
Man's cure invented misery for myself.
But penalties not these did I expect:
To see myself rotting beneath the sky,
The lonely tenant of this lifeless peak.
But now, I pray, no more lament my state.
Sit here with me while I predict the march
Of destiny, and so learn all to the end.
I plead with you, I plead. Take on my load
Who now do suffer. Fortune's darkling wing
May touch or god or man with anything.

CHORUS (*sings*): Prometheus, to your bitter cry
My heart responds, and daintily
I step upon this rocky place
From rapid car that late did trace
The highways of the flashing bird.
Now wait I till the final word
Of your ordeal is spoken.

(*They dismount and retire to the rear of the stage, right and left.*)

EPISODE FIVE

PROMETHEUS and GENESIS

(*Enter* PRIMAL GENESIS *in a flying car drawn by a griffin (perhaps a sphinx). He is parent of the* DAUGHTERS OF GENESIS, *who form the* CHORUS, *and like them he represents the powers both of the atmosphere through which he flies and of the subterranean regions from which he issues. His Greek name "Okeanos" is the symbol not of salt water but of that circular stream or current which was supposed to surround the world, and also to generate it. He may perhaps be thought of as representing the Far Horizon which, while dividing sky from earth, seems also to be the original of both, and hence also of sea and "regions under the earth." Though reduced to anthropomorphic form, he is already in Homer the traditional "Genesis of All," a cosmic power anterior to Zeus but now, like other natural forces, subservient to the rule Zeus has established over the elements. The pomposity of his manner is in proportion to his real loss of former power.*)

GENESIS (*sings*): Through time and distances prolonged,
Traversing stage on stage, I come
  To you, Prometheus, voyaging.
Behold my steed, this bird that flies
By sheer volition of my mind;
  No bit or bridle holds him.
With you I surely sympathize
In your mishap. Relationship
Renders this unavoidable.
And ties of family apart,
To none am I more partial than
To you. And you shall realize
  How genuine this statement.
I cannot bring myself to speak
In honeyed flatteries. So make
It clear what I must undertake
To help you. For a better friend
Than Genesis you'll never find
  Reliable to serve you.

PROMETHEUS: What's here? Has my reverse drawn even you
To inspect me? Have you perilously come
Leaving your self-named streams, and rock-recessed
Ceilings of caves primaeval, to set foot
Here where the iron mines are? Did you come to view

In sympathy my sufferings' spectacle?
Then here it is, the friend who aided Zeus
In joint foundation of his tyranny.
What torments in return are laid on me!

GENESIS: I see, Prometheus, and I have a mind
To counsel you despite your subtlety.
Know thou thyself, and shape thy character
Anew, to fit new tyranny in heaven.
These edged and whetted sentences you fling,
If still continued, Zeus may even hear
Although he sit far off. And present trouble
As child's play in your sight will then appear.
O sufferer, put off the mood you have,
And seek from these afflictions to be freed.
Time-worn perhaps my sentiments may seem,
But what you've paid, Prometheus, is the wage
Earned by a rash, an overweening tongue.
And you are not yet humbled, nor will bow
Before defeat, but rather make it worse.
If you will be my pupil, you must stop
Kicking the goad with your heel, and realize
Despot's authority is absolute.
Now for my own part will I go and try
To see if I can free you from these toils.
Do thou refrain, nor furiously protest.
You are the mastermind, and you should know
How with tongue's vanity a price must go.

PROMETHEUS: Yourself exempt are enviable indeed
Who once with me shared perilous consequence.
Better dismiss my problem from your thought.
You cannot sway him. He is pitiless.
But watch yourself for trouble on the road.

GENESIS: Your wits can make your friends intelligent
Far better than yourself. This I infer
From the facts themselves. But my resolve you need
Not now restrain. For I am proud to say
Zeus will to me your gift of freedom pay.

PROMETHEUS: I do commend you now, and ever shall;
Your zeal leaves nothing lacking. But I say
Labor thou not for me. For laboring
You cannot help even if you have a mind.
Rather refrain and so protect yourself.
For my misfortunes cannot make me wish
That all the world should be unfortunate.

I have a brother Atlas and his fate
Afflicts my heart. By western shores he stands
Propping the pillar that holds heaven from earth,
A load too large for his exhausted hands.

In caves primaeval of Cilicia
The hundred-headed prisoner have I seen,
Typhoon the terrible, his giant might
Forcefully overcome, and pitied him.

He rose in insurrection 'gainst the gods.
His ghastly dragon jaws hissed scorching death.
Flame from his eyes he launched inflammable
That Zeus his onslaught might succumb beneath.

But him the unsleeping thunder-flame of Zeus
Descendant and inevitable smote
Through to the midriff and the inward parts,
Blasting the boastful utterance in his throat.

And now a sprawled and smouldering thing he lies
Useless, in shattered ruin of his might,
Hard by the passage of the narrow seas.
And all the weight of Aetna grips him tight.

High on the peak Hephaestus has his forge,
That peak whence flaming fire one day shall spout,
And torrid streams eat up the level fields,
And all the bloom of Sicily put out.

This fire shall be the anger of Typhoon
Skyward in rain of molten lava thrown,
E'en though the bolt of Zeus has struck him down.

(*The following dialogue is framed with savage irony.* GENESIS *briefly attempts the role of* PROMETHEUS, *relying on "formulas," foresight, and intellectual "courage."* PROMETHEUS *rejoins with that short-range common sense and caution appropriate to the mind of* GENESIS. *Hence there is a double entendre in the dialogue:* PROMETHEUS *himself illustrates those perils against which he utters caution. It does not take* GENESIS *long to revert to character.*)

But as for you, experience need not learn
From me. Preserve yourself: you have the skill.
My present bitter draught I'll drink alone
Until Zeus's wrath relax its purpose.

GENESIS: But soft, Prometheus. Do you not agree
That wrath distempered formulas can cure?
PROMETHEUS: Yes, if in season one assuage the mood,
Nor swollen temper forcefully reduce.
GENESIS: To take Promethean care, yet courage too—
What hazard do you see in this? Explain.
PROMETHEUS: Work thrown away, and silly sentiment.
GENESIS: If that be weakness, then let me indulge.
Fair thoughts can profit if they're fairly hid.
PROMETHEUS: The offense that you may give will look like mine.
GENESIS: Your words suggest
that homeward road is best.
PROMETHEUS: Grieve not for me:
my case spells enmity.
GENESIS: You mean from one
who sits the imperial throne?
PROMETHEUS: Your cautious path
should always skirt his wrath.
GENESIS: Prometheus' fate
our course can educate.
PROMETHEUS: Quick! Homeward start,
before sound sense depart!
GENESIS: I go, your cry still ringing in my ear,
Where level roadways of the air appear.
My winged steed four-footed strides the sky
Eager her homeward path to trace and in her stall to lie.
(*Exit.*)

EPISODE SIX

CHORUS

FIRST SEMI-CHORUS (*sings*): O thou afflicted,
When shall I cease thy lot lamenting?
See where the bitter springs of sorrow,
Well-springs of grief, my visage furrow.
When shall your light arise?
When shall I dry my eyes?

These stark repellent pains
Zeus's private law ordains,
So to the gods he may

That were before his day
Valor make manifest and all vainglory.
SECOND SEMI-CHORUS (*sings*): Far voices calling,
Grief of the stones and trees, calling uncomforted:
Ancient magnificence and honor splendid—
These, even these, were yours, and these are ended:
Prerogatives ill-starred
You and your brethren shared.

And mankind that afar
Inhabit Asia's shore,
Beneath an alien sun,
Join universal moan,
In all your agonies themselves conspiring.
FIRST SEMI-CHORUS: The Amazon by Colchis keeps
Her intrepid habitation:
Far off beside Crimea's sea
The Scythian holds his frontier station:
People unto people cry
Communion in your agony.
SECOND SEMI-CHORUS: And Arabia has sons,
Mighty men of valor dwelling
Nigh unto the Caucasus
In embattled fortresses.
Through clash of spears and battle shock
They sense the travail on your rock.
CHORIC LEADER: That other once I saw,
Your forerunner in great affliction, your sole exemplar in great tribulation;
Sore constraint was upon him, yea, in irrefragable bondage
Bowed I beheld him:
Even the Titan Atlas, his giant strength holding, straining,
Against the weight of the dome of the sky on his shoulders turning—
Desperate his bursting groan,
Extreme his exhaustion.
UNISON: The surf of the concurrent sea
Cries aloud, the water-deeps
Moan, and the vast chambers the earth beneath
Quake and tremble, those darkling mansions of death.
And the solemn river fountains cry
Their lamentation bitterly.

(*As the song ends, the* CHORUS *partially retire to either side, and there is a short period of profound silence.*)

EPISODE SEVEN

PROMETHEUS and CHORUS

PROMETHEUS: My silence is not idle willfulness.
Pray you, believe, my thought's intensity,
Seeing myself abused, gnaws at my heart.
Surely none else but I set out for these
The newest gods their rights and privileges?
But you know all the story. Let me rather
Relate to you the tragedy of man:
How from the silly creature that he was
I made him conscious and intelligent.
I speak the human race not to condemn
But to explain my kindness in what I gave to them.

Seeing they did not see, nor hearing grasp
That which they heard. Like shapes of dreams they lived

The random planless years, all ignorant

Of houses built of brick to catch the sun
Or timber fashioning. Like little ants
They dwelt in holes of sunless cavities.

They had no signs reliable to mark
Winter and scented spring and harvest-time,
Mindless was all they did, until I showed
The dubious rise and setting of the stars.

That triumph next of scientific mind
The count numerical for man I find,
And history's instrument, skill of the bard,
That great compositor the written word.

I was the first to yoke the animals
In service to the strap, and lay on them
Inheritance of man's excessive toil.
Between the shafts I led the obedient horse,
That ornament of luxury and wealth.
The gleaming sail that wafts across the sea
The intrepid mariner was my device.

The inventor I, who many a shape did show
Of science to mankind, now do not know
What science will my own release allow.
CHORUS: Your wits do wander in your sore despite,
And mind unseated plunges in despair,

Even as a fumbling doctor finds himself
Diseased, not knowing his own remedy.
PROMETHEUS: Hear yet again, and marvel what resource,
What science sprang from my intelligence.
Here was the greatest: if a man fell sick,
Where was his remedy of application?
Potions, alembics, messes, poultices—
All were to seek. The sufferer pined and sank
In stark emaciation, till I brought
The soothing unguent and the restoring draught
To man the battlements against disease.

Procedures intricate I plotted out
Of the diviner's skill, and how to tell
The waking vision from the idle dream.
Of chance word's augury and journeying sign
The sense obscure did I communicate.

The divers figures of the flights of birds,
Those matched with luck, and those made otherwise,
The regimen of their respective groups,
Conjunctions, oppositions, amities,
With strict exactness did I designate.

And the smooth look of entrails, and correct
Color of bile to please the gods withal,
And the prediction of the liver's lobe
Shown in the lineaments' complexities.

By smoke of sacrifice of loin and thigh
Wrapped in the fat I did initiate
Man in a dark and intricate technique,
And the hidden bloodshot eye of the sign by fire
I did unmask, that had been veiled before.

So much for these. Turn next and contemplate
Those great utilities beneath the earth,
Copper and iron, silver and yellow gold.
Who before me dare claim discovery
Of these, unless a madman? None, I trow.

One sentence short proclaims the truth unique:
Prometheus gave, what man received, technique.
CHORUS: Why such utility for man effect
Unseasonably, to your own neglect?
Your power emancipated yet will prove
Zeus's equal disputant. This I believe.

PROMETHEUS: Not so, not yet, is the last sentence written
In Fate's methodical book. I shall go free
After affliction of ten thousand years.
Technology's resource cannot withstand
Necessity's remorseless iron hand.

FIRST CHORIC LEADER: Who then is pilot of Necessity?

PROMETHEUS: The triple Fates and the avenging Weirds.

SECOND LEADER: You mean, the power of Zeus is less than theirs?

PROMETHEUS: Yes, he may not infringe on what is written.

FIRST LEADER: Does not his portion read perpetual power?

PROMETHEUS: That question goes unanswered. Ask not why.

SECOND LEADER: What solemn thing is this your bosom hides?

PROMETHEUS: Bethink you of some other word to speak.
For this thing that you ask there comes not yet
The appointed hour to cry it out aloud.
The secret must be hugged, that so I may
These bonds despiteful loose at last, and put my griefs away.

EPISODE EIGHT

CHORUS

FIRST SEMI-CHORUS (*sings*): Grant, oh my willful soul,
Zeus the omnipotent prove thy antagonist never.
Service of sacrifice and prayer be thy constant endeavor,
And the victim slain at the feast
That the high gods hold at the edge of the world by the timeless river.
"From frantic word to be saved":
This the inscription graved
On my heart forever.

SECOND SEMI-CHORUS (*sings*): Confident spring to keep
Fresh in one's heart till the fall of the year, a reveler tasting
The well-spread table of life, is joy everlasting.
But I feel the breath of fear
When I look on Prometheus bound, his pride and his power on the mountain wasting;
Who awe to Zeus denied
And privately sanctified

The estate of mortals.

FIRST SEMI-CHORUS: O labor of love thrown away!
Who now, dear head, shall defend thee?
Why so unschooled in the state of ephemeral man?
How feeble he is, how resourceless,
How like a dream he passes
Blinded in all his ways, and in all his acts prevented!
Nor, though one still take thought, can the grand design
By his thinking be circumvented.

SECOND SEMI-CHORUS: The truth of it all comes home,
Your own dark fate beholding:
Through the dirge that I raise for you now I seem to hear
Faint melody persistent
Son of a day how distant—
Bridal bath of our sister Hesioné, song at her wedding
Sung as the maid whose hand you had wooed and won
Came home to be bride at your bidding.

EPISODE NINE

PROMETHEUS and the WANDERER

(Enter a WANDERING WOMAN. *She is later revealed to be wearing cows' horns, and* PROMETHEUS *then identifies her as Io, daughter of Inachus, a river of Greece, sprung (like the* CHORUS*) from* GENESIS, *but anthropomorphically represented as king of Argos. The symbolism of her role is complex. She wears horns as the Sacred Cow, destined bride of Zeus, but also as his scapegoat, a woman turned into an animal, outcast and "devoted." The animal parasite which pursues her is in her imagination likewise a demon cattle-driver (Argus) appointed to goad her away from Zeus's embraces. It is also referred to as an infection, and as the instrument of insanity. Its persecution of her is described in terms which suggest both the jealousy of Hera and also the pursuit of Zeus. Moreover, the "touch" of Zeus which is one day to heal her is to prove also the occasion, perhaps of the restoration of her humanity, certainly of her impregnation.*

These ambiguities are deliberate. Her condition is half-bestial, half-human, and the symbolism of the myth in these aspects would appear to be sexual. But at other times the metaphor of her wanderings changes to suggest the career of land-explorer, and of navigator. Her origin is Hellenic, but her destination, and perhaps the manner of her doom, is revealed to be Egyptian. Her concluding historical function is to be Egypto-Hellenic. Her part, like that of PROMETHEUS, *has universal overtones. Like him she represents mortality in competition with sovereignty. As* PROMETHEUS *has elevated man's condition to his own sorrow, so she with equal affliction explores man's earthly habitation. Both endure torments of a peculiar refinement which are complementary; he is exhausted by immobility, she by unresting activity. Her role therefore cannot be played with the realism appropriate to a single consistent character. She is the supreme mummer in the masque, and her utterances and gestures should correspond. The floor on which she moves is the world map, and she dances upon it with a certain crazy and unpredictable formalism.*)

WANDERER: Where have I come? Who are the men
That here inhabit? And who the stranger
Exposed on these rocks? The stone has seized him!
Stranger, declare, what crime of thine demands
    This protracted death?
Stranger, speak, name this port of call
    In my everlasting journey.
For I too am storm-beaten and heavy-laden.

(*She screams.*)

    Oh horror!
  That touch again, that flying filthy touch!
Look how he walks, look how he stalks, look at his thousand eyes,
    Look at his roving eye
    The demon dragon-fly!
  He is my keeper, he is my cattle-man:
Look he is dead! eyes of the dead! eyes that pursue.

(*Screams again.*)

    Death keep him back! earth hold him down!
    See how he haunts me, hunts me, see him approach.
    Plodding the barren land, treading the thirsty sand, tracking the silent shore,
    Where shall I lay me? How shall I save me? What shall I pray me?
    What shall I do?

(*She sings in a style alternating between hypnosis and frenzy.*)

First Monody of the WANDERER:

Breath of the pipe comes stealing soothing, pan-pipes clear, now far, now near,
How full of fear, how calm, how crazy!
Ah no! not yet! not more! not further pipe ye my ever-lasting journey!—
Son of Kronos, did ever my heart deceive thee?
Was my guilt uncovered before thee,
That you build me a prison of everlasting pain?
Why send this filthy parasite's infection
To drive mē through the wilderness insane?
O fire, consume me! Deep mountains smother me!
Give my flesh to the fish of the seas to devour!
Lord of the sky,
Sanction my desperate cry.
I have run my race, I have trodden the prints and the pain of my everlasting journey.
I am now beyond all resource to outrun my affliction.
Hear what is said by the hornéd maid,
The ox-eyed maiden, the heavy-laden.

PROMETHEUS: Yes, I can hear. It is the whirling maid
Who dances to the demon dragon-fly:
Daughter of Inachus, passion of Zeus;
Who now across the world endures perforce
By Hera's malice her appalling course.

Second Monody of the WANDERER: Name of my father, cried from the mountain! name, true name, in the silence heard—
Stranger, who are you? How do you name me?
How does thy anguish know my anguish? How I am pierced by thy spoken word!
You have named that other name, God's filthy agent,
That barbed and hovering infection
Which saps my strength and drives me over the earth
In starving contumely, cringing and reeling
Under the lash of Hera's studied wrath,
Sped wild and lost from coast to coast.
Who is afflicted as I am afflicted?
Speak, thou stranger!
Speak and declare if danger

Waits in the dark unseen. Show the device I may use,
and the balm that may cure me.
Speak, can you speak? Make your prognostic fairly.
Friend, if you know, bethink thee of utter woe,
Of mine, the maid world-weary, the heavy-laden.

EPISODE TEN

PROMETHEUS, the WANDERER, and CHORUS

PROMETHEUS: My answer shall be full and fair indeed,
Nor make some mystery of your anxious need.
A friend has right frank utterance to inspire:
Know that Prometheus speaks, whose gift to man was fire!
WANDERER: Thou great utility of social man,
His brightest light since history began,
Prometheus, steadfast in your works revealed,
What spells this punishment, these fetters sealed?
PROMETHEUS: The song of my own sorrows is just done.
WANDERER: And yet there is one favor I would ask—
PROMETHEUS: What is it? I would tell you everything—
WANDERER: His name who nailed you to this precipice.
PROMETHEUS: What Zeus designed Hephaestus did perform.
WANDERER: What was the quality of such offense?
PROMETHEUS: Enough! The curtain can be raised no more.
WANDERER: There is one other thing. What goal, what term
Shall end my wild career across the world?
PROMETHEUS: Knowledge of this is worse than ignorance.
WANDERER: Ah! keep not back the path that I must tread.
PROMETHEUS: Think not that I do grudge to give it you.
WANDERER: Then tell it all. Why do you hesitate?
PROMETHEUS: Why should I strike a sword into your heart?
WANDERER: Your forethought need not spare what I find sweet.
PROMETHEUS: You press: I must comply. The tale begins—
CHORUS: Prometheus, wait! If she wants luxury,
Then so do I. For surely her disease
Calls for investigation medical.
Let fortune's violence the patient tell,
Ere you predict the discipline required to make her well.
PROMETHEUS: Io, these women are your father's sisters.
Be yours, this service to perform for them.

Is it not true that the lamenting tear
    To audience shown
    That sheds tears of its own own,
Does then no idle luxury appear?

WANDERER: What you and they do urge I cannot doubt
Must be obeyed. In plainest form I speak
All you desire to know. And yet hot shame
Of my corruption still sweeps over me:
My reckless maidenhood's catastrophe
And shape subverted by God's agency . . .

It was at night the haunting visions came
Entering my bedchamber, and spoke to me
Caressingly: O maid most fortunate,
Why hold your maidenhood when you can win
Marriage magnificent? The heart of Zeus
By passion's barb inflamed desires to engage
    With you the works of love.
My child, thrust not away the bed of Zeus.
Go out among your father's sheep and kine,
The water-meadows where the cattle lie.
So shall the eye divine be satisfied
    Of its desire.
These were the dreams that kept me company
Through all the hours of dark, until one day
I took my courage in my hands and told
My father how the nights had haunted me.
To Pytho and Dodona he dispatched
Wise men and prophets many to inquire
What word or deed might in the sight of gods
Find pleasure. And they brought back oracles
Dark and involved and spoken doubtfully.
At last to him the clear cold word returned
Of conjuration and of prophecy:

"Thrust forth your daughter from the hearth and home.
Outcast the corners of the world to roam,
Or else from Zeus shall thunderbolt descend
In scorching flame your lineage to end."

He bowed to Apollo's word and drove me out,
And shut the door against my heart and his.
He could not otherwise. Zeus's bridle rein
Forcefully held him to the course he took.
My mind and body straightway were deformed,
Twisted into the hornéd shape you see.

And touched and tortured by the insect's sting,
Leaping and starting wildly, I made off
To where Cerchnea's stream and Lerna's spring
Flow for the thirsty. And that earth-born giant
Who kept the cattle herded me along,
Argus the fiend, whose eyes infuriate
And multiform spied every track I made.
But him did sudden doom and unforeseen
Of life deprive. And through the world go I
Scourged by the parasite and lashed by Zeus.

You've heard the history. If you have news
Of what I still must meet, O tell it me,
Nor let compassion comfort me with lies.
The cunning composition of the word
That swindles is infection worst of all.

CHORIC LEADER (*sings*): Child of sorrow
Heaven defend thee!

FULL CHORUS (*sings*): Never, never thought I
I should ever hear
Tale so wild and alien,
Tale so charged with fear.
Sight to eyes forbidden,
Heart cannot bear:
Pain, degradation, and despair.

CHORIC LEADER: The forked tongue of pain
Draws the blood from my heart.
Cry fortune! Cry fate!
Behold Io's estate.
But my fortitude fails
And my vision recoils.

EPISODE ELEVEN

PROMETHEUS, CHORUS, and the WANDERER

(*During the discourse of* PROMETHEUS, *the* WANDERER *may perform certain responsive dances upon the stations of the world map.*)

PROMETHEUS: As one betrayed by fear you sigh too soon. Delay you, till you hear the bitter end.

CHORUS: Show what you mean. It helps the sick to offer

Prognostic clear of what they still must suffer.
PROMETHEUS: The first of your petitions I could heed
At small cost to myself. For your first need
Was that her previous course by her own mouth
Be told. But next comes tale of Hera's wrath.

For now shall prophecy complete be made
Of trials that still do lie before this maid.
Inachus' seed, mark well the word I bring
Of goals and bounds of your far journeying.

Turn hence towards the risings of the sun
And through domains unfurrowed take your way,
And you will reach the ranging Scythians
Whose homes are moving platforms raised on wheels.
These are their covered wagons, and they shoot
With a powerful bow. Give them wide room, and, skirting
In sound of the surf on the shore, get through beyond.
Off to your left are the artisans of iron,
The Chalybes. These are wild men. Beware.

Next comes the River Outrageous, fitly named.
Ford not its waters. They are not fordable,
Until you reach the actual Caucasus,
World's highest mountain. From its streaming crown
The torrents on the frontal surfaces
Their foaming strength discharge. These strenuous peaks
That touch the stars you must surmount, and take
The southerly route:

where you will next encounter
The Amazon army of the breastless women
That hate all men. These one day will be found
At a place called Themiscyra, at the flow
Of the Thermodon. There the projecting jaw
Of Salmydessus thrusting into the sea
Gives ships and crews dire hospitality.
They will assist your route, and be glad of it.

Then the Crimean isthmus will you reach
Right at the narrows of the inland sea.
Here you must summon nerve to launch from land
Through the Maeotic straits, to the other side.

This enterprise shall live in later days:
The passage shall in fame and name be yours
Forever, *Bosporus*, the *Heifer's Ford.*

Then Europe's plain is left behind, and so
At Asia's mainland you at last arrive.

(*To the* CHORUS)

What think ye of it all? Chorus, reply.
Does Zeus force tyranny identical
On gods and men alike? This mortal woman
He being god had need to marry. Therefore
He cast on her these world-wide wanderings.

(*To the* WANDERER)

Maiden, a cruel suitor for your hand
Have you obtained. For know that when I've said
All this, the overture has scarce begun.

WANDERER: Oh woe, woe.
What shall I do?

PROMETHEUS: That gasp! That strangled cry! How can you take
The tale of tribulation yet to come?

CHORUS: You say you have more miseries for her?

PROMETHEUS: Storms of affliction and a sea of pain.

WANDERER: Why should I go on living? What's to lose
Hurling myself head first from this stark peak?
My body thudding to the ground below
Would sleep at last. Better die once and for all
Than day on day to go on suffering.

PROMETHEUS: Trials such as mine you could not even face—
Mine, who 'tis writ must wince but may not die.
Death would indeed be rest from weariness.
But as it is, the distance I must go
Lasts on and on, until Zeus's overthrow.

WANDERER: Zeus's power be broken? Is that possible?

PROMETHEUS: Perhaps that's one calamity you'd like!

WANDERER: Why should I not, being thus by him abused?

PROMETHEUS: Make merry then. The thing's as good as done.

WANDERER: What hand could rob him of his tyranny?

PROMETHEUS: His own, his empty-headed purposes.

WANDERER: Show me the way of it, unless there's risk.

PROMETHEUS: He'll make a match one day shall prove his ruin.

WANDERER: With god or mortal? Can it be revealed?

PROMETHEUS: Why do you ask that? No, my lips are sealed.

WANDERER: Is it the wife will thrust him from his throne?

PROMETHEUS: A greater one than Zeus himself—her son!

WANDERER: Has he no way to avert calamity?
PROMETHEUS: None, unless I from bondage am set free.
WANDERER: Whence can come rescue that his will defies?
PROMETHEUS: From your own seed my rescuer shall arise.
WANDERER: From mine? By child of mine are you released?
PROMETHEUS: When your twelfth generation shall have ceased.
WANDERER: Now can your riddle's meaning scarce be read.
PROMETHEUS: Your future too is better left unsaid.
WANDERER: Ah! having promised me the light, take it not back instead!
PROMETHEUS: Of matched alternatives I grant but one.
WANDERER: Explain what two you mean, and let me choose.
PROMETHEUS: I will. Either your labors' end you hear,
Or else, the account of my deliverer.
CHORUS: I pray you, as to one, consent to her,
And for the other favor me, and give
To history its due. So she will learn
The sweep of her far-flung route, and I shall hear
Your champion named, the thing for which I long.
PROMETHEUS: You both do press and I must needs release
All the intelligence you feel you need.
First Io's route adventurous shall unfold:
Let mind and memory now inscribe the tale as it is told

There lies a strait two continents between:
Cross this and toward the flaming sunrise go
Beyond the roaring sea:
until you come
To Gorgon-land, Cisthene's littoral.
There dwell the witches three, the Phorcydes,
With shapes like swans, one eye between the three
And a single tooth. The light of day shines not
Upon this place nor e'er the moon by night.

And nigh to them that flapping trilogy
The Gorgon goddesses, whom men abhor.
Their hair is serpentine, and one fell look
Strikes a man dead! They guard the perilous route
Lying in wait. Be you yourself on guard!
There is another and a fearsome thing
That travelers have seen. Beware I say
The voiceless and envenomed hounds of Zeus,
The griffins,

and that one-eyed horde beware,
The horseback riders of the plain, who keep
The Stygian ferry and the streams of gold,
The Arimaspians.

And you will reach
A frontier land afar, of swarthy men
Who live beside the sources of the sun.

The river Aethiopian there is found.
Proceed along its bank until you come
To the cataract amid the Bybline peaks

Where from the welling mountain are discharged
The streams august and potable of Nile.
Nile will conduct you to his rich terrain
Triangular, where, as the fates decree,
Shall you and yours found far-flung colony.

If my report goes stumbling or obscure,
Repeat your inquiry till you are sure.
I have more time to lend to you than I can well endure.
CHORUS: If there are things omitted or postponed
In telling of this ghastly pilgrimage,
Communicate them now to her. But if
Her story's finished, then you have a pledge
To fill for me. Remember what it is.
PROMETHEUS: The goal of all her journeying is now
Complete. But that my right to speak be known,
Her previous ordeal ere she reached this place
I will divine, to prove my prophecies.

(To the WANDERER):

Troublesome detail I omit from speech,
The goal decisive of your route to reach.
For when your feet trod the Molossian plain
And came to high Dodona's deep ravine,
The seat oracular of Thresprotian Zeus
And cult incredible of the talking oaks,
You heard infallible voices in the trees
Calling to you, "O wife of Zeus to be,
Famous thy name!" Can you still feel the glow
Of that far hour?

From there you fled along
The coastal road, demented by the thing
That stung and poisoned you, to the great gulf

Of Rhea, and then back again your course
Storm-driven returned.

Therefore in future fame
That corner of the sea shall bear the name
Ionian after you, and men shall say
In time to come: "Io once passed that way."

Such are the evidences that my mind
Sees further than the obvious can find.
Let me retrace to where I stopped before
And give you public news that all must share.
Canopus is a city far away
Fringing the silted sandbars of the Nile.
That is where Zeus shall make you sane again
With lightest touch of his untrembling hand.

And you shall bear a son called Epaphus
Named for that touch. For Zeus engendered him—
The swarthy lord of all fertility
That overflow of Nile does irrigate.

The fifty daughters, born in fifth descent
From him, to Argos shall one day return
Fleeing reluctant union with their kin,
Even their cousins: who in ardent love,
Like hawks upon the heels of fleeing doves,
Shall come in hot pursuit of an embrace
Prohibited, God grudging their desire.

Hellas shall welcome them, and woman's hand
Poised in the night shall overcome and slay.
Each bride shall take away her bridegroom's life,
Driving the smoking sword into his throat.
May love so visit my own enemies!

But one of them shall strong desire seduce
Of children unbegotten. She shall stay
Her blunted purpose, as effeminate
Choosing to rate rather than murderess.
She shall in Argos found a royal line.
But systematic history would take
Too long. At any rate, the stock will bear
One day a warrior of high renown
Armed with the bow, and he from these my bonds
Shall set me free.

So much in oracle
My mother Themis did translate to me
She, the Titanic Wisdom, ancient of days.

But more detail would take too long to tell
And yield you little benefit as well.

WANDERER (*sings hysterically, as she dances*): O God, yet again, yet again!
I can feel it come,
The limb distorted, the lips that foam,
The brain corrupted, the wits cast free,
And the thin hot flame of insanity:
The barb unpurified, the sting implanted,
Is poisoning me.

The panicked heart kicks in wild amaze,
The eyeball glares and the pupil strays:
Of course I carry before the blast
Deranged, and as tongue's control is lost,
Thick streams of strangled utterance strive
Against self-destruction's mounting wave.
(*Exit.*)

EPISODE TWELVE

CHORUS

FIRST SEMI-CHORUS (*sings*): Prudent indeed his skill
Who currency gave to the truth he had weighed in the scales of his wisdom:
"Marry within your rank." No sentence is stronger written.
They that in wealth do flourish wantonly,
Those high born that are lofty in their degree—
Let not the hand of the laboring man
Engage their connection.

SECOND SEMI-CHORUS (*sings*): O thou perpetual fate,
Suffer me never with Zeus to embrace in connubial union.
Never may I draw near as a bride to a heavenly bridegroom.
For my eye recoils before Io's maidenhead
That loves not man nor by man is visited:
By Hera whirled through a dark and stormy world:
Laid waste in affliction.

UNISON: If equal be the marriage tie

Fearless I go. But if destiny woo
With passionate glance of the lordly eye,
  Then shall I fear irresistibly.
For who when the battle is hopeless can reap any fruit in the sowing of tares?
  Or know how divinity's purpose appears?
That can change and transform and dishonor,
  But ruthless, relentless, unswerving pursues.

EPISODE THIRTEEN

PROMETHEUS and CHORUS

PROMETHEUS: Doom waits for Zeus. His proud and violent heart
Shall verily stoop, what time he furbishes
A matrimony that shall furnish cause
To topple his tyranny and efface his power.
Then, then, shall curse pronounced when Kronos fell
From ancient throne be utterly fulfilled.
This is the jeopardy no other god
Can extricate for him except myself.
Mine is the crucial knowledge. Let him now
In face of this sit cheerful in the sky
Trusting loud noise and waving thunderbolts
    High in his smoky hand.

These cannot fend away his coming fall
And scandal dire and unendurable.
For now himself he raises up against
Himself a combatant impregnable.

This prodigy shall flame and clangor furnish
Stronger than thunderclap and lightning flash;
His spear point shall Poseidon's trident shiver;
Seas shall be stirred and earth's foundations crash.

Colliding with disaster, Zeus shall see
What bondage means for one who has been free.

CHORIC LEADER: Your wish is father to your spoken threat.

PROMETHEUS: The truth and my own wish can coincide.

CHORUS: Must one indeed foresee Zeus's overthrow?

PROMETHEUS: He'll find a load on his neck will stagger him.

CHORUS: Your words strike like the lightning. O beware.

PROMETHEUS: What should I fear whose fate is not to die?
CHORUS: Suppose he lay a harder trial on you?
PROMETHEUS: Well, let him. I can foresee anything.
CHORUS: A sop to Nemesis, they say, is wise.
PROMETHEUS: Go cringe and kiss authority, and fall
Prostrate. To me Zeus matters not at all.
Let him play out his little act of power.
His role in heaven lasts but for an hour.

But soft. I think I spy his errand boy:
His recent highness sends a deputy.
Indeed he must have brought some news with him.

EPISODE FOURTEEN

HERMES, PROMETHEUS, and CHORUS

(*Enter* HERMES, *the* DEPUTY *of Zeus who, like* POWER *and* FORCE, *represents in this masque one of the extensions of absolutism exercised by remote control. He is characterized by* PROMETHEUS *as the* DEPUTY *and the* MINISTER. *At the end of the episode the* CHORUS *name him as "Hermes," traditionally the "herald" of the gods, and his mask and dress presumably express this function. Despite the personal label, he is less a "character" than a person converted into an instrument of the policy of someone else. He is commissioned to make certain important "policy announcements," but on the other hand everything he says is a reflection at secondhand of what he conceives that policy to be, and he is treated with corresponding contempt. Part of his exchange with* PROMETHEUS, *like the earlier exchange between* PROMETHEUS *and* GENESIS, *is designed as the nearest equivalent to comic relief that the Greeks could manage in a tragedy. The descent to the thrust and parry of repartee briefly lifts the tension before the emotional climax of the finale.*)

HERMES: Mr. Acidity, I'm addressing you.
(But you overdo it, don't you!) Attention, please!
The scientific sinner, are you not?
The thief who stole and gave ephemeral man
The privilege of fire, an insult to heaven?
The almighty father orders you to state
That matrimonial tie which, so you boast,

May prove the occasion of his fall from power;
Explain moreover unambiguously
In all detail. Don't give me double cause
To visit you, Prometheus. You can see
How unrelieved Zeus's punishment can be.

PROMETHEUS: How full of arrogance and angry wind
The words of heaven's minister come out!
How new are all of you! How newly fledged
The power that dreams of aery citadels
Beyond the reach of grief. Have I not seen
Two tyrannies cast headlong to the ground?
And shall this third authority not end
In automatic ruin? Do you think
I'd ever cringe before these newest gods?
The truth is far far otherwise. So you,
Please to retrace your overzealous steps.
You'll gather no enlightenment from me!

HERMES: Look how already has your stubborn course
Struck on these hopeless reefs. Is once enough?

PROMETHEUS: When I compare the wages that you earn
With mine, believe me, I would not exchange!

HERMES: These rocks perhaps reward your patience better
Than loyal service at the Father's side?

PROMETHEUS: The fire of arrogance must be fought with fire.

HERMES: You seem to find your fate enjoyable.

PROMETHEUS: Enjoyable! I could wish for all my foes.
A like content! And I include you, sir!

HERMES: What part have I in your predicament?

PROMETHEUS: All gods I hate who benefit repay
With injury, scorning the rightful way.

HERMES: In what you have just said I think I hear
A note of stark insanity appear.

PROMETHEUS: Insane! so be it. If they are mad who crave
Requital for their foes, then let me rave!

HERMES: Lucky the fortune that affects you thus!
No one could tolerate you prosperous.

PROMETHEUS: Alas, for fortune lost.

HERMES: Alas, you cry?
That word is not in Zeus's vocabulary!

PROMETHEUS: Time that grows ever old will teach him yet.

HERMES: Sense and propriety you still forget!

PROMETHEUS: I know. I should not argue with a slave.

HERMES: To his request, then, no reply you have?

PROMETHEUS: Owing him debt, I'd make the payment fair.

HERMES: How dare you patronize Zeus's messenger!

PROMETHEUS: A child could not be sillier than you
If you expect enlightenment from me.
No stroke of malice or ingenious skill,
Till these outrageous fetters fall away,
Shall make me tell Zeus what he wants to know.

In face of this, let incandescent flame
Hurtle to earth: let wings of flying snow
Blot out the sky: let the deep thunder churn
Primaeval chaos. I shall still remain
Unmoved amid it all, refusing to show
Whose fated hand shall execute his tyranny's overthrow.
HERMES: Ask yourself first what good this does to you.
PROMETHEUS: Long since I looked the issue full in the face.
HERMES: O fool! must you persist? Can you not find
In sheer disaster's face a better mind?
PROMETHEUS: You might as well convince an ocean wave
As me, whom you embarrass fruitlessly.
Let not the thought beguile you that I might
In fear of Zeus's dire purposes break down
And his detested power importunate
With supplicating spread of womanish hands
To set me free. I am far away from that.
HERMES: The more I speak, more useless seems the effect.
My prayers can neither touch nor soften you.
You take the bit in your teeth like a horse untamed,
Fighting against the rein to have your way.
And yet how frail, for all your vehemence,
That science seems on which you do rely.
Simple self-will falls strengthless to the ground
When isolated from a mind that's sound.

Consider, if my warning you ignore,
How the successive and stupendous wave
Of mounting agony breaks on your head.

The almighty Zeus with flame and thunder shock
This place shall assault, and rock uproot from rock.
Your plunging form, locked in the stone ravine,
Doomed shall preside over the awful scene.

By time's slow agony in darkness vexed
Light shall at last receive you back. But next
High in the heaven the vulpine scream is heard,
Your body's butcher, the atrocious bird.

Swooping he settles to the furious feast,

From dawn to dark an uninvited guest,
Tearing your flesh in strips to reach his prey,
The oozing liver that he eats away.

Look not for any terminus to these
Your tortures till some god appear to take
Your load upon him and consent to pass
Beneath the earth to Hades' sunless depths
  And vasty halls of Hell.

In face of this take counsel. These are facts
Not fiction. What I've said is true—too true.
The lips of Zeus do lack the power to lie;
His words always succeed. So presently
Do thou beware, look round, take cognizance,
Nor think self-will stronger than common sense.
  CHORUS: What Hermes speaks we think appropriate.
Self-will he bids you sacrifice, and rate
The skill of common sense highest of all.
For that the skillful mind should err is surely pitiful.

EPISODE FIFTEEN

PROMETHEUS, HERMES, and CHORUS

(*During the preceding episode, preliminary warnings of storm and earthquake to come are heard offstage. These intensify as* PROMETHEUS *opens his first song. The five lyrics are arranged responsively and symmetrically in the order* a b c b a. *When the* CHORUS *sings, there may be imagined to occur a brief lull in the storm.* HERMES, after delivering his second song, retires from the scene just before it becomes chaotic, and the CHORUS *at the same time crouch round* PROMETHEUS, *clasping rocks and boulders for protection. During* PROMETHEUS' *second song the catastrophe intensifies and becomes total.*)

  PROMETHEUS (*first song*): Now has the messenger tongued and told
The news I already knew of old.
To suffer is not such sore despite
By the hand that hates me, and whom I hate.
In face of this I defy the flame
Of the flickering tongue of the lightning flash.
Let it strike two-forked, let the thunder crash,

Let the wild typhoon and the hurricane
Disrupt the space of the sky. Let shock
Of air imprisoned blast rock from rock,
And tear the infernal roots apart
Till the whole earth quake to its very heart,
And the seas erupting in spouting roar
Wash down the heavens to ocean's floor.
Let its force the very stars confound
Of the cosmic scene in its annual round.

Let total dark be my body's fate,
Hurled into hell precipitate,
Caught in unyielding vortices
Of Necessity's cosmic purposes.
Whatever the peril, the doom, the pain,
Self-existent I still remain.
Zeus's hand can never destroy me.

HERMES (*first song*): Surely is now the frenzy heard
Of the wandering wit and the distraught word
Surely these boasts, these jarring cries,
This desperate vision that truth denies,
Relax no rein of his wild career—
Surely insanity is near.
But as for you, ye divinities
Who here partake in his miseries
As your own load, go fly before
The ascending storm and the thunder's roar.
Soon, soon, shall the fury of this place
All reason vanquish, all light efface
And daze and destroy you wholly.

CHORUS: Speak, if you must, some other note
That would beguile me to your side.
How shall I give my gentle vote
To your torrential charge, or guide
My conduct by that infamy
That would this sufferer desert?
Beside him I prefer to stay
Whate'er the peril or the hurt.
Never a trust to undermine—
I learned that lesson long ago,
Nor would to any other sin
Sooner my fierce derision show.

HERMES (*second song*): And yet, remember the word I say,
The warning given, the price to pay,
Nor when self-destroyed for release you strive,

Calamity's desperate fugitive,
Blame fate or fortune or Zeus's design
For perils that compass unforeseen.
No, the design it is your own,
Yours the gauge, the defiance thrown,
Yours the initiative cold and clear,
The wide-eyed choice, the presumption sheer,
That cast you in toils infatuate
Of self-destruction's unfathomed net.
(*Exit.*)

PROMETHEUS (*second song*): Prologue is over: the play's begun—
The first low rumble of mounting storm!
The earthquake's subterranean roar,
The answering shock of the ocean floor,
As deep on deep thunders reply
To the massed battalions of the sky.
Now lightning's incandescent spark
Igniting streaks the onrushing dark
With filaments of flame, now whirls
The dizzy dust in flying coils.
Now the four quarters of the sky
Blasting collide; the space on high
Seaward descends in cosmic wreck.
I am engulfed! Zeus's hand has struck.
Each shape of fear by his might displayed
Tells me, "Now tremble and be afraid."

O Mother Earth that my lips have kissed,
Thou space of sky where the morning mist
Does socially upon all below
Enkindle the heaven's revolving show,
Hear now from chaos the cry begun:
"Behold Prometheus! on him alone
What acts of unrighteousness are done!"

(*As the last lines are uttered, the colossal figure of the* FORE-THINKER, *with its cliff, topples into the abyss.*)

Sophocles:
OEDIPUS THE KING

To those who have never read *Oedipus the King* but have heard the name in connection with Freud, the play is about Oedipus' hostility toward Laïus, his father, and his lust for Jocasta, his mother. But before we can evaluate this or any other interpretation we ought to be familiar with the plot which lies behind Sophocles' drama.

Because the tale of Oedipus was well-known to the audience which assembled to see the play, Sophocles relied, not on the narrative thread, but rather on an ironical retelling (on dramatic irony, see p. 13), for the audience came not to hear a new story but to see an old one presented in a new manner. Homer had mentioned Oedipus in the eleventh book of the *Odyssey,* and Aeschylus had written a trilogy (of which only one play survives) on the house of Laïus; but though the outlines of the story were fixed, Sophocles was free to see in the fate of the unlucky king whatever he wished. "One thing," Browning wrote of Greek myths, "has many sides,"

> But no good supplants a good,
> Nor beauty undoes beauty. Sophokles
> Will carve and carry a fresh cup, brimful
> Of beauty and good, firm to the altar-foot,
> And glorify the Dionusiac shrine.

Briefly, Oedipus' father, Laïus, abducted a boy and was later told that only if he died childless would Thebes avoid ruin. Further, he was told that he would die by his child's hand, and that the child would wed his own mother, Laïus' wife. Laïus begot a child, and thus the prophesied events came to pass. Oedipus, having been abandoned by Laïus and Jocasta with his feet fettered, was cared for by Polybus and Merope of Corinth. Ridiculed because he did not resemble his parents, he consulted Apollo's oracle at Delphi and was told that he would kill his father and marry his mother. Horrified, he immediately fled from his supposed parents and journeyed toward Thebes. On the way he met Laïus (who was, of course, unknown to him). Laïus ordered him out of the road and struck him. Oedipus thereupon killed Laïus and then proceeded to solve the riddle of the Sphinx. A creature with the head of a woman, the body of a lion, the wings of an eagle, and the tail of a serpent, the Sphinx had been terrorizing Thebes (because of Laïus' criminal abduction) by devouring each passer who was unable to tell what creature walks on four legs in the morning, two in the afternoon, and three in the evening. The Sphinx destroyed herself when Oedipus answered "Man," for man walks on all fours in infancy, two legs in maturity, and is aided by a cane or some sort of guide in his declining hours. Because of his success, the Thebans, lacking a king, made Oedipus their ruler and gave him Jocasta, the old king's wife. Later, because an unclean person (Oedipus) was in the land, a plague fell upon the city, and it is here that the drama opens.

Aeschylus probably saw in the myth a justification of Zeus's ways to man, for Laïus sinned when he abducted a boy, a sin for which he and his house were punished. But Sophocles' play does not seem to follow this moral interpretation, for whereas in some of the pre-Sophoclean versions the oracle is conditional—*if* Laïus begets a son, the boy will slay him—we read in *King Oedipus* merely that Laïus consulted an oracle and was told of his destiny. Jocasta has, perhaps, already conceived Oedipus, or must inevitably conceive him. A basic problem, then, is whether Oedipus was fated to perform certain actions—in which case he is not morally responsible—or whether his crimes are the result only of his own will. If he was destined to kill Laïus and marry Jocasta, the gods may be malicious or they may have moral purposes undiscernible by man's inferior mind. If Oedipus is morally guilty, the gods are just, for they punish him. But these are extreme assumptions; it is possible that Oedipus is guilty but his punishment disproportionate, or that he is guilty but his guilt is unrelated to his suffering.

A modern discussion of the play probably should first note that Freud's theory of the Oedipus complex (the view that the play dramatizes our universal hostility toward the parent of the same sex and our universal sexual desire for the parent of the opposite sex), whether right or wrong, is inappropriately named, for Oedipus killed Laïus without knowing who the man was, and, in fact, fled from Corinth in fear that he might kill his father. Similarly, Oedipus does not seem to have had any sexual interest in Jocasta; she was given to him along with the kingdom when he was offered the rule of Thebes. Freud accounted for the uncanny hold which the play exercises upon us by suggesting that in it we see ourselves, for the oracle given to Oedipus is also, he said, given to every man.

Other students of the play have seen other images of our destiny in the tragedy. Some, like Freud, imply that man's deeds are largely inherent in his nature, and that the prophecy indicates not that Apollo *wills* Oedipus to do certain things, but that he foresees Oedipus' necessary or inevitable actions. Thus a doctor might predict the early death of a child, but the prediction does not represent the doctor's *will.* On the other hand, some of the characters in the play feel that the gods are responsible for Oedipus' actions, and surely Oedipus is innocent of all intent to commit parricide or incest. He may not even be guilty of murder, but only of manslaughter or unpremeditated killing, for Laïus perhaps wrongfully tried to drive him from the road.

The prophecies would seem to suggest divine responsibility, yet as we see or read the drama we feel that it is a profoundly human play. Oedipus, one of the best-characterized figures in Greek tragedy, is presented as the kind of man who might well have killed another in a dispute over the right of way. Maxwell Anderson, writing of *Oedipus,* says that the play teaches that evil actions revenge themselves on the doer. If this assumption that Oedipus is justly punished is too pat an evaluation, we nevertheless feel that the king in the play accords with the Oedipus of the antecedent action—intelligent, self-confident, quick to act. These gifts, however, can be tragic as well as useful, and though the gods move in the background, as we read the drama we almost see a man forging his own destiny. The characters may be puppets from a divine point of view, but they engage in clashes of personality so human that the gods almost disappear. Yet the gods, of course, are never completely removed from our minds, and perhaps the fact that Oedipus suffers for his deeds (we cannot call them crimes) is, though terrible, in a degree reassuring. At least there is a system in nature; effects have causes, and horrible and pitiable though the effects are, they may be better than a chaotic universe.

When Oedipus solved the riddle, in the enigma he saw man. And the play is about Oedipus' further discovery—a discovery partly about man but chiefly about himself. Thomas De Quincey, an English essayist, suggested a further relation between the riddle and the play: When Oedipus answered the riddle he saw Man; years later, when his life was closing, he might have answered, De Quincey suggests, not "Man" but

"Oedipus." For who so weak at birth as the abandoned infant with feet pinned together, who so powerful and upright at noon, and who so in need of assistance in his last blind years?

Sophocles: Biographical Note. Born about 496 B.C., Sophocles entered a world in which Athens was the rising power. He died in 406 B.C.; thus his life spans Athens' greatness and he was spared the horror of seeing her fall to Sparta. Handsome and athletic, learned and musical, he apparently enjoyed the esteem of his contemporaries. He is often referred to as "serene," but his dramas suggest a deep rather than a complacent view of life. Although he wrote more than a hundred plays and won eighteen victories in the dramatic contests, only seven of his tragedies survive.

Oedipus the King

TRANSLATED BY J. T. SHEPPARD

Characters

OEDIPUS, *King of Thebes, son of Laïus, reputed son of Polybus.*

JOCASTA, *widow of Laïus, now wife of Oedipus.*

CREON, *her brother, a prince of Thebes.*

TEIRESIAS, *a blind soothsayer.*

A PRIEST of ZEUS.

A MESSENGER *from Corinth.*

A HERDSMAN.

A MESSENGER *from the Palace.*

ANTIGONE and ISMENE, *children of Oedipus.*

CHORUS of THEBAN CITIZENS.

SUPPLIANTS, GUARDS, and SERVANTS.

(*An open place before the Royal Palace at Thebes. Enter a company of suppliants, old men, youths, and children, who take their places at the altars before the Palace. Enter to them, from the Palace,* OEDIPUS.)

OEDIPUS: My children, sons of Cadmus and his care,
Why thus, in suppliant session, with the boughs
Enwreathed for prayer, throng you about my feet,
While Thebes is filled with incense, filled with hymns
To the Healer, Phoebus, and with lamentation?—
Whereof I would not hear the tale, my children,
From other lips than yours. Look! I am here,
I, who am called 'the All-Famous Oedipus'!
Tell me, old priest, you who by age are fit
To speak for these, in what mood stand ye here—
Of panic—or good courage? Speak! For I,
You know, would give all aid. Hard were my heart,
Pitying not such a petitioning.

A PRIEST: King, Master of my country, Oedipus,
You see us, in our several ages, ranged
About your altars. Some are not yet fledged
For long flight, others old and bowed with years,
Priests—I of Zeus—and yonder, of our youth
A chosen band. Thebes, garlanded for prayer,
Sits in the markets, at the shrines of Pallas,
And by Ismenus' oracle of fire.
With your own eyes you see, the storm is grown
Too strong, and Thebes can no more lift her head
Out of the waves, clear from the surge of death.
A blight is on her budding fruit, a blight
On pastured cattle, and the barren pangs
Of women: and the fiery fever-god
Hath struck his blow—Pestilence sweeps the city,
Empties the house of Cadmus and makes rich
With tears and wailings the black house of Death.
We count you not a god, I and these children,
That thus we seek your hearth. Of human kind
We judge you first in the common accident
Of fate; in the traffic of the gods with man
Greatest of men;—who came to Cadmus' town
And loosed the knot and quit us of the toll
To that grim singer paid. No hint from us,
No schooling, your own wit, touched by some god,
Men say and think, raised us and gave us life.
So now, great Oedipus, mighty in the world,

We stand and pray. If you have any knowledge
From god or man, find help! The tried man's thought,
And his alone, springs to the live event!
Oh, noblest among men, raise up our state!
Oh, have a care! To-day for that past zeal
Our country calls you Saviour. Shall your sway
Be thus remembered—that you raised us high
Only to fall? Not so! Lift up our state
Securely, not to fall. With promise good
You brought us fortune. Be the same to-day!
Would you be Prince, as you are Master, here?
Better to master men than empty walls.
The desolate ship is nothing, ramparts nothing,
Deserted, with no men to people them.

OEDIPUS: Alas, my sons! I know with what desire
You seek me. Well I know the hurt whereby
You all are stricken—and not one of you
So far from health as I. Your several griefs
Are single and particular, but my soul
Mourns for myself, for you, and for all Thebes.
You rouse not one that sleeps. Through many tears
And many searchings on the paths of thought,
By anxious care, at last, one way of cure
I found:—and put in action. . . . I have sent
Menoeceus' son, Creon, my own wife's brother,
To ask of Phoebus, in his Pythian shrine,
'By word or deed how shall I rescue Thebes?'
And when I mark the distance and the time,
It troubles me—what does he? Very long—
Beyond his time, he lingers. . . . When he comes,
Then call me base if I put not in act
What thing soever Phoebus showeth me.

PRIEST: Good words and seasonable. In good time—
Look! my companions tell me, Creon comes!

OEDIPUS: O King Apollo, as his looks are glad
So may he bring us glad and saving fortune.

PRIEST: I think he bears us good. Else were his head
Not thus enwreathed, thick with the clustered laurel.

OEDIPUS: He is in earshot. We'll not think, but know!

(*He raises his voice as* CREON *approaches.*)

Prince, and my kinsman, son of Menoeceus, speak!
What message bring you for us from the god?

CREON: Good news! I count all news as fortunate,

However hard, that issues forth in good.

OEDIPUS: 'Tis a response that finds me undismayed,
And yet not overbold. What says the god?

CREON: If you would hear now, with this company
Here present, I will speak—or go within?

OEDIPUS: Speak it to all, since it is their distress
I care for—aye, more than for my own life.

CREON: So be it. As I heard from the god, I speak.
Phoebus the King enjoins with clear command:
A fell pollution, fed on Theban soil,
Ye shall drive out, not feed it past all cure.

OEDIPUS: How drive it out? In what way came misfortune?

CREON: There must be banishment, or blood for blood
Be paid. 'Tis murder brings the tempest on us.

OEDIPUS: Blood—for what blood? Whose fate revealeth he?

CREON: My Lord, in former days, our land was ruled—
Before you governed us—by Laïus.

OEDIPUS: I know—men tell me so—I never saw him.

CREON: He fell. Apollo chargeth us to strike
His murderers, whoe'er they be, with vengeance.

OEDIPUS: The task is hard. How can we hope to track
A crime so ancient? Where can they be found?

CREON: Here, said the god, in Thebes. To seek is oft
To find—neglected, all escapes the light.

OEDIPUS: Was it in Thebes, or on the countryside
Of Thebes, the King was murdered, or abroad?

CREON: Abroad, on sacred mission, as he said,
He started—then, as he went, returned no more.

OEDIPUS: Came none with news? Came none who journeyed with him
Back, to report that you might learn and act?

CREON: All slain.... One panic-stricken fugitive
Told naught that he saw—knew naught—save one thing only.

OEDIPUS: What thing? One clue, disclosing many more,
The first small promise grasped, may teach us all.

CREON: Robbers, he told us, met the King and slew him—
Not just one man, but a great company.

OEDIPUS: What brought the robber ... what, unless 'twas pay, ...
Something contrived from Thebes! ... to such a deed?

CREON: Some thoughts of that there were. Yet, in our troubles,
For Laïus dead no man arose with aid.

OEDIPUS: Some thoughts! For a King dead! A pressing trouble,

To put you off with less than certainty!

CREON: It was the Sphinx—whose riddling song constrained us
To leave the unknown unknown, and face the present.

OEDIPUS: Then I'll go back and fetch all to the light!
'Tis very just in Phoebus—and in you
'Tis a just zeal for the cause of that slain man.
And right it is in me that ye shall see me
Fighting that cause for Phoebus and for Thebes.
Not for some distant unknown friend,—myself,
For my own sake, I'll drive this evil out,
Since he that slew this King were fain perchance
Again, by the same hand, to strike . . . at me!
So, fighting for your King, I serve myself.
Come then, my children, lift your prayerful boughs,
And leave the altar-steps. Up! No delay!
Go, someone, gather Cadmus' people here!
I will do all. Then as the god gives aid,
We'll find Good Luck . . . or else calamity!

(*Exit.*)

PRIEST: Up, children, let us go! The King's own word,
You hear it, grants the boon for which we came.
Now Phoebus, who sent the oracle,
Himself to stay the plague and save us all.

(*The* SUPPLIANTS *leave the altars. The* THEBAN CITIZENS, *summoned by the King's messengers, gather in front of the Palace.*)

CHORUS: Glad Message of the voice of Zeus,
From golden Pytho travelling to splendid Thebes, what burden bringest thou?
Eager, am I, afraid, heart-shaken with fear of thee—
(Healer, Apollo of Delos, God of the Cry, give ear!)
Shaken with reverent fear. Is it some new task to be done?
Or is it some ancient debt thou wilt sweep in the fulness of time to the payment?
Tell me thy secret, Oracle deathless, Daughter of golden Hope!
First call we on the child of Zeus,
Deathless Athene; then on her that guards our land, her Sister, Artemis,
Lady of Good Report, whose throne is our market place;
Aye, and Apollo! I cry thee, Shooter of Arrows, hear!

Three that are strong to deliver, appear! Great Fighters of Death,
Now, if in ancient times, when calamity threatened, ye came to help us,
Sweeping afar the flame of affliction,—strike, as of old, to-day!

II

Alas! Alas! Beyond all reckoning
My myriad sorrows!
All my people sick to death, yet in my mind
No shaft of wit, no weapon to fight the death.
The fruits of the mighty mother Earth increase not.
Women from their tempest of cries and travail-pangs
Struggle in vain . . . no birth-joy followeth.
As a bird on the wing, to the west, to the coast of the sunset god
Look, 'tis the soul of the dead that flies to the dark, nay, soul upon soul,
Rushing, rushing, swifter and stronger in flight than the race of implacable fire,
Myriads, alas, beyond all reckoning,—
A city dying!
None has pity. On the ground they lie, unwept,
Spreading contagious death; and among them wives
That wail, but not for them, aye, and grey mothers
Flocking the altar with cries, now here, now there,
Shrilling their scream of prayer . . . for their own lives.
And a shout goeth up to the Healer; and, cleaving the air like fire.
Flashes the Paean, above those voices that wail in a piping tune.
Rescue! Rescue! Golden One! Send us the light of thy rescuing, Daughter of Zeus!

III

Turn to flight that savage War-God, warring not with shield and spear,
But with fire he burneth when his battle-cry is loud,
Turn him back and drive him with a rushing into flight,
Far away, to exile, far, far away from Thebes,
To the great sea-palace of Amphitrite,
Perchance to the waves of the Thracian sea and his own barbaric shore

He spareth us not. Is there aught that the night has left?
Lo! Day cometh up to destroy.
King and Lord, O Zeus, of the lightning fires,
Father of all! Thine is the Might. Take up the bolt and slay!
Phoebus, King Lycean, I would see thee string thy golden bow,
Raining on the monster for our succour and defence
Shafts unconquered. I would see the flashing of the fires
From the torch of Artemis, that blazeth on the hills
When she scours her mountains of Lycia.
And another I call, the Golden-Crowned, and his name is a name of Thebes;
He is ruddy with wine, and his cry is the triumph cry,
And his train are the Maenades;—
Come, great Bacchus, come! With a splendour of light,
Blazing for us, strike at the god cursed among gods, and save!

(*Re-enter* OEDIPUS.)

OEDIPUS: You pray! And for your prayer . . . release, perchance,
And succour you shall find; if you will aid
My nursing of this malady, and attend,
Obedient, to the words which I shall speak
Touching a story strange to me. I stand
A stranger to the fact, could not have proved it,
A foreigner, with no hint to guide me to it,
Yet now, a Theban among Thebans, speak
To you, to Thebes, my solemn proclamation.
Is there among you one who knows what hand
Did murder Laïus, son of Labdacus?
That man I charge unfold the truth to me.
Say that he fear by utterance to bring
Himself in accusation . . . why, his payment
Shall not be harsh; he shall depart unharmed.
Doth any know another, citizen
Or stranger, guilty? Hide it not. Reward
I'll pay, and Thebes shall add her gratitude.
What! You are silent still? If any fear
For a friend or for himself, and will not speak,
Then I must play my part. Attend what follows.
This man, whoe'er he be, from all the land
Whose government and sway is mine, I make
An outlaw. None shall speak to him, no roof
Shall shelter. In your sacrifice and prayer
Give him no place, nor in drink-offerings,

But drive him out of doors . . . for it is he
Pollutes us, as the oracle Pythian
Of Phoebus hath to-day revealed to me.
Thus I take up my fight for the dead man's cause
And for the god, adding this malediction
Upon the secret criminal—came the blow
By one man's hand, or aid of many hands—
As was the deed, so be his life, accurst!
Further, if, with my knowledge, in my house
He harbour at my hearth, on mine own head
Fall every imprecation here pronounced.
On you I lay my charge. Observe this ban
For my sake and the god's, and for your country
Now sunk in ruin, desolate, god-forsaken.
Why—such a business, even had the gods
Not moved therein, 'twas ill to leave uncleansed.
A noble gentleman, a King had perished . . .
Matter enough for probing. Well, you failed.
To-day, since I am King where he was King,
The husband of his bride, from whose one womb,
Had he been blest with progeny, had sprung
Near pledges of our bond, his fruit and mine . . .
Not so . . . fell Fortune leapt upon her prey,
And slew him. Therefore I will fight for him
As for my father; face all issues; try
All means, to find the slayer, and avenge
That child of Labdacus and Polydorus,
Agenor's offspring and great Cadmus' son.
If any shirk this task, I pray the gods
Give to their land no increase, make their wives
Barren, and with the like calamities,
Nay, worse than ours to-day, so let them perish.
On you, the rest of Thebes, who make my will
Your own—may Righteousness, who fight for us,
And all the gods wait on you still with good.

CHORUS: O King, as bound beneath thy curse I speak.
I neither slew, nor can I point to him
That slew. The quest . . . Apollo, he that sent
The oracle, should tell who is the man.

OEDIPUS: 'Twere just. Yet lives there any man so strong,
Can force unwilling gods to do his will?

CHORUS: I think, the second best . . . if I may speak . . .

OEDIPUS: Aye, if you have a third best, speak it! speak it!

CHORUS: The great Teiresias, more than other men,
Sees as great Phoebus sees. From him, great King,

The searcher of this case were best instructed.
OEPIDUS: There I have not been slothful. I have sent—
Creon advising—I have sent for him
Twice . . . It is very strange . . . Is he not yet come?
CHORUS: Well, well. The rest's old vague unmeaning talk.
OEPIDUS: What talk? What talk? I must neglect no hint.
CHORUS: He died, they said, at the hand of travellers.
OEDIPUS: I heard it too. And he that saw . . . none sees him!
CHORUS: Nay, if he have the touch of fear, he'll not
Abide thy dreadful curse. He needs must speak.
OEDIPUS: Phrases to frighten him that dared the doing?
CHORUS: Yet hath he his accuser. See! They bring
The sacred prophet hither, in whose soul,
As in no other mortal's, liveth truth.

(*Enter* TEIRESIAS, *led by a boy.*)

OEPIDUS: Teiresias, thou that judgest all the signs
That move in heaven and earth—the secret things,
And all that men may learn—thine eyes are blind,
Yet canst thou feel our city's plight, whereof
Thou art the champion, in whom alone,
Prophet and Prince, we find our saving help!
Phoebus hath sent—perchance my messengers
Spoke not of it—this answer to our sending.
One only way brings riddance of the plague:—
To find, and kill or banish, them that killed
King Laïus. Come! Be lavish of thy skill.
By hint of birds, by all thy mantic arts,
Up! Save thyself and me, save Thebes, and heal
All the pollution of that murdered King!
See, we are in thy hands. 'Tis good to serve
Thy fellows by all means, with all thou hast.

TEIRESIAS: Ah me! It is but sorrow to be wise
When wisdom profits not. All this I knew,
Yet missed the meaning. Else I had not come.
OEDIPUS: Why, what is this? How heavily thou comest!
TEIRESIAS: Dismiss me home. Be ruled by me. The load
Will lighter press on thee, as mine on me.
OEDIPUS: Dost thou refuse us? In thy words I find
Small love for Thebes, thy nurse, and for her law.
TEIRESIAS: 'Tis that I see thy own word quit the path
Of safety, and I would not follow thee.

OEDIPUS: Oh, if thy wisdom knows, turn not away!
We kneel to thee. All are thy suppliants.
TEIRESIAS: For none of you is wise, and none shall know
From me this evil . . . call it mine, not thine!
OEDIPUS: Thou knowest? And thou wilt not tell? Thy mind
Is set, to play us false, and ruin Thebes?
TEIRESIAS: I spare myself and thee. Why question me?
'Tis useless, for I will not answer thee.
OEDIPUS: Not answer me! So, scoundrel! . . . Thou wouldst heat
A stone. . . . Thou wilt not? Can we wring from thee
Nothing but stubborn hopeless heartlessness?
TEIRESIAS: My stubborn heart thou chidest, and the wrath
To which thy own is mated, canst not see.
OEDIPUS: Have I no cause for anger? Who unmoved
Could brook the slight such answers put on Thebes?
TEIRESIAS: Though I hide all in silence, all must come.
OEDIPUS: Why, if all must, more cause to tell me all.
TEIRESIAS: I speak no more. So, if it pleasure thee,
Rage on in the full fury of thy wrath!
OEDIPUS: Aye, so I will—speak out my wrath, and spare
No jot of all I see. Listen! I see
In thee the plotter of the deed, in thee,
Save for the blow, the doer. Hadst thou eyes,
Then had I said—the killing too was thine.
TEIRESIAS: So! Is it so?—I bid thee, by the words
Of thy decree abiding, from this day
That lights thee now, speak not to these or me:
Since thou art foul, and thou pollutest Thebes.
OEDIPUS: So bold, so shameless? Can you dare to launch
Such impudent malice, and still look for safety?
TEIRESIAS: Safe am I now. The truth in me is strong.
OEDIPUS: The truth? Who taught it you? 'Twas not your art.
TEIRESIAS: Thyself. I would not speak. Thou madest me.
OEDIPUS: Once more. What was it? I must have it plain.
TEIRESIAS: Spoke I not plainly? Art thou tempting me?
OEDIPUS: I am not sure I took it. Speak again.
TEIRESIAS: Thou seekest, and thou art, the murderer!
OEDIPUS: A second time that slander! You shall rue it.
TEIRESIAS: Shall I add more to make thee rage the more?
OEDIPUS: Add all you will. Say on. 'Tis wasted breath.
TEIRESIAS: I tell thee, with thy dearest, knowing nought,
Thou liv'st in shame, seeing not thine own ill.
OEDIPUS: You talk and talk and fear no punishment?
TEIRESIAS: Aye, none, if there be any strength in truth.

OEDIPUS: 'Tis strong enough for all, but not for thee.
Blind eyes, blind ears, blind heart, thou hast it not.
TEIRESIAS: And *thou* hast . . . misery, this to mock in me
Which soon shall make all present mock at thee.
OEDIPUS: Night, endless night is on thee. How canst thou
Hurt me or any man that sees the light?
TEIRESIAS: Thou art not doomed to fall by me. Apollo,
Who worketh out this end, sufficeth thee—
OEDIPUS:—Creon!—Was this invention his, or thine?—
TEIRESIAS: Nor is thy ruin Creon. 'Tis thyself!
OEDIPUS: O Wealth, O Kingship and thou, gift of Wit
That conquers in life's rivalry of skill,
What hate, what envy come with you! For this,
The government, put in my hand by Thebes,
A gift I asked not,—can it be for this;
Creon, the true, Creon, so long my friend,
Can plot my overthrow, can creep and scheme
And set on me this tricking fraud, this quack,
This crafty magic-monger—quick to spy
Ill-gotten gain, but blind in prophecy.
Aye . . . Where have you shown skill? Come, tell me. Where?
When that fel[illegible]ch was here with riddling hymn
Why were you silent? Not one word or hint
To save this people? Why? That puzzle cried
For mantic skill, not common human wit;
And skill, as all men saw, you had it not;
No birds, no god informed you. I, the fool,
Ignorant Oedipus,—no birds to teach me—
Must come, and hit the truth, and stop the song;—
The man whom you would banish—in the thought
To make yourself a place—by Creon's throne!
You and your plotter will not find, I think,
Blood-hunting pays! You have the look of age:
Else, your own pain should teach you what you are!
CHORUS: We think the prophet's word came but from wrath,
And, as we think, O King, from wrath thine own.
We need not this. Our need is thought, how best
Resolve the god's decree, how best fulfill it.
TEIRESIAS: Though thou be master, thou must brook one right's
Equality—reply! Speech yet is mine,
Since I am not thy slave, nor Creon's man
And client, but the slave of Loxias.
I speak then. Thou hast taunted me for blind,

Thou, who hast eyes and dost not see the ill
Thou standest in, the ill that shares thy house,—
Dost know whose child thou art?—nor see that hate
Is thine from thy own kin, here and below.
Twin-scourged, a mother's Fury and thy father's,
Swift, fatal, dogging thee, shall drive thee forth,
Till thou, that seest so true, see only night,
And cry with cries that every place shall harbour,
And all Cithaeron ring them back to thee,
When thou shalt know thy Marriage . . . and the end
Of that blithe bridal-voyage, whose port is death!
Full many other evils that thou know'st not
Shall pull thee down from pride and level thee
With thy own brood, aye, with the thing thou art!
So then, rail on at Creon: if thou wilt,
Rail on at me who speak: yet know that thou
Must perish, and no man so terribly.

OEDIPUS: Can this be borne? This, and from such as he?
Go, and destruction take thee! Hence! Away!
Quick! . . . Leave my house . . . begone the way thou camest.

TEIRESIAS: That way I had not come hadst thou not called me.

OEDIPUS: I little thought to hear such folly; else I had made little haste to summon thee.

TEIRESIAS: Such as thou say'st I am; for thee a fool,
But for thy parents that begat thee, wise.

OEDIPUS: My parents! Stay! Who is my father? . . . Speak!

TEIRESIAS: This day shall give thee birth and shall destroy thee.

OEDIPUS: Riddles again! All subtle and all vague!

TEIRESIAS: Thou can'st read riddles as none other can.

OEDIPUS: Aye, taunt me there! There thou shalt find me great.

TEIRESIAS: 'Tis just that Luck of thine hath ruined thee.

OEDIPUS: What matter? I saved Thebes, and I care nothing.

TEIRESIAS: Then I will go. Come, lad, conduct me hence.

OEDIPUS: Aye. Bid him take thee hence. Here thou dost clog
And hinder—once well sped, wilt harm no more!

TEIRESIAS: I go, yet speak my message, fearing not
Thee and thy frown. No way canst thou destroy me.
Wherefore I tell thee . . . He whom thou this while
Hast sought with threatenings and with publishings
Of Laïus' murder—that same man is here,
Now called a stranger in our midst, but soon
He shall be known, a Theban born, yet find
Small pleasure in it. Blind, that once had sight,

A beggar, once so rich, in a foreign land
A wanderer, with a staff groping his way,
He shall be known—the brother of the sons
He fathered; to the woman out of whom
He sprang, both son and husband;—and the sire
Whose bed he fouled, he murdered! Get thee in,
And think, and think. Then, if thou find'st I lie,
Then say I have no wit for prophecy!

(*Exit* TEIRESIAS. OEDIPUS, *deeply moved, withdraws into the Palace.*)

CHORUS: Who is the man of wrong, seen by the Delphian Crag oracular?
Seen and guilty—blood on his hand—from a sin unspeakable!
Now shall he fly!
Swifter, stronger than horses of storm,
Fly! It is time!
Armed with the fire and the lightning, the Child of Zeus leapeth upon him:
After the god swarm the dreadful Fates unerring.
Swift as a flame of light, leapeth a Voice, from the snows Parnassian,
Voice of Phoebus, hunting the sinner that lurks invisible.
Lost in the wild,
Rock and forest and cavernous haunt
Rangeth the bull,
Lost and alone—to escape from the words that fly, swift from Apollo's
Oracle shrine:—stinging words that swarm and die not.
The prophet wise, reader of bird and sign,
Terribly moveth me.
I cannot deny. I cannot approve. I knew not what to say.
I brood and waver. I know not the truth of the day or the morrow.
I know not any quarrel that the Labdacids have, or have ever had, with the son of Polybus,
Nor proof to make me stand against the praise men give to Oedipus,
Though I fight for the Labdacids, to avenge the King's strange death,
The only Wise, Zeus and Apollo, know
Truth and the way of man,

They know! Can a prophet know? Can a man know
more than common men?
No proof is found. Yet a man may be wiser, I know, than
his fellow.
Until the charge be proven good, let the world cry "Guilty,"
never will I consent with it.
We saw the maid of fatal wing: we know the helper.
Wise and true
To the city of Thebes, he came. I will never call him false.

(*Enter* CREON.)

CREON: Good citizens, news of a monstrous charge
Spoken by Oedipus the King against me
Brings me indignant here. Can he believe
That I am guilty in this perilous time
Of act or word conducting to his hurt?
I care no more for life, with such a tale
Abroad—no vexing trifle, but a charge
Of great concern and import—to be called
By you, my country, and my friends, a traitor!
CHORUS: It was not reasoned judgment, but the stress,
Perhaps, of anger, forced the bitter words.
CREON: So, then, the words were uttered, that I plotted
And won the seer to make his tale a lie?
CHORUS: 'Twas spoken so. I know not with what thought.
CREON: Was the mind steady, was the eye unchanged,
When the King spoke against my loyalty?
CHORUS: I know not. What my masters do, I see not.

(*Enter* OEDIPUS.)

Look! In good time, the King himself is come!
OEDIPUS: Fellow, what brings you here? Are you so bold,
Unblushingly to venture to the house
Of him you would destroy, proved murderer,
Brigand, and traitor, that would steal my throne?
Tell me, come, tell me. When you plotted this,
Seemed I a fool or coward? Did you think
I should not see the crime so cunningly
Preparing, or could see and not prevent?
What! Without friends or money did you hunt
A Kingdom? 'Twas a foolish enterprise.
Kingdoms are caught by numbers and by gold!
CREON: This right I bid thee do. As thou hast spoken,
So hear me. Then, when thou hast knowledge, judge.

OEDIPUS: Glib art thou . . . and I slow to learn—from thee,
In whom I find so harsh an enemy.

CREON: This one thing first, this one thing let me say—

OEDIPUS: This one thing never—that thou art not false.

CREON: Nay, if you think unreasoned stubbornness
A thing to value, 'tis an evil thought.

OEDIPUS: Nay, if you think to do your kinsman wrong
And scrape the penalty . . . 'tis a mad thought.

CREON: Aye, true, and justly spoken. But the hurt
You think that I have done you, tell it me.

OEDIPUS: Did you, or did you not, urge me 'twas best
To summon his grand reverence, the prophet?

CREON: Even as I first advised, so I think still.

OEDIPUS: How long ago, tell me, did Laïus . . .

CREON: What, that he did? I have not understood.

OEDIPUS: Pass, by that stroke that slew him, from men's sight?

CREON: 'Tis a long count of many long-sped days.

OEDIPUS: This prophet—well! Was he in practice then?

CREON: Honoured as now, wise as he is to-day.

OEDIPUS: So? In those days spoke he at all of me?

CREON: Never, when I was present, aught of thee.

OEDIPUS: And did you make no question for the dead?

CREON: Question, be sure, we made—but had no answer.

OEDIPUS: That day this wise man did not breathe it! Why?

CREON: I know not. Where I am not wise, I speak not.

OEDIPUS: One thing you know.—Be wise, then, and confess it.

CREON: What is it? If I know I'll not deny.

OEDIPUS: Had you not been with him, he had not hinted
My name, my compassing of Laïus' fall.

CREON: Doth he so? You best know. Nay, let me ask,
And do you answer, as I answered you.

OEDIPUS: Ask! You will never prove me murderer!

CREON: First, then:—is not your wedded wife my sister?

OEDIPUS: A truth allowed and not deniable!

CREON: Joint partner of your honours and your lands?

OEDIPUS: Freely she has her every wish of me.

CREON: Am not I third, in equal partnership?

OEDIPUS: Aye, and 'tis that proves thee a traitor friend.

CREON: No! Reason with thyself, as reason I,
And, first, consider—Who would be a King
That lives with terrors, when he might sleep sound,
Knowing no fear, and wield the selfsame sway?
Not such an one as I. My nature craves

To live a King's life, not to be a King:—
And so think all who know what Wisdom is.
Through you, all unafraid, I win my will;
To crown me were to lay constraints on me.
What can the despot's throne confer more sweet
Than peaceful sway and princely influence?
When all clean gains of honourable life
Are mine, must I run mad, and thirst for more?
"Good-day" cries all the world, and open-armed
Greets me! The King's own suitors call for me,
Since that way lies success! What? Leave all this,
To win that Nothing? No, Disloyalty
Were neither reason nor good policy.
My nature holds no lust for that high thought,
And loathes the man who puts that thought in act.
Thus you may prove it—go to Pytho: Ask
If well and truly I have brought my message:
Or thus—discover plot or plan wherein
The seer and I joined council—I'll pronounce
The sentence, add my voice to thine, for death!
Only, on vague suspicion charge me not.
It is not fair, it is not just, for nothing
To call a true man false, a false man true!
To cast a good friend off—it is as if
You cast the very life you love away.
Well, Time shall teach you surely. For 'tis Time,
And only Time, can prove a true man's worth,
Where one short day discovers villainy!
CHORUS: Good words, O King, for one that hath a care
To scrape a fall. Hot thoughts are dangerous!
OEDIPUS: Ah! Where a secret plotter to his end
Moves hot, as hotly must I counter him.
Shall I sit still and bide his time? My all
Were lost, in error mazed, and his work done.
CREON: Come then. What is your will? To cast me forth . . .
OEDIPUS: Not so! My will is death, not banishment.
CREON: Still so unmoved? Can you not trust my word?
OEDIPUS: No, you must prove the folly of ambition!
CREON: Have *you* such wisdom?
OEDIPUS: I can play my hand!
CREON: But should play fair with me! . . .
OEDIPUS: —who are so false!
CREON: If you are blinded . . .
OEDIPUS: Still I must be King!
CREON: Better unkinged, than Tyrant . . .

OEDIPUS: Thebes—my Thebes!

CREON: *My* Thebes, as thine! Both are her citizens!

CHORUS: Peace, princes! See where from the palace comes
Jocasta, in your time of need. With her
Turn into good the evil of this quarrel.

(*Enter* JOCASTA.)

JOCASTA: O foolish! foolish! Why this rioting
Of ill-conditioned words? For shame, with Thebes
So suffering, to open private sores!
Come in! . . . Go, Creon, home! . . . You must not turn
What matters nothing into a great wrong.

CREON: Sister, your husband Oepidus claims right
To do me grievous wrong—his fatal choice,
To thrust me from my country, or to slay me!

OEPIDUS: Aye, wife, 'tis true. I find him practising
Against my person craft and treachery.

CREON: An oath! If aught in all this charge be true,
Desert me good! May my own oath destroy me!

JOCASTA: Believe, believe him, Oedipus! Respect
My prayer, and these, thy friends, that pray to thee,
And, if not these, that oath's solemnity!

I

CHORUS: King, we are thy suppliants. Yield, be kind, be wise.

OEDIPUS: What would you have me yield?

CHORUS: Spurn not him that never yet was false, and now is strong in his great oath.

OEDIPUS: Know you the thing you ask?

CHORUS: We know.

OEDIPUS: Speak on!

CHORUS: Thy friend, so terribly bound by his oath to truth,
For mere suspicion's sake,
Cast not away, blamed and disgraced.

OEDIPUS: Be not deceived. As thus you ask, for me
You ask destruction, or my flight from Thebes.

CHORUS: Never! By him that is prince of the gods, the Sun,
If that thought be in us,
Hopeless, godless, friendless, may we perish!
Not so! Our hearts are heavy. The land we love is perishing.
And how shall a hurt yourselves have made be added to the wrong?

OEDIPUS: So! Let him go . . . though I be slain for it,

Or shamed, and violently thrust from Thebes.
It is your pleading voice, 'tis not his oath,
Hath moved me. Him I shall hate where'er he be.

CREON: You yield, but still you hate; and as you pass
From passion, you are hard. 'Tis very plain.
Such men—'tis just—reap for themselves most pain!

OEDIPUS: Go! Get you gone, and leave me!

CREON: I will go!
You know not, pity not. These trust me still, and know!

(*Exit* CREON.)

II

CHORUS: Lady, stay no longer! Take your lord within. 'Tis time!

JOCASTA: First tell me what has happened.

CHORUS: Words that bred conjecture lacking knowledge, charges whose injustice galls.

JOCASTA: Came they from both?

CHORUS: From both.

JOCASTA: Tell me, what words?

CHORUS: Enough! Already the land is afflicted sore!
For me, enough that strife
Fell, as it fell. There let it lie!

OEDIPUS: See where it leads you, though the thought was kind,
To stay my hand and blunt my purposes.

CHORUS: King, we have told it thee often, again we tell.
Could we put thee from us,
Call us fools and bankrupt of all wisdom.
Not so! When this dear land on a sea of woes was perishing,
You brought her a wind of Fortune. Steer the ship once more safe home!

JOCASTA: I pray you, husband, give me also leave
To know the cause of this so steadfast wrath.

OEDIPUS: I'll tell it. You are more to me than these.
'Twas Creon, and his plotting for my hurt.

JOCASTA: Speak on, my lord. Make charge and quarrel plain.

OEDIPUS: He says I am the murderer of Laïus.

JOCASTA: Of his own knowledge? Or on evidence?

OEDIPUS: No, he has brought a rascal prophet in
To speak, and save his own lips from the lie!

JOCASTA: Then leave these thoughts. . . . Listen to me and learn,
Listen . . . I'll give my proof.—On soothsaying

Nothing depends. An oracle once came
To Laïus—I'll not say it came from Phoebus,
But from his ministers—that he should die
Some day, slain by a son of him and me.
Now, the King . . . strangers, robbers murdered him,
So runs report, at a place where three roads meet.
And the child, not yet three days from the birth,
He took, and pierced his ankles, fettered him,
And cast him out to die on the barren hills.
Phoebus fulfilled not that; made not the son
His father's murderer; wrought not the thing
That haunted Laïus, death by that son's hand.
So dread, so false was prophecy! And you
Regard it not. The god will easily
Bring to the light whate'er he seeks and wills.

OEDIPUS: Wife, as I heard you speak, within my soul
What trouble stirred! What fearful doubt was born!

JOCASTA: What moves you to speak thus? What is your fear?

OEDIPUS: I seemed to hear you say that Laïus
Was murdered at a place where three roads meet.

JOCASTA: So it was said, and so it still is said.

OEDIPUS: Tell me the country where this thing was done?

JOCASTA: Phocis the land is called, where meet the roads
That run from Delphi and from Daulia.

OEDIPUS: Tell me how long ago?

JOCASTA: 'Twas punishéd
Just before you were known as King in Thebes.

OEDIPUS: O Zeus, what is it thou wilt do with me!

JOCASTA: What is it, Oedipus, in this, that moves you?

OEDIPUS: Ask nothing yet. Tell me of Laïus—
What was his stature? Tell me, how old was he?

JOCASTA: Tall, and his hair turning to grey, his shape
Not unlike yours—

OEDIPUS: My curse! Oh, ignorant!
Alas! I see it was myself I cursed.

JOCASTA: Speak! When I look at you I am afraid—

OEDIPUS: My thoughts are heavy. Had the prophet eyes
Help me to make it clear: one answer more—

JOCASTA: I am afraid, but ask! If I know, I'll tell.

OEDIPUS: How travelled Laïus? Went he out, alone,
Or, like a King, with retinue and guard?

JOCASTA: They were five, five in all, and one of them
A herald—and one chariot for the King.

OEDIPUS: All out, alas! All clear! Come, tell me, wife,
Who brought the news? Who gave you that report?

JOCASTA: One servant who alone escaped alive.
OEDIPUS: Where is that servant now? Here, in my house?
JOCASTA: No, no! He is not here. When he came home,
And saw you on the throne, and Laïus dead,
He touched me by the hand, beseeching me
To send him out into some pasture lands
Far off, to live far from the sight of Thebes.
And I—I sent him—he deserved, my lord,
Though but a slave, as much, nay more, than this.
OEDIPUS: Come, we must have him back, and instantly!
JOCASTA: 'Tis easy. . . . Yet—What would you with the man?
OEDIPUS: I fear myself, dear wife; I fear that I
Have said too much, and therefore I must see him.
JOCASTA: Then he shall come. Yet, have not I some claim
To know the thought that so afflicts my lord?
OEDIPUS: I'll not refuse that claim, so deep am I
Gone in forebodings. None so close as you,
To learn what ways of destiny are mine.
My father was of Corinth, Polybus;
My mother Merope, Dorian. As a prince
I lived at first in Corinth, till there fell
A stroke of Fortune, very strange, and yet
Not worth such passion as it moved in me.
Some fellow, at a banquet, flown with wine,
Called me my father's bastard, drunkenly;
And I was angry, yet for that one day
Held myself back, though hardly. Then I sought
Mother and father, questioning; and they
Were hot in their resentment of the taunt;
And I was glad to see them angry. Still
It rankled, and I felt the rumour grow.
I told my parents nothing, but set out
For Pytho. Phoebus, for my journey's pains,
Gave me no clue—dismissed me—yet flashed forth,
In words most strange and sad and horrible:—
'Thou shalt defile thy mother, show mankind
A brood by thee begot intolerable,
And shalt be thy own father's murderer.'
When this I heard, I fled. Where Corinth lay
Henceforth I guessed but by the stars. My road
Was exile, where I might escape the sight
Of that foul's oracle's shame fulfilled on me.
And as I went, I came to that same land
In which you tell me that your King was slain.
Wife, I will tell you all the truth. I passed

Close by that meeting of three ways, and there
A herald met me, and a man that drove
Steeds and a car, even as you have said.
The leader and the old man too were fain
To thrust me rudely from the road. But I,
When one that led the horses jostled me,
Struck him in anger. This the old man saw,
And, from the car—watching for me to pass—
Dashed down his forking goad full on my head—
But paid me double for it. Instantly,
Out from the car, my staff and this right hand
Smote him and hurled him backward to the ground,
And all of them I slew.
If there be aught
That makes that stranger one with Laïus,
There lives no wretch to-day so sad as I,
Nor ever can be one more scorned of heaven
Than I, whom none may welcome, citizen
Or stranger, to his home; nor speak to me;
But only drive me out. And this—'twas I,
No other, on myself invoked this curse.
These hands, by which he died, pollute his bed
And her that shared it. Am I vile enough?
Am I not all uncleanness. I must fly;
And, though I fly from Thebes, must never set
My foot in my own country, never see
My people there, or else I must be joined
In marriage with my mother, and must kill
My father, Polybus, that got and reared me.
If any judge my life and find therein
Malignant stars at work, he hath the truth.
No, No! Ye pure and awful gods, forbid
That I should see that day! Oh, let me pass
Out from the world of men, before my doom
Of living set so foul a blot on me!

CHORUS: O King, we fear thy words, yet bid thee hope,
Till he that saw the deed bring certainty.

OEDIPUS: Why—hope, one little hope, remains. 'Tis this:—
To wait that herdsman's coming; nothing more.

JOCASTA: What—if he comes—what would you have of him?

OEDIPUS: Listen, and I will tell you. If it prove
He speaks as you have spoken, I am saved.

JOCASTA: Tell me, what was it in my words?

OEDIPUS: You said
This was his tale, that robbers slew the King,

Robbers. If he confirm it, if he speak
Of robbers still, it was not I, not I,
That slew. One man is not a company.
But if he names one lonely wayfarer,
Then the deed sways to me, and all is true.

JOCASTA: No. It is certain. When he brought his news
He told it thus. Not I alone, but all
The city heard. He cannot take it back.
And should he swerve a little from his story,
He cannot show, my King, that Laïus died
As prophets would have had him. Loxias
Declared a son of mine must murder him;—
And then that poor lost creature never lived
To kill him. Long ere that, my child was dead.
Since that, for all the soothsayers can tell,
I go straight on, I look not left nor right.

OEDIPUS: 'Tis well. 'Tis very well. And yet—that slave—
Send for him. Have him fetched. Do not neglect it.

JOCASTA: I'll send without delay. Let us go in.
I will do nothing, nothing, but to please you.

(*Exeunt* OEDIPUS *and* JOCASTA.)

CHORUS: Be the prize of all my days
In every word, in every deed,
Purity, with Reverence.
Laws thereof are set before us.
In the heights they move.
They were born where Heaven is,
And Olympus fathered them.
Mortal parent have they none.
Nor shall man's forgetfulness ever make them sleep.
A god in them is great. He grows not old.

Insolence it is that breeds
A tyrant, Insolence enriched
Overmuch with vanities,
Gains unmeet, that give no profit.
So he climbs the height,
So down to a destiny
Evil utterly he leaps,
Where there is no help at all.
True Ambition, for the State, quench it not, O God!
Apollo, still in thee is my defence.

True Ambition, yes! But if a man
Tread the ways of Arrogance;

Fear not Justice, honour not the gods enshrined;
Evil take him! Ruin be the prize
Of his fatal pride!
If his gain be gain of wrong,
If he know not reverence,
If in vanity he dare profane
Sanctities inviolate.
Then from the arrows of the gods what mortal man shall save his soul alive?
If doings such as these be countenanced,
What mean religion's holy dance and hymn?

No more shall I seek in reverence
Earth's inviolate Central Shrine;
No more go to Abai, nor Olympia;
If before all eyes the oracle
Fit not the event!
Zeus, if thou art rightly named,
King and Master over all,
Save thine honour! Let not this escape
Thine eternal governance!
Look to thy oracles of old concerning Laïus; put to nought by man,
They fade, nor is Apollo glorified
In worship any more. Religion dies!

(*Enter* JOCASTA.)

JOCASTA: Prince of Thebes, the thought has come to me
To seek the temples of the gods with boughs
Of supplication and these offerings
Of incense. Oedipus, much overwrought,
And every way distracted, cannot judge
The present sanely by the past, but lends
All ears to every voice that bids him fear.
So, since my words are spent in vain, I come
To thee, Apollo—thou art near to us,
Lycean!—and I pray thee, take the gift,
And grant some clean way of deliverance!
We are afraid; for Oedipus, the guide
And captain of us all, runs mad with fear.

(*Enter a* MESSENGER *from Corinth.*)

MESSENGER: Can you direct me, strangers, to the house
Of Oedipus, your Master?—Better still,
Perchance you know where I may find the King?

CHORUS: This is the house, and he within. The Queen,
His wife and mother of his home, is here.
MESSENGER: His wife, and blest with offspring! Happiness
Wait on her always, and on all her home!
JOCASTA: I wish you happy too. Your gracious speech
Deserves no less. Tell me, with what request
You are come hither, or what news you bring.
MESSENGER: Lady, good news for him and all his house.
JOCASTA: Why, what good news is this? Who sent you here?
MESSENGER: I come from Corinth, and have that to tell
I think will please, though it be partly sad.
JOCASTA: How can a sad tale please? Come, tell it me!
MESSENGER: The people of that country, so men said,
Will choose him monarch of Corinthia.
JOCASTA: What? Is old Polybus no longer King?
MESSENGER: No longer King. Death has him in the grave.
JOCASTA: Dead! Say you so? Oedipus' father dead?
MESSENGER: If he be not so, may I die myself!
JOCASTA: Quick! To your master, girl; tell him this news!
O oracles of the gods, where are you now!
This was the man that Oedipus so feared
To slay, he needs must leave his country. Dead!
And 'tis not Oedipus, but Fortune slew him!

(*Enter* OEDIPUS.)

OEDIPUS: Tell me, Jocasta, wife of my dear love,
Why you have called me hither, out of doors.
JOCASTA: Let this man speak; and as you listen, judge
The issue of the god's grand oracles!
OEDIPUS: This man, who is he? What has he to tell?
JOCASTA: He comes from Corinth, and will tell you this:—
Polybus is no more. Your father's dead.
OEDIPUS: What! Is this true, sir? Answer for yourself!
MESSENGER: If this must needs come first in my report,
'Tis true enough. King Polybus is dead
OEDIPUS: By treachery? Or did sickness visit him?
MESSENGER: A little shift of the scale, and old men sleep.
OEDIPUS: Ah! My poor father died, you say, by sickness?
MESSENGER: Yes, and by reason of his length of days.
OEDIPUS: Ah, me! Wife, why should any man regard
The Delphic Hearth oracular, and the birds
That scream above us—guides, whose evidence
Doomed me to kill my father, who is dead,
Yes, buried under ground, and I stand here,

And have not touched my weapon.—Stay! Perchance
'Twas grief for me. I may have slain him so.
Anyhow, he is dead, and to his grave
Has carried all these oracles—worth nothing!

JOCASTA: Worth nothing. Did I not tell you so long since?

OEDIPUS: You told me, but my fears misguided me.

JOCASTA: Banish your fears, and think no more of them.

OEDIPUS: No, no! Should I not fear my mother's bed?

JOCASTA: Why, what should a man fear? Luck governs all!
There's no foreknowledge, and no providence!
Take life at random. Live as best you can.
That's the best way. What! Fear that you may wed
Your mother? Many a man has dreamt as much,
And so may you! The man who values least
Such scruples, lives his life most easily.

OEDIPUS: All this were well enough, that you have said,
Were not my mother living. Though your words
Be true, my mother lives, and I must fear.

JOCASTA: Your father's death at least is a great hope.

OEDIPUS: Yes, but she lives, and I am still afraid.

MESSENGER: What woman is the cause of all these terrors?

OEDIPUS: Merope, sir, that dwelt with Polybus.

MESSENGER: What find you both to fear in Merope?

OEDIPUS: An oracle from the gods, most terrible.

MESSENGER: May it be told, or did the gods forbid?

OEDIPUS: No, you may hear it. Phoebus hath said that I
Must come to know my mother's body, come
To shed with my own hand my father's blood.
Therefore I have put Corinth this long time
Far from me. Fortune has been kind, and yet
To see a parent's face is best of all.

MESSENGER: Was this the fear that drove you from your home?

OEDIPUS: This, and my will never to slay my father.

MESSENGER: Then since I only came to serve you, sir,
Why should I hesitate to end your fear?

OEDIPUS: Ah! If you could, you should be well rewarded!

MESSENGER: Why, that was my chief thought in coming here,
To do myself some good when you come home.

OEDIPUS: No, where my parents are, I'll not return!

MESSENGER: Son, I can see, you know what you do.

OEDIPUS: 'Fore God, what mean you, sir? Say what you know.

MESSENGER: If this be all that frightens you from home!—

OEDIPUS: All? 'Tis the fear Apollo may prove true—

MESSENGER: And you polluted, and your parents wronged?
OEDIPUS: Aye, it is that, good man! Always that fear!
MESSENGER: Can you not see the folly of such fancies?
OEDIPUS: Folly? Why folly, since I am their son?
MESSENGER: Because King Polybus was nothing to you!
OEDIPUS: How now? The father that begot me, nothing?
MESSENGER: No more, no less, than I who speak to you!
OEDIPUS: How should my father rank with nought—with you?
MESSENGER: He never was your father, nor am I.
OEDIPUS: His reason, then, for calling me his son?
MESSENGER: You were a gift. He had you from these arms.
OEDIPUS: He gave that great love to a stranger's child?
MESSENGER: Because he had none of his own to love.
OEDIPUS: So. Did you buy this child,—or was it yours?
MESSENGER: I found you where Cithaeron's valleys wind.
OEDIPUS: Our Theban hills! What made you travel here?
MESSENGER: Once on these very hills I kept my flocks.
OEDIPUS: A shepherd? Travelling to earn your wages?
MESSENGER: Yes, but your saviour too, my son, that day!
OEDIPUS: What ailed me, that you found me in distress?
MESSENGER: Ask your own feet. They best can answer that.
OEDIPUS: No, no! Why name that old familiar hurt?
MESSENGER: I set you free. Your feet were pinned together!
OEDIPUS: A brand of shame, alas! from infancy!
MESSENGER: And from that fortune comes the name you bear.
OEDIPUS: Who named me? Who? Father or mother? Speak!
MESSENGER: I know not. He that gave you to me—may!
OEDIPUS: You found me not? You had me from another?
MESSENGER: Another shepherd bade me take you. True.
OEDIPUS: What shepherd? Can you tell me? Do you know?
MESSENGER: I think they called him one of Laïus' people.
OEDIPUS: Laïus? The same that once was King in Thebes?
MESSENGER: Aye. 'Twas the same. For him he shepherded.
OEDIPUS: Ah! Could I find him! Is he still alive?
MESSENGER: You best can tell, you, natives of the place!
OEDIPUS: Has any man here present knowledge of
The shepherd he describes? Has any seen,
Or here or in the pastures, such an one?
Speak! It is time for full discovery!
CHORUS: I think, my lord, he means that countryman
Whose presence you desired. But there is none,
Perchance, can tell you better than the Queen.
OEDIPUS: You heard him, wife. Think you he means the man
Whom we await already? Was it he?

JOCASTA: What matter what he means? Oh, take no heed,
And waste no thoughts, I beg you, on such tales.
OEDIPUS: For me it is not possible—to hold
Such clues as these, and leave my secret so.
JOCASTA: No! By the gods, no; leave it, if you care
For your own life. I suffer. 'Tis enough.
OEDIPUS: Take heart. *Your* noble blood is safe, although
I prove thrice bastard, and three times a slave!
JOCASTA: Yet, I beseech you, yield, and ask no more.
OEDIPUS: I cannot yield my right to know the truth.
JOCASTA: And yet I speak—I think—but for your good.
OEDIPUS: And this same good, I find, grows tedious.
JOCASTA: Alas! I pray you may not know yourself.
OEDIPUS: Go, someone, fetch the herdsman! Let the Queen
Enjoy her pride in her fine family!
JOCASTA: O Wretched, Wretched utterly! That name
I give you, and henceforth no other name!

(*Exit.*)

CHORUS: Why went the Queen so swiftly, Oedipus,
As by some anguish moved? Alas! I fear
Lest from that silence something ill break forth.
OEDIPUS: Break what break will! My will shall be to see
My origin however mean! For her,
She is a woman, proud, and woman's pride
Likes not perhaps a husband humbly got!
I am Luck's child. Deeming myself her son,
I shall not be disowned. She lavishes
Good gifts upon me, she's my nature's mother!
Her moons, my cousins, watched my littleness
Wax and grow great. I'll not deny my nature
But be myself and prove my origin.

CHORUS: To-morrow brings full moon!
All hail, Cithaeron! Hail!
If there be wit in me, or any prophet-power,
To-morrow bringeth thee
Fresh glory. Oedipus the King
Shall sing thy praise and call thee his!
His mother and his nurse!
All Thebes shall dance to thee, and hymn thy hill,
Because it is well-pleasing to the King.
Apollo, hear us! Be this thing thy pleasure too!

Who is thy mother, child?

Is it a maid, perchance,
Of that fair family that grows not old with years,
Embraced upon the hills
By roving Pan? Or else a bride
Of Loxias, who loveth well
All upland pasturage?
Did Hermes, or that dweller on the hills,
Bacchus, from one of Helicon's bright Nymphs,
His chosen playmates, take the child for his delight?

OEDIPUS: If I may guess—I never met the man—
I think, good friends, yonder I see the herd
Whom we so long have sought. His many years
Confirm it, for they tally with the years
Of this our other witness; and the guides
I know for men of mine. Can *you,* perchance,
Be certain? You have seen, and know the man.

(*Enter* HERDSMAN.)

CHORUS: Indeed I know him. Laïus trusted him,
Though but a shepherd, more than other men.
OEDIPUS: This question first to you, Corinthian:—
Is this the man you mean?
MESSENGER: Aye, this is he.
OEDIPUS: Look hither, sir, and answer everything
That I shall ask. Were you once Laïus' man?

HERDSMAN: I was, a house-bred servant, no bought slave!
OEDIPUS: What was your work? What was your way of life?
HERDSMAN: The chief part of my life I kept the flocks.
OEDIPUS: Which were the regions where you camped the most?
HERDSMAN: Cithaeron—or sometimes the country round.
OEDIPUS: Ah, then you know this man? You saw him there?
HERDSMAN: I saw him? Saw him when? What man, my lord?
OEDIPUS: Yonder!—Did nothing ever pass between you?
HERDSMAN: No—speaking out of hand, from memory.
MESSENGER: Small wonder he forgets! Come, I'll remind
His ignorance, my lord. I make no doubt
He knows that once around Cithaeron's hills
He tended his two flocks—I had but one—
Yet served for company three summer-times,
The six long months from spring to autumn nights.
And when at last the winter came, I drove
Down to my farm, and he to Laïus' folds.

Was it so done as I have said, or no?

HERDSMAN: 'Tis very long ago. Yes, it is true.

MESSENGER: Now tell me this:—You know you gave me once
A boy, to rear him as a child of mine?

HERDSMAN: What do you mean? Why do you ask me?

MESSENGER: Why?
Because, my friend, that child is now your King!

HERDSMAN: A curse upon you! Silence! Hold your peace.

OEDIPUS: No, no! You must not chide him, sir! 'Tis you
That should be chid, not he, for speaking so.

HERDSMAN: Nay, good my master, what is my offence?

OEDIPUS: This: that you answer nothing—of the child.

HERDSMAN: 'Tis nothing. He knows nothing. 'Tis but talk.

OEDIPUS: You will not speak to please me? Pain shall make you!

HERDSMAN: No! By the gods, hurt me not! I am old.

OEDIPUS: Come, one of you. Quick! Fasten back his arms!

HERDSMAN: O Wretched, Wretched! Why? What would you know?

OEDIPUS: Did you, or did you not, give him the child?

HERDSMAN: I gave it him. Would I had died that day.

OEDIPUS: This day you shall, unless you speak the truth.

HERDSMAN: Alas! And if I speak, 'tis worse, far worse.

OEDIPUS: Ah! So the fellow means to trifle with us!

HERDSMAN: No, No! I have confessed I gave it him.

OEDIPUS: How came you by it? Was the child your own?

HERDSMAN: It was not mine. Another gave it me.

OEDIPUS: Another? Who, and of what house in Thebes?

HERDSMAN: Nay, for the gods' love, Master, ask no more.

OEDIPUS: Make me repeat my question, and you die!

HERDSMAN: The answer is:—a child of Laïus' house.

OEDIPUS: Slave born? Or kinsman to the royal blood?

HERDSMAN: Alas!
So it has come, the thing I dread to tell.

OEDIPUS: The thing I dread to hear. Yet I must hear it.

HERDSMAN: Thus then:—they said 'twas . . . Laïus' son. . . . And yet
Perhaps Jocasta best can answer that.

OEDIPUS: Jocasta gave it you?

HERDSMAN: She gave it me.

OEDIPUS: For what?

HERDSMAN: She bade me do away with it.

OEDIPUS: Its mother! Could she?

HERDSMAN: Fearing prophecies—

OEDIPUS: What prophecies?

HERDSMAN: His father he must kill!
OEDIPUS: And yet you let this old man take him? Why?
HERDSMAN: 'Twas pity, sir. I thought: he dwells afar,
And takes him to some distant home. But he
Saved him to suffer! If you are the child
He saith, no man is more unfortunate.
OEDIPUS: Alas! It comes! It comes! And all is true!
Light! Let me look my last on thee, for I
Stand naked now. Shamefully was I born:
In shame I wedded: to my shame I slew.

(*Exeunt all except the* CHORUS.)

CHORUS: Ah! Generations of mankind!
Living, I count your life as nothingness.
None hath more of happiness,
None that mortal is, than this:
But to seem to be and then,
Having seemed, to fail.
Thine, O unhappy Oedipus,
Thine is the fatal destiny,
That bids me call no mortal creature blest.

Zeus! To the very height of wit
He shot, and won the prize of perfect life;
Conqueror that slew the maid,
Who, with crooked claw and tongue
Riddling, brought us death, when he
Rose and gave us life.
That day it was that hailed thee King,
Preferred above mankind in state
And honour, Master of the Might of Thebes.

To-day, alas! no tale so sad as thine!
No man whom changing life hath lodged
So close with Hell, and all her plagues, and all her sorrowing!
Woe for the fame of Oedipus!
For the Son hath lain where the Father lay,
And the bride of one is the bride of both.
How could the field that the father sowed endure him
So silently so long?

Time knoweth all. Spite of they purposing,
Time hath discovered thee, to judge,
The monstrous mating that defiled the father through the son.
Woe for the babe that Laïus got.
And I would I never had looked on thee,

And the songs I sing are a dirge for thee.
This is the end of the matter: he that saved me,
Hath made me desolate.

(*Enter a* MESSENGER *from the Palace.*)

MESSENGER: Great Lords, that keep the dignities of Thebes,
What doings must ye hear, what sights must see,
And oh! what grief must bear, if ye are true
To Cadmus and the breed of Labdacus!
Can Ister or can Phasis wash this house—
I trow not—, with their waters, from the guilt
It hides? . . . Yet soon shall publish to the light
Fresh, not unpurposed evil. 'Tis the woe
That we ourselves have compassed, hurts the most.

CHORUS: That which we knew already, was enough
For lamentation. What have you besides?

MESSENGER: This is the briefest tale for me to tell,
For you to hear:—your Queen Jocasta's dead.

CHORUS: Alas! Poor lady! Dead! What was the cause?

MESSENGER: She died by her own hand. Of what befell
The worst is not for you, who saw it not.
Yet shall you hear, so much as memory
Remains in me, the sad Queen's tragedy.
When in her passionate agony she passed
Beyond those portals, straight to her bridal-room
She ran, and ever tore her hair the while;
Clashed fast the doors behind her; and within,
Cried to her husband Laïus in the grave,
With mention of that seed whereby he sowed
Death for himself, and left to her a son
To get on her fresh children, shamefully.
So wept she for her bridal's double woe,
Husband of husband got, and child of child.
And after that—I know not how—she died.
We could not mark her sorrows to the end,
For, with a shout, Oedipus broke on us,
And all had eyes for him. Hither he rushed
And thither. For a sword he begged, and cried:
"Where is that wife that mothered in one womb
Her husband and his children! Show her me!
No wife of mine!" As thus he raged, some god—
'Twas none of us—guided him where she lay.
And he, as guided, with a terrible shout,
Leapt at her double door; free of the bolts

Burst back the yielding bar,—and was within.
And there we saw Jocasta. By a noose
Of swaying cords, caught and entwined, she hung.
He too has seen her—with a moaning cry
Looses the hanging trap, and on the ground
Has laid her. Then—Oh, sight most terrible!—
He snatched the golden brooches from the Queen,
With which her robe was fastened, lifted them,
And struck. Deep to the very founts of sight
He smote, and vowed those eyes no more should see
The wrongs he suffered, and the wrong he did.
"Henceforth," he cried, "be dark!—since ye have seen
Whom ye should ne'er have seen, and never knew
Them that I longed to find." So chanted he,
And raised the pins again, and yet again,
And every time struck home. Blood from the eyes
Sprinkled his beard, and still fresh clammy drops
Welled in a shower unceasing, nay, a storm
With blood for rain, and hail of clotting gore.
So from these twain hath evil broken; so
Are wife and husband mingled in one woe.
Justly their ancient happiness was known
For happiness indeed; and lo! to-day—
Tears and Disasters, Death and Shame, and all
The ills the world hath names for—all are here.

CHORUS: And hath he found some respite now from pain?

MESSENGER: He shouts, and bids open the doors, and show
To all his Thebes this father-murderer,
This mother— . . . Leave the word. It is not clean.
He would be gone from Thebes, nor stay to see
His home accursèd by the curse he swore;
Yet hath he not the strength. He needs a guide,
Seeing his griefs are more than man can bear.
Nay, he himself will show you. Look! The gates
Fall open, and the sight that you shall see
Is such that even hate must pity it.

(*Enter* OEDIPUS, *blind.*)

CHORUS: O sight for all the world to see
Most terrible! O suffering
Of all mine eyes have seen most terrible!
Alas! What Fury came on thee?
What evil Spirit, from afar,

O Oedipus! O Wretched!
Leapt on thee, to destroy?
I cannot even Alas! look
Upon thy face, though much I have
To ask of thee, and much to hear,
Aye, and to see—I cannot!
Such terror is in thee!

OEDIPUS: Alas! O Wretched! Whither go
My steps? My voice? It seems to float
Far, far away from me.
Alas! Curse of my Life, how far
Thy leap hath carried thee!

CHORUS: To sorrow none can bear to see or hear.

OEDIPUS: Ah! The cloud!
Visitor unspeakable! Darkness upon me horrible!
Unconquerable! Cloud that may not ever pass away!
Alas!
And yet again, alas! How deep they stab—
These throbbing pains, and all those memories.

CHORUS: Where such afflictions are, I marvel not,
If soul and body made one doubled woe.

OEDIPUS: Ah! My friend!
Still remains thy friendship. Still thine is the help that comforts me,
And kindness, that can look upon these dreadful eyes unchanged.
Ah me!
My friend, I feel thy presence. Though mine eyes
Be darkened, yet I hear thy voice, and know.

CHORUS: Oh, dreadful deed! How wert thou steeled to quench
Thy vision thus? What Spirit came on thee?

OEDIPUS: Apollo! 'Twas Apollo, friends,
Willed the evil, willed, and brought the agony to pass!
And yet the hand that struck was mine, mine only, wretched.
Why should I see, whose eyes
Had no more any good to look upon?

CHORUS: 'Twas even as thou sayest.

OEDIPUS: Aye. For me . . . Nothing is left for sight.
Nor anything to love:
Nor shall the sound of greetings any more

Fall pleasant on my ear.
Away! Away! Out of the land, away!
Banishment, Banishment! Fatal am I, accursed,
And the hate on me, as on no man else, of the gods!
CHORUS: Unhappy in thy fortune and the wit
That shows it thee. Would thou hadst never known.

OEDIPUS: A curse upon the hand that loosed
In the wilderness the cruel fetters of my feet,
Rescued me, gave me life! Ah! Cruel was his pity,
Since, had I died, so much
I had not harmed myself and all I love.
CHORUS: Aye, even so, 'twere better.
OEDIPUS: Aye, for life never had led me then
To shed my father's blood;
Men had not called me husband of the wife
That bore me in the womb.
But now—but now—Godless am I, the son
Born of impurity, mate of my father's bed,
And if worse there be, I am Oedipus! It is mine!
CHORUS: In this I know not how to call thee wise,
For better wert thou dead than living—blind.

OEDIPUS: Nay, give me no more counsel. Bid me not
Believe my deed, thus done, is not well done.
I know 'tis well. When I had passed the grave,
How could those eyes have met my father's gaze,
Or my unhappy mother's—since on both
I have done wrongs beyond all other wrong?
Or live and see my children?—Children born
As they were born! What pleasure in that sight?
None for these eyes of mine, for ever, none.
Nor in the sight of Thebes, her castles, shrines
And images of the gods, whereof, alas!
I robbed myself—myself, I spoke that word,
I that she bred and nurtured, I her prince,
And bade her thrust the sinner out, the man
Proved of the gods polluted—Laïus' son.
When such a stain by my own evidence
Was on me, could I raise my eyes to them?
No! Had I means to stop my ears, and choke
The wells of sound, I had not held my hand,
But closed my body like a prison-house
To hearing as to sight. Sweet for the mind
To dwell withdrawn, where troubles could not come.

Cithaeron! Ah, why didst thou welcome me?
Why, when thou hadst me there, didst thou not kill,
Never to show the world myself—my birth!
O Polybus, and Corinth, and the home
Men called my father's ancient house, what sores
Festered beneath that beauty that ye reared,
Discovered now, sin out of sin begot.
O ye three roads, O secret mountain-glen,
Trees, and a pathway narrowed to the place
Where met the three, do you remember me?
I gave you blood to drink, my father's blood,
And so my own! Do you remember that?
The deed I wrought for you? Then, how I passed
Hither to other deeds?
O Marriage-bed
That gave me birth, and, having borne me, gave
Fresh children to your seed, and showed the world
Father, son, brother, mingled and confused,
Bride, mother, wife in one, and all the shame
Of deeds the foulest ever known to man.
No. Silence for a deed so ill to do
Is better. Therefore lead me hence, away!
To hide me or to kill. Or to the sea
Cast me, where you shall look on me no more.
Come! Deign to touch me, though I am a man
Accurséd. Yield! Fear nothing! Mine are woes
That no man else, but I alone, must bear.

(*Enter* CREON, *attended.*)

CHORUS: Nay, for your prayer, look! in good season comes
Creon, for act or counsel. In your place
He stands, the sole protector of the land.
OEDIPUS: Alas! What words have I for him? What plea
That I can justify? Since all the past
Stands proved, and shows me only false to him.
CREON: I come not, Oedipus, in mockery.
Nor with reproach for evils that are past.—
Nay, if ye have no reverence for man,
Have ye no shame before our Lord the Sun,
Who feeds the world with light, to show unveiled
A thing polluted so, that neither Earth
Nor Light nor Heaven's rain my welcome it.
Stay not. Convey him quickly to his home:
Save his own kindred, none should see nor hear—

So piety enjoins—a kinsman's woe.

OEDIPUS: Ah, since thou hast belied my thought and come
As noblest among men to me, so vile,
Grant me one boon, for thine own weal, not mine.

CREON: What is thy prayer? What boon can I bestow?

OEDIPUS: Cast me from Thebes, aye, cast me quickly forth
Where none may see, and no man speak with me.

CREON: This had I done, be sure, save that I first
Would ask the god what thing is right to do.

OEDIPUS: His word was published, and 'twas plain:—
'Destroy
The guilty one, the parricide!'—'tis I!

CREON: So runs the word; and yet, to ask the god
For guidance in such utter need is best.

OEDIPUS: What? Will you ask for one so lost as I?

CREON: Surely, and you will now believe the god.

OEDIPUS: Aye, and on thee I lay this charge, this prayer:
For her that is within make burial
As pleaseth thee. 'Tis fitting. She is thine.
For me, ah! never doom this land of Thebes,
My father's town, to harbour me alive.
Leave me to haunt the mountains, where the name
Is known of my Cithaeron—proper tomb
By mother and by father set apart
For me, their living child. So let me die
Their victim still that would have slain me there.
And yet this much I know. There is no hurt
Nor sickness that can end me. Since from death
I lived, it was to finish some strange woe. . . .
So let my Fortune, where it goeth, go!
But for my children, Creon,—for the sons
Think not at all. Men are they; anywhere
Can live, and find sufficiency for life.
But for my sad daughters, that dear pair
That never found my table spread apart
From them, nor missed their comrade, but must share
Always the very food their father had:
Be all your care for them. Oh! Best of all,
Let me but touch them, and so weep my full.
Grant it, my prince,
O noble spirit, grant it. But one touch,
And I could think them mine, as when I saw.

(*Enter* ANTIGONE *and* ISMENE.)

Ah! What is this?
That sound? Oh, can it be? Are these my loves,
Weeping? Has Creon pitied me, and fetched
The children of my dearest love to me?
Can it be true?

CREON: 'Tis true; 'twas I so ordered it. I knew
The joy thou hadst in them. 'Tis with thee still.

OEDIPUS: Be happy, and for treading this good way
A kinder fate than mine defend thy steps.
Children, where are you? Come. Ah, come to me!
These arms that wait you are your brother's arms,
Their kindness bade these eyes that were so bright,
Your father's eyes, to see as now they see,
Because 'tis known, my children, ignorant
And blind, your father sowed where he was got.
For you I weep, for you. I have not strength
To see you, only thoughts of all the life
That waits you in the cruel world of men.
No gathering of Thebes, no festival
That you shall visit, but shall send you home
With tears, instead of happy holiday.
And when you come to marriage-days, ah! then
Who will be found to wed you? Who so brave
Will shoulder such reproach of shame as I
Put on my parents, and must leave with you?
Is any woe left out? Your father killed
His father, took the mother of his life
And sowed the seed on her, begetting you
From the same womb whereof himself was born.
This your reproach must be. Lives there a man,
Children, to wed you? None, alas! 'Tis plain:
Unwedded and unfruitful must you die.
Son of Menoeceus, thou art left to them,
Their only father now, for we, their own,
Who gave them life, are dead. Suffer not these,
That are thy kin, beggared and husbandless
To wander, laid as low as I am laid.
Have pity on them. See how young they are,
And, save for thy good part, all desolate.
Promise me, loyal friend. Give me thy hand
In token of it. Children, out of much
I might have told you, could you understand,
Take this one counsel: be your prayer to live.
Where fortune's modest measure is, a life
That shall be better than your father's was.

CREON: It is enough! Go in! Shed no more tears, but go!
OEDIPUS: I would not, yet must yield.
CREON: Measure in all is best.
OEDIPUS: Know you the pledge I crave?
CREON: Speak it, and I shall know.
OEDIPUS: This:—that you banish me!
CREON: That is the gods' to give.
OEDIPUS: The gods reject me!
CREON: Then, perchance, you *shall* have banishment.
OEDIPUS: You promise?
CREON: Knowing not, 'tis not my wont to speak.
OEDIPUS: Then take me, take me, hence!
CREON: Come! Quit your children. Come!
OEDIPUS: No! No! You shall not.
CREON: Ah! Seek not the mastery
In all. Too brief, alas! have proved your masteries.
CHORUS: Look, ye who dwell in Thebes. This man was Oedipus.
That Mighty King, who knew the riddle's mystery,
Whom all the city envied, Fortune's favourite.
Behold, in the event, the storm of his calamities,
And, being mortal, think on that last day of death,
Which all must see, and speak of no man's happiness
Till, without sorrow, he hath passed the goal of life.

(*Exeunt omnes.*)

Euripides:
HIPPOLYTUS

The *Hippolytus* which has come down to us in the revised version, performed in 428 B.C., of a play that Euripides had earlier presented. The first version, wherein Phaedra (rather than the Nurse) told Hippolytus, her stepson, of her illicit passion for him, outraged the audience, and the drama is said to have been hissed off the stage.

Behind the events presented in Euripides' play is the earlier career of Theseus, king of Athens, who had conquered the Amazons (a tribe of female warriors), seized, or married in a loose manner, their queen, and sired Hippolytus. Back in Athens, and desirous of making a political alliance, Theseus legally married Phaedra, the sister of the king of Crete. Hippolytus, inheriting the Amazon love of nature and hunting, grew up a devotee to Artemis, goddess of the hunt and of chastity.

Euripides' play begins with a formal prologue spoken by Aphrodite, goddess of passion or love. Announcing that she will destroy Hippolytus for slighting her, she explains that Phaedra will supply the means. Aphrodite has caused Phaedra to fall in love with her stepson and thus will undo him. Phaedra, too, Aphrodite says, will be destroyed, but her death is a mere unfortunate necessity in the goddess' eyes. The conflict, then, begins as one between two deities, Aphrodite and Artemis, and it concludes on this note, for after Phaedra and Hippolytus are destroyed, Artemis announces that in retaliation she will set about to ruin one of Aphrodite's devotees. But within this divine framework lies a drama about human beings whom many critics have found more realistic than the characters of Sophocles. While we may say the conflict between the gods or between passion on the one hand and restraint or even barren asceticism on the other is made concrete in the persons of Phaedra and Hippolytus, we cannot help noting that Phaedra is more than a mere cardboard cutout labeled "the power of sexual desire." She struggles against her impulse and—in the revised version of the play—does not even tell Hippolytus of her love but allows the Nurse, who has convinced her of the futility of struggle, to convey her message to her stepson. Phaedra, then, far from being a miniature version of Aphrodite, is a woman in self-conflict.

Phaedra's inner conflict, and the Nurse's arguments which persuade the queen to yield, reflect new developments in Greek thinking. The older traditional values were, in these years, being questioned, and the problems of suffering and guilt and legal responsibility were being re-examined. Despite the fact that Aphrodite speaks of the use she will make of Phaedra, we feel that Aphrodite is a part of Phaedra's nature. That is, wrongdoing is not forced upon the innocent, nor is man fully responsible for his deeds. In moments of passion, Euripides suggests, human beings perform terrible acts. Socrates, contemporary of Euripides, insisted that no man knowingly does evil; wrongdoing, he says, is the result of our ignorance, and if we truly know the good we will pursue it. But Phaedra cries out that she knows what she should do but is *unable* to do it. Reason does not have the command over the passions which Socrates attributed to it. Against the Socratic view that recognition of the good necessarily results in good actions, we can juxtapose Phaedra's typically Euripidean admission of powerlessness, and perhaps we may see in Euripides something analogous to St. Paul's statement (Romans 7:19): "For the good that I would I do not: but the evil which I would not, that I do."

Euripides brings the gods down to earth, incarnates them, but the people in whom these "gods" dwell are, as we see in *Hippolytus,* not the happier for harboring divinity. Phaedra's suggestion that she is not responsible for her actions must not be taken as the dramatist's concluding moral tag, and, indeed, she *is* responsible for some of her deeds. In addition to being accused of libeling the gods and blaming them for our misdeeds, Euripides was charged with engaging in clever rhetoric, arguments which were persuasive but unsound. Doubtless he was influenced by the rhetoricians of his day, who engaged in the practice of creating forceful rather than logically valid arguments in defense of accused persons, but this is not to say that he valued intellectual agility more than morality. In fact, although his characters argue subtly and at length, in the final analysis their acts (as Phaedra laments) are governed *not* by intellect but by other forces. Euripides thus deals not so much with broad moral problems as with specifically human difficulties, and it is probably for this reason that Cardinal Newman found him less majestic but more pathetic than Sophocles.

Although most of this discussion has centered on Phaedra, and later dramatists and critics have frequently regarded her as the central character, Hippolytus is the titular hero of the play. Phaedra is indisputably more interesting and complex than Hippolytus, but she drops out sooner, and, just as at the outset she was a mere tool, so the conclusion of the drama focuses not on her but on Hippolytus and, to some degree, Theseus. The play is not so much about Phaedra as about what a particular elemental force, embodied in her nature (Phaedra touches on her heredity), is capable of doing, and at the conclusion we see not Phaedra but the ruin created by frustrated passion. Nor is there any suggestion that evil has worked itself out to its end, for the conflicting principles are neither good nor evil but partial goods, or, perhaps more accurately, amoral facts of life which will, Artemis says, continue to conflict, though the mortals come to a tardy understanding. And this tardy understanding, coupled with Phaedra's attempts to struggle against her own divinely disordered nature, is perhaps what Browning perceived when he wrote that

> Euripides shrank not to teach,
> If gods be strong and wicked, man, though weak,
> May prove their match by willing to be good.

Euripides: Biographical Note. Euripides' approximate dates (484-406 B.C.) mark him as a younger contemporary of Sophocles. Thus, while Sophocles was already old when the disastrous struggle between Greek city-states, the Peloponnesian War, began in 431 B.C., Euripides was in his maturity. More agitated by current trends than Sophocles, Euripides reflects a doubting, skeptical mood. Unpopular in his day (he won only five prizes, though he wrote ninety-two plays) and often maligned, he was of a retiring and bookish nature. In his last months he voluntarily left Athens and settled in Macedonia, where he may have enjoyed the excellent company of other great self-exiled Athenians, including Zeuxis, the painter, and Thucydides, the historian. His extant dramas are of more varied kinds than those of Sophocles, for in addition to tragedies we have some of his tragicomedies and melodramas.

Hippolytus

TRANSLATED BY F. L. LUCAS

Characters

APHRODITE.

ARTEMIS.

THESEUS, *King of Athens.*

HIPPOLYTUS, *his natural son by the Queen of the Amazons.*

PHAEDRA, *daughter of Minos and wife of Theseus.*

HER NURSE.

OLD HUNTSMAN.

SERVANT OF HIPPOLYTUS.

CHORUS OF HUNTSMEN.

CHORUS OF WOMEN OF TROEZĒN.

ATTENDANTS.

(*The palace of Troezēn. Before it, on opposite sides, images of* APHRODITE *and of* ARTEMIS. *Above it appears* APHRODITE *herself.*)

APHRODITE: Great upon earth and high in Heaven endures
My power, nor dim my glory, that am called
The Cyprian Queen. To all that live and look
Upon the sunlight, 'twixt the Pontic surge
To eastward and, to west, the Atlantic Gates,
Favour I give if they revere my greatness,
But, if they flout me—ruin!
For thus is the nature even of the Gods—
To be well pleased with honour from mankind.
And soon, that my words are truth, my deeds shall show.
For Theseus' son by the Queen of Amazons,
Hippolytus, by the blameless Pittheus bred
Here in Troezēn, alone throughout the land
Dares to call *me* of all Gods evillest!—
And spurns at love and shuns the touch of wedlock.
Instead, as greatest of all Gods, he honours
Apollo's sister, Zeus-born Artemis;
And dedicated to that fellowship
Higher than human, he follows his Maiden Queen,
With his swift hounds, through the green woods for ever,
Clearing the land of beasts.
For *that* I care not. What is *that* to me?
But, for his sin against myself, this day
I will smite Hippolytus. Long since pursued
My purpose was; and little's left to do.
For once from Pittheus' hall Hippolytus came
To the land of King Pandīon, there to see
The Holy Mysteries, as initiate.
And there, by my own devising, his father's wife,
The noble Phaedra, saw him; and her heart
Was gripped by passion's anguish.
So even then, in the days before she came
Here to Troezēn,
She raised a shrine beside the Rock of Pallas
To me, the Cyprian, looking toward this land,
Because her love was far. For *his* sake there
She made that shrine, henceforth to bear his name.
But now—since Theseus, to escape pollution
From the blood of Pallas' sons, has bowed himself
To a year of banishment from Cĕcrops' land,
And brought her hither with him—his poor Queen,

Goaded by passion, sighs and wastes to death,
In silence. None of all her household knows.
Yet not in silence shall her passion end.
I will open Theseus' eyes, and the truth be known,
So that he kills this son of his I hate,
By his own prayer; according to the promise
Vouchsafed him once by the sea's lord, Poseidon—
That whatsoever boons Theseus should ask,
Three times the God would grant them.
  And Phaedra, noble princess as she is,
Must perish too. *Her* griefs I cannot weigh
Against such vengeance on my enemies
As sates my soul.
But here I see, from the sweat of the chase returning,
This Theseus' son, Hippolytus—I go.
Thick at his heels a rout of scrvitors
Come bawling out their hymns to Artemis;
But little he knows that already the Gate of Hades
Gapes; and, above him, stands the last sun he sees.

(APHRODITE *disappears and* HIPPOLYTUS *enters with his huntsmen. They pass Aphrodite's image without doing it reverence.*)

HIPPOLYTUS: Praise, as ye come, on Her heavenly throne,
  Praise to the Zeus-born Artemis!—
To Her that loves us as Her own!
  HUNTSMEN: Hail, O Queen revered, adored
  Maid most fair!—
Daughter of Creation's Lord,
Child of Zeus, that Lēto bare!
Beside Thy Father in Heaven's height,
Where His walls gleam golden-bright,
  Thy dwelling is.
Fairest, fairest Thou of all
Maids that tread Olympus' hall,
  Hail, Artemis!

(HIPPOLYTUS *brings a wreath to the image of* ARTEMIS.)

HIPPOLYTUS: To Thee I bring this garland, mistress mine,
Twined from the flowers of an untrodden field,
Where never shepherd dares to feed his flock,
Nor scythe of mower came. The bee alone
Wings in the spring across that virgin meadow,
Which Purity herself keeps watered green.

And none may pluck its flowers—no evil heart—
But those alone whose inbred, unschooled nature
Still loves, in all life's ways, self-mastery.
Mistress beloved, take Thou, from a hand revering,
This garland to enclasp Thy locks of gold.
To me alone of men Thou grantest this—
To be beside Thee and to talk with Thee,
Hearing Thy voice, although Thy face be hid.
As in the beginning of my race of life,
So be it to the end!

HUNTSMAN: My lord—for the name of 'master' fits alone The Gods—may I proffer you a word of counsel?

HIPPOLYTUS: Why, surely! Else, I should show but little wisdom.

HUNTSMAN: Know you a rule that governs all men's hearts?

HIPPOLYTUS: Not I! What means your question?

HUNTSMAN: This!—to resent unfriendliness and pride.

HIPPOLYTUS: Rightly. What pride is not insufferable?

HUNTSMAN: Far different from the grace of courteous lips?

HIPPOLYTUS: Most true—a precious thing, of little cost.

HUNTSMAN: Think you the like may hold true of the Gods?

HIPPOLYTUS: Yes. If our human ways resemble theirs.

HUNTSMAN: Yet there is *one* dread Goddess *you* ignore.

HIPPOLYTUS: Whom then! Take care now, lest your tongue should trip!

HUNTSMAN: She stands here at your gate—the Cyprian!

HIPPOLYTUS: From far I honour *her.* My hands are pure.

HUNTSMAN: Yet dread is She, and honoured in the world.

HIPPOLYTUS: I love not Gods whose powers are of the night.

HUNTSMAN: *All* Gods, my son, should have due reverence.

HIPPOLYTUS: Yet men, like Gods, love better some than others.

HUNTSMAN: May happiness be yours!—and wit to find it!

HIPPOLYTUS: Go now, my men!—indoors and take your meal!
After the hunt a well-filled table's welcome.
And see my horses groomed—when I have eaten,
I will yoke them to my car for exercise.
As for your Cyprian—fare she well, for me!

(*He goes out. The old* HUNTSMAN *turns to the image of* APHRODITE.)

HUNTSMAN: But *I*—for not for *us* to imitate
The young and thoughtless—humbly as fits a slave,
O Cyprian Queen, before Thy image here

Bow down in prayer. Thou shouldst be merciful,
If any in the headstrong heat of youth,
Speaks idly of Thy name. Seem not to hear him.
Surely the Gods should be more wise than men.

(*He too goes out. There enters the* CHORUS OF WOMEN OF TROEZĒN.)

strophe 1

A WOMAN OF THE CHORUS: From Ocean's hidden deeps, men say,
uprushing,
A water subterrene
Fills, from the rock-face gushing,
Our pitchers in Troezēn:
And there by that waterside
I met with a friend I knew—
Mantles of purple hue
She dipped in the stream, and dried
On rocks where the sun beat warm. 'Twas she
First told me our Queen's calamity—

That in her palace now, by sickness faded, *antistrophe* 1
She wastes upon her bed;
With soft veils overshaded,
Dark lies her golden head.
Now the third day she lives
With lips divine sealed fast—
Through them not once hath passed
The bread Earth's Mother gives.
Suffering and still, she hasteneth
Towards that grim harbour whose name is Death.

ANOTHER: Has a God then, lady, possessed thee?—

strophe 2

Is it Pan, or Hecate?
Has the Mountain Mother oppressed thee,
Or the dread Corybants, maybe?

ANOTHER: Or hast thou angered Dictynna,
The Huntress-queen, not keeping
Her rites, and her dues denied?
For far She can follow the sinner,
By water, by land, overleaping
The Swirl of the eddying tide.

ANOTHER: Or thy lord, the long-descended *antistrophe* 2
Prince of Erechtheus' line—
Has *he* by stealth offended,
As he crept to a bed not thine?

ANOTHER: Or comes there some seafarer
From a Cretan haven sailing,
To hospitable Troezēn?—
Of bitter news the bearer,
That in sorrow unavailing
Chains to her couch the Queen?

ANOTHER: Yet frail is woman; hard to guide, *epode*
Her nature's jarring elements;
Hers, for her sorrow, still abide
Labouring womb and craving sense.
Such travail-storms ere now oppressed
Me too—but on Her that easeth birth,
Queen of the Bow, I cried distrest.
She heard—and for ever I hymn Her worth,
Where She walks among the Blest.

CHORUS-LEADER: But see—the Queen comes from her room.
Out of the palace her old nurse brings her—
Her own brow dark with a deepened gloom.
Ah, would to God some tongue could say
What evil wrings her,
That her beauty wastes away!

(PHAEDRA *is led in by the* NURSE. *Her women follow.*)

NURSE: Ah, sickness!—the sorrows that life must see!
What now can I do? Or leave undone?
Here is your bed where you wished to be—
Outside, where Heaven arches free,
And shines the sun.

Hither you needs must come! In vain.
You will only long for your room again.
Nothing can please your fickleness.
You crave what you lack; what you possess,
But brings you pain.

(*The attendants help their mistress to a couch.*)

Still worse to nurse the sick than bear
The sickness! A nurse has double grief—
Arms that ache and a heart of care.

Yet life brings sorrow for all to share,
And for labour no relief.
And if, after life, aught better abides,
Mists enfold it and darkness hides.
Vainly we yearn for some thing unknown,
Behind the grave we glimpse its gleam;
Yet hidden is life beyond our own,
And mystery over the tomb is thrown,
And we drift on tales of dream.
  PHAEDRA: Raise up my body. Lift my head,
My women. Take these hands still fair—
The strength that knit my limbs is fled.
Unbind my coif—it aches to wear;
And over my shoulders loose my hair.
  NURSE: Take courage, child!—not fretfully
Toss to and fro!
Nothing can ease this pain for thee
But a brave heart's tranquillity.
All born must suffer so.
  PHAEDRA: Ah for some cool spring in a meadow!—
  To drink clear waters plunging past!
There underneath the poplar-shadow,
  In the long grass to lie at last!
  NURSE: What means this moan,
My daughter? With so wild a tone
Cry not mad words in ears unknown.
  PHAEDRA: Take me up, to the hills, to the hunting-grounds,
To the high pine-woods—with hunting-hounds
Athirst for slaughter, let me follow
    The dappled deer!
Ah God, to shout the huntsman's hollo,
  Gripping a lance of Thessaly!—
  To feel my yellow hair toss free,
    To fling my spear!
  NURSE: But, child, what folly blinds thy brain!
What has the hunt to do with thee?
  Why crave for torrents of the hills?
  This green slope by our palace spills
Clear streams to drink, and drink again.
  PHAEDRA: O Lady of Limne by the sea—
  Tracks where the hammering horse-hoofs gleam!
  To be there, with a wild Enétian team!—
And break them to my mastery!
  NURSE: How swiftly thy folly changes fashion!

But now, thy fancy turned thy feet
To hunt the hills—now is thy passion
For steeds, on the sands where no waves beat!
Wise indeed were the seer could say
What spirit drives thy heart astray
And robs thee of thy senses, sweet.
PHAEDRA: What have I done? Ah, misery!
Where have I wandered in my mind?
Crazed, fallen, by God's hand struck blind!
O dear nurse, veil again my head.
I blush for the words that broke from me.
Cover my face, and the tears I shed,
And the shame that bows my forehead low.
The sane have too much suffering;
Yet madness—'tis a fearful thing.
Better to die, and not to know!
NURSE: I veil thy head, then—would the earth
Hid mine, at rest!
Of all life's lessons, from my birth,
None true as this—that happiest
Are they that never love too deep
And give their hearts to none to keep!
Better the passion that passes by,
Lightly come and lightly fled.
Too bitter the burden, when *one* must try
To bear the griefs of two; as I,
For this dear head.
The loyalty that loves unchanging ever,
Brings life, they tell, small happiness;
Sick grows the soul with its endeavour;
I praise, past all that seeks excess,
The middle way—
And the wise will witness what I say.
LEADER: Old dame, the faithful nurse, these many years,
Of our unhappy Queen, we see her sorrow,
But what it is that ails her—*that* lies hidden.
May we not know?—not hear it from your lips?
NURSE: All questionings are vain—she will not tell.
LEADER: Not even how her trouble first began?
NURSE: It is all the same. She will not speak a word.
LEADER: How faint she lies there, in her faded beauty!
NURSE: How should she not? Three days she has tasted nothing.
LEADER: Is she distracted? Or resolved on death?
NURSE: On death—at least, this fast she keeps grows deadly.

LEADER: Strange! But her husband?—can he leave her so?
NURSE: Ah, but she hides it—will not own she suffers.
LEADER: Can he not *see* the whole truth in her face?
NURSE: No. For it happens he has left Troezēn.
LEADER: Can you not wring it from her, by compulsion,
Find what it is that ails her—clouds her mind?
NURSE: I have tried all; and tried it all in vain.
Yet I will *not* give over, *not* lose heart.
Come, you shall see yourself if I am true
To my mistress in her trouble.
Listen, dear daughter. Let us both forget
What we have said—but be not so forbidding!
Smooth out that brow of gloom, and change your thoughts.
And I—if before I too much shared your sadness,
Now I will turn to try a wiser way.
Come!—if your sickness is a secret one,
These women here will help to bring you through it.
But if a man may hear it, then speak out,
And we will tell the truth to your physicians.

(PHAEDRA *does not answer.*)

Ah God, still silent! Silence is wrong, my child!
If what I say is false, point out my error;
If it is true—why, then accept the truth.
Oh speak! Look in my face! Ah bitterness!
See, women of Troezēn, we lose our labour,
And gain no ground at all. My former pleadings
Left her unmoved; and still she will not listen.
Yet hear me now—to this too, if you can,
Be deafer than the sea! If thus you die
Abandoning your children, *they* will forfeit
All birthright from their father—yes! I swear it
By that bold-riding Queen of the Amazons
Whose son shall be their master—well you know him!—
That bastard with a soul of true-born honour,
Hippolytus—
PHAEDRA: My God!
NURSE: So *that* can touch you?
PHAEDRA: Nurse, thy words kill me. Now, by Heaven above,
Never again breathe *that* man's name to me!
NURSE: You see the danger!—yet, with open eyes,
Will neither save yourself, nor help your children!
PHAEDRA: I love them. This storm that sinks me blows not *thence.*

NURSE: There is no blood-stain, child, upon your hands?
PHAEDRA: My hands are clean: the stain is on my heart.
NURSE: Is there some enemy has done you wrong?
PHAEDRA: One I love ruins me. Neither of us willed it.
NURSE: Is Theseus guilty of some fault against you?
PHAEDRA: Never may *he* have fault to find with *me*!
NURSE: Why then, what fear makes you resolved to die?
PHAEDRA: Leave me to err! I err not against *thee.*
NURSE: Leave you! I *will* not. It is I that am left—forsaken!

(*She kneels before* PHAEDRA.)

PHAEDRA: What! Will you force me!—clinging to my hand!
NURSE: And to thy knees! I will not let thee go.
PHAEDRA: Bitter, poor nurse, you would find the truth—too bitter!
NURSE: What bitterer pain to bear than losing thee?
PHAEDRA: You will be my ruin! I do this for my honour.
NURSE: Yet what I ask is good—can you refuse?
PHAEDRA: I am struggling to pluck honour out of shame.
NURSE: Speak then—your fame shall only stand the fairer.
PHAEDRA: In God's name leave me now—let go my hand.
NURSE: No! You deny me the trust that is my due.
PHAEDRA (*slowly*): I give it then. I am ashamed to grudge your prayer.
NURSE (*rising*): I say no more. *Your* tongue must speak the rest.
PHAEDRA: Ah mother! What a passion once was thine!
NURSE: What do you mean, my child? The Bull of Crete!
PHAEDRA: You too, poor sister—bride of Dionysus!
NURSE: What ails you, child? These tales that blot your race!
PHAEDRA: And now I am the third to be undone.
NURSE: This grows too horrible! What follows next?
PHAEDRA: Thence falls an ancient curse on all our blood.
NURSE: But still this leaves my questioning unanswered.
PHAEDRA: Ah!
Would God that *you* could say this thing, not I!
NURSE: *I* have no prophet's gift, to read such riddles.
PHAEDRA: Ah, what is this strange thing that men call "love"?
NURSE: The sweetest thing in life; yet bitter too.
PHAEDRA: But mine, I fear, must be its bitterness.
NURSE: What are you saying, child? In love! With whom?
PHAEDRA: The Queen of Amazons—she had a son. . . .
NURSE: Hippolytus!

PHAEDRA: *Thou* namest him, not I.

NURSE: Child! What comes *now*? Your words are death to me.
O friends!—unbearable!—I *cannot* bear
Life any longer! Light of day, I curse thee—
I curse thee, Sun in Heaven. Let me go,
And hurl me headlong, and be quit of life,
Laid with the dead. Farewell! This is the end.
For now I know that even honest women,
Fight how they may, can still grow passionate
With love of evil. Ah, Love is no Goddess,
But a thing more powerful than any God,
Destroying her, and me, and all her race.

ONE OF THE CHORUS: Marked you the Queen!
Ah, when have been
Words of such anguish spoken?

ANOTHER: For me, dear Lady, better death
Than what thy madness suffereth!

ANOTHER: Poor heart, by its sorrows broken!

ANOTHER: Ah pain, that is man's daily bread!

ANOTHER: Lost!—thou art lost!—such horrors to disclose!

ANOTHER: What shall this long day bring thee, ere it goes?

ANOTHER: Sure, for this house some doom of dread.

ANOTHER: Too clear, poor child of Crete, to what dark end
This curse of the Cyprian must at last descend.

PHAEDRA: Ah women of Troezēn, that have your dwelling
Here at this outer gate of Pĕlops' land,
Oft in the night's long watches I have pondered
What cause it is brings human lives to ruin.
I cannot think it is defect of reason
Leaves us undone. For many have discernment.
To me the truth seems other.
We well know what is good; we understand,
Yet will not face the struggle—some are idle,
Some sacrifice their honour for the sake
Of pleasure—life can bring so much of pleasure—
Long hours of talk; and idleness, sweet poison.
[And our own sense of pride. Two kinds there are
Of pride—one not dishonourable; but one—
False, and a household curse. If men judged rightly,
They could not use one word to name them both.]
Now since I hold this certain, no enchantment
Could have the potency to overturn
My sure conviction. So, in my present trouble,
I reasoned thus:

When first Love wounded me, I asked myself
How best I might endure. In the beginning
My choice was silence, and to hide my hurt.
For how could I trust my tongue? Our tongues are glib
To school the hearts of others with advice,
And yet most deadly for our own undoing.
Next, I resolved that I would bear my madness
Nobly, and crush it out by self-control.
Lastly, when both these remedies proved vain
Against Love's violence, I vowed to die.
And this—past all denial!—is the best.
I would not see obscured my better actions;
But few be the eyes that see me sink dishonoured!
I knew that all I did now—all I suffered—
Would bring me shame; knew, too, I was a woman,
And so a thing men hate. Accurst the wife
Who first dared to defile her marriage-bed
With a seducer! Such iniquity
First took its rise with women of noble blood;
For once the high-born turn them to foul ways,
Quickly the base will find them fair enough.
Curst, too, be all those modest-spoken wives
That yet in secret dare all shamelessness!
How can they bear, O sea-born Cyprian Queen,

(*She turns to the image of* APHRODITE.)

To look unblenching in their husbands' eyes?
Nor shudder at the darkness their accomplice,
Nor fear the very walls will cry aloud?
Dear friends, *this* is the cause that brings my death—
That never I may shame before the world
My husband, and my children. Let them live
In glorious Athens with free hearts, frank faces,
And honour unblemished from their mother's side.
For a father's guilt, or mother's, makes a man,
Stout-hearted though he be, creep like a slave.
Well it is said, that naught stands up to life
But a spirit that is just and honourable;
For Time, one day, confronts the base with all
His baseness; as a girl sees her young beauty
Clear in her mirror. God keep *that* from me!

LEADER: O Heaven, how lovely, always, goodness is—
A flower whose fruit is honour!

NURSE: Ah mistress mine, how you did frighten me

At first with your misfortune!
But now I see, I was poor-spirited,
And second thoughts are wiser. This your passion
Is nothing so unheard of, nor past reason.
It is Aphrodite's anger falls upon you.
You are in love? What wonder? Many are.
Because you are in love, why talk of death?
Fine end for all the lovers in the world—
And all that shall love hereafter—just to die!
Love's Goddess is too hard for human strength,
When She puts forth Her power. Gently She comes
To those that bow to Her; but when She finds
A heart presumptuous and arrogant,
Why, then—what would you?—then She tramples it.
Her path is through the Heavens; Her feet are set
Upon the surging seas; all springs from Her.
For still She sows love's seed, still quickens passion
From which we children of this earth are born.
They that have turned the scrolls of ancient lore,
Conversing with the Muses, know full well
How Zeus once fell in love with Sémele,
And how fair-glittering Dawn once snatched to Heaven
Her darling Céphalus. Yet those they loved
Abide in Heaven still—*they* do not flee
From their immortal lovers—well content,
Methinks, with what befell them.
Will *you,* then, still be stubborn? Ah, if you
Will not accept these laws that rule our nature,
Your father should have sealed some covenant,
Before he got you—made a pre-condition
Your life should bow to other Gods than ours.
How many, think you, most sagacious husbands
See well that their marriage ails, but shut their eyes!
How many fathers stand accessory
To the passions of their children! Worldly wisdom
Warns us to let unhandsome things lie hid.
Vain to be *too* elaborate in life.
Even the beam that bears the roof aloft
Cannot lie wholly straight. What hope, for you,
To swim from such deep waters safe to shore?
You are but human—rest you well content
If the goodness in your heart outweighs the evil.
  And so, dear daughter, cease this black despair,
Cease from this pride of heart—for pride it is
To think you can be stronger than the Gods.

Have the courage of your passion. For a God
Hath willed it so. And since your soul is sick,
Deal wisely with the sickness.
There are, for such things, magic words and charms
And we will find some sovereign remedy.
Ay, truly men would be hard put to it,
Without us women to find out a way.

LEADER: Phaedra, in this thy grief thy nurse's tongue
Speaks the more shrewdly—but *thou* hast still my praise.
And yet my praise must be less pleasant hearing,
And colder comfort, than her counsel is.

PHAEDRA: Ah, this it is brings ruin on human homes
And prosperous cities—too fine-sounding phrases.
Men need, not speeches pleasant to the ear,
But what will lead them on the path of honour.

NURSE: What lofty talk! It is not specious words
You need—it is the *man*! We must see clear
At once, by speaking out the truth about you.
If it was not your *life* that hung imperilled,
If *you* were a woman mistress of herself,
So far I would not lead you, for the sake
Of passion, or of pleasure.
But now—to save you needs a crowning effort;
And who shall blame me?

PHAEDRA: O monstrous words! Will you not hold your tongue!
Have done with uttering such foulnesses.

NURSE: Foul they may be: foul means will serve you now
Far more than fair.
Better the act that saves you—if it can—
Than some fine name to deck you when you die.

PHAEDRA: No more, by Heaven! You speak too cleverly
Such words of shame! I have subdued my soul
To bear my love; but with your specious tempting
I shall be sunk in the very sin I hate.

NURSE: If that's your mind, your heart should not have sinned;
But since it *has,* now hear. Not much to grant me!
There in the house I have—now I remember—
Philtres with power to charm all love asleep.
And these shall cure you, if you have the courage;
Nor touch your honour; nor derange your mind.

PHAEDRA: This drug of yours—is it a salve or potion?

NURSE: I know not, child. You need a cure; not questions.

PHAEDRA: I fear this air of over-subtlety.

NURSE: *You* would fear anything! Afraid of what?
PHAEDRA: That you may breathe some word to Theseus' son.
NURSE: Let me alone, child. I will manage all.

(*She turns to the image of* APHRODITE.)

Only do Thou, O sea-born Cyprian Queen,
Grant me Thy help. What else I have in mind—
Enough to speak of *that* to friends within.

(*She goes into the palace.*)

CHORUS: Ah Eros, Eros, whose hand distils *strophe* 1
Into our eyes the grace that fills
With sweetness hearts Thou wouldst assail,
Come not with Evil on Thy trail,
Come not too wild!
There is no star so blasting, fire so hot,
As are the shafts that Love hath shot,
The Thunderer's child.

In vain by Phoebus' Pythian shrine *antistrophe* 1
Hellas heaps high her slaughtered kine,
And by Alphēus' stream in vain,
While Eros, all earth's suzerain,
We worship not—
Guard of sweet Aphrodite's bridal door,
Whose onset racks with ruin and war
Our mortal lot!

Thus by the Cyprian's will *strophe* 2
Was given, virgin still
And innocent, as bride to Hēracles,
Oechalia's daughter torn
From her father's house, forlorn
As maddened Maenad, or shy Nymph that flees.
Mid smoke and blood, that from men slain
Ran steaming red,
With battle-cries to sound her bridal strain,
Poor maid, she wed!

What Cypris' coming brings, *antistrophe* 2
You too, O Dirce's springs,
And, hallowed towers of Thebes, too well you know—
How with thunder and lightning's flame
To Sémele Love came,
Mother of twice-born Bacchus, and laid her low;
The bride at last of Doom was she,

With death for dower.
Fierce through the world flies Love, as flies a bee
From flower to flower.

(*Voices within.* PHAEDRA *goes to the door and listens.*)

PHAEDRA: Hush! O my friends, now I am lost indeed!
LEADER: What terror shakes you, Phaedra? What's within?
PHAEDRA: Wait!—let me catch their voices.
LEADER: I say no more. This prelude's grim enough!
PHAEDRA: Oh, oh, oh!
O misery of my fate!
LEADER: What means your cry? What voice is there?
Tell me, good lady!
What are these words that bring despair?
PHAEDRA: Ah, I am ruined! Come hither to the door!
Listen to that wild outcry there within!
LEADER: Nay, *thou* art nearer. It is for thee
To catch their speech.
What is this new calamity?
PHAEDRA: The son of that bold-riding Amazon,
Hippolytus, heaps curses on my woman.
LEADER: I hear a shouting—yet cannot hear
What words they are
That break through the doors upon thine ear.
PHAEDRA: Ah, clear enough! "Accursed go-between,"
He calls her—"traitress to her master's bed."
LEADER: Alas, dear heart! Betrayed and sold!
What counsel now?
'Tis ruin for thee—thy secret's told!
PHAEDRA: Oh, oh!
LEADER: Betrayed by her that you loved of old!
PHAEDRA: She has destroyed me, telling my misfortune.
Her love sought healing—but it brings me shame.
LEADER: And now what will you do, in this despair?
PHAEDRA: Only one way I know. One cure alone
For what has come upon me—quickest death!

(HIPPOLYTUS *rushes forth through the door, followed by the* NURSE.)

HIPPOLYTUS: O Mother Earth! O all-revealing Sun!
What have I heard—what things unutterable!
NURSE: Be quiet, my son! Your shouting will be heard.
HIPPOLYTUS: Too hideous what I heard, to keep it quiet!
NURSE: By this right hand, by this fair arm I beg you——

(*She clings to him.*)

HIPPOLYTUS: Keep off your hand. Dare not to touch my garment.

NURSE: I *beseech* you!—by your knees! Do not destroy me!

HIPPOLYTUS: What frightens you? You *say* you have done no wrong!

NURSE: Son, what I said is not for common ears.

HIPPOLYTUS: What's well is but the better, told abroad.

NURSE: Dear son, do not dishonour your sworn word.

HIPPOLYTUS: My tongue it was, but not my heart, that swore.

NURSE: What will you do, son? Ruin those that love you?

HIPPOLYTUS: Faugh! Never evil heart had love of mine.

NURSE: Forgive, my son! All frailty is but human.

HIPPOLYTUS: Ah God, why hast Thou set beneath the sun
This curse of man, this counterfeit called "woman"?
If Thy will *was* to multiply mankind,
It should have been by other means than that!
Better if men made offering in Thy temples—
Gold, iron, or massy bronze—and bought thereby
Offspring to match its value. Then their homes
Could have been free from women's tyranny.
The curse they are is clear enough by this—
That the very fathers who begot and bred them,
Must give rich dowries to be rid of them.
Then wretched men take home these pests—rejoicing,
Wasting their wealth, their happiness, to deck
With finery and fairest of adornment
These foulest idols!
The lightest lot is his that keeps at home
Some futile fool, some nothing of a wife;
But the clever ones I loathe—may hearth of mine
Never be cursed with a woman that thinks too much!
It is in nimble brains the Cyprian breeds
Readiest mischief; while a stupid woman
Is saved from such follies by mere want of wit.
But never wives should have she-servants' visits—
Better it were they lived with dumb, brute beasts
And never a soul to talk or listen to.
For these adulteresses hatch at home
Plots that their women carry forth abroad;
As thou, base wretch, hast come to me to traffic
With the inviolate bed of my own father.
Faugh! Let me find some stainless running water
To wash my ears of it!

How couldst thou dream that I would stoop to listen,
Who feel myself polluted but to hear it!
Be thankful, woman, that my scruples save thee!
Hadst thou not trapped me unawares with oaths,
Nothing should have withheld me from revealing
All to my father. As it is, so long
As *he* is from Troezēn, I quit this palace.
I *will* keep silence. But the day I come,
Returning with King Theseus, I shall watch
How you and your mistress dare to meet his eyes—
Then I shall know, and taste, your brazenness.
Curse you! No, never can I utter all
My loathing of women!—not though I be blamed
For harping on one theme eternally;
For *they* no less repeat their infamy.
Let *them* learn modesty, or be it mine
To cry their shame for ever.

(*Ignoring the silent* PHAEDRA, *he goes out.*)

PHAEDRA: Ah, desolate
Is woman's fate!
What now can I do, or say,
To loose this noose of doom drawn tight—
My punishment? O Earth, O light,
Where flee away?
Such suffering grows too hard to hide.
What God, what man, will help me now, my friends?
Lend me his hand, or gather to my side?
Evil I did—and thus it ends!
Past all escape comes ruin on me.
When knew a woman such agony?

LEADER: Alas, it is finished. All your nurse's arts
Are gone to wreck, dear mistress. Evil hour!

PHAEDRA (*turning on her* NURSE): Accursed wretch! The ruin of those that loved you!
What have you done to me! May Zeus my grandsire
With his lightning blast thee to annihilation!
Did I not bid you—yes, I guessed your purpose—
Say not a word of what has stained my name?
But *you* must talk! Gone now my hope of dying
With honour! I must find some new defence.
For now this man, whetted to sharpest anger,
Will denounce me to his father for your fault—
Denounce all my misfortune to old Pittheus—

Fill the whole world with foulest accusations!
A curse upon you and all meddling friends
That force their ignoble help on the unwilling!
NURSE: Mistress, you well may chide my ill success.
It stings you to the heart; and blinds your judgment.
But even to this I have—if you will but listen—
An answer still. I nursed you and I love you.
I tried to heal your pain. But failed to reach
What I had hoped for. If I had, ah then
How wise you would have called me! Wisdom's credit
Hangs merely on the luck that crowns the issue.
PHAEDRA: Ha, this is fair, you think?—and should content me?
You cut me to the heart—then bandy words!
NURSE: We talk too much. True, I have played the wanton;
Yet even now, my child, there is chance of safety.
PHAEDRA: Have done! Your first advice to me was evil;
Vile your attempt. Begone! Think of yourself.
And I will set my own affairs to rights.

(*The* NURSE *creeps out.*)

But grant me, noble daughters of Troezēn,
This my one prayer—
To hide all you have heard, in secrecy.
LEADER: I swear by Artemis, dread child of Zeus,
Never to bring your sorrows to the light.
PHAEDRA: Thanks to you all. One way alone I find,
In this disaster, that will give my children
An honourable life, and help myself,
As things have fallen now.
I will not shame the royal race of Crete,
Nor blush before the face of my own husband,
For one life's sake.
LEADER: Some plan of evil irretrievable—?
PHAEDRA: Yes. Death! But how?—*that* must be *my* decision.
LEADER: Ah, say not so!
PHAEDRA: Yes, friends! From you at least
Let me have *good* advice.
Since the Cyprian destroys me, I this day
Will take my leave of life—yes, She shall triumph,
And I fall victim to love's cruelty.
And yet, dead though I am, I will be deadly
To one that lives.
So he shall learn not to look down in pride

Upon my ruin. He *had* part in my sickness—
He too shall learn the need for modesty!

(*She enters the palace.*)

CHORUS: God, to some trackless mountain-hollow *strophe* 1
Would I had wings to fly!—
Wings, where the wild birds flock, to follow
Across the western sky,
To where Érídanus' waters
Sweep down to Adria's wave,
And the Sun-god's sorrowing daughters
Bewail their brother's grave,
While gleaming through that purple deep
Amber fall the tears they weep!

Or where, while apples round them redden, *antistrophe* 1
Chant the Hesperides,
And the Sea-god guards, to ships forbidden,
His purple waste of seas!
For there, in Atlas' keeping,
Lies Heaven's sacred bound,
There springs divine rise leaping
By walls where Zeus hath found
Peace, and the kindly Earth doth bless
The Gods' immortal happiness.

Ah white-winged ship of Crete, *strophe* 2
That over the surges' beat
Through wastes of sea conveyed
My Queen, from out the home of happy years,
A happy bride—and yet the bride of tears!
Curst was that keel, the day from Crete she weighed
To fly like some dark bird of bane
Towards glorious Athens and the strand
Of Mūnychus; curst, when her sailors made
Her fast again,
And trod the Attic land!

For now, by a love perverse *antistrophe* 2
And Aphrodite's curse,
Beneath her misery
Our Queen lies broken. Soon shall a rope be cast
From the beams of her bridal-chamber, and made fast
About the throat that was so white to see.
Bowed by her shame, by Love opprest,
She has chosen still the better part;

Honoured at least she leaves her memory.
And lays to rest
That ache within her heart.

(*Cries are heard within the palace.*)

A WOMAN'S VOICE (*within*): Help, help!
Come quickly, hasten!—here within the palace!
Our mistress—the Queen of Theseus—she is hanged!

ONE OF THE CHORUS: Ah, all is over! Round her neck the noose,
Dead is our royal lady.

THE VOICE (*within*): Will you not hurry! Quick, a two-edged knife,
To cut away the cord!

ANOTHER OF THE CHORUS: Ah friends, what shall we do? Enter the palace?—
Loose from the Queen this knot that strangles her?

ANOTHER: What use? Has she not her young men-servants there?
And life is perilous for meddling hands.

THE VOICE (*within*): Straighten the limbs of the unhappy dead—
This bitter thing that keeps house for our Lord!

ANOTHER: Poor woman! Life is over. I can hear—
As a dead body, now, they straighten her.

(KING THESEUS *enters with his followers; his head garlanded, for he is returning from a pilgrimage to some shrine.*)

THESEUS: What means this clamour, women?—can you tell me?—
There in the palace? Loud with grief I hear
My servants' voices. And the doors are closed,
That should stand wide with welcome to a pilgrim
Come from the House of God.
Has anything befallen Pittheus' age?
Far gone in years he is; yet a bitter blow
It would be, still to know our house had lost him.

LEADER: Theseus, what now has happened touches not
The old. It is yours to mourn for death in youth.

THESEUS: God! Has a child of mine been robbed of life?

LEADER: *They* live. Their mother's dead. Most bitterly.

THESEUS: What! My wife gone! How did she come to die?

LEADER: Within a hanging rope she noosed her neck.

THESEUS: Some cold despair of life? Or some disaster?

LEADER: We know no more. Only this moment, Theseus,
I reached your threshold here—to share your grief.
THESEUS: Oh, misery! Unhappiest of pilgrims,
What serves me now this garland round my head?

(*He tears it off.*)

Undo the bolts, men, fling the doors wide open!
Bring to my eyes this sight of bitterness—
My wife!—that, dying, leaves me, too, destroyed!

(*The palace door opens, revealing* PHAEDRA *on her bier with mourning women round her.*)

ONE OF THE CHORUS: What hast thou suffered, what hast done,
Sad, suffering heart!—
A deed to wreck the royal line of our land!
ANOTHER: To an evil end so rashly run!
Poor wrestler, overthrown thou art
By thine own hand.
Who *was* it darkened from thy days the sun?
THESEUS: Ah burden of sorrow! Ah Troezēn! *strophe*
No grief like this my life hath seen!

How hard on this house, O Fate, thy foot hath trod!
O brand burnt deep by some Avenging God!

Ruin of my life!—no life for me,
Before whom spreads a boundless sea

Of sorrows, wave on wave, for evermore;
I drown in it, far off from sight of shore!

Wife that I loved, what word shall guess
This secret of thy dim distress?

Slipped from my hands, as some bird fluttereth,
Thou hast plunged headlong down the Gulfs of Death.

Alas my sorrow! This sure is sent
By the high Gods upon my head
As punishment
For sins forgot of my fathers dead.
LEADER: Lord, thou art not alone in suffering so;
Many a husband weeps a true wife dead.
THESEUS: Out of the light, out of the light *antistrophe*
Would God I were laid, in House of Night.

Since I am left without thee, sweet, alone!
Death though hast dealt me!—bitterer than thine own!

Ah but to know—what was it woke
This thought of death in thy heart that broke?

Can *no* man tell me? Are ye useless all,
Servants of mine that crowd this royal hall?

Alas, my lost one! Oh despair
Too deep for words, too black to bear,

Darkening my home! Now all my life lies ended;
Orphaned, my children; and my hearth unfriended
Thou hast left them alone now—left them forgot!
Ah best and dearest, the like of thee
The sun sees not,
Nor all night's starry eyes can see.

ONE OF THE CHORUS: Unhappy king, with tears my eyes are blind
To watch thy fate,
And all thy house left desolate.
Yet I shudder to think what waits behind.

THESEUS: But look!
What can it mean, this tablet hanging here
From her dear hand? Maybe, it can tell us more?
Or, rather, has she left some last request,
Poor Queen, about our children; or my marrying
Some other after her?
Fear not, poor heart! There lives no other woman
Shall share the home of Theseus, or his bed.

(*He lifts the tablet.*)

How smiles on me the old familiar seal
From the gold ring of her that's gone for ever!
Now to unwind the threads that wrap the wax,
And see what it will tell me.

(*He reads.*)

ANOTHER WOMAN: Alas and alas, how ill on ill is hurled!
Disaster on disaster Heaven brings!
After such misery
Life loses worth for me.

ANOTHER: Lost and undone—no longer of this world—
I count the race of our ancestral kings.

LEADER: God, if it may be, hearken to my prayer—
Wreck not this house! For now, as a prophet marks
Some boding bird, I see the signs of doom.

THESEUS: Horror on horror! Unendurable

Unspeakable! what wretchedness is mine!

LEADER: What is it? Say, my lord—if I may hear?

THESEUS: It cries out things unutterable—it cries,
This tablet. How escape such agony!
These characters traced here before my eyes
Wail out a dirge to me.

LEADER: Ah *there* speaks what a prelude to disaster!

THESEUS: It sticks at the gates of speech, this word
Of horror. Yet it *shall* be heard!
Hear, all Troezēn!
Hippolytus has dared by force befoul
My bed!—defied the dreadful eye of God!
But Thou, Poseidon!—Father!—that hast promised
Fulfillment to three prayers that I should pray,
Hear this one now!
Destroy my son!—yea, let him not outlive
This day!—if indeed Thy gift was not a dream.

LEADER: In Heaven's name, my lord!—call back your prayer!
The future shall yet confute you. Trust my word!

THESEUS: Impossible! To exile, too, I doom him.
One fate, or other, surely shall strike him down.
Either Poseidon, hearkening to my curse,
Shall thrust him dead to Hades;
Or else, a homeless exile from Troezēn,
He shall drag a bitter life through alien lands.

LEADER: But look! Your son himself—Hippolytus!
Timely he comes. Ah, Theseus, lay aside
This fatal anger—think of your royal line.

HIPPOLYTUS (*entering*): Father, I heard your voice—raised loud in sorrow—
And hurried here. Tell me—for I know nothing—
What is your grief?

(*He sees the dead* PHAEDRA.)

Ha, what is this! My father! Your own Queen,
Dead! But how strange! One that I only left
A moment since—that looked upon the sunlight
So short a while ago!
What happened to her, then? What brought her death?
I beg you, father!—tell me!
Silence? What use is it to grieve in silence?
The human heart, that longs to know all truth,
Even when truth is bitter craves it still;
And, father, *you* are wrong to hide your sorrows

From those that are your friends—and more than friends.

THESEUS: O race of men
So often erring, yet no wiser still!
What use are all the thousand arts you teach—
All your devices and discoveries,
When this one thing
You neither know nor ever tried to know—
How to plant sense within the brain of fools!

HIPPOLYTUS: It would be a master of his art, indeed,
That could compel a fool to quit his folly!
But this is no time for subtleties, my father.
I fear this grief has left you overwrought.

THESEUS: Would God that men had but some certain sign
To put to proof the hearts of those they love,
And know which was the loyal, and which the traitor!—
Ay, would we all had *two* tones in our speech—
One for true dealing, and the other merely
To serve occasion; so the lying tongue
Might stand revealed beside the tones of truth,
And we no more be duped!

HIPPOLYTUS: What!—has some friend been breathing in your ear
Slanders of *me*!—tainting my guiltless honour!
This thing grows ghastly. Yes, aghast they leave me,
Your words that ramble from a brain distracted.

THESEUS: Ah heart of man—what lengths will it not go to?
What limits to its wanton shamelessness?
For if it swells with each new generation,
If in extravagance of villainy
The sons outdo the fathers, to this earth
Heaven must add some other world to hold
Its ruffians and scoundrels.
Behold this man that, born a son of mine,
Defiled my bed!—now by my dead wife's word
Convicted, past all doubt, of infamy!
Look in my face, since you have sunk indeed
To this pollution. Meet your father's eye!
Is it *you* that are no ordinary man,
But walk with Gods? Yes, *you,* the self-controlled,
The pure of heart! Ask not that *I* believe
Your boasting; or be fool enough to think
The Gods so blind as *that*!
Go, swell your pride, purchase a peddling glory
By meals kept pure from flesh! Cry "Lord" to Orpheus!
Pursue your pious vapours—hold in honour

The holy books of Bacchus!
Now you are caught! And I bid the world beware
Of you and all your like—schemers of vileness,
That with fine phrases hunt your private ends.
My Queen is dead—do you hope her death shall save you?
Scoundrel! It shall but brand your little guilt the deeper.
What oaths, what pleadings, in your own defence
Can weigh against *her* witness?
Will you say she hated you?—that bastard sons
Can find no favour with a wedded wife?
Truly she held life cheap, if just for spite
She sacrificed the dearest thing men have!
Will you plead that men are no such fools of passion,
but 'tis inbred in women? Yet I know
Young men that are as little to be trusted,
Whenever the Cyprian troubles youth's hot blood.
Their very manhood makes them but the bolder.
So now—but why should I bandy words with you,
When the dead bears this clearest testimony?
Begone from this land, at once!—to banishment!
Dare not to tread the earth of god-built Athens,
Nor any frontier subject to my sword.
For if I let you triumph, this outrage done,
Not even the witness of the Isthmian Sĭnis
Can leave men sure I did not boast but idly
His overthrow; and those sea-bordering rocks
Of Scīron will in vain proclaim aloud
That *I* bring death to villains.

LEADER: How from this day dare I call any man
"Happy"?—for now our noblest are brought low.

HIPPOLYTUS: Father, this gathered fury in your soul
Is terrible. Your charge may lend itself
To lofty-sounding phrases; yet, laid bare,
It shows but ugly. All unskilled am I
To speak before a crowd. I could plead better
In presence of a few—as young as I.
But men whom the wise hold cheap—so fate has willed it—
Are cleverer at haranguing multitudes.
Yet since this ill has chanced, I must perforce
Give my tongue rein. First for this first indictment
You sprang upon me—hoping I should be crushed
And struck too dumb to answer. Look you there
Upon this sun above, this earth beneath us—
No living man they know, say what you will,
More pure of heart than I. For I have learnt,

First, reverence for Heaven: next, to choose
For friends of mine, not men with a love of evil,
But hearts too honourable to tempt to wrong,
Or by base services repay their comrades.
Nor am I, father, one that mocks his fellows,
But loyal in their absence as their sight;
And, above all, untouched by that one sin
Of which you would convict me. To this day
My flesh is virgin. Nothing I know of love—
Except by talk and seeing pictures of it.
And little zest have I for even that,
Being maiden still in spirit.
Little, maybe, you care for my restraint;
Yet show, at least, what was there here to tempt me?
Could I find no woman's body in the world.
Lovely as hers? Could *I* hope to inherit
Your house by wedding *her*?—your Queen and heiress!
I should have been mere fool—no, downright mad.
The sweetness of a throne? Who cares for that,
Whose soul is upright—though it *can* corrupt
Minds that are dazzled by mere sovereignty.
Far rather *I* would choose to stand the first
In our Greek games; but hold a second rank
In my own city—and so live at ease,
Friends to its noblest. *There's* a life of action,
Yet free of danger—happier than a king's.
You have my answer—save for one thing more:
Had I some witness to my own true nature,
Were *she* but living still to plead against,
The facts themselves would *make* you see the guilty.
But now—by Zeus and by this Earth beneath us,
I swear I never touched your marriage-bed—
Nor could have wished it—no, not dreamed of it!
Were I so villainous, then let me perish,
Nameless and fameless, homeless, cityless—
A banished outlaw wandering through the world!
And, even dead, let sea and land alike
Reject my carrion!
But as for *her*—if fear drove her to death,
I do not know. And more I must not say.
Honour she had not; yet she died with honour:
But I that have it, kept it all in vain!

LEADER: You have made full answer to your accusation.
Weighty indeed, this oath you have sworn by Heaven.

THESEUS: Now is he not a wizard!—a magician!—

That dreams mere smooth assurance must prevail
On *me*—the parent he has left dishonoured!

HIPPOLYTUS: *You* give me, father, no less cause for wonder.
If *you* were a son of mine, and *I* your father,
And *I* believed you had dared to touch my wife,
You would have paid your crime with more than exile.
I should have killed you.

THESEUS: Well said, well said! Yet not so *you* shall die!—
Not by the penalty thus self-invoked
(For speedy death is kindest for the wretched);
But as a beggared outcast from your home.

HIPPOLYTUS: Ha, what's your will?—not even wait till Time
Can witness to the truth! Banished at once!

THESEUS: Yes, if I could, beyond the Pontic Sea,
Beyond the bounds of Atlas!—I so hate you.

HIPPOLYTUS: Not put to proof my oath—my sworn denial!
Consult no prophet! Cast me out untried!

THESEUS: This tablet here needs no diviner's arts,
It stands your sure accuser. What care I
For all the fowls that fly above my head?

HIPPOLYTUS: Ah God, can I not at last unseal my lips?—
Since, honouring Thee, I only find my ruin?
But no! I should break in vain the oath I swore—
Not even *that* would touch this heart I plead with.

THESEUS: Heavens, you choke me with your sanctimony!
Go! Go, I say! Out of your father's kingdom!

HIPPOLYTUS: Where shall I turn my wretched steps? What stranger.
Can I beg to give me shelter?—charged with *this*!

THESEUS: Find one who loves to welcome as his guests
Seducers that defile the hearth they share.

HIPPOLYTUS: Ah *that* cuts to the heart! Yes, I could weep
To seem to men so vile. And you believe it!

THESEUS: *Then* was the time to weep and fear the future,
When first you dared to shame your father's wife.

HIPPOLYTUS: Ah walls of home, could *you* but cry aloud
In witness whether I am vile or no!

THESEUS: Wisely you call to witness speechless things.
But *without* tongue the facts denounce you guilty.

HIPPOLYTUS: Ah, were I *you,* judging my son before me,
How I should weep for what that son endures!

THESEUS: Always self-worship! *That* you have learnt far better
Than the honour due to those that gave you life!

HIPPOLYTUS: Ah my poor mother! Ah my bitter birth!

God save all those I love from bastardy!

THESEUS: Out with him, men! Have you not heard my sentence,
Pronouncing, long ago, his banishment!

HIPPOLYTUS: Let them touch me if they dare!—they shall repent it.
Do it yourself, if you have heart enough.

THESEUS: I will, if still you disregard my orders.
Your exile stirs in me no touch of pity.

HIPPOLYTUS: No hope, it seems, to move you. Ah my sorrow,
To know the truth, and yet not how to tell it!

(THESEUS *goes out with his guards. The palace closes on the dead Queen.* HIPPOLYTUS *pauses before the image of* ARTEMIS.)

Daughter of Lēto, Goddess best-loved.
My comrade in the chase, comrade in life,
I must be banished, then, from glorious Athens.
Farewell, dear land and city of Erechtheus!
Farewell, Troezēn!—most happy of all homes
For years of youth! I take my last sight of you,
The last of all farewells.
Youths of Troezēn, friends of my boyhood, come,
Bid me good-bye. And cheer me on my way.
You will not ever find another friend
More honourable—though not so thinks my father!

(*He goes out with his friends.*)

CHORUS: The load on my heart grows lighter, when I trust in the care of Heaven; *strophe* 1
Yet that hid hope in some all-guiding Mind
Falters, to see how mortals have suffered still, and striven—
How upon change there follows change, and all man's days are driven
Down wandering ways and blind.

antistrophe 1

This is the lot I long for, would the Gods but heed my crying—
A fortune kind; a soul from sorrows free;
A judgment not too narrow, nor counterfeit and lying;
An easy heart, with chance and change from day to day complying;
And friends to be glad with me.

strophe 2

But I see what I had not dreamed of—the peace of my soul is vanished.
For now to foreign lands afar
There wanders forth, alone and banished,
Of Athens, and Greece, the brightest star,
A son by his angry sire denied.
Ah sands of Troezēn, with your ripples playing!
Woods of the hills where he wandered, slaying
Beasts of the wild with his swift hounds baying,
At dread Dictynna's side!

antistrophe 2

Never again shall the beaches of Limne echo ringing
With thy Enétian coursers' flight;
Hushed now thy harp, hushed is thy singing
That waked through watches of the night
Thy father's hall. For Lēto's child,
No hands with garlands now shall cover
Those bowers She haunts when hunting's over;
No jealous maids crave now for lover
This wanderer far exiled.

A MAIDEN: And mine must be, for thy sorrow,
A destiny of pain.
Ah my unhappy mother,
You gave me life in vain!
I rage at the Gods! Fair Graces,
That join true hearts in one,
Why was it that you tore him
Away from the land that bore him?
What evil had he done?

LEADER: But look! A servant of Hippolytus Comes hurrying, with a face all wrapped in gloom.

(*The* MESSENGER *enters.*)

MESSENGER: Speak, women!—if you know it, tell me where To find King Theseus, sovereign of Troezēn? Within the palace?

(THESEUS *comes forth.*)

LEADER: See, from its door he comes himself to meet you.

MESSENGER: Theseus, I have a heavy tale to utter, Alike for you and for all those that dwell In the walls of Athens and Troezēn's marches.

THESEUS: What is it now? Has some disaster fallen On our two neighbour-cities?

MESSENGER: Hippolytus—'tis almost truth to say—
Is dead! For by a hair yet hangs his life.
THESEUS: Who killed him? Had he made some enemy,
Whose wife he violated—like his father's?
MESSENGER: He was destroyed by his own chariot-team,
And by the curses that your own lips cried
To the God of Sea, your sire, against your son.
THESEUS: Ah Heaven! Ah Poseidon, then indeed
Thou art my Father, thus to hear my prayers!
How did he perish? Tell me how the blow
Of Justice felled this shamer of my blood.
MESSENGER: Down by the beach with its great rollers breaking
We all were combing out our horses' manes,
In tears. For word had reached us that our master,
Hippolytus, was forced to quit Troezēn,
Sentenced by you to bitter banishment.
Soon came the prince himself, tears in his voice,
Like ours; and with him followed to the shore
An endless stream of friends and young companions.
Awhile he wept; then, mastering his sorrow,
"Why this despair?" he said. "I must obey.
Men, put the horses to my chariot.
Troezēn henceforward is no home for me."
Then every one of us sprang quick to work
And, sooner than tongue could tell it, to our master
We brought his mares all harnessed.
From off the chariot-rail he caught the reins
And standing there, with sandalled feet well braced,
Lifted his hands to Heaven, crying: "Zeus,
Let me die, if I am guilty!
Oh grant that my father find how he has wronged me,
Before my death—or at least when life is done."
With that he gripped the goad and struck his team;
And we that served him followed, crowding close
About his car and by the horses' heads,
Along the road to Argos and Epidaurus.
But when we came where, in the desert lands
Beyond Troezēn's frontier, the coast falls shelving
Towards the Sarōnic Gulf—just then we caught
A sullen roar like subterranean thunder—
Grisly to hear. The horses raised their heads
And pricked their ears. And we in consternation,
Wondering from whence it came, looked towards the breakers;
And lo! to Heaven towered a wave prodigious,

So high it masked from sight the Rocks of Scīron
And hid the Isthmus, hid Asclēpius' crag.
Swirling aloft and spewing jets of spray,
It rolled in shoreward, where the chariot stood;
And as it broke, in one great crash of foam,
Out of its midst there rose a monstrous bull,
That lifted up its voice till all the land
Re-echoed with a shudder—as we looked,
It seemed too horrible for eyes to bear.
At sight of it, our master's team went wild
With terror. But he, well skilled in handling horses,
Gripped hard the reins and leaning all his weight
Backward, like rower heaving at his oar,
Tugged; yet his coursers, taking in their teeth
The forged iron bits, swept him away, unheeding
Alike his guiding hand, and their own harness,
And the chariot behind them. If he tried
To rein them towards the softer ground, the bull
Headed them off and each time turned them back
In madder frenzy still; but when, in panic,
They swerved to the rocks again, the monster followed
And drew, in silence, nearer, ever nearer,
Until he forced one wheel against a crag
And flung our master headlong—all was chaos—
Naves, linchpins, hurled to Heaven; but the driver,
Caught miserably within the tangling reins,
Was dragged—his dear head pounding on the boulders,
His flesh ripped from him—fearful came his cries:
"Stand!—do not tear me—you that I bred myself!
Woe for my father's curse! Will no one save me?—
Innocent as I am!" But we, though eager,
Lagged far away behind; till—God knows how!—
He slipped from the reins that held him, hardly breathing.
But fatal bull and horses disappeared
Amid the hidden places of the hills.
  Sire, I am only a servant in your house,
But nothing on earth shall ever make me think
This son of yours was guilty of dishonour—
Not though I saw the total race of women
Hanged!—nor all Ida's pine-woods felled for tablets
Of accusation! For I *know* him noble.
  LEADER: Alas! Now falls a new calamity.
None can escape his fate and the destined hour.
  THESEUS: At first, my hate for him that has suffered this
Made your words welcome. Yet, in respect for Heaven,

Even for *him*—for still he is my son—
I take his doom with neither joy nor sorrow.

MESSENGER: But now? Shall we bring him, this unfortunate?—
Or what's your pleasure?
Decide, my lord. And yet, would you only hear me,
You will *not* be harsh to your unhappy son.

THESEUS: Bring him!—this man who swore he had not shamed
My bed!—that my eyes may see him, and my mouth
Confute him with the judgment of the Gods.

(*The* MESSENGER *goes.*)

CHORUS: The hearts of men, the hearts of Gods that yield not,
O Cyprian, own Thy sway!
Beside Thee, swift on glancing pinions
That circle round His prey,
Love soars across the lands—across
The thundering ocean-spray.

Swooping on wings of gleaming gold,
He maddens, and soothes, with His sorcery
Creatures alike of hill and wold,
Of earth and sea.
All life beneath the blaze of sun—
And men! They are subdued, each one,
O Cyprian, to Thee!

(*Above the palace appears the Goddess* ARTEMIS*; though to the mortals on the stage she remains invisible.*)

ARTEMIS: Son of King Aegeus, so proudly descended,
Give ear to my voice!
Lo, I am Artemis, daughter of Lēto.
Thrice-miserable Theseus, in folly exulting
Over this son thou hast foully slain—
Believing the lies of a wife that told thee
Things all unproven—thou proven fool,
Go now and hide in the darkness of Hades
Thy guilty head!
Or soar aloft like a bird to Heaven,
Away from this sorrow that snares thy feet!
For never again among men of honour
Shall place be found for *thee*.

Listen now, Theseus. Hear thy tale of ruin.
True, I can help thee nothing; only grieve thee.
Yet I am come to show thy son's true heart,
That *he* may die in honour,
And Phaedra's frenzy—that yet, in certain sort,
Was noble. Though passion seized her for thy son,
To it her heart was goaded by that Goddess
Most loathed of us whose joy is maidenhood.
And though she strove to overpower by reason
The Cyprian's violence, despite her will
She was worsted by the cunning of her nurse;
Who told thy son what ailed her, under oath
Of secrecy. But, being honourable,
Hippolytus was deaf to all her prayers;
And yet too godfearing to break his pledge,
For all thy fury. But meanwhile thy Queen,
Dreading discovery, forged her own false tale
And by that treachery destroyed thy son.
And yet thou couldst believe her!

THESEUS: Oh misery!

ARTEMIS: Does it bite thee to the heart? But, Theseus, wait
To hear what follows—and to mourn yet more!
Rememberest thou those three sure prayers thy father
Promised to grant thee? One, ignoble fool,
Thou hast misused to strike—no enemy—
But thine own son!
Thy sire, Poseidon, in His wisdom, duly
Performed what He had promised. Thine the guilt,
In *His* eyes, as in mine. So mad thy haste,
That would not wait for proof, nor prophet's word—
Searched not the matter—left not the truth for Time
To bring to light—but launched upon thy son
This curse that killed him!

THESEUS: Ah Lady, let me die!

ARTEMIS: Heinous thy sin;
Yet, for thee too, not unforgivable.
Thus was the will of Cypris. Thus She wreaked
Her anger. And in Heaven this is law—
No God may thwart another God's resolve;
We must let it take its course.
Be sure, had I not feared the wrath of Zeus,
Never could *I* have sunk so low in shame
As to let perish him that I loved the best
Of all on earth. Yet pardoned is thy folly,
First, that it knew not what it did—and then

Phaedra, by death escaping from all question,
Left thee deceived.
So now on thee there falls this heaviest sorrow.
Yet *my* heart too must mourn. For good men's deaths
Can bring the Gods no gladness: but the wicked
Our wrath consumes—their children and their homes.

LEADER: Look, he draws near us, this son of sorrow.
Torn now, and mangled, is that young body,
That golden head. Ah house of destruction,
What double disaster the hand of Heaven
Has wrought upon thy roof!

(*The injured* HIPPOLYTUS *enters, leaning on the shoulders of two attendants.*)

HIPPOLYTUS: Oh, oh!
Wretch that I am, thus torn and tortured
By the unjust doom of an unjust father!
This is the end.
It shoots through my head, this stabbing anguish,
The spasms shudder across my brain,
Stop, let me rest!—for my limbs give way.
Oh, oh!
Accursed team!—with my hands I fed you,
With death and destruction ye have repaid.
Ah, by the Gods, good fellows, gently,
Where on my wounds your hands take hold!
Who is there standing upon my right?
Carry me carefully—draw me on evenly—
Curst and destroyed by my father's fault!
Ah Zeus, ah Zeus, hast Thou eyes to see?
I, the godfearing, the stainless in honour,
Who lived more purely than all beside,
Go down to the pit that gapes before me,
A broken creature. In righteousness
Towards all men I laboured—
And all for naught!
Ah, ah!
Again it pierces, the pain, the pain!
Let go!—for my anguish,
O Death, come as Healer!
Kill me now, kill me! I long for the stab
Of two-edged steel,
To cleave me and lay me, at last, to my rest,
Oh fatal prayer that my father prayed!

Sin of my sires, from ages forgotten—
Why has it fallen
Thus on the guiltless years of my youth?
Ah, what can I utter?
How to escape from this merciless torture?
Oh that the doom, in darkness enfolded,
Of sunless Hades might give me sleep!

ARTEMIS: Unhappy one! Bowed to what misery!
And ruined, too, by thy own noble heart!

HIPPOLYTUS: Ah!
What fragrant breath divine! Through all my pain
I breathe it—and this load of flesh grows lightened.
Is this the deathless Artemis beside me?

ARTEMIS: She *is,* poor heart—the Goddess thou lovest best.

HIPPOLYTUS: Seest Thou, Mistress, my calamity?

ARTEMIS: I see. Yet eyes immortal may not weep.

HIPPOLYTUS: None now shall serve Thee; none shall lead Thy hunt—

ARTEMIS: Too true. But I love thee—even in thy death.

HIPPOLYTUS:—none guard Thy images; nor watch Thy steeds.

ARTEMIS: So willed, in her wickedness, the Cyprian.

HIPPOLYTUS: Ah? Now I know what Power it was destroyed me!

ARTEMIS: Stung by thy scorn. Hating thy purity.

HIPPOLYTUS: So *Her* sole hand has brought three lives to ruin!

ARTEMIS: Thee, and thy father, and thy father's queen.

HIPPOLYTUS: My father's grief—*that* too I sorrow for.

ARTEMIS: Yes, he was blinded by a power divine.

HIPPOLYTUS: Ah my poor father! What unhappiness!

THESEUS: Son, I am broken. Life has lost its joy.

HIPPOLYTUS: Both so deceived!—but you I pity more.

THESEUS: Would I could die, my son!—die in your stead!

HIPPOLYTUS: A bitter gift your sire Poseidon gave!

THESEUS: Ah, that my lips had never breathed of it!

HIPPOLYTUS: What matter now? Your anger could have killed me.

THESEUS: Too true! Such madness Heaven sent upon me.

HIPPOLYTUS: Ah!
If only human lips could curse the Gods!

ARTEMIS: Let be! Though thy soul descend to nether darkness,
Not unavenged shall be the Cyprian's anger
That dared to strike thee down—so pure of heart,
So reverent of the Gods!

This hand of mine with its unerring arrows
Shall smite in retribution that one man
She in Her turn holds dearest.
But *thou* poor suffering heart—in recompense
For all thou hast endured, I promise thee
Honour supreme in this Troezēnian land.
For, in thy name its brides, long years hereafter,
Shall shear their tresses ere the wedding-morn
And pay thee solemn tribute of their tears.
Thou shalt be a theme eternal for the songs
Of maiden lips; and Phaedra's love for thee
Shall perish never from the mouths of men.
Now, ancient Aegeus' child, take up thy son
And clasp him in thy arms. Thou hast destroyed him,
Not knowing what thou didst. When Heaven wills it,
Man needs must err. And thou, Hippolytus,
Hate not thy father. For thy doom ordained
This end for thee. Farewell! It is not lawful
That I should look on death, nor let these eyes
Be sullied with a mortal's agony.
And well I see that thou art near thy hour.

(ARTEMIS *disappears.*)

HIPPOLYTUS: Farewell to Thee, O happy Maiden Queen.
Lightly Thou leavest our long companionship!
But at Thy bidding I forgive my father—
Never these ears were deaf to word of Thine.
Ah, fast the night falls now across my eyes.
Clasp me, my father! Stay me in your arms!

THESEUS: My son, my son! What will you do to me?

HIPPOLYTUS: My end is come. I see Death's gates before me.

THESEUS: Will you leave me?—with this stain upon my hands?

HIPPOLYTUS: Ah no! For I acquit you of my death.

THESEUS: Truly! Release me from all guilt of blood?

HIPPOLYTUS: So witness Artemis, the Archer-queen!

THESEUS: My dearest son, how generous to your father!

HIPPOLYTUS: Pray that your *true*-born sons may be the same.

THESEUS: Ah noble and upright heart!

HIPPOLYTUS: Farewell, you too, my father—a long farewell!

THESEUS: My son, do not forsake me! Still endure!

HIPPOLYTUS: To the end I have endured. It is finished now.
Quick, father!—lay the clothes above my face!

THESEUS: Ah glorious land of Pallas and of Athens,

What a son is lost to you! Wretch that I am!
Long, Cypris, long till I forget Thy curse!

(*He follows the body of* HIPPOLYTUS *into the palace.*)

CHORUS: Sudden and strange this sorrow came
On all Troezēn.
Many a tear this death shall claim;
Long must memory mourn the name
Of greatness that has been.

William Shakespeare: *KING LEAR*

Like the Greeks, the Elizabethans were less insistent that their dramatists devise new stories than that they retell old ones more effectively. Dryden's description, in 1668, of Shakespeare's contemporary, Ben Jonson, is as appropriate to Shakespeare as to Jonson: "He has done his robberies so openly that we may see that he fears not to be taxed by any law. He invades authors like a monarch, and what would be theft in other poets is only victory in him."

The victory which Shakespeare achieved in the creation of *King Lear* is rooted partly in Elizabethan history books and partly in an anonymous Elizabethan play, *King Leir.* The legend of Lear, a king in Britain before the Roman conquest, who had disowned Cordelia, his virtuous daughter, and exposed himself to her two wicked sisters, Goneril and Regan, was sanctified as history. But historical accounts and the anonymous drama are untragic, for their hero was finally restored to the throne by the devotion of the daughter whom he had rejected. Although the old drama of *King Leir* ended happily with the king's restoration, history books carried the story further, and related that after his peaceful death Cordelia was deposed and died in prison.

Such was the raw material which Shakespeare appropriated, and to it he added a subplot, borrowed from Sir Philip Sidney's *Arcadia,* a courtly Elizabethan novel by the ideal gentleman (scholar, poet, soldier) of the age. To the story of Lear and his daughters, Shakespeare joined a tale of a man (Gloucester, in the play) who trusted his wicked son and rejected his loyal one, and he linked these two stories by having the villainous son (Edmund) engage in intrigues with Lear's two ferocious daughters. And, instead of ending (as the old play did) with justice triumphant, Shakespeare so darkened both tales that some of his most perceptive and sympathetic critics have felt that his play is not tragic but pessimistic.

In 1681 Nahum Tate, finding Shakespeare's *Lear* "A Heap

of Jewels, unstrung and unpolisht," decided to improve it. In his version he not only restored Lear to the throne, but he had Lear's fair daughter, Cordelia, wed to Gloucester's honest son, Edgar. This happy ending held the stage until 1823, when Edmund Kean reverted to the tragic conclusion; but after three performances Kean took up Tate's ending again, and not until 1838 did William Macready set Shakespeare's own play back on the boards. Even Dr. Johnson, the finest critic of eighteenth-century England and one of the most perceptive students of Shakespeare's plays, found the tragic ending unsatisfactory. Admitting that justice does not always triumph on earth, he insisted nevertheless that a play is not worsened if it conforms to our hopes rather than to our experience. "A play in which the wicked prosper, and the virtuous miscarry, may doubtless be good, because it is a just representation of the common events of human life: but since all reasonable beings naturally love justice, I cannot easily be persuaded that the observation of justice makes a play worse." Johnson's words deserve careful thought, and though few people would now go back to Tate's happier text, many readers have felt that in *Lear* Shakespeare was needlessly brutal.

But the picture in *Lear* is tragic, not brutal, and Johnson somewhat misstated the case when he asserted that "the wicked prosper." True, Goneril and Regan, Lear's "tigers, not daughters," treat the old king barbarously, and Lear and Cordelia die; Gloucester, too, who foolishly relied on Edmund and mistrusted Edgar, dies in the course of the drama. But if the good people perish, so, too, do the wicked, and at the end of the play, though the greatest people are no more, the kingdom returns to the hands of the righteous. The cataclysm subsides, and evil has—at least for a while—expired in the holocaust which it created.

The play begins with Lear's abdication; portioning out his kingdom to his daughters, he blindly rejects Cordelia, his favorite, when she refuses—or is unable—to publicly pronounce her love for him. Because Kent, a faithful courtier, interposes, Lear banishes him, too, and calls upon the goddess Nature to witness his rejection of Cordelia. But he soon finds that Goneril and Regan, the daughters who freely professed their love, are in reality monsters of ingratitude, and he who gave them a kingdom learns that he has no place to rest his head. Again he calls on Nature, now to make Goneril sterile, and if this time he has indeed been mistreated, we nevertheless perceive that he has not yet learned all that he must before his tragic life is over. Out on the heath he wanders about in the storm, but the rain which beats down on his head is far weaker than the storm which rages in his mind.

Tragedy, Edith Hamilton has said in *The Greek Way,* is the suffering of a soul that can suffer greatly, and Lear's anguish is dramatically counterpoised against Gloucester's pain. The Gloucester subplot parallels the main plot, but Gloucester never reaches Lear's heights. Gloucester's blinding, horrible though it be, is only the physical counterpart to the more painful, yet more noble, suffering of Lear. Still further removed from the tragic hero, Kent—who, with the Fool, sometimes plays a role corresponding to a Greek chorus—is bound in the stocks, but with a patient shrug (which was never Lear's way) he asks simply that Fortune turn her wheel.

It is precisely Lear's *im*patience which makes him potentially tragic. Every inch a king, his curses are cosmic (though as unnatural as the cruel acts which he asks Nature to witness), and his early appeal to the gods is that they should touch him with noble anger. But Lear must acquire patience and wisdom, not anger. As the tragedy progresses he does indeed become a man more sinned against than sinning, and if at the beginning of the play Regan astutely remarks that Lear "hath ever but slenderly known himself," Lear acquires some self-knowledge through his suffering. But the consequences of folly cannot be undone by tardy knowledge, and the evil forces work their course. Cordelia dies, and the hope that she and Lear might dwell in an almost mystical union is shattered. Lear, however, has seen too much of life to remain in this world, and his death is as appropriate as it is inevitable. The best comment on the impertinence of Tate's revised happy ending is Charles Lamb's: "A happy ending!—as if the living martyrdom that Lear had gone through,—the flaying of his feelings alive, did not make a fair dismissal from the stage of life the only decorous thing for him. . . . As if the childish pleasure of getting his gilt robes and sceptre again could tempt him to act over again his misused station—as if, at his years and with his experience, anything was left but to die."

Shakespeare: Biographical Note. William Shakespeare (1564–1616) has left us few biographical facts, but, more important, he left us a stout book of great plays. Born in Stratford of a middle-class family, he probably received an adequate education in his early years, and later (about 1588) went to London. He wrote two long narrative poems and the greatest sonnets in the language, but could scarcely hope to support a family on the gains of such poetry. In London he became connected with the theater, and while he was writing his early plays he probably was acting in other people's. As the last decade of the sixteenth century progressed, he gained in stature, and by the turn of the century he was one of England's most popular playwrights. He continued to write until about 1611 (*King Lear,* whose exact date is uncertain, was probably written in 1605), and then retired, having enriched himself by his pen and his part ownership in the Globe Theatre. Modern attempts to deny his authorship of the plays are mostly based on the assumption that an ignorant Stratford rustic (which he was not) could not have written such superb dramas. Ben Jonson, the greatest comic writer of the English Renaissance, and a great classical scholar, knew Shakespeare well and several times refers to him. Shakespeare, Jonson says in a memorial poem, had small Latin and less Greek but nevertheless deserves a place with the ancient dramatists, for "he was not of an age but for all time!"

King Lear

Characters

LEAR, *King of Britain.*

KING OF FRANCE.

DUKE OF BURGUNDY.

DUKE OF CORNWALL.

DUKE OF ALBANY.

EARL OF KENT.

EARL OF GLOUCESTER.

EDGAR, *son of Gloucester.*

EDMUND, *bastard son to Gloucester.*

CURAN, *a courtier.*

OLD MAN, *tenant to Gloucester.*

DOCTOR.

LEAR'S FOOL.

OSWALD. *steward to Goneril.*

A CAPTAIN *under Edmund's command.*

GENTLEMEN.

A HERALD.

SERVANTS *to Cornwall.*

GONERIL, REGAN, CORDELIA — daughters to Lear.

KNIGHTS *attending on Lear,* OFFICERS, MESSENGERS, SOLDIERS, ATTENDANTS.

ACT I

Scene I (Lear's *Palace.*)

(*Enter* KENT, GLOUCESTER, *and* EDMUND.)

KENT: I thought the King had more affected[1] the Duke of Albany than Cornwall.

GLOUCESTER: It did always seem so to us; but now, in the division of the kingdom, it appears not which of the Dukes he values most, for equalities are so weighed that curiosity in neither can make choice of either's moiety.[2]

KENT: Is not this your son, my lord?

GLOUCESTER: His breeding, sir, hath been at my charge. I have so often blushed to acknowledge him that now I am brazed[3] to't.

KENT: I cannot conceive you.

GLOUCESTER: Sir, this young fellow's mother could; whereupon she grew round-wombed, and had indeed, sir, a son for her cradle ere she had a husband for her bed. Do you smell a fault?

KENT: I cannot wish the fault undone, the issue of it being so proper.

GLOUCESTER: But I have a son, sir, by order of law, some year elder than this, who yet is no dearer in my account. Though this knave came something saucily into the world before he was sent for, yet was his mother fair, there was good sport at his making, and the whoreson must be acknowledged. Do you know this noble gentleman, Edmund?

EDMUND: No, my lord.

GLOUCESTER: My Lord of Kent. Remember him hereafter as my honorable friend.

EDMUND: My services to your lordship.

KENT: I must love you, and sue to know you better.

EDMUND: Sir, I shall study deserving.

GLOUCESTER: He hath been out nine years, and away he shall again.

(*Sound a sennet.*)

[1]Favored.

[2]Their shares are so equal that neither man can, by scrutiny, prefer the other's.

[3]Hardened.

The King is coming.

(*Enter one bearing a coronet, then* LEAR, ALBANY, CORNWALL, GONERIL, REGAN, CORDELIA, *with* FOLLOWERS.)

LEAR: Attend the lords of France and Burgundy, Gloucester.
GLOUCESTER: I shall, my lord.

(*Exeunt* GLOUCESTER *and* EDMUND.)

LEAR: Meantime we shall express our darker[1] purpose.
Give me the map there. Know that we have divided
In three our kingdom; and 'tis our fast intent
To shake all cares and business from our age,
Conferring them on younger strengths while we
Unburthened crawl toward death. Our son of Cornwall,
And you, our no less loving son of Albany,
We have this hour a constant will to publish
Our daughters' several dowers, that future strife
May be prevented now. The princes, France and Burgundy,
Great rivals in our youngest daughter's love,
Long in our court have made their amorous sojourn,
And here are to be answered. Tell me, my daughters
(Since now we will divest us both of rule,
Interest[2] of territory, cares of state),
Which of you shall we say doth love us most,
That we our largest bounty may extend
Where nature doth with merit challenge.[3] Goneril,
Our eldest-born, speak first.
GONERIL: Sir, I love you more than words can wield the matter;
Dearer than eyesight, space, and liberty;
Beyond what can be valued, rich or rare;
No less than life, with grace, health, beauty, honor;
As much as child e'er loved, or father found;
A love that makes breath poor, and speech unable.
Beyond all manner of so much I love you.
CORDELIA (*aside*): What shall Cordelia speak? Love, and be silent.
LEAR: Of all these bounds, even from this line to this,
With shadowy forests and with champains[4] riched,
With plenteous rivers and wide-skirted meads,
We make thee lady. To thine and Albany's issues

[1]Secret. [2]Possession.

[3]To her whose merit, reinforced by my natural affection, has the best claim.

[4]Fields.

Be this perpetual. What says our second daughter,
Our dearest Regan, wife of Cornwall?
REGAN: I am made of the selfsame metal that my sister is,
And prize me[1] at her worth. In my true heart
I find she names my very deed of love,
Only she comes too short, that I profess
Myself an enemy to all other joys
Which the most precious square[2] of sense possesses,
And find I am alone felicitate
In your dear Highness' love.
CORDELIA (*aside*): Then poor Cordelia!
And yet not so; since I am sure my love's
More richer than my tongue.
LEAR: To thee and thine hereditary ever
Remain this ample third of our fair kingdom,
No less in space, validity,[3] and pleasure
Than that conferred on Goneril. Now, our joy,
Although our last, and least, to whose young love
The vines of France and milk of Burgundy
Strive to be interessed,[4] what can you say to draw
A third more opulent than your sisters? Speak.
CORDELIA: Nothing, my lord.
LEAR: Nothing?
CORDELIA: Nothing.
LEAR: Nothing can come of nothing; speak again.
CORDELIA: Unhappy that I am, I cannot heave
My heart into my mouth. I love your Majesty
According to my bond,[5] no more nor less.
LEAR: How, how, Cordelia? Mend your speech a little,
Lest it may mar your fortunes.
CORDELIA: Good my lord,
You have begot me, bred me, loved me; I
Return those duties back as are right fit,
Obey you, love you, and most honor you.
Why have my sisters husbands, if they say
They love you all? Haply, when I shall wed,
That lord whose hand must take my plight[6] shall carry
Half my love with him, half my care and duty.
Sure I shall never marry like my sisters,
To love my father all.
LEAR: But goes thy heart with this?

[1]Appraise myself.
[2]Criterion.
[3]Value.
[4]Have a claim.
[5]Obligation.
[6]Pledge

CORDELIA: Ay, good my lord.
LEAR: So young, and so untender?
CORDELIA: So young, my lord, and true.
LEAR: Let it be so! Thy truth then be thy dower!
For, by the sacred radiance of the sun.
The mysteries of Hecate[1] and the night,
By all the operation of the orbs
From whom we do exist and cease to be,
Here I disclaim all my paternal care,
Propinquity and property of blood,
And as a stranger to my heart and me
Hold thee from this for ever. The barbarous Scythian,
Or he that makes his generation[2] messes
To gorge his appetite, shall to my bosom
Be as well neighbored, pitied, and relieved
As thou my sometime daughter.
KENT: Good my liege—
LEAR: Peace, Kent!
Come not between the dragon and his wrath.
I loved her most, and thought to set my rest
On her kind nursery.[3] Hence and avoid my sight!
So be my grave my peace as here I give
Her father's heart from her! Call France? Who stirs?
Call Burgundy! Cornwall and Albany,
With my two daughters' dowers digest the third;
Let pride, which she calls plainness, marry her.
I do invest you jointly with my power,
Preëminence, and all the large effects
That troop with majesty. Ourself, by monthly course,
With reservation of an hundred knights,
By you to be sustained, shall our abode
Make with you by due turns. Only we still retain
The name, and all the addition[4] to a king; the sway,
Revenue, execution of the rest,
Beloved sons, be yours, which to confirm
This coronet part between you.
KENT: Royal Lear,
Whom I have ever honored as my king,
Loved as my father, as my master followed,
As my great patron thought on in my prayers—
LEAR: The bow is bent and drawn; make from the shaft.
KENT: Let it fall rather, though the fork invade

[1]Goddess of the Lower World.
[2]Offspring.
[3]Tender care.
[4]Titles.

The region of my heart! Be Kent unmannerly
When Lear is mad. What wouldst thou do, old man?
Think'st thou that duty shall have dread to speak
When power to flattery bows? To plainness honor's bound
When majesty falls to folly. Reserve thy state,[1]
And in thy best consideration check
This hideous rashness. Answer my life my judgment,
Thy youngest daughter does not love thee least,
Nor are those empty-hearted whose low sounds
Reverb[2] no hollowness.

LEAR: Kent, on thy life, no more!

KENT: My life I never held but as a pawn
To wage against thine enemies; nor fear to lose it,
Thy safety being the motive.

LEAR: Out of my sight!

KENT: See better, Lear, and let me still remain
The true blank[3] of thine eye.

LEAR: Now by Apollo—

KENT: Now by Apollo, King,
Thou swearest thy gods in vain.

LEAR: O vassal! miscreant!

(*Laying his hand on his sword.*)

ALBANY, CORNWALL: Dear sir, forbear!

KENT: Kill thy physician, and thy fee bestow
Upon the foul disease. Revoke thy gift,
Or, whilst I can vent clamor from my throat,
I'll tell thee thou dost evil.

LEAR: Hear me, recreant!
On thine allegiance, hear me!
Since thou has sought to make us break our vow,
Which we durst never yet, and with strained pride
To come betwixt our sentence and our power,
Which nor our nature nor our place can bear,
Our potency made good, take thy reward.
Five days we do allot thee for provision
To shield thee from disasters of the world,
And on the sixth to turn thy hated back
Upon our kingdom. If, on the tenth day following,
Thy banished trunk be found in our dominions,
The moment is thy death. Away! By Jupiter,
This shall not be revoked.

KENT: Fare thee well, King; since thus thou wilt appear,

[1]Retain thy power.

[2]Reverberate.

[3]Target.

Freedom lives hence, and banishment is here.
(*To* CORDELIA) The gods to their dear shelter take thee, maid,
That justly think'st and hast most rightly said!
(*To* REGAN *and* GONERIL) And your large speeches may your deeds approve,
That good effects may spring from words of love.
Thus Kent, O princes, bids you all adieu;
He'll shape his old course in a country new.
(*Exit.*)
(*Flourish. Enter* GLOUCESTER *with* FRANCE *and* BURGUNDY, ATTENDANTS.)

GLOUCESTER: Here's France and Burgundy, my noble lord.
LEAR: My Lord of Burgundy,
We first address toward you, who with this king
Hath rivalled for our daughter. What in the least
Will you require in present dower with her,
Or cease your quest of love?
BURGUNDY: Most royal Majesty,
I crave no more than hath your Highness offered,
Nor will you tender[1] less.
LEAR: Right noble Burgundy,
When she was dear to us, we did hold her so,
But now her price is fallen. Sir, there she stands.
If aught within that little seeming substance,
Or all of it, with our displeasure pieced,
And nothing more, may fitly like your Grace,
She's there, and she is yours.
BURGUNDY: I know no answer.
LEAR: Will you, with those infirmities she owes,[2]
Unfriended, new adopted to our hate,
Dowered with our curse, and strangered with our oath,
Take her, or leave her?
BURGUNDY: Pardon me, royal sir;
Election makes not up[3] on such conditions.
LEAR: Then leave her, sir, for by the power that made me
I tell you all her wealth. (*To* FRANCE) For you, great King,
I would not from your love make such a stray
To match you where I hate; therefore beseech you
To avert your liking a more worthier way
Than on a wretch whom nature is ashamed
Almost to acknowledge hers.

[1]Offer
[2]Owns.
[3]Choice is not made.

FRANCE: This is most strange,
That she that even but now was your best object,
The argument[1] of your praise, balm of your age,
Most best, most dearest, should in this trice of time
Commit a thing so monstrous to dismantle
So many folds of favor. Sure her offence
Must be of such unnatural degree
That monsters[2] it, or your fore-vouched affection
Fallen into taint; which to believe of her
Must be a faith that reason without miracle
Should never plant in me.

CORDELIA: I yet beseech your Majesty,
If for I want that glib and oily art
To speak and purpose not, since what I well intend,
I'll do't before I speak—that you make known
It is no vicious blot, murther, or foulness,
No unchaste action or dishonored step,
That hath deprived me of your grace and favor;
But even for want of that for which I am richer,
A still-soliciting eye, and such a tongue
As I am glad I have not, though not to have it
Hath lost me in your liking.

LEAR: Better thou
Hadst not been born than not to have pleased me better.

FRANCE: Is it but this—a tardiness in nature
Which often leaves the history unspoke
That it intends to do? My Lord of Burgundy,
What say you to the lady? Love's not love
When it is mingled with regards that stand
Aloof from the entire point.[3] Will you have her?
She is herself a dowry.

BURGUNDY: Royal King,
Give but that portion which yourself proposed,
And here I take Cordelia by the hand,
Duchess of Burgundy.

LEAR: Nothing. I have sworn; I am firm.

BURGUNDY: I am sorry then you have so lost a father
That you must lose a husband.

CORDELIA: Peace be with Burgundy!
Since that respects of fortune are his love,
I shall not be his wife.

FRANCE: Fairest Cordelia, that art most rich, being poor;

[1]Subject.
[2]Makes monstrous.
[3]Mixed with irrelevant considerations.

Most choice, forsaken; and most loved, despised!
Thee and thy virtues here I seize upon.
Be it lawful I take up what's cast away.
God's, gods! 'tis strange that from their coldest neglect
My love should kindle to inflamed respect.
Thy dowerless daughter, King, thrown to my chance,
Is queen of us, of ours, and our fair France.
Not all the dukes of waterish Burgundy
Can buy this unprized precious maid of me.
Bid them farewell, Cordelia, though unkind;
Thou losest here, a better where[1] to find.

LEAR: Thou hast her, France; let her be thine; for we
Have no such daughter, nor shall ever see
That face of hers again. Therefore be gone
Without our grace, our love, our benison.[2]
Come, noble Burgundy.

(*Flourish. Exeunt* LEAR, BURGUNDY, CORNWALL, ALBANY, GLOUCESTER, *and* ATTENDANTS.)

FRANCE: Bid farewell to your sisters.

CORDELIA: The jewels of our father, with washed eyes
Cordelia leaves you. I know you what you are;
And like a sister am most loath to call
Your faults as they are named. Use well our father;
To your professed[3] bosoms I commit him;
But yet, alas, stood I within his grace,
I would prefer him to a better place.
So farewell to you both.

GONERIL: Prescribe not us our duty.

REGAN: Let your study
Be to content your lord, who hath received you
At fortune's alms. You have obedience scanted,[4]
And well are worth the want that you have wanted.[5]

CORDELIA: Time shall unfold what plighted[6] cunning hides.
Who cover faults, at last shame them derides.
Well may you prosper!

FRANCE: Come, my fair Cordelia.

(*Exeunt* FRANCE *and* CORDELIA).

GONERIL: Sister, it is not little I have to say of what most

[1]Place.
[2]Blessing.
[3]Professing (love).
[4]Been lacking in.
[5]The lack (of affection) which you yourself lack.
[6]Folded.

nearly appertains to us both. I think our father will hence to-night.

REGAN: That's most certain, and with you; next month with us.

GONERIL: You see how full of changes his age is. The observation we have made of it hath not been little. He always loved our sister most, and with what poor judgment he hath now cast her off appears too grossly.

REGAN: 'Tis the infirmity of his age; yet he hath ever but slenderly known himself.

GONERIL: The best and soundest of his time hath been but rash; then must we look from his age to receive not alone the imperfections of long-ingraffed condition,[1] but therewithal the unruly waywardness that infirm and choleric years bring with them.

REGAN: Such unconstant starts are we like to have from him as this of Kent's banishment.

GONERIL: There is further compliment of leave-taking between France and him. Pray you let us hit together. If our father carry authority with such dispositions as he bears, this last surrender of his will but offend us.

REGAN: We shall further think of it.

GONERIL: We must do something, and i'th'heat.

(*Exeunt.*)

SCENE II

(GLOUCESTER'S *Castle.*)

(*Enter* EDMUND *the Bastard alone, with a letter.*)

EDMUND: Thou, Nature, art my goddess; to thy law
My services are bound. Wherefore should I
Stand in the plague[2] of custom, and permit
The curiosity of nations to deprive me,
For that I am some twelve or fourteen moonshines
Lag of[3] a brother? Why bastard? wherefore base?
When my dimensions are as well compact,
My mind as generous, and my shape as true,
As honest madam's issue? Why brand they us

[1]Old habits.

[2]Submit to the vexation of.

[3]Behind.

With base? with baseness? bastardy? base, base?
Who, in the lusty stealth of nature, take
More composition[1] and fierce quality
Than doth, within a dull, stale, tired bed,
Go to the creating a whole tribe of fops
Got 'tween asleep and wake? Well then,
Legitimate Edgar, I must have your land.
Our father's love is to the bastard Edmund
As to the legitimate. Fine word "legitimate"!
Well, my legitimate, if this letter speed,[2]
And my invention thrive, Edmund the base
Shall top the legitimate. I grow, I prosper:
Now, gods, stand up for bastards!

(*Enter* GLOUCESTER.)

GLOUCESTER: Kent banished thus? and France in choler parted?
And the King gone to-night? prescribed[3] his power?
Confined to exhibition?[4] All this done
Upon the gad?[5] Edmund, how now? What news?

EDMUND: So please your lordship, none. (*Pocketing the letter.*)

GLOUCESTER: Why so earnestly seek you to put up that letter?

EDMUND: I know no news, my lord.

GLOUCESTER: What paper were you reading?

EDMUND: Nothing, my lord.

GLOUCESTER: No? What needed then that terrible dispatch of it into your pocket? The quality of nothing hath not such need to hide itself. Let's see. Come, if it be nothing, I shall not need spectacles.

EDMUND: I beseech you, sir, pardon me. It is a letter from my brother that I have not all o'er-read; and for so much as I have perused, I find it not fit for your o'erlooking.

GLOUCESTER: Give me the letter, sir.

EDMUND: I shall offend, either to detain or give it. The contents, as in part I understand them, are to blame.

GLOUCESTER: Let's see, let's see.

EDMUND: I hope, for my brother's justification, he wrote this but as an essay[6] or taste of my virtue.

GLOUCESTER (*reads*): "This policy and reverence[7] of age

[1]Strength.
[2]Succeed.
[3]Limited.
[4]A pension.
[5]Spur of the moment..
[6]Test.
[7]Policy of revering.

makes the world bitter to the best of our times; keeps our fortunes from us till our oldness cannot relish them. I begin to find an idle and fond[1] bondage in the oppression of aged tyranny, who sways, not as it hath power, but as it is suffered. Come to me, that of this I may speak more. If our father would sleep till I waked him, you should enjoy half his revenue for ever, and live the beloved of your brother, Edgar."
Hum! Conspiracy? "Sleep till I waked him, you should enjoy half his revenue." My son Edgar! Had he a hand to write this? a heart and brain to breed it in? When came you to this? Who brought it?

EDMUND: It was not brought me, my lord: there's the cunning of it. I found it thrown in at the casement of my closet.

GLOUCESTER: You know the character[2] to be your brother's?

EDMUND: If the matter were good, my lord, I durst swear it were his; but in respect of that, I would fain think it were not.

GLOUCESTER: It is his?

EDMUND: It is his hand, my lord; but I hope his heart is not in the contents.

GLOUCESTER: Has he never before sounded you in this business?

EDMUND: Never, my lord. But I have heard him oft maintain it to be fit that, sons at perfect age, and fathers declined, the father should be as ward to the son, and the son manage his revenue.

GLOUCESTER: O villain, villain! His very opinion in the letter! Abhorred villain! Unnatural, detested, brutish villain! worse than brutish! Go, sirrah, seek him; I'll apprehend him. Abominable villain! Where is he?

EDMUND: I do not well know, my lord. If it shall please you to suspend your indignation against my brother till you can derive from him better testimony of his intent, you should run a certain course; where, if you violently proceed against him, mistaking his purpose, it would make a great gap in your own honor and shake in pieces the heart of his obedience. I dare pawn down my life for him that he hath writ this to feel my affection to your honor, and to no further pretence of danger.

GLOUCESTER: Think you so?

EDMUND: If your honor judge it meet, I will place you where you shall hear us confer of this and by an auricular assurance[3] have your satisfaction, and that without any further delay than this very evening.

[1]Foolish.

[2]Handwriting.

[3]Hearing the evidence.

GLOUCESTER: He cannot be such a monster.

EDMUND: Nor is not, sure.

GLOUCESTER: To his father, that so tenderly and entirely loves him. Heaven and earth! Edmund, seek him out; wind me into him,[1] I pray you; frame the business after your own wisdom. I would unstate myself to be in a duo resolution.[2]

EDMUND: I will seek him, sir, presently; convey the business as I shall find means, and acquaint you withal.

GLOUCESTER: These late eclipses in the sun and moon portend no good to us. Though the wisdom of nature can reason it thus and thus, yet nature finds itself scourged by the sequent effects. Love cools, friendship falls off, brothers divide. In cities, mutinies; in countries, discord; in palaces, treason; and the bond cracked 'twixt son and father. This villain of mine comes under the prediction; there's son against father: the King falls from bias of nature; there's father against child. We have seen the best of our time. Machinations, hollowness, treachery, and all ruinous disorders follow us disquietly to our graves. Find out this villain, Edmund; it shall lose thee nothing; do it carefully. And the noble and true-hearted Kent banished! his offence, honesty! 'Tis strange. (*Exit.*)

EDMUND: This is the excellent foppery of the world, that, when we are sick in fortune, often the surfeit of our own behavior, we make guilty of our disasters the sun, the moon, and the stars; as if we were villains on necessity, fools by heavenly compulsion, knaves, thieves, and treachers by spherical predominance,[3] drunkards, liars, and adulterers by an enforced obedience of planetary influence; and all that we are evil in, by a divine thrusting on. An admirable evasion of whoremaster man, to lay his goatish disposition to the charge of a star! My father compounded with my mother under the Dragon's Tail, and my nativity was under Ursa Major, so that it follows I am rough and lecherous. Fat! I should have been that I am, had the maidenliest star in the firmament twinkled on my bastardizing. Edgar—

(*Enter* EDGAR.)

and pat! he comes, like the catastrophe of the old comedy. My cue is villainous melancholy, with a sigh like Tom o' Bedlam.[4] O these eclipses do portend these divisions. Fa, sol, la, mi.

EDGAR: How now, brother Edmund? What serious contemplation are you in?

[1]Gain his confidence.

[2]Dispossess myself to be free of doubts.

[3]Planetary influence.

[4]A crazy beggar.

EDMUND: I am thinking, brother, of a prediction I read this other day, what should follow these eclipses.

EDGAR: Do you busy yourself with that?

EDMUND: I promise you, the effects he writes of succeed unhappily, as of unnaturalness between the child and the parent; death, dearth, dissolutions of ancient amities; divisions in state, menaces and maledictions against king and nobles; needless diffidences, banishment of friends, dissipation of cohorts, nuptial breaches, and I know not what.

EDGAR: How long have you been a sectary astronomical?[1]

EDMUND: Come, come, when saw you my father last?

EDGAR: The night gone by.

EDMUND: Spake you with him?

EDGAR: Ay, two hours together.

EDMUND: Parted you in good terms? Found you no displeasure in him by word or countenance?

EDGAR: None at all.

EDMUND: Bethink yourself wherein you may have offended him; and at my entreaty forbear his presence until some little time hath qualified[2] the heat of his displeasure, which at this instant so rageth in him that with the mischief of[3] your person it would scarcely allay.

EDGAR: Some villain hath done me wrong.

EDMUND: That's my fear. I pray you have a continent forbearance[4] till the speed of his rage goes slower; and, as I say, retire with me to my lodging, from whence I will fitly bring you to hear my lord speak. Pray ye, go; there's my key. If you do stir abroad, go armed.

EDGAR: Armed, brother?

EDMUND: Brother, I advise you to the best. Go armed. I am no honest man if there be any good meaning toward you. I have told you what I have seen and heard; but faintly, nothing like the image and horror of it. Pray you, away!

EDGAR: Shall I hear from you anon?

EDMUND: I do serve you in this business.

(*Exit* EDGAR).

A credulous father, and a brother noble,
Whose nature is so far from doing harms
That he suspects none; on whose foolish honesty
My practices ride easy! I see the business.
Let me, if not by birth, have lands by wit;

[1]Believer in astrology.
[2]Modified.
[3]Harm to.
[4]Self-control.

All with me's meet that I can fashion fit.

(*Exit.*)

SCENE III

(ALBANY'S *Palace.*)

(*Enter* GONERIL *and* OSWALD, *her Steward.*)

GONERIL: Did my father strike my gentleman for chiding of his fool?

OSWALD: Ay, madam.

GONERIL: By day and night he wrongs me. Every hour
He flashes into one gross crime or other
That sets us all at odds; I'll not endure it.
His knights grow riotous, and himself upbraids us
On every trifle. When he returns from hunting
I will not speak with him; say I am sick.
If you come slack of former services,
You shall do well; the fault of it I'll answer.

OSWALD: He's coming, madam; I hear him. (*Horns within.*)

GONERIL: Put on what weary negligence you please,
You and your fellows; I'd have it come to question.
If he distaste it, let him to our sister,
Whose mind and mine I know in that are one,
Not to be overruled. Idle old man,
That still would manage those authorities
That he hath given away! Now, by my life,
Old fools are babes again, and must be used
With checks as flatteries, when they are seen abused.[1]
Remember what I have said.

OSWALD: Very well, madam.

GONERIL: And let his knights have colder looks among you;
What grows of it, no matter. Advise your fellows so.
I would breed from hence occasions, and I shall,
That I may speak. I'll write straight to my sister
To hold my very course. Prepare for dinner.
(*Exeunt.*)

[1]Old fools must be checked as well as flattered when they are under a misapprehension.

Scene IV

(The Same.)

(Enter KENT, *disguised.)*

KENT: If but as well I other accents borrow,
That can my speech defuse,[1] my good intent
May carry through itself to that full issue
For which I razed[2] my likeness. Now, banished Kent,
If thou canst serve where thou dost stand condemned,
So may it come, thy master, whom thou lovest,
Shall find thee full of labors.

(Horns within. Enter LEAR, KNIGHTS, *and* ATTENDANTS.)

LEAR: Let me not stay a jot for dinner; go get it ready. *(Exit an* ATTENDANT.) How now? What art thou?

KENT: A man, sir.

LEAR: What dost thou profess? What wouldst thou with us?

KENT: I do profess to be no less than I seem, to serve him truly that will put me in trust, to love him that is honest, to converse with him that is wise and says little, to fear judgment, to fight when I cannot choose, and to eat no fish.[3]

LEAR: What art thou?

KENT: A very honest-hearted fellow, and as poor as the King.

LEAR: If thou be'st as poor for a subject as he's for a king, thou art poor enough. What wouldst thou?

KENT: Service.

LEAR: Who wouldst thou serve?

KENT: You.

LEAR: Dost thou know me, fellow?

KENT: No, sir; but you have that in your countenance which I would fain call master.

LEAR: What's that?

KENT: Authority.

LEAR: What services canst thou do?

KENT: I can keep honest counsel, ride, run, mar a curious tale in telling it and deliver a plain message bluntly. That which ordinary men are fit for, I am qualified in, and the best of me is diligence.

LEAR: How old art thou?

[1]Disguise.

[2]Erased.

[3]To be a Protestant.

KENT: Not so young, sir, to love a woman for singing, nor so old to dote on her for anything. I have years on my back forty-eight.

LEAR: Follow me; thou shalt serve me. If I like thee no worse after dinner, I will not part from thee yet. Dinner, ho, dinner! Where's my knave? my fool? Go you and call my fool hither.
(*Exit an* ATTENDANT.)

(*Enter* OSWALD.)

You, you, sirrah, where's my daughter?

OSWALD: So please you— (*Exit.*)

LEAR: What says the fellow there? Call the clotpoll[1] back. (*Exit a* KNIGHT.) Where's my fool, ho? I think the world's asleep.

(*Enter* KNIGHT.)

How now? Where's that mongrel?

KNIGHT: He says, my lord, your daughter is not well.

LEAR: Why came not the slave back to me when I called him?

KNIGHT: Sir, he answered me in the roundest manner, he would not.

LEAR: He would not?

KNIGHT: My lord, I know not what the matter is, but to my judgment your Highness is not entertained with that ceremonious affection as you were wont. There's a great abatement of kindness appears as well in the general dependants as in the Duke himself also and your daughter.

LEAR: Ha! say'st thou so?

KNIGHT: I beseech you pardon me, my lord, if I be mistaken; for my duty cannot be silent when I think your Highness wronged.

LEAR: Thou but rememberest me of mine own conception. I have perceived a most faint neglect of late, which I have rather blamed as mine own jealous curiosity[2] than as a very pretence and purpose of unkindness; I will look further into't. But where's my fool? I have not seen him this two days.

KNIGHT: Since my young lady's going into France, sir, the fool hath much pined away.

LEAR: No more of that; I have noted it well. Go you and tell

[1]Blockhead.

[2]Suspicious watchfulness.

my daughter I would speak with her. (*Exit* KNIGHT). Go you, call hither my fool. (*Exit an* ATTENDANT.)

(*Enter* OSWALD.)

O, you, sir, you, come you hither, sir. Who am I, sir?

OSWALD: My lady's father.

LEAR: "My lady's father"? My lord's knave! You whoreson dog! you slave! you cur!

OSWALD: I am none of these, my lord; I beseech your pardon.

LEAR: Do you bandy looks with me, you rascal? (*Strikes him.*)

OSWALD: I'll not be strucken, my lord.

KENT: Nor tripped neither, you base football player. (*Trips up his heels.*)

LEAR: I thank thee, fellow. Thou servest me, and I'll love thee.

KENT: Come, sir, arise, away! I'll teach you differences. Away, away! If you will measure your lubber's length again, tarry; but away! Go to! Have you wisdom? So. (*Pushes him out.*)

LEAR: Now, my friendly knave, I thank thee. There's earnest[1] of thy service. (*Gives money.*)

(*Enter* FOOL.)

FOOL: Let me hire him too. Here's my coxcomb. (*Offers* KENT *his cup.*)

LEAR: How now, my pretty knave? How dost thou?

FOOL: Sirrah, you were best take my coxcomb.

KENT: Why, fool?

FOOL: Why? For taking one's part that's out of favor. Nay, an thou canst not smile as the wind sits, thou'lt catch cold shortly. There, take my coxcomb! Why, this fellow has banished two on's[2] daughters, and did the third a blessing against his will. If thou follow him, thou must needs wear my coxcomb. How now, nuncle?[3] Would I had two coxcombs and two daughters!

LEAR: Why, my boy?

FOOL: If I gave them all my living, I'ld keep my coxcombs myself. There's mine! beg another of thy daughters.

LEAR: Take heed, sirrah—the whip.

FOOL: Truth's a dog must to kennel; he must be whipped out, when the Lady brach[4] may stand by th' fire and stink.

LEAR: A pestilent gall to me!

[1]Advance wages.

[2]Of his.

[3]Mine uncle.

[4]Bitch.

FOOL: Sirrah, I'll teach thee a speech.

LEAR: Do.

FOOL: Mark it, nuncle.

Have more than thou showest,
Speak less than thou knowest,
Lend less than thou owest,[1]
Ride more than thou goest,
Learn more than thou trowest,[2]
Set less than thou throwest,[3]
Leave thy drink and thy whore,
And keep in-a-door,
And thou shalt have more
Than two tens to a score.

KENT: This is nothing, fool.

FOOL: Then 'tis like the breath of an unfeed lawyer—you gave me nothing for't. Can you make no use of nothing, nuncle?

LEAR: Why, no, boy. Nothing can be made out of nothing.

FOOL (*to* KENT): Prithee tell him, so much the rent of his land comes to. He will not believe a fool.

LEAR: A bitter fool!

FOOL: Dost thou know the difference, my boy, between a bitter fool and a sweet one?

LEAR: No, lad; teach me.

FOOL: That lord that counselled thee
To give away thy land,
Come place him here by me—
Do thou for him stand.
The sweet and bitter fool
Will presently appear;
The one in motley here,
The other found out there.

LEAR: Dost thou call me fool, boy?

FOOL: All thy other titles thou hast given away; that thou wast born with.

KENT: This is not altogether fool, my lord.

FOOL: No, faith, lords and great men will not let me. If I had a monopoly out, they would have part on't. And ladies too, they will not let me have all the fool to myself; they'll be snatching. Give me an egg, nuncle, and I'll give thee two crowns.

[1]Ownest.
[2]Believest.
[3]Wager less than you win at a throw.

LEAR: What two crowns shall they be?

FOOL: Why, after I have cut the egg i' th' middle and eat up the meat, the two crowns of the egg. When thou clovest thy crown i' th' middle and gavest away both parts, thou borest thine ass on thy back o'er the dirt. Thou hadst little wit in thy bald crown when thou gavest thy golden one away. If I speak like myself in this, let him be whipped that first finds it so.

(*Sings*) Fools had ne'er less grace in a year,
For wise men are grown foppish,
And know not how their wits to wear,
Their manners are so apish.

LEAR: When were you wont to be so full of songs, sirrah?

FOOL: I have used it, nuncle, ever since thou madest thy daughters thy mother, for when thou gavest them the rod, and puttest down thine own breeches,

(*Sings*) Then they for sudden joy did weep,
And I for sorrow sung,
That such a king should play bo-peep
And go the fools among.

Prithee, nuncle, keep a schoolmaster that can teach thy fool to lie. I would fain learn to lie.

LEAR: An[1] you lie, sirrah, we'll have you whipped.

FOOL: I marvel what kin thou and thy daughters are. They'll have me whipped for speaking true; thou'lt have me whipped for lying; and sometimes I am whipped for holding my peace. I had rather be any kind o' thing than a fool, and yet I would not be thee, nuncle. Thou hast pared thy wit o' both sides and left nothing i' th' middle. Here comes one o' the parings.

(*Enter* GONERIL.)

LEAR: How now, daughter? What makes that frontlet[2] on? Methinks you are too much o' late i' th' frown.

FOOL: Thou wast a pretty fellow when thou hadst no need to care for her frowning; now thou art an O without a figure. I am better than thou art now; I am a fool, thou art nothing. (*To* GONERIL) Yes, forsooth, I will hold my tongue. So your face bids me, though you say nothing. Mum, mum!

He that keeps nor crust nor crumb,
Weary of all, shall want some.

[1]If. [2]Frown.

(*Points at* LEAR.) That's a shealed peascod.[1]

GONERIL: Not only, sir, this your all-licensed fool,
But other of your insolent retinue
Do hourly carp and quarrel, breaking forth
In rank, and not-to-be-endured riots. Sir,
I had thought, by making this well known unto you,
To have found a safe redress, but now grow fearful,
By what yourself, too, late have spoke and done,
That you protect this course, and put it on[2]
By your allowance; which if you should, the fault
Would not scape censure, nor the redresses sleep,
Which, in the tender[3] of a wholesome weal,[4]
Might in their working do you that offence
Which else were shame, that then necessity
Must call discreet proceeding.

FOOL: For you know, nuncle,

The hedge-sparrow fed the cuckoo so long
That it had it[5] head bit off by it[5] young.

So out went the candle, and we were left darkling.

LEAR: Are you our daughter?

GONERIL: I would you would make use of your good wisdom,
Whereof I know you are fraught,[6] and put away
These dispositions which of late transport you
From what you rightly are.

FOOL: May not an ass know when the cart draws the horse?
Whoop, Jug, I love thee!

LEAR: Does any here know me? This is not Lear.
Does Lear walk thus? speak thus? Where are his eyes?
Either his notion[7] weakens, his discernings
Are lethargied—Ha! waking? 'Tis not so!
Who is it that can tell me who I am?

FOOL: Lear's shadow.

LEAR: I would learn that, for by the marks of sovereignty,
Knowledge, and reason, I should be false persuaded
I had daughters.

FOOL: Which they will make an obedient father.

LEAR: Your name, fair gentlewoman?

GONERIL: This admiration,[8] sir, is much o' th' savor

[1]Shelled pea-pod.
[2]Encourage it.
[3]Care.
[4]Commonwealth.
[5]Its.
[6]Supplied.
[7]Mind.
[8]Astonishment.

Of other your new pranks. I do beseech you
To understand my purposes aright.
As you are old and reverend, you should be wise.
Here do you keep a hundred knights and squires;
Men so disordered, so deboshed,[1] and bold
That this our court, infected with their manners,
Shows like a riotous inn. Epicurism and lust
Make it more like a tavern or a brothel
Than a graced palace. The shame itself doth speak
For instant remedy. Be then desired
By her that else will take the thing she begs
A little to disquantity[2] your train,
And the remainders that shall still depend
To be such men as may besort[3] your age,
Which know themselves, and you.

LEAR: Darkness and devils!
Saddle my horses; call my train together!
Degenerate bastard, I'll not trouble thee;
Yet have I left a daughter.

GONERIL: You strike my people, and your disordered rabble
Make servants of their betters.

(*Enter* ALBANY.)

LEAR: Woe that too late repents! O, sir, are you come?
Is it your will? Speak, sir! Prepare my horses.
Ingratitude, thou marble-hearted fiend,
More hideous when thou show'st thee in a child
Than the sea-monster!

ALBANY: Pray, sir, be patient.

LEAR (*to* GONERIL): Detested kite, thou liest!
My train are men of choice and rarest parts,
That all particulars of duty know
And in the most exact regard support
The worships[4] of their name. O most small fault,
How ugly didst thou in Cordelia show,
Which, like an engine,[5] wrenched my frame of nature
From the fixed place, drew from my heart all love
And added to the gall. O Lear, Lear, Lear!
Beat at this gate that let thy folly in (*strikes his head*)
And thy dear judgment out! Go, go, my people.

ALBANY: My lord, I am guiltless, as I am ignorant

[1]Debauched.
[2]Diminish.
[3]Suit.
[4]Honors.
[5]Machine (the rack).

Of what hath moved you.
LEAR: It may be so, my lord.
Hear, Nature, hear, dear goddess, hear!
Suspend thy purpose, if thou didst intend
To make this creature fruitful;
Into her womb convey sterility;
Dry up in her the organs of increase,
And from her derogate[1] body never spring
A babe to honor her! If she must teem,
Create her child of spleen, that it may live
And be a thwart disnatured[2] torment to her.
Let it stamp wrinkles in her brow of youth,
With cadent[3] tears fret channels in her cheeks,
Turn all her mother's pains and benefits
To laughter and contempt, that she may feel
How sharper than a serpent's tooth it is
To have a thankless child! Away, away! (*Exit.*)
ALBANY: Now, gods that we adore, whereof comes this?
GONERIL: Never afflict yourself to know more of it,
But let his disposition have that scope
That dotage gives it.

(*Enter* LEAR.)

LEAR: What, fifty of my followers at a clap?
Within a fortnight?
ALBANY: What's the matter, sir?
LEAR: I'll tell thee. (*To* GONERIL) Life and death! I am ashamed
That thou hast power to shake my manhood thus,
That these hot tears, which break from me perforce,
Should make thee worth them. Blasts and fogs upon thee!
Th' untented[4] woundings of a father's curse
Pierce every sense about thee! Old fond eyes,
Beweep this cause again, I'll pluck ye out,
And cast you, with the waters that you lose,
To temper clay. Yea, is it come to this?
Let it be so. Yet have I left a daughter,
Who I am sure is kind and comfortable.
When she shall hear this of thee, with her nails
She'll flay thy wolvish visage. Thou shalt find
That I'll resume the shape which thou dost think
I have cast off for ever.

[1]Corrupt.
[2]Perverse, unnatural.
[3]Falling.
[4]Incurable.

(*Exeunt* LEAR, KENT, *and* ATTENDANTS.)

GONERIL: Do you mark that, my lord?

ALBANY: I cannot be so partial, Goneril,
To the great love I bear you—

GONERIL: Pray you, content. What, Oswald, ho!
(*To the* FOOL) You, sir, more knave than fool, after your master!

FOOL: Nuncle Lear, nuncle Lear, tarry! Take the fool with thee.

A fox, when one has caught her,
And such a daughter,
Should sure to the slaughter,
If my cap would buy a halter.
So the fool follows after. (*Exit.*)

GONERIL: This man hath had good counsel! A hundred knights?
'Tis politic and safe to let him keep
At point[1] a hundred knights; yes, that on every dream,
Each buzz, each fancy, each complaint, dislike,
He may enguard his dotage with their powers
And hold our lives in mercy.—Oswald, I say!

ALBANY: Well, you may fear too far.

GONERIL: Safer than trust too far.
Let me still take away the harms I fear,
Not fear still to be taken. I know his heart.
What he hath uttered I have writ my sister.
If she sustain him and his hundred knights,
When I have showed the unfitness—

(*Enter* OSWALD.)

How now, Oswald?
What, have you writ that letter to my sister?

OSWALD: Ay, madam.

GONERIL: Take you some company, and away to horse!
Inform her full of my particular fear,
And thereto add such reasons of your own
As may compact it more. Get you gone,
And hasten your return. (*Exit* OSWALD.) No, no, my lord,
This milky gentleness and course of yours,
Though I condemn it not, yet, under pardon,
You are much more at task[2] for want of wisdom

[1]Fully armed. [2]Blamed.

Than praised for harmful mildness.

ALBANY: How far your eyes may pierce I cannot tell;
Striving to better, oft we mar what's well.

GONERIL: Nay then—

ALBANY: Well, well; the event. (*Exeunt.*)

SCENE V

(*Court before* ALBANY'S *Palace.*)

(*Enter* LEAR, KENT, *and* FOOL.)

LEAR: Go you before to Gloucester with these letters. Acquaint my daughter no further with anything you know than comes from her demand out of the letter. If your diligence be not speedy, I shall be there afore you.

KENT: I will not sleep, my lord, till I have delivered your letter. (*Exit.*)

FOOL: If a man's brains were in's heels, weren't not in danger of kibes?[1]

LEAR: Ay, boy.

FOOL: Then I prithee be merry; thy wit shall ne'er go slipshod.

LEAR: Ha, ha, ha!

FOOL: Shalt see thy other daughter will use thee kindly;[2] for though she's as like this as a crab's[3] like an apple, yet I can tell what I can tell.

LEAR: What canst tell, boy?

FOOL: She'll taste as like this as a crab does to a crab. Thou canst tell why one's nose stands i'th' middle on's face?

LEAR: No.

FOOL: Why, to keep one's eyes of either side's nose, that what a man cannot smell out, he may spy into.

LEAR: I did her wrong.

FOOL: Canst tell how an oyster makes his shell?

LEAR: No.

FOOL: Nor I neither; but I can tell why a snail has a house.

LEAR: Why?

FOOL: Why, to put's head in; not to give it away to his daughters, and leave his horns without a case.

[1]Chilblains.

[2]According to her nature.

[3]Crabapple.

LEAR: I will forget my nature. So kind a father!—Be my horses ready?

FOOL: Thy asses are gone about 'em. The reason why the seven stars are no more than seven is a pretty reason.

LEAR: Because they are not eight?

FOOL: Yes indeed. Thou wouldst make a good fool.

LEAR: To tak't again perforce! Monster ingratitude!

FOOL: If thou wert my fool, nuncle, I'ld have thee beaten for being old before thy time.

LEAR: How's that?

FOOL: Thou shouldst not have been old till thou hadst been wise.

LEAR: O, let me not be mad, not mad, sweet heaven!
Keep me in temper; I would not be mad!

(*Enter* GENTLEMAN.)

How now? Are the horses ready?

GENTLEMAN: Ready, my lord.

LEAR: Come, boy.

FOOL: She that's a maid now, and laughs at my departure,
Shall not be a maid long, unless things be cut shorter.
(*Exeunt.*)

ACT II

SCENE I

(GLOUCESTER'S *Castle.*)

(*Enter* EDMUND *and* CURAN, *meeting.*)

EDMUND: Save thee, Curan.

CURAN: And you, sir. I have been with your father, and given him notice that the Duke of Cornwall and Regan his Duchess will be here with him this night.

EDMUND: How comes that?

CURAN: Nay, I know not. You have heard of the news abroad—I mean the whispered ones, for they are yet but ear-kissing[1] arguments?

EDMUND: Not I. Pray you, what are they?

[1]Whispered.

CURAN: Have you heard of no likely wars toward[1] 'twixt the two Dukes of Cornwall and Albany?

EDMUND: Not a word.

CURAN: You may do, then, in time. Fare you well, sir. (*Exit.*)

EDMUND: The Duke be here to-night? The better! best!
This weaves itself perforce into my business.
My father hath set guard to take my brother;
And I have one thing, of a queasy question,[2]
Which I must act. Briefness and fortune, work!
Brother, a word! Descend! Brother, I say!

(*Enter* EDGAR.)

My father watches. O sir, fly this place;
Intelligence is given where you are hid;
You have now the good advantage of the night.
Have you not spoken 'gainst the Duke of Cornwall?
He's coming hither, now i'th' night, i'th' haste,
And Regan with him. Have you nothing said
Upon his party 'gainst the Duke of Albany?
Advise yourself.

EDGAR: I am sure on't, not a word.

EDMUND: I hear my father coming. Pardon me;
In cunning I must draw my sword upon you;
Draw, seem to defend yourself; now quit you well.—
Yield! Come before my father. Light, ho, here!
Fly, brother.—Torches, torches!—So farewell.

(*Exit* EDGAR.)

Some blood drawn on me would beget opinion
Of my more fierce endeavor. (*Stabs his arm.*) I have seen drunkards
Do more than this in sport.—Father, father!—
Stop, stop! No help?

(*Enter* GLOUCESTER, *and* SERVANTS *with torches.*)

GLOUCESTER: Now, Edmund, where's the villain?

EDMUND: Here stood he in the dark, his sharp sword out,
Mumbling of wicked charms, conjuring the moon
To stand auspicious mistress.[3]

GLOUCESTER: But where is he?

[1]Imminent.
[2]Requiring great care.
[3]To give him her favors.

EDMUND: Look, sir, I bleed.
GLOUCESTER: Where is the villain, Edmund?
EDMUND: Fled this way, sir. When by no means he could—
GLOUCESTER: Pursue him, ho! Go after. (*Exeunt some* SERVANTS.) By no means what?
EDMUND: Persuade me to the murther of your lordship;
But that I told him the revenging gods
'Gainst parricides did all their thunders bend;
Spoke with how manifold and strong a bond
The child was bound to th' father—sir, in fine,
Seeing how loathly opposite I stood
To his unnatural purpose, in fell[1] motion
With his prepared sword he charges home
My unprovided body, lanced mine arm;
And when he saw my best alarumed spirits,
Bold in the quarrel's right, roused to th'encounter,
Or whether gasted[2] by the noise I made,
Full suddenly he fled.
GLOUCESTER: Let him fly far.
Not in this land shall he remain uncaught;
And found—dispatch. The noble Duke my master,
My worthy arch[3] and patron, comes to-night.
By his authority I will proclaim it,
That he which finds him shall deserve our thanks,
Bringing the murderous coward to the stake;
He that conceals him, death.
EDMUND: When I dissuaded him from his intent
And found him pight[4] to do it, with curst speech
I threatened to discover him. He replied,
"Thou unpossessing bastard, dost thou think,
If I would stand against thee, would the reposal
Of any trust, virtue, or worth in thee
Make thy words faithed?[5] No. What I should deny
(As this I would; ay, though thou didst produce
My very character), I'ld turn it all
To thy suggestion, plot, and damned practice;
And thou must make a dullard of the world,
If they not thought the profits of my death
Were very pregnant and potential spurs
To make thee seek it."

[1]Foul.
[2]Frightened.
[3]Lord.
[4]Determined.
[5]Believed.

GLOUCESTER: O strange and fastened[1] villain,
Would he deny his letter? I never got him.

(*Tucket within.*)

Hark, the Duke's trumpets! I know not why he comes.
All ports I'll bar; the villain shall not scape;
The Duke must grant me that. Besides, his picture
I will send far and near, that all the kingdom
May have due note of him, and of my land,
Loyal and natural boy, I'll work the means
To make thee capable.[2]

(*Enter* CORNWALL, REGAN, *and* ATTENDANTS.)

CORNWALL: How now, my noble friend? Since I came hither
(Which I can call but now) I have heard strange news.
REGAN: If it be true, all vengeance comes too short
Which can pursue the offender. How dost, my lord?
GLOUCESTER: O madam, my old heart is cracked, it's cracked!
REGAN: What, did my father's godson seek your life?
He whom my father named, your Edgar?
GLOUCESTER: O lady, lady, shame would have it hid!
REGAN: Was he not companion with the riotous knights
That tended upon my father?
GLOUCESTER: I know not, madam. 'Tis too bad, too bad!
EDMUND: Yes, madam, he was of that consort.[3]
REGAN: No marvel then though he were ill affected.
'Tis they have put him on the old man's death,
To have the expense and waste of his revenues.
I have this present evening from my sister
Been well informed of them, and with such cautions
That, if they come to sojourn at my house,
I'll not be there.
CORNWALL: Nor I, assure thee, Regan.
Edmund, I hear that you have shown your father
A childlike[4] office.
EDMUND: It was my duty, sir.
GLOUCESTER: He did bewray[5] his practice, and received
This hurt you see, striving to apprehend him.
CORNWALL: Is he pursued?

[1]Hardened.
[2]Able to inherit.
[3]Company.
[4]Filial.
[5]Betray.

GLOUCESTER: Ay, my good lord.
CORNWALL: If he be taken, he shall never more
Be feared of doing harm. Make your own purpose,
How in my strength you please. For you, Edmund,
Whose virtue and obedience doth this instant
So much commend itself, you shall be ours.
Natures of such deep trust we shall much need;
You we first seize on.
EDMUND: I shall serve you, sir,
Truly, however else.
GLOUCESTER: For him I thank your Grace.
CORNWALL: You know not why we came to visit you—
REGAN: Thus out of season, threading dark-eyed night.
Occasions, noble Gloucester, of some prize,[1]
Wherein we must have use of your advice.
Our father he hath writ, so hath our sister,
Of differences, which I best thought it fit
To answer from[2] our home; the several messengers
From hence attend dispatch. Our good old friend,
Lay comforts to your bosom, and bestow
Your needful counsel to our businesses,
Which craves the instant use.
GLOUCESTER: I serve you, madam.
Your Graces are right welcome.

(*Exeunt. Flourish.*)

SCENE II

(*Before* GLOUCESTER'S *Castle.*)

(*Enter* KENT *and* OSWALD, *severally.*)

OSWALD: Good dawning to thee, friend; art of this house?
KENT: Ay.
OSWALD: Where may we set our horses?
KENT: I'th mire.
OSWALD: Prithee, if thou lov'st me, tell me.
KENT: I love thee not.
OSWALD: Why then, I care not for thee.

[1]Importance.
[2]Away from.

KENT: If I had thee in Lipsbury Pinfold,[1] I would make thee care for me.

OSWALD: Why dost thou use me thus? I know thee not.

KENT: Fellow, I know thee.

OSWALD: What dost thou know me for?

KENT: A knave, a rascal, an eater of broken meats; a base, proud, shallow, beggarly, three-suited, hundred-pound, filthy worsted-stocking knave; a lily-livered, action-taking,[2] whoreson, glass-gazing, superserviceable, finical rogue; one-trunk-inheriting slave; one that wouldst be a bawd in way of good service, and art nothing but the composition of a knave, beggar, coward, pander, and the son and heir of a mongrel bitch; one whom I will beat into clamorous whining, if thou deny'st the least syllable of thy addition.

OSWALD: Why, what a monstrous fellow art thou, thus to rail on one that's neither known of thee nor knows thee!

KENT: What a brazen-faced varlet art thou, to deny thou knowest me! Is it two days ago since I tripped up thy heels and beat thee before the King? (*Draws his sword.*) Draw, you rogue, for though it be night yet the moon shines. I'll make a sop o'th' moonshine of you. Draw, you whoreson cullionly barbermonger,[3] draw!

OSWALD: Away! I have nothing to do with thee.

KENT: Draw, you rascal! You come with letters against the King, and take Vanity the puppet's part against the royalty of her father. Draw, you rogue, or I'll so carbonado[4] your shanks; draw, you rascal! Come your ways!

OSWALD: Help, ho! murther! help!

KENT: Strike, you slave! Stand, rogue! Stand, you neat slave! Strike! (*Beats him.*)

OSWALD: Help, ho! murther! murther!

(*Enter* EDMUND, *with his rapier drawn,* GLOUCESTER, CORNWALL, REGAN, SERVANTS.)

EDMUND: How now? What's the matter? Part.

KENT: With you, goodman boy, if you please! Come, I'll flesh ye; come on, young master!

GLOUCESTER: Weapons? arms? What's the matter here?

CORNWALL: Keep peace, upon your lives! He dies that strikes again. What is the matter?

REGAN: The messengers from our sister and the King.

CORNWALL: What is your difference? Speak.

OSWALD: I am scarce in breath, my lord.

[1]Between my jaws (?).

[2]Taking refuge in the law.

[3]Fop.

[4]Slice.

KENT: No marvel, you have so bestirred your valor. You cowardly rascal, nature disclaims in[1] thee; a tailor made thee.

CORNWALL: Thou art a strange fellow. A tailor make a man?

KENT: A tailor, sir; a stonecutter or a painter could not have made him so ill, though he had been but two years o' the trade.

CORNWALL: Speak yet, how grew your quarrel?

OSWALD: This ancient ruffian, sir, whose life I have spared
At suit of his gray beard—

KENT: Thou whoreson zed![2] thou unnecessary letter! My lord, if you will give me leave, I will tread this unbolted villain into mortar and daub the walls of a jakes[3] with him. "Spare my gray beard," you wagtail?

CORNWALL: Peace, sirrah!
You beastly knave, know you no reverence?

KENT: Yes, sir, but anger hath a privilege.

CORNWALL: Why art thou angry?

KENT: That such a slave as this should wear a sword,
Who wear no honesty. Such smiling rogues as these,
Like rats, oft bite the holy cord atwain
Which are too intrinse[4] t' unloose; smooth every passion
That in the natures of their lords rebel,
Bring oil to fire, snow to their colder moods;
Renege, affirm, and turn their halcyon beaks
With every gale and vary of their masters,
Knowing naught (like dogs) but following.
A plague upon your epileptic visage!
Smile you my speeches, as I were a fool?
Goose, an I had you upon Sarum[5] Plain,
I'ld drive ye cackling home to Camelot.

CORNWALL: What, art thou mad, old fellow?

GLOUCESTER: How fell you out? Say that.

KENT: No contraries hold more antipathy
Than I and such a knave.

CORNWALL: Why dost thou call him knave? What is his fault?

KENT: His countenance likes me not.

CORNWALL: No more perchance does mine, or his, or hers.

KENT: Sir, 'tis my occupation to be plain;
I have seen better faces in my time
Than stands on any shoulder that I see
Before me at this instant.

[1]Disowns.
[2]Letter Z.
[3]Latrine.
[4]Intricate.
[5]Salisbury.

CORNWALL: This is some fellow
Who, having been praised for bluntness, doth affect
A saucy roughness, and constrains the garb[1]
Quite from his nature. He cannot flatter, he!
An honest mind and plain, he must speak truth!
An they will take it, so; if not, he's plain.
These kind of knaves I know which in this plainness
Harbor more craft and more corrupter ends
Than twenty silly-ducking observants[2]
That stretch their duties nicely.
KENT: Sir, in good faith, in sincere verity,
Under the allowance of your great aspect,
Whose influence, like the wreath of radiant fire
On flickering Phoebus' front—
CORNWALL: What mean'st by this?

KENT: To go out of my dialect, which you discommend so much. I know, sir, I am no flatterer. He that beguiled you in a plain accent was a plain knave, which for my part I will not be, though I should win your displeasure to entreat me to't.

CORNWALL: What was th' offence you gave him?
OSWALD: I never gave him any.
It pleased the King his master very late
To strike at me, upon his misconstruction;
When he, conjunct,[3] and flattering his displeasure,
Tripped me behind; being down, insulted, railed
And put upon him such a deal of man
That worthied[4] him, got praises of the King
For him attempting who was self-subdued,
And, in the fleshment[5] of this dread exploit,
Drew on me here again.
KENT: None of these rogues and cowards
But Ajax is their fool.
CORNWALL: Fetch forth the stocks!
You stubborn ancient knave, you reverent braggart,
We'll teach you—
KENT: Sir, I am too old to learn.
Call not your stocks for me; I serve the King,
On whose employment I was sent to you.
You shall do small respect, show too bold malice
Against the grace and person of my master,
Stocking his messenger.

[1]Puts on the appearance.
[2]Parasites.
[3]Taking his part.
[4]Won him honor.
[5]Excitement.

CORNWALL: Fetch forth the stocks! As I have life and honor,
There shall he sit till noon.

REGAN: Till noon? Till night, my lord, and all night too!

KENT: Why, madam, if I were your father's dog,
You should not use me so.

REGAN: Sir, being his knave, I will.

CORNWALL: This is a fellow of the selfsame color
Our sister speaks of. Come, bring away the stocks!

(*Stocks brought out.*)

GLOUCESTER: Let me beseech your Grace not to do so.
His fault is much, and the good King his master
Will check him for't. Your purposed low correction
Is such as basest and contemnedest wretches
For pilferings and most common trespasses
Are punished with. The King must take it ill
That he, so slightly valued in his messenger,
Should have him thus restrained.

CORNWALL: I'll answer that.

REGAN: My sister may receive it much more worse,
To have her gentleman abused, assaulted,
For following her affairs. Put in his legs.

(KENT *is put in the stocks.*)
Come, my good lord, away.

(*Exeunt all but* GLOUCESTER *and* KENT.)

GLOUCESTER: I am sorry for thee, friend; 'tis the Duke's
pleasure,
Whose disposition, all the world well knows,
Will not be rubbed nor stopped. I'll entreat for thee.

KENT: Pray do not, sir. I have watched and travelled hard;
Some time I shall sleep out, the rest I'll whistle;
A good man's fortune may grow out at heels.
Give you good morrow!

GLOUCESTER: The Duke's to blame in this; 'twill be ill taken.

(*Exit.*)

KENT: Good King, that must approve the common saw,[1]
Thou out of heaven's benediction comest
To the warm sun!
Approach, thou beacon to this under globe,
That by thy comfortable beams I may

[1]Prove true the common proverb.

Peruse this letter. Nothing almost sees miracles
But misery. I know 'tis from Cordelia,
Who hath most fortunately been informed
Of my obscured course; and [*reads*] "shall find time
From this enormous state, seeking to give
Losses their remedies." All weary and o'erwatched,
Take vantage, heavy eyes, not to behold
This shameful lodging.
Fortune, good night; smile once more, turn thy wheel.

(*Sleeps.*)

Scene III

(*Near* GLOUCESTER's *Castle*)

(*Enter* EDGAR.)

EDGAR: I heard myself proclaimed,
And by the happy hollow of a tree
Escaped the hunt. No port is free, no place
That guard and most unusual vigilance
Does not attend my taking.[1] Whiles I may scape,
I will preserve myself; and am bethought
To take the basest and most poorest shape
That ever penury, in contempt of man,
Brought near to beast. My face I'll grime with filth,
Blanket my loins, elf all my hair in knots,
And with presented nakedness outface
The winds and persecutions of the sky.
The country gives me proof and precedent
Of Bedlam[2] beggars, who, with roaring voices,
Strike in their numbed and mortified bare arms
Pins, wooden pricks, nails, sprigs of rosemary;
And with this horrible object, from low farms,
Poor pelting[3] villages, sheepcotes, and mills,
Sometime with lunatic bans, sometime with prayers,
Enforce their charity. "Poor Turlygod! poor Tom!"
That's something yet! Edgar I nothing am. (*Exit.*)

[1]Wait to capture me.

[2]From Bethlehem Hospital for the insane.

[3]Paltry.

Scene IV

(*Before* GLOUCESTER'S *Castle;* KENT *in the Stocks.*)

(*Enter* LEAR, FOOL, *and* GENTLEMAN.)

LEAR: 'Tis strange that they should so depart from home,
And not send back my messenger.
GENTLEMAN: As I learned,
The night before there was no purpose in them
Of this remove.
KENT: Hail to thee, noble master!
LEAR: Ha!
Mak'st thou this shame thy pastime?
KENT: No, my lord.
FOOL: Ha, ha! he wears cruel[1] garters.
Horses are tied by the head, dogs and bears by the neck, monkeys by the loins, and men by the legs. When a man's overlusty at legs, then he wears wooden nether-stocks.[2]
LEAR: What's he that hath so much thy place mistook
To set thee here?
KENT: It is both he and she—
Your son and daughter.
LEAR: No.
KENT: Yes.
LEAR: No, I say.
KENT: I say yea.
LEAR: No, no, they would not!
KENT: Yes, they have.
LEAR: By Jupiter, I swear no!
KENT: By Juno, I swear ay!
LEAR: They durst not do't;
They could not, would not do't. 'Tis worse than murther
To do upon respect[3] such violent outrage.
Resolve me with all modest haste which way
Thou mightst deserve or they impose this usage,
Coming from us.
KENT: My lord, when at their home
I did commend your Highness' letters to them,
Ere I was risen from the place that showed
My duty kneeling, came there a reeking post,
Stewed in his haste, half breathless, panting forth

[1]Pun on *crewel,* worsted.
[2]Stockings.
[3]Against the respect owed to Lear.

From Goneril his mistress salutations;
Delivered letters, spite of intermission,[1]
Which presently they read; on whose contents,
They summoned up their meiny,[2] straight took horse,
Commanded me to follow and attend
The leisure of their answer, gave me cold looks,
And meeting here the other messenger,
Whose welcome I perceived had poisoned mine—
Being the very fellow which of late
Displayed so saucily against your Highness—
Having more man than wit about me, drew;
He raised the house with loud and coward cries.
Your son and daughter found this trespass worth
The shame which here it suffers.

FOOL: Winter's not gone yet, if the wild geese fly that way.

Fathers that wear rags
  Do make their children blind,
But fathers that bear bags
  Shall see their children kind.
Fortune, that arrant whore,
Ne'er turns the key to the poor.

But for all this, thou shalt have as many dolors for thy daughters as thou canst tell in a year.

LEAR: O, how this mother swells up toward my heart!
Hysterica passio![3] Down, thou climbing sorrow!
Thy element's below! Where is this daughter?

KENT: With the Earl, sir, here within.

LEAR: Follow me not;
Stay here. (*Exit.*)

GENTLEMAN: Made you no more offence but what you speak of?

KENT: None.
How chance the King comes with so small a number?

FOOL: An thou hadst been set i'th' stocks for that question, thou'dst well deserved it.

KENT: Why, fool?

FOOL: We'll set thee to school to an ant, to teach thee there's no laboring i'th' winter. All that follow their noses are led by their eyes but blind men, and there's not a nose among twenty but can smell him that's stinking. Let go thy hold when a great wheel runs down a hill, lest it break thy neck with following

[1]In spite of interruption.

[2]Retinue.

[3]Hysterical passion.

it; but the great one that goes upward, let him draw thee after. When a wise man gives thee better counsel, give me mine again. I would have none but knaves follow it, since a fool gives it.

That sir which serves and seeks for gain,
And follows but for form,
Will pack when it begins to rain
And leave thee in the storm.
But I will tarry, the fool will stay,
And let the wise man fly.
The knave turns fool that runs away;
The fool no knave, perdy.

KENT: Where learned you this, fool?
FOOL: Not i'th' stocks, fool.

(*Enter* LEAR *and* GLOUCESTER.)

LEAR: Deny to speak with me? They are sick? they are weary?
They have travelled all the night? Mere fetches,[1]
The images[2] of revolt and flying off!
Fetch me a better answer.
GLOUCESTER: My dear lord,
You know the fiery quality of the Duke,
How unremovable and fixed he is
In his own course.
LEAR: Vengeance! plague! death! confusion!
Fiery? What quality? Why, Gloucester, Gloucester,
I'd speak with the Duke of Cornwall and his wife.
GLOUCESTER: Well, my good lord, I have informed them so.
LEAR: Informed them? Dost thou understand me, man?
GLOUCESTER: Ay, my good lord.
LEAR: The King would speak with Cornwall; the dear father
Would with his daughter speak, commands her service.
Are they informed of this? My breath and blood!
Fiery? the fiery Duke? Tell the hot Duke that—
No, but not yet! May be he is not well;
Infirmity doth still neglect all office[3]
Whereto our health is bound. We are not ourselves
When nature, being oppressed, commands the mind
To suffer with the body. I'll forbear,
And am fallen out with my more headier[4] will,

[1]Pretexts.
[2]Signs.
[3]Duty.
[4]Too impetuous.

To take the indisposed and sickly fit
For the sound man.—Death on my state! Wherefore
Should he sit here? This act persuades me
That this remotion[1] of the Duke and her
Is practice only. Give me my servant forth.
Go tell the Duke and's wife I'ld speak with them—
Now, presently. Bid them come forth and hear me,
Or at their chamber door I'll beat the drum
Till it cry sleep to death.

GLOUCESTER: I would have all well betwixt you. (*Exit.*)

LEAR: O me, my heart, my rising heart! But down!

FOOL: Cry to it, nuncle, as the cockney did to the eels when she put 'em i'th' paste alive. She knapped 'em o'th' coxcombs with a stick and cried "Down, wantons, down!" 'Twas her brother that, in pure kindness to his horse, buttered his hay.

(*Enter* CORNWALL, REGAN, GLOUCESTER, SERVANTS.)

LEAR: Good morrow to you both.
CORNWALL: Hail to your Grace!

(KENT *here set at liberty.*)

REGAN: I am glad to see your Highness.

LEAR: Regan, I think you are; I know what reason
I have to think so. If thou shouldst not be glad,
I would divorce me from thy mother's tomb,
Sepulchring an adultress. (*To* KENT) O, are you free?
Some other time for that.—Beloved Regan,
Thy sister's naught.[2] O Regan, she hath tied
Sharp-toothed unkindness, like a vulture, here!

(*Points to his heart.*)

I can scarce speak to thee. Thou'lt not believe
With how depraved a quality—O Regan!

REGAN: I pray you, sir, take patience. I have hope
You less know how to value her desert
Than she to scant[3] her duty.

LEAR: Say, how is that?

REGAN: I cannot think my sister in the least
Would fail her obligation. If, sir, perchance
She have restrained the riots of your followers,
'Tis on such ground, and to such wholesome end,

[1]Removal.
[2]Wicked.
[3]Fall short of.

As clears her from all blame.
LEAR: My curses on her!
REGAN: O, sir, you are old!
Nature in you stands on the very verge
Of her confine. You should be ruled, and led
By some discretion that discerns your state
Better than you yourself. Therefore I pray you
That to our sister you do make return;
Say you have wronged her, sir.
LEAR: Ask her forgiveness?
Do you but mark how this becomes the house:[1]
"Dear daughter, I confess that I am old; (*Kneels.*)
Age is unnecessary;[2] on my knees I beg
That you'll vouchsafe me raiment, bed, and food."
REGAN: Good sir, no more! these are unsightly tricks.
Return you to my sister.
LEAR: (*rises*): Never, Regan!
She hath abated me of half my train,
Looked black upon me, struck me with her tongue,
Most serpent-like, upon the very heart.
All the stored vengeances of heaven fall
on her ingrateful top; strike her young bones,
You taking[3] airs, with lameness!
CORNWALL: Fie, sir, fie!
LEAR: You nimble lightnings, dart your blinding flames
Into her scornful eyes; infect her beauty,
You fen-sucked fogs, drawn by the powerful sun,
To fall and blast her pride!
REGAN: O the blest gods! so will you wish on me
When the rash mood is on.
LEAR: No, Regan, thou shalt never have my curse;
Thy tender-hefted[4] nature shall not give
Thee o'er to harshness. Her eyes are fierce, but thine
Do comfort, and not burn. 'Tis not in thee
To grudge my pleasures, to cut off my train,
To bandy hasty words, to scant my sizes,[5]
And, in conclusion, to oppose the bolt
Against my coming in. Thou better know'st
The offices of nature, bond of childhood,
Effects of courtesy, dues of gratitude.
Thy half o'th' kingdom hast thou not forgot,

[1]The royal family.
[2]Old people are not wanted.
[3]Malignant.
[4]Gentle.
[5]To reduce my allowances.

Wherein I thee endowed.
REGAN: Good sir, to the purpose.

(*Tucket within.*)

LEAR: Who put my man i'th' stocks?
CORNWALL: What trumpet's that?
REGAN: I know't—my sister's. This approves her letter,
That she would soon be here.

(*Enter* OSWALD.)

Is your lady come?
LEAR: This is a slave, whose easy-borrowed pride
Dwells in the fickle grace of her he follows.
Out, varlet, from my sight!
CORNWALL: What means your Grace?

(*Enter* GONERIL.)

LEAR: Who stocked my servant? Regan, I have good hope
Thou didst not know on't.—Who comes here? O heavens!
If you do love old men, if your sweet sway
Allow obedience, if you yourselves are old,
Make it your cause! Send down, and take my part!
(*To* GONERIL) Art not ashamed to look upon this beard?—
O Regan, wilt thou take her by the hand?
GONERIL: Why not by the hand, sir? How have I offended?
All's not offence that indiscretion finds
And dotage terms so.
LEAR: O sides, you are too tough!
Will you yet hold? How came my man i'th' stocks?
CORNWALL: I set him there, sir; but his own disorders
Deserved much less advancement.
LEAR: You? Did you?
REGAN: I pray you, father, being weak, seem so.
If, till the expiration of your month,
You will return and sojourn with my sister,
Dismissing half your train, come then to me.
I am now from home, and out of that provision
Which shall be needful for your entertainment.
LEAR: Return to her, and fifty men dismissed?
No, rather I abjure all roofs, and choose
To wage against the enmity of the air,
To be a comrade with the wolf and owl—
Necessity's sharp pinch! Return with her?
Why, the hot-blooded France, that dowerless took
Our youngest born, I could as well be brought

To knee his throne, and squire-like, pension beg
To keep base life afoot. Return with her?
Persuade me rather to be slave and sumpter[1]
To this detested groom. (*Points at* OSWALD.)
GONERIL: At your choice sir.
LEAR: I prithee, daughter, do not make me mad.
I will not trouble thee, my child; farewell.
We'll no more meet, no more see one another.
But yet thou art my flesh, my blood, my daughter,
Or rather a disease that's in my flesh.
Which I must needs call mine. Thou art a boil,
A plague sore, an embossed[2] carbuncle
In my corrupted blood. But I'll not chide thee;
Let shame come when it will, I do not call it;
I do not bid the Thunder-bearer shoot
Nor tell tales of thee to high-judging Jove.
Mend when thou canst; be better at thy leisure;
I can be patient, I can stay with Regan,
I and my hundred knights.
REGAN: Not altogether so.
I looked not for you yet, nor am provided
For your fit welcome. Give ear, sir, to my sister,
For those that mingle reason with your passion
Must be content to think you old, and so—
But she knows what she does.
LEAR: Is this well spoken?
REGAN: I dare avouch it, sir. What, fifty followers?
Is it not well? What should you need of more?
Yea, or so many, sith that both charge[3] and danger
Speak 'gainst so great a number? How in one house
Should many people, under two commands,
Hold amity? 'Tis hard, almost impossible.
GONERIL: Why might not you, my lord, receive attendance
From those that she calls servants, or from mine?
REGAN: Why not, my lord? If then they chanced to slack[4] ye,
We could control them. If you will come to me
(For now I spy a danger), I entreat you
To bring but five-and-twenty; to no more
Will I give place or notice.
LEAR: I gave you all—
REGAN: And in good time you gave it!
LEAR: Made you my guardians, my depositaries,

[1]Drudge (literally, a pack horse).
[2]Swollen.
[3]Expense.
[4]Neglect.

But kept a reservation to be followed
With such a number. What, must I come to you
With five-and-twenty? Regan, said you so?
REGAN: And speak't again, my lord. No more with me.
LEAR: Those wicked creatures yet do look well-favored
When others are more wicked; not being the worst
Stands in some rank of praise. (*To* GONERIL) I'll go with thee.
Thy fifty yet doth double five-and-twenty,
And thou art twice her love.
GONERIL: Hear me, my lord;
What need you five-and-twenty, ten, or five,
To follow in a house where twice so many
Have a command to tend you?
REGAN: What need one?
LEAR: O, reason not the need! Our basest beggars
Are in the poorest thing superfluous,[1]
Allow not nature more than nature needs,
Man's life is cheap as beast's. Thou art a lady;
If only to go warm were gorgeous,
Why, nature needs not what thou gorgeous wear'st,
Which scarcely keeps thee warm. But, for true need—
You heavens, give me that patience, patience I need!
You see me here, you gods, a poor old man,
As full of grief as age, wretched in both;
If it be you that stirs these daughters' hearts
Against their father, fool me not so much
To bear it tamely; touch me with noble anger,
And let not women's weapons, water drops,
Stain my man's cheeks! No, you unnatural hags!
I will have such revenges on you both
That all the world shall—I will do such things—
What they are yet, I know not, but they shall be
The terrors of the earth! You think I'll weep;
No, I'll not weep.
I have full cause of weeping, but this heart (*Storm and*
Shall break into a hundred thousand flaws[2] *tempest.*)
Or ere I'll weep. O fool, I shall go mad!

(*Exeunt* LEAR, GLOUCESTER, KENT, *and* FOOL.)

CORNWALL: Let us withdraw; 'twill be a storm.
REGAN: This house is little; the old man and's people
Cannot be well bestowed.

[1]Have more than is absolutely necessary.
[2]Fragments.

GONERIL: 'Tis his own blame hath put himself from rest
And must needs taste his folly.
REGAN: For his particular,[1] I'll receive him gladly,
But not one follower.
GONERIL: So am I purposed.
Where is my Lord of Gloucester?
CORNWALL: Followed the old man forth.

(*Enter* GLOUCESTER.)

He is returned.
GLOUCESTER: The King is in high rage.
CORNWALL: Whither is he going?
GLOUCESTER: He calls to horse, but will I know not whither.
CORNWALL: 'Tis best to give him way; he leads himself.
GONERIL: My lord, entreat him by no means to stay.
GLOUCESTER: Alack, the night comes on, and the bleak winds
Do sorely ruffle. For many miles about
There's scarce a bush.
REGAN: O, sir, to wilful men
The injuries that they themselves procure
Must be their schoolmasters. Shut up your doors.
He is attended with a desperate train,
And what they may incense him to, being apt
to have his ear abused, wisdom bids fear.
CORNWALL: Shut up your doors, my lord; 'tis a wild night.
My Regan counsels well. Come out o'th' storm.

(*Exeunt.*)

ACT III

SCENE I

(A Heath.)

(*Storm still. Enter* KENT *and a* GENTLEMAN *severally.*)

KENT: Who's there besides foul weather?
GENTLEMAN: One minded like the weather, most unquietly.
KENT: I know you; where's the King?
GENTLEMAN: Contending with the fretful elements,

[1]As for himself.

Bids the wind blow the earth into the sea,
Or swell the curléd waters 'bove the main,[1]
That things might change or cease, tears his white hair,
Which the impetuous blasts, with eyeless rage,
Catch in their fury and make nothing of,
Strives in his little world of man to outscorn
The to-and-fro-conflicting wind and rain.
This night, wherein the cub-drawn bear[2] would couch,
The lion and the belly-pinched wolf
Keep their fur dry, unbonneted he runs,
And bids what will take all.

KENT: But who is with him?

GENTLEMAN: None but the fool, who labors to outjest
His heart-struck injuries.

KENT: Sir, I do know you,
And dare upon the warrant of my note
Commend a dear[3] thing to you. There is division
(Although as yet the face of it is covered
With mutual cunning) 'twixt Albany and Cornwall,
Who have (as who have not, that their great stars
Throned and set high?) servants, who seem no less,
Which are to France the spies and speculations[4]
Intelligent of our state. What hath been seen,
Either in snuffs and packings[5] of the Dukes,
Or the hard rein which both of them have borne
Against the old kind King, or something deeper,
Whereof, perchance, these are but furnishings—
But, true it is, from France there comes a power
Into this scattered kingdom, who already,
Wise in our negligence, have secret feet
In some of our best ports and are at point
To show their open banner. Now to you:
If on my credit you dare build so far
To make your speed to Dover, you shall find
Some that will thank you, making just report
Of how unnatural and bemadding sorrow
The King hath cause to plain.[6]
I am a gentleman of blood and breeding,
And from some knowledge and assurance offer

[1]Land.

[2]A bear sucked dry by cubs, hungry.

[3]Important [4]Informers.

[5]Quarrels and plots.

[6]Complain.

This office to you.

GENTLEMAN: I will talk further with you.

KENT: No, do not.
For confirmation that I am much more
Than my out-wall, open this purse and take
What it contains. If you shall see Cordelia
(As fear not but you shall), show her this ring,
And she will tell you who your fellow is
That yet you do not know. Fie on this storm!
I will go seek the King.

GENTLEMAN: Give me your hand. Have you no more to say?

KENT: Few words, but, to effect,[1] more than all yet:
That, when we have found the King (in which your pain
That way, I'll this), he that first lights on him
Holla the other.

(*Exeunt severally.*)

Scene II

(Another part of the Heath.)

(*Storm still. Enter* LEAR *and* FOOL.)

LEAR: Blow, winds and crack your cheeks! rage, blow,
You cataracts and hurricanoes, spout
Till you have drenched our steeples, drowned the cocks![2]
You sulphurous and thought-executing[3] fires,
Vaunt-couriers[4] of oak-cleaving thunderbolts,
Singe my white head! And thou, all-shaking thunder,
Strike flat the thick rotundity o'th' world,
Crack Nature's molds, all germains[5] spill at once,
That make ingrateful man!

FOOL: O nuncle, court holy water[6] in a dry house is better than this rain water out o' door. Good nuncle, in, and ask thy daughters' blessing! Here's a night pities neither wise men nor fools.

LEAR: Rumble thy bellyful! Spit, fire; spout, rain!
Nor rain, wind, thunder, fire are my daughters;
I tax not you, you elements, with unkindness;

[1]In importance.
[2]Weather vanes.
[3]Killing quick as thought.
[4]Forerunners
[5]Seeds.
[6]Flattery.

I never gave you kingdom, called you children;
You owe me no subscription.[1] Then let fall
Your horrible pleasure. Here I stand your slave,
A poor, infirm, weak, and despised old man;
But yet I call you servile ministers,
That will with two pernicious daughters join
Your high-engendered battles 'gainst a head
So old and white as this. O! O! 'tis foul!

FOOL: He that has a house to put's head in has a good head-piece.

The codpiece that will house
  Before the head has any,
The head and he shall louse:
  So beggars marry many.
The man that makes his toe
  What he his heart should make
Shall of a corn cry woe,
  And turn his sleep to wake.

For there was never yet fair woman but she made mouths in a glass.[2]

(*Enter* KENT.)

LEAR: No, I will be the pattern of all patience;
I will say nothing.

KENT: Who's there?

FOOL: Marry, here's grace and a codpiece; that's a wise man and a fool.

KENT: Alas, sir, are you here? Things that love night
Love not such nights as these. The wrathful skies
Gallow[3] the very wanderers of the dark
And make them keep their caves; since I was man,
Such sheets of fire, such bursts of horrid thunder,
Such groans of roaring wind and rain, I never
Remember to have heard; man's nature cannot carry
The affliction nor the fear.

LEAR: Let the great gods,
That keep this dreadful pudder[4] o'er our heads,
Find out their enemies now. Tremble, thou wretch,
That hast within thee undivulged crimes
Unwhipped of justice. Hide thee, thou bloody hand,

[1]Obedience.
[2]Practised smiling.
[3]Terrify.
[4]Turmoil.

Thou perjured, and thou simular[1] man of virtue
That are incestuous; caitiff, in pieces shake
That under covert and convenient seeming
Hast practised on man's life. Close pent-up guilts,
Rive your concealing continents,[2] and cry
These dreadful summoners grace. I am a man
More sinned against than sinning.

KENT: Alack, bareheaded?
Gracious my lord, hard by here is a hovel;
Some friendship will it lend you 'gainst the tempest;
Repose you there, while I to this hard house
(More harder than the stones whereof 'tis raised,
Which even but now, demanding after you,
Denied me to come in) return, and force
Their scanted courtesy.

LEAR: My wits begin to turn.
Come on, my boy. How dost, my boy? Are cold?
I am cold myself. Where is this straw, my fellow?
The art of our necessities is strange,
That can make vile things precious. Come, your hovel.
Poor fool and knave, I have one part in my heart
That's sorry yet for thee.

FOOL (*sings*):

> He that has and a little tiny wit—
>   With hey, ho, the wind and the rain—
> Must make content with his fortunes fit,
>   For the rain it raineth every day.

LEAR: True, boy. Come bring us to this hovel.

(*Exeunt* LEAR *and* KENT.)

FOOL: This is a brave night to cool a courtesan. I'll speak a prophecy ere I go:

> When priests are more in word than matter;
> When brewers mar their malt with water;
> When nobles are their tailors' tutors,
> No heretics burned, but wenches' suitors;
> When every case in law is right,
> No squire in debt nor no poor knight;
> When slanders do not live in tongues,
> Nor cutpurses come not to throngs;
> When usurers tell their gold i'th' field,

[1]Hypocritical. [2]Split your containers.

And bawds and whores do churches build:
Then shall the realm of Albion
Come to great confusion.
Then comes the time, who lives to see't,
That going shall be used with feet.

This prophecy Merlin shall make, for I live before his time.

(*Exit.*)

Scene III

(GLOUCESTER's *Castle.*)

(*Enter* GLOUCESTER *and* EDMUND *with lights.*)

GLOUCESTER: Alack, alack, Edmund, I like not this unnatural dealing. When I desired their leave that I might pity him, they took from me the use of mine own house, charged me on pain of perpetual displeasure neither to speak of him, entreat for him, nor any way sustain him.

EDMUND: Most savage and unnatural!

GLOUCESTER: Go to; say you nothing. There is division betwixt the Dukes, and a worse matter than that. I have received a letter this night—'tis dangerous to be spoken—I have locked the letter in my closet. These injuries the King now bears will be revenged home; there is part of a power already footed;[1] we must incline to the King. I will seek him and privily relieve him. Go you and maintain talk with the Duke, that my charity be not of him perceived; if he ask for me, I am ill and gone to bed. If I die for't, as no less is threatened me, the King my old master must be relieved. There is strange things toward, Edmund; pray you be careful. (*Exit*)

EDMUND: This courtesy, forbid thee, shall the Duke
Instantly know, and of that letter too.
This seems a fair deserving, and must draw me
That which my father loses—no less than all;
The younger rises when the old doth fall. (*Exit.*)

[1]On the march.

SCENE IV

(*The Heath. Before a Hovel.*)

(*Storm still. Enter* LEAR, KENT, *and* FOOL.)

KENT: Here is the place, my lord; good my lord, enter.
The tyranny of the open night's too rough
For nature to endure.
LEAR: Let me alone.
KENT: Good my lord, enter here.
LEAR: Wilt break my heart?
KENT: I had rather break mine own; good my lord, enter.
LEAR: Thou think'st 'tis much that this contentious storm
Invades us to the skin; so 'tis to thee;
But where the greater malady is fixed,
The lesser is scarce felt. Thou'dst shun a bear,
But if thy flight lay toward the raging sea,
Thou'dst meet the bear i'th' mouth. When the mind's free,
The body's delicate; the tempest in my mind
Doth from my senses take all feeling else
Save what beats there. Filial ingratitude!
Is it not as this mouth should tear this hand
For lifting food to't? But I will punish home!
No, I will weep no more. In such a night
To shut me out! Pour on; I will endure.
In such a night as this! O Regan, Goneril!
Your old kind father, whose frank heart gave all!
O, that way madness lies; let me shun that!
No more of that.
KENT: Good my lord, enter here.
LEAR: Prithee go in thyself, seek thine own ease;
This tempest will not give me leave to ponder
On things would hurt me more. But I'll go in.
(*To the* FOOL): In boy, go first.—You houseless poverty—
Nay, get thee in; I'll pray, and then I'll sleep. (*Exit* FOOL.)
Poor naked wretches, wheresoe'er you are,
That bide the pelting of this pitiless storm,
How shall your houseless heads and unfed sides,
Your looped[1] and windowed raggedness, defend you
From seasons such as these? O, I have ta'en
Too little care of this! Take physic, pomp;
Expose thyself to feel what wretches feel,

[1]Full of holes.

That thou mayst shake the superflux[1] to them
And show the heavens more just.

EDGAR (*within*): Fathom and half, fathom and half! Poor Tom!

(*Enter* FOOL *from the hovel.*)

FOOL: Come not in here, nuncle, here's a spirit. Help me, help me!

KENT: Give me thy hand. Who's there?

FOOL: A spirit, a spirit! He says his name's poor Tom.

KENT: What art thou that dost grumble there i'th' straw? Come forth.

(*Enter* EDGAR *disguised as a madman.*)

EDGAR: Away, the foul fiend follows me! Through the sharp hawthorn blows the cold wind. Humh; go to thy bed and warm thee.

LEAR: Didst thou give all to thy daughters, and art thou come to this?

EDGAR: Who gives anything to poor Tom, whom the foul fiend hath led through fire and through flame, through ford and whirlpool, o'er bog and quagmire; that hath laid knives under his pillow and halters in his pew, set ratsbane by his porridge, made him proud of heart, to ride on a bay trotting horse over four-inched bridges, to course[2] his own shadow for a traitor. Bless they five wits, Tom's acold. O, do de, do de, do de; bless thee from whirlwinds, star-blasting, and taking![3] Do poor Tom some charity, whom the foul fiend vexes. There could I have him now—and there—and there again—and there!

(*Storm still.*)

LEAR: What, have his daughters brought him to this pass?
Couldst thou save nothing? Wouldst thou give 'em all?

FOOL: Nay, he reserved a blanket, else we had been all shamed.

LEAR: Now all the plagues that in the pendulous air
Hang fated o'er men's faults light on thy daughters!

KENT: He hath no daughters, sir.

LEAR: Death, traitor! nothing could have subdued nature
To such a lowness but his unkind daughters.
Is it the fashion that discarded fathers

[1]Superfluity.
[2]Pursue.
[3]Infection.

Should have thus little mercy on their flesh?
Judicious punishment, 'twas this flesh begot
Those pelican[1] daughters.

EDGAR: Pillicock sat on Pillicock's Hill. 'Allow, 'allow, loo, loo!

FOOL: This cold night will turn us all to fools and madmen.

EDGAR: Take heed o'th' foul fiend; obey thy parents; keep thy word justly; swear not; commit not with man's sworn spouse; set not thy sweet heart on proud array. Tom's acold.

LEAR: What hast thou been?

EDGAR: A servingman, proud in heart and mind; that curled my hair, wore gloves in my cap, served the lust of my mistress' heart and did the act of darkness with her; swore as many oaths as I spake words, and broke them in the sweet face of heaven; one that slept in the contriving of lust, and waked to do it. Wine loved I deeply, dice dearly, and in woman outparamoured the Turk. False of heart, light of ear, bloody of hand, hog in sloth, fox in stealth, wolf in greediness, dog in madness, lion in prey! Let not the creaking of shoes nor the rustling of silks betray thy poor heart to woman. Keep thy foot out of brothels, thy hand out of plackets,[2] thy pen from lender's books, and defy the foul fiend. Still through the hawthorn blows the cold wind; says suum, mun, hey nonny. Dolphin my boy; boy, sessa! let him trot by.

(*Storm still*).

LEAR: Thou wert better in a grave than to answer with thy uncovered body this extremity of the skies. Is man no more than this? Consider him well. Thou owest the worm no silk, the beast no hide, the sheep no wool, the cat[3] no perfume. Ha, here's three on's are sophisticated! Thou art the thing itself; unaccommodated[4] man is no more but such a poor, bare, forked animal as thou art. Off, off, you lendings! Come, unbutton here.

(*Tears at his clothes.*)

FOOL: Prithee, nuncle, be contented; 'tis a naughty night to swim in. Now a little fire in a wild field were like an old lecher's heart—a small spark, all the rest on's body cold. Look, here comes a walking fire.

(*Enter* GLOUCESTER *with a torch.*)

[1]Young pelicans were thought to feed on their mother's blood.
[2]Opening in a petticoat. [3]Civet cat. [4]Undressed.

EDGAR: This is the foul fiend Flibbertigibbet; he begins at curfew, and walks till the first cock. He gives the web and the pin,[1] squints the eye, and makes the harelip; mildews the white wheat, and hurts the poor creature of earth.

Saint Withold footed thrice the 'old;[2]
He met the nightmare, and her nine fold;
Bid her alight
And her troth plight,
And aroint[3] thee, witch, aroint thee!

KENT: How fares your Grace?

LEAR: What's he?

KENT: Who's there? What is't you seek?

GLOUCESTER: What are you there? Your names?

EDGAR: Poor Tom, that eats the swimming frog, the toad, the tadpole, the wall-newt and the water; that in the fury of his heart, when the foul fiend rages, eats cow-dung for sallets, swallows the old rat and the ditch-dog, drinks the green mantle of the standing pool; who is whipped from tithing[4] to tithing, and stock-punished and imprisoned; who hath had three suits to his back, six shirts to his body, horse to ride, and weapon to wear;

But mice and rats, and such small deer,[5]
Have been Tom's food for seven long year.

Beware my follower; peace, Smulkin, peace, thou fiend!

GLOUCESTER: What, hath your Grace no better company?

EDGAR: The prince of darkness is a gentleman!
Modo he's called, and Mahu.

GLOUCESTER: Our flesh and blood, my lord, is grown so vile,
That it doth hate what gets[6] it.

EDGAR: Poor Tom's acold.

GLOUCESTER: Go in with me; my duty cannot suffer
To obey in all your daughters' hard commands.
Though their injunction be to bar my doors
And let this tyrannous night take hold upon you,
Yet have I ventured to come seek you out
And bring you where both fire and food is ready.

LEAR: First let me talk with this philosopher;
What is the cause of thunder?

KENT: Good my lord, take his offer; go into the house.

[1]Eye disease.
[2]Wold, field.
[3]Be gone.
[4]District.
[5]Animals.
[6]Begets.

LEAR: I'll talk a word with this same learned Theban.
What is your study?

EDGAR: How to prevent the fiend and to kill vermin.

LEAR: Let me ask you one word in private.

KENT: Importune him once more to go, my lord.
His wits begin to unsettle.

GLOUCESTER: Canst thou blame him?

(*Storm still.*)

His daughters seek his death. Ah, that good Kent!
He said it would be thus—poor banished man!
Thou sayest the King grows mad: I'll tell thee, friend,
I am almost mad myself. I had a son,
Now outlawed from my blood; he sought my life
But lately, very late. I loved him, friend,
No father his son dearer; true to tell thee,
The grief hath crazed my wits. What a night 's this!
I do beseech your Grace—

LEAR: O, cry you mercy,[1] sir.
Noble philosopher, your company.

EDGAR: Tom's acold.

GLOUCESTER: In, fellow, there, into th' hovel; keep thee warm.

LEAR: Come, let's in all.

KENT: This way, my lord.

LEAR: With him!
I will keep still with my philosopher.

KENT: Good my lord, soothe him; let him take the fellow.

GLOUCESTER: Take him you on.

KENT: Sirrah, come on; go along with us.

LEAR: Come, good Athenian.

GLOUCESTER: No words, no words! hush.

EDGAR: Child Rowland to the dark tower came;
His word was still

Fie, foh, and fum!
I smell the blood of a British man.

(*Exeunt.*)

[1] I beg your pardon.

Scene V

(GLOUCESTER's *Castle.*)

(Enter CORNWALL *and* EDMUND.)

CORNWALL: I will have my revenge ere I depart his house.

EDMUND: How, my lord, I may be censured, that nature thus gives way to loyalty, something fears me to think of.

CORNWALL: I now perceive it was not altogether your brother's evil disposition made him seek his[1] death, but a provoking merit, set awork by a reproveable badness in himself.

EDMUND: How malicious is my fortune that I must repent to be just! This is the letter he spoke of, which approves him an intelligent party to the advantages of France. O heavens! that this treason were not—or not I the detector!

CORNWALL: Go with me to the Duchess.

EDMUND: If the matter of this paper be certain, you have mighty business in hand.

CORNWALL: True or false, it hath made thee Earl of Gloucester. Seek out where thy father is, that he may be ready for our apprehension.

EDMUND (*aside*): If I find him comforting the King, it will stuff his suspicion more fully.—I will persevere in my course of loyalty, though the conflict be sore between that and my blood.

CORNWALL: I will lay trust upon thee, and thou shalt find a dearer father in my love.

(*Exeunt.*)

Scene VI

(*A Building near* GLOUCESTER's *Castle.*)

(*Enter* KENT *and* GLOUCESTER.)

GLOUCESTER: Here is better than the open air; take it thankfully. I will piece out the comfort with what addition I can; I will not be long from you.

KENT: All the power of his wits have given way to his impatience. The gods reward your kindness! (*Exit* GLOUCESTER.)

[1]Gloucester's.

(*Enter* LEAR, EDGAR, *and* FOOL.)

EDGAR: Frateretto calls me, and tells me Nero is an angler in the lake of darkness. Pray, innocent, and beware the foul fiend.

FOOL: Prithee, nuncle, tell me whether a madman be a gentleman or a yeoman.

LEAR: A king, a king!

FOOL: No, he's a yeoman that has a gentleman to his son, for he's a mad yeoman that sees his son a gentleman before him.

LEAR: To have a thousand with red burning spits
Come hizzing in upon 'em—

EDGAR: The foul fiend bites my back.

FOOL: He's mad that trusts in the tameness of a wolf, a horse's health, a boy's love, or a whore's oath.

LEAR: It shall be done; I will arraign them straight.
(*To* EDGAR) Come, sit thou here, most learned justicer.
(*To* the FOOL) Thou, sapient sir, sit here. Now, you she-foxes!

EDGAR: Look, where he stands and glares! Want'st thou eyes at trial, madam?

Come o'er the bourn,[1] Bessy, to me.

FOOL: Her boat hath a leak,
And she must not speak
Why she dares not come over to thee.

EDGAR: The foul fiend haunts poor Tom in the voice of a nightingale. Hopdance cries in Tom's belly for two white herring. Croak not, black angel; I have no food for thee.

KENT: How do you, sir? Stand you not so amazed.
Will you lie down and rest upon the cushions?

LEAR: I'll see their trial first; bring in their evidence.
(*To* EDGAR) Thou, robed man of justice, take thy place.
(*To the* FOOL) And thou, his yokefellow of equity,
Bench by his side. (*To* KENT) You are o'th' commission,
Sit you too.

EDGAR: Let us deal justly.

Sleepest or wakest thou, jolly shepherd?
Thy sheep be in the corn;
And for one blast of thy minikin[2] mouth
Thy sheep shall take no harm.

Purr! the cat is gray.

LEAR: Arraign her first; 'tis Goneril. I here take my oath be-

[1]Brook. [2]Tiny.

fore this honorable assembly, she kicked the poor King her father.

FOOL: Come hither, mistress; is your name Goneril?

LEAR: She cannot deny it.

FOOL: Cry you mercy, I took you for a joint-stool.

LEAR: And here's another whose warped looks proclaim
What store her heart is made on. Stop her there!
Arms, arms! sword! fire! Corruption in the place!
False justicer, why hast thou let her scape?

EDGAR: Bless thy five wits!

KENT: O pity, sir, where is the patience now
That you so oft have boasted to retain?

EDGAR (*aside*): My tears begin to take his part so much
They mar my counterfeiting.

LEAR: The little dogs and all,
Tray, Blanch, and Sweetheart, see, they bark at me.

EDGAR: Tom will throw his head at them. Avaunt, you curs!

By thy mouth or black or white,
Tooth that poisons if it bite;
Mastiff, greyhound, mongrel grim,
Hound or spaniel brach[1] or lym,[2]
Bobtail tyke or trundle-tail—[3]
Tom will make them weep and wail;
For, with throwing thus my head,
Dogs leap the hatch, and all are fled.

Do de, de de. Sessa! Come, march to wakes and fairs and market towns. Poor Tom, thy horn is dry.

LEAR: Then let them anatomize Regan. See what breeds about her heart. Is there any cause in nature that makes these hard hearts? (*To* EDGAR) You, sir, I entertain for one of my hundred; only I do not like the fashion of your garments. You'll say they are Persian; but let them be changed.

KENT: Now, good my lord, lie here and rest awhile.

LEAR: Make no noise, make no noise; draw the curtains.
So, so, we'll go to supper i'th' morning.

FOOL: And I'll go to bed at noon.

(*Enter* GLOUCESTER.)

GLOUCESTER: Come hither, friend; where is the King my master?

KENT: Here, sir, but trouble him not; his wits are gone.

[1]Bitch.
[2]Bloodhound.
[3]Kinds of dogs.

GLOUCESTER: Good friend, I prithee take him in thy arms;
I have o'erheard a plot of death upon him;
There is a litter ready; lay him in't
And drive toward Dover, friend, where thou shalt meet
Both welcome and protection. Take up thy master.
If thou shouldst dally half an hour, his life,
With thine, and all that offer to defend him,
Stand in assured loss. Take up, take up,
And follow me, that will to some provision
Give thee quick conduct.

KENT: Oppressed nature sleeps;
This rest might yet have balmed thy broken senses,
Which, if convenience will not allow,
Stand in hard cure.[1] (*To the* FOOL) Come, help to bear thy master;
Thou must not stay behind.

GLOUCESTER: Come, come, away!

(*Exeunt all but* EDGAR.)

EDGAR: When we our betters see bearing our woes,
We scarcely think our miseries our foes.
Who alone suffers suffers most i'th' mind,
Leaving free things and happy shows behind;
But then the mind much sufferance doth o'erskip
When grief hath mates, and bearing[2] fellowship.
How light and portable my pain seems now.
When that which makes me bend makes the King bow.
He childed as I fathered! Tom, away!
Mark the high noises, and thyself bewray[3]
When false opinion, whose wrong thought defiles thee,
In thy just proof repeals and reconciles thee.
What will hap more to-night, safe scape the King!
Lurk, lurk.

(*Exit.*)

[1]Are in a dangerous condition.
[2]Endurance.
[3]Reveal.

Scene VII

(GLOUCESTER'S *Castle.*)

(*Enter* CORNWALL, REGAN, GONERIL, EDMUND, *and* SERVANTS.)

CORNWALL (*to* GONERIL): Post speedily to my lord your husband; show him this letter: the army of France is landed.—Seek out the traitor Gloucester.

(*Exeunt some of the* SERVANTS.)

REGAN: Hang him instantly.
GONERIL: Pluck out his eyes.
CORNWALL: Leave him to my displeasure. Edmund, keep you our sister company. The revenges we are bound to take upon your traitorous father are not fit for your beholding. Advise the Duke where you are going, to a most festinate[1] preparation; we are bound to the like. Our posts shall be swift and intelligent betwixt us. Farewell, dear sister; farewell, my Lord of Gloucester.

(*Enter* OSWALD.)

How now? Where's the King?
OSWALD: My Lord of Gloucester hath conveyed him hence.
Some five or six and thirty of his knights,
Hot questrists[2] after him, met him at gate,
Who, with some other of the lord's dependants,
Are gone with him toward Dover, where they boast
To have well-armed friends.
CORNWALL: Get horses for your mistress.
GONERIL: Farewell, sweet lord, and sister.
CORNWALL: Edmund, farewell.

(Exeunt GONERIL, EDMUND, *and* OSWALD.)

Go seek the traitor Gloucester,
Pinion him like a thief, bring him before us.

(*Exeunt other* SERVANTS.)

Though well we may not pass upon his life
Without the form of justice, yet our power
Shall do a courtesy to our wrath, which men
May blame, but not control.

[1]Speedy.
[2]Searchers.

(*Enter* GLOUCESTER, *brought in by two or three.*)

Who's there? the traitor?

REGAN: Ingrateful fox! 'tis he.

CORNWALL: Bind fast his corky[1] arms.

GLOUCESTER: What mean your Graces? Good my friends, consider
You are my guests. Do me no foul play, friends.

CORNWALL: Bind him, I say.

(SERVANTS *bind him.*)

REGAN: Hard, hard. O filthy traitor!

GLOUCESTER: Unmerciful lady as you are, I'm none.

CORNWALL: To this chair bind him. Villain, thou shalt find—

(REGAN *plucks his beard.*)

GLOUCESTER: By the kind gods, 'tis most ignobly done
To pluck me by the beard.

REGAN: So white, and such a traitor!

GLOUCESTER: Naughty lady,
These hairs which thou dost ravish from my chin
Will quicken,[2] and accuse thee. I am your host.
With robber's hands my hospitable favors
You should not ruffle thus. What will you do?

CORNWALL: Come, sir, what letters had you late from France?

REGAN: Be simple-answered, for we know the truth.

CORNWALL: And what confederacy have you with the traitors
Late footed[3] in the kingdom?

REGAN: To whose hands have you sent the lunatic King:
Speak.

GLOUCESTER: I have a letter guessingly set down,
Which came from one that's of a neutral heart,
And not from one opposed.

CORNWALL: Cunning.

REGAN: And false.

CORNWALL: Where hast thou sent the King?

GLOUCESTER: To Dover.

REGAN: Wherefore to Dover? Wast thou not charged at peril—

CORNWALL: Wherefore to Dover? Let him first answer that.

GLOUCESTER: I am tied to th' stake, and I must stand the course.[4]

REGAN: Wherefore to Dover, sir?

GLOUCESTER: Because I would not see thy cruel nails

[1]Withered.
[2]Come to life.
[3]Landed.
[4]Endure the attack.

Pluck out his poor old eyes; nor thy fierce sister
In his anointed flesh stick boarish fangs.
The sea, with such a storm as his bare head
In hell-black night endured, would have buoyed[1] up
And quenched the stelled fires.[2]
Yet, poor old heart, he holp the heavens to rain.
If wolves had at thy gate howled that stern time,
Thou shouldst have said, "Good porter, turn the key."
All cruels else subscribe.[3] But I shall see
The wingéd vengeance overtake such children.

CORNWALL: See't shalt thou never. Fellows, hold the chair.
Upon these eyes of thine I'll set my foot.

GLOUCESTER: He that will think to live till he be old,
Give me some help!—O cruel! O you gods!

REGAN: One side will mock another. Th' other too!

CORNWALL: If you see vengeance—

FIRST SERVANT: Hold your hand, my lord!
I have served you ever since I was a child;
But better service have I never done you
Than now to bid you hold.

REGAN: How now, you dog?

FIRST SERVANT: If you did wear a beard upon your chin, I'ld shake it on this quarrel.

REGAN: What do you mean?

CORNWALL: My villain!

(*Draw and fight.*)

FIRST SERVANT: Nay, then, come on, and take the chance of anger.

REGAN: Give me thy sword. A peasant stand up thus?

(*She takes a sword and runs at him behind.*)

FIRST SERVANT: O, I am slain! My lord, you have one eye left
To see some mischief on him. O! (*He dies.*)

CORNWALL: Lest it see more, prevent it. Out, vile jelly!
Where is thy luster now?

GLOUCESTER: All dark and comfortless! Where's my son Edmund?
Edmund, enkindle all the sparks of nature
To quit[4] this horrid act.

REGAN: Out, treacherous villain!
Thou call'st on him that hates thee. It was he

[1]Swelled.

[2]Stars

[3]All other cruel creatures are forgiven.

[4]Avenge.

That made the overture[1] of thy treasons to us,
Who is too good to pity thee.

GLOUCESTER: O my follies! Then Edgar was abused.
Kind gods, forgive me that, and prosper him!

REGAN: Go thrust him out at gates, and let him smell
His way to Dover.

(*Exit* one with GLOUCESTER.)

How is't, my lord? How look you?

CORNWALL: I have received a hurt; follow me, lady.
Turn out that eyeless villain; throw this slave
Upon the dunghill. Regan, I bleed apace;
Untimely comes this hurt. Give me your arm.

(*Exit* CORNWALL, *led by* REGAN.)

SECOND SERVANT: I'll never care what wickedness I do,
If this man come to good.

THIRD SERVANT: If she live long,
And in the end meet the old course of death,
Women will all turn monsters.

SECOND SERVANT: Let's follow the old Earl, and get the bedlam
To lead him where he would. His roguish madness
Allows itself to anything.

THIRD SERVANT: Go thou. I'll fetch some flax and whites of eggs
To apply to his bleeding face. Now heaven help him!

(*Exeunt.*)

ACT IV

SCENE I

(*The Heath.*)

(*Enter* EDGAR.)

EDGAR: Yet better thus, and known to be contemned,[2]
Than still contemned[2] and flattered. To be worst,
The lowest and most dejected thing of fortune,

[1]Disclosure. [2]Despised

Stands still in esperance,[1] lives not in fear.
The lamentable change is from the best;
The worst returns to laughter. Welcome then,
Thou unsubstantial air that I embrace!
The wretch that thou hast blown unto the worst
Owes nothing to thy blasts.

(*Enter* GLOUCESTER, *led by an* OLD MAN.)

But who comes here?
My father, poorly led? World, world, O world!
But that thy strange mutations make us hate thee,
Life would not yield to age.

OLD MAN: O my good lord,
I have been your tenant, and your father's tenant,
These fourscore years.

GLOUCESTER: Away! Get thee away! Good friend, be gone;
Thy comforts can do me no good at all;
Thee they may hurt.

OLD MAN: You cannot see your way.

GLOUCESTER: I have no way, and therefore want no eyes;
I stumbled when I saw. Full oft 'tis seen
Our means secure us,[2] and our mere defects
Prove our commodities.[3] Oh dear son Edgar,
The food[4] of thy abused father's wrath,[4]
Might I but live to see thee in my touch,
I'ld say I had eyes again!

OLD MAN: How now? Who's there?

EDGAR (*aside*): O gods! Who is't can say "I am at the worst"?
I am worse than e'er I was.

OLD MAN: 'Tis poor mad Tom.

EDGAR (*aside*): And worse I may be yet. The worst is not
So long as we can say "This is the worst."

OLD MAN: Fellow, where goest?

GLOUCESTER: Is it a beggarman?

OLD MAN: Madman and beggar too.

GLOUCESTER: He has some reason, else he could not beg.
I'th' last night's storm I such a fellow saw,
Which made me think a man a worm. My son
Came then into my mind, and yet my mind
Was then scarce friends with him. I have heard more since.

[1]Hope.
[2]Our means make us careless.
[3]Advantages. [4]Object.

As flies to wanton boys are we to th' gods.
They kill us for their sport.

EDGAR (*aside*): How should this be?
Bad is the trade that must play fool to sorrow,
Angering itself and others.—Bless thee, master!

GLOUCESTER: Is that the naked fellow?

OLD MAN: Ay, my lord.

GLOUCESTER: Then, prithee, get thee away. If for my sake
Thou wilt o'ertake us hence a mile or twain
I'th'way toward Dover, do it for ancient love,
And bring some covering for this naked soul,
Who I'll entreat to lead me.

OLD MAN: Alack, sir, he is mad!

GLOUCESTER: 'Tis the time's plague when madmen lead the blind.
Do as I bid thee, or rather do thy pleasure.
Above the rest, be gone.

OLD MAN: I'll bring him the best 'parel that I have,
Come on't what will. (*Exit.*)

GLOUCESTER: Sirrah naked fellow—

EDGAR: Poor Tom's acold. (*Aside*) I cannot daub[1] it further.

GLOUCESTER: Come hither, fellow.

EDGAR (*aside*): And yet I must.—Bless thy sweet eyes, they bleed.

GLOUCESTER: Know'st thou the way to Dover?

EDGAR: Both stile and gate, horseway and footpath. Poor Tom hath been scared out of his good wits. Bless thee, good man's son, from the foul fiend! Five fiends have been in poor Tom at once: of lust, as Obidicut; Hobbididence, prince of dumbness; Mahu, of stealing; Modo, of murder; Flibbertigibbet, of mopping and mowing, who since possesses chambermaids and waiting women. So, bless thee, master!

GLOUCESTER: Here, take this purse, thou whom the heavens' plagues
Have humbled to all strokes; that I am wretched
Makes thee the happier. Heavens deal so still!
Let the superfluous and lust-dieted man,
That slaves your ordinance,[2] that will not see
Because he does not feel, feel your power quickly;
So distribution should undo excess,
And each man have enough. Dost thou know Dover?

EDGAR: Ay, master.

[1]Dissemble.

[2]Who makes your commands subservient to himself.

GLOUCESTER: There is a cliff, whose high and bending head
Looks fearfully in the confined deep.
Bring me but to the very brim of it,
And I'll repair the misery thou dost bear
With something rich about me. From that place
I shall no leading need.
EDGAR: Give me thy arm;
Poor Tom shall lead thee.
(*Exeunt.*)

SCENE II

(*Before the* DUKE OF ALBANY'S *Palace.*)

(*Enter* GONERIL *and* EDMUND.)

GONERIL: Welcome, my lord. I marvel our mild husband
Not met us on the way.
(*Enter* OSWALD.)
Now, where's your master?
OSWALD: Madam, within, but never man so changed.
I told him of the army that was landed:
He smiled at it. I told him you were coming:
His answer was, "The worse." Of Gloucester's treachery
And of the loyal service of his son
When I informed him, then he called me sot
And told me I had turned the wrong side out.
What most he should dislike seems pleasant to him;
What like, offensive.
GONERIL (*to* EDMUND): Then shall you go no further.
It is the cowish terror of his spirit
That dares not undertake; he'll not feel wrongs
Which tie him to an answer. Our wishes on the way
May prove effects. Back, Edmund, to my brother;
Hasten his musters and conduct his powers.
I must change arms at home and give the distaff[1]
Into my husband's hands. This trusty servant
Shall pass between us; ere long you are like to hear
(If you dare venture in your own behalf)
A mistress's command. Wear this; (*Gives a favor.*)
spare speech;

[1]Spinning staff, i.e., symbol of womanhood.

Decline your head. This kiss, if it durst speak,
Would stretch thy spirits up into the air.
Conceive, and fare thee well.
EDMUND: Yours in the ranks of death! (*Exit.*)
GONERIL: My most dear Gloucester!
(EDMUND *exits.*)
O, the difference of man and man!
To thee a woman's services are due;
A fool usurps my bed.
OSWALD: Madam, here comes my lord. (*Exit.*)

(*Enter* ALBANY.)

GONERIL: I have been worth the whistle.
ALBANY: O Goneril,
You are not worth the dust which the rude wind
Blows in your face; I fear your disposition.
That nature which contemns its origin
Cannot be bordered certain[1] in itself;
She that herself will sliver and disbranch
From her material[2] sap, perforce must wither
And come to deadly use.[3]
GONERIL: No more! The text is foolish.
ALBANY: Wisdom and goodness to the vile seem vile;
Filths savor but themselves. What have you done?
Tigers, not daughters, what have you performed?
A father, and a gracious aged man,
Whose reverence even the head-lugged bear would lick,
Most barbarous, most degenerate, have you madded.
Could my good brother suffer you to do it?
A man, a prince, by him so benefited!
If that the heavens do not their visible spirits
Send quickly down to tame these vile offences,
It will come,
Humanity must perforce prey on itself,
Like monsters of the deep.
GONERIL: Milk-livered man!
That bearest a cheek for blows, a head for wrongs,
Who hast not in thy brows an eye discerning
Thine honor from thy suffering; that not knowest
Fools do those villains pity who are punished
Ere they have done their mischief. Where's thy drum?
France spreads his banners in our noiseless[4] land,

[1]Confined.
[2]Essential.
[3]Destruction.
[4]Peaceful.

With plumed helm thy state begins to threat,
Whilst thou, a moral fool, sit'st still, and criest
"Alack, why does he so?"
ALBANY: See thyself, devil!
Proper[1] deformity seems not in the fiend
So horrid as in woman.
GONERIL: O vain fool!
ALBANY: Thou changed and self-covered[2] thing, for shame!
Bemonster not thy feature! Weren't my fitness
To let these hands obey my blood,[3]
They are apt enough to dislocate and tear
Thy flesh and bones. Howe'er thou art a fiend,
A woman's shape doth shield thee.
GONERIL: Marry, your manhood mew!

(*Enter a* GENTLEMAN.)

ALBANY: What news?
GENTLEMAN: O, my good lord, the Duke of Cornwall's dead,
Slain by his servant, going to put out
The other eye of Gloucester.
ALBANY: Gloucester's eyes?
GENTLEMAN: A servant that he bred, thrilled with remorse,
Opposed against the act, bending his sword
To his great master, who thereat enraged,
Flew on him, and amongst them felled him dead;
But not without that harmful stroke which since
Hath plucked him after.
ALBANY: This shows you are above,
You justicers, that these our nether crimes
So speedily can venge! But O poor Gloucester!
Lost he his other eye?
GENTLEMAN: Both, both, my lord.
This letter, madam, craves a speedy answer.
'Tis from your sister.
GONERIL (*aside*): One way I like this well;
But being widow, and my Gloucester with her,
May all the building in my fancy pluck[4]
Upon my hateful life. Another way
The news is not so tart.—I'll read, and answer. (*Exit.*)
ALBANY: Where was his son when they did take his eyes?
GENTLEMAN: Come with my lady hither.
ALBANY: He is not here.

[1]Natural.
[2]Hypocrital.
[3]Passion.
[4]May all my castles in the air pull down.

GENTLEMAN: No, my good lord, I met him back again.
ALBANY: Knows he the wickedness?
GENTLEMAN: Ay, my good lord; 'twas he informed against him,
And quit the house on purpose, that their punishment
Might have the freer course.
ALBANY: Gloucester, I live
To thank thee for the love thou showedst the King,
And to revenge thine eyes. Come hither, friend.
Tell me what more thou knowest. (*Exeunt.*)

SCENE III

(*A French Camp near Dover.*)

(*Enter* KENT *and a* GENTLEMAN.)

KENT: Why the King of France is so suddenly gone back know you no reason?

GENTLEMAN: Something he left imperfect in the state, which since his coming forth is thought of, which imports to the kingdom so much fear and danger that his personal return was most required and necessary.

KENT: Who hath he left behind him general?

GENTLEMAN: The Marshal of France, Monsieur la Far.

KENT: Did your letters pierce the Queen to any demonstration of grief?

GENTLEMAN: Ay, sir; she took them, read them in my presence,
And now and then an ample tear trilled down
Her delicate cheek. It seemed she was a queen
Over her passion, who, most rebel-like,
Sought to be king o'er her.
KENT: O, then it moved her?
GENTLEMAN: Not to a rage; patience and sorrow strove
Who should express her goodliest. You have seen
Sunshine and rain at once: her smiles and tears
Were like, a better way.[1] Those happy smiles
That played on her ripe lip seemed not to know
What guests were in her eyes, which parted thence
As pearls from diamonds dropped. In brief,

[1]Like sunshine and rain, but better.

Sorrow would be a rarity most beloved,
If all could so become it.
KENT: Made she no verbal question?
GENTLEMAN: Faith, once or twice she heaved the name of father
Pantingly forth, as if it pressed her heart,
Cried "Sisters, sisters! Shame of ladies! Sisters!
Kent! father! sisters! What, i'th' storm? i'th' night?
Let pity not be believed!" There she shook
The holy water from her heavenly eyes,
And clamor moistened.[1] Then away she started
To deal with grief alone.
KENT: It is the stars,
The stars above us, govern our conditions,[2]
Else one self mate and mate[3] could not beget
Such different issues. You spoke not with her since?
GENTLEMAN: No.
KENT: Was this before the King returned?
GENTLEMAN: No, since.
KENT: Well, sir, the poor distressed Lear's i'th' town,
Who sometime, in his better tune, remembers
What we are come about, and by no means
Will yield to see his daughter.
GENTLEMAN: Why, good sir?
KENT: A sovereign shame so elbows him; his own unkindness,
That stripped her from his benediction, turned her
To foreign casualties,[4] gave her dear rights
To his dog-hearted daughters—these things sting
His mind so venomously that burning shame
Detains him from Cordelia.
GENTLEMAN: Alack, poor gentleman!
KENT: Of Albany's and Cornwall's powers you heard not?
GENTLEMAN: 'Tis so; they are afoot.
KENT: Well, sir, I'll bring you to our master Lear
And leave you to attend him. Some dear cause
Will in concealment wrap me up awhile.
When I am known aright, you shall not grieve
Lending me this acquaintance. I pray you go
Along with me.
(*Exeunt.*)

[1]Her exclamations turned to tears.
[2]Characters.
[3]The parents.
[4]Risks.

SCENE IV

(*The French Camp.*)

(*Enter, with drum and colors,* CORDELIA, DOCTOR, *and* SOLDIERS.)

CORDELIA: Alack, 'tis he! Why, he was met even now
As mad as the vexed sea, singing aloud,
Crowned with rank fumiter and furrow weeds,
With hardocks, hemlock, nettles, cuckoo flowers,
Darnel[1], and all the idle weeds that grow
In our sustaining corn. A century[2] send forth;
Search every acre in the high-grown field
And bring him to our eye. (*Exit an* OFFICER.) What can man's wisdom
In the restoring his bereaved sense?
He that helps him take all my outward worth.
DOCTOR: There is means, madam.
Our foster nurse of nature is repose,
The which he lacks. That to provoke in him
Are many simples operative,[3] whose power
Will close the eye of anguish.
CORDELIA: All blest secrets,
All you unpublished virtues of the earth,
Spring with my tears! be aidant and remediate[4]
In the good man's distress! Seek, seek for him!
Lest his ungoverned rage dissolve the life
That wants the means to lead it.
(*Enter* MESSENGER.)
MESSENGER: News, madam.
The British powers are marching hitherward.
CORDELIA: 'Tis known before. Our preparation stands
In expectation of them. O dear father,
It is thy business that I go about.
Therefore great France
My mourning and importuned tears hath pitied.
No blown ambition doth our arms incite,
But love, dear love, and our aged father's right.
Soon may I hear and see him!
(*Exeunt.*)

[1]Kinds of weeds and wild flowers.
[2]Company of soldiers.
[3]Medicinal herbs.
[4]Helpful remedies.

Scene V

(GLOUCESTER'S *Castle.*)

(*Enter* REGAN *and* OSWALD.)

REGAN: But are my brother's powers set forth?
OSWALD: Ay, madam.
REGAN: Himself in person there?
OSWALD: Madam, with much ado.
Your sister is the better soldier.
REGAN: Lord Edmund spake not with your lord at home?
OSWALD: No, madam.
REGAN: What might import my sister's letter to him?
OSWALD: I know not, lady.
REGAN: Faith, he is posted hence on serious matter.
It was great ignorance, Gloucester's eyes being out,
To let him live; where he arrives he moves
All hearts against us. Edmund, I think, is gone,
In pity of his misery, to dispatch
His nighted[1] life; moreover, to descry
The strength o'th' enemy.
OSWALD: I must needs after him, madam, with my letter.
REGAN: Our troops set forth to-morrow. Stay with us;
The ways are dangerous.
OSWALD: I may not, madam.
My lady charged my duty in this business.
REGAN: Why should she write to Edmund? Might not you
Transport her purposes by word? Belike,
Something—I know not what—I'll love thee much—
Let me unseal the letter.
OSWALD: Madam, I had rather—
REGAN: I know your lady does not love her husband;
I am sure of that; and at her late being here
She gave strange eliads[2] and most speaking looks
To noble Edmund. I know you are of her bosom.
OSWALD: I, madam?
REGAN: I speak in understanding. Y'are; I know't,
Therefore I do advise you take this note.
My lord is dead; Edmund and I have talked,
And more convenient is he for my hand
Than for your lady's. You may gather more.
If you do find him, pray you give him this;

[1]Blinded. [2]Loving glances.

And when your mistress hears thus much from you,
I pray desire her call her wisdom to her.
So fare you well.
If you do chance to hear of that blind traitor,
Preferment falls on him that cuts him off.
OSWALD: Would I could meet him, madam; I should show
What party I do follow.
REGAN: Fare thee well. (*Exeunt.*)

SCENE VI

(*The country near Dover.*)

(*Enter* GLOUCESTER, *and* EDGAR *dressed like a peasant.*)

GLOUCESTER: When shall I come to the top of that same hill?
EDGAR: You do climb up it now. Look how we labor.
GLOUCESTER: Methinks the ground is even.
EDGAR: Horrible steep.
Hark, do you hear the sea?
GLOUCESTER: No, truly.
EDGAR: Why, then, your other senses grow imperfect
By your eyes' anguish.
GLOUCESTER: So may it be indeed.
Methinks thy voice is altered, and thou speakest
In better phrase and matter than thou didst.
EDGAR: Y'are much deceived. In nothing am I changed
But in my garments.
GLOUCESTER: Methinks y'are better spoken.
EDGAR: Come on, sir, here's the place; stand still. How fearful
And dizzy 'tis to cast one's eyes so low!
The crows and choughs[1] that wing the midway air
Show scarce so gross as beetles. Halfway down
Hangs one that gathers sampire[2]—dreadful trade!
Methinks he seems no bigger than his head.
The fishermen that walk upon the beach
Appear like mice; and yond tall anchoring bark,
Diminished to her cock;[3] her cock, a buoy
Almost too small for sight. The murmuring surge
That on th'unnumbered idle pebble chafes

[1]Jackdaws. [2]A plant. [3]Dinghy.

Cannot be heard so high. I'll look no more,
Lest my brain turn, and the deficient sight
Topple down headlong.

GLOUCESTER: Set me where you stand.

EDGAR: Give me your hand. You are now within a foot
Of th'extreme verge. For all beneath the moon
Would I not leap upright.

GLOUCESTER: Let go my hand.
Here, friend, 's another purse; in it a jewel
Well worth a poor man's taking. Fairies and gods
Prosper it with thee! Go thou further off;
Bid me farewell, and let me hear thee going.

EDGAR: Now fare ye well, good sir.

GLOUCESTER: With all my heart.

EDGAR (*aside*): Why I do trifle thus with his despair
Is done to cure it.

GLOUCESTER: O you mighty gods! (*He kneels.*)
This world I do renounce, and, in your sights,
Shake patiently my great affliction off.
If I could bear it longer and not fall
To quarrel with your great opposeless[1] wills,
My snuff[2] and loathed part of nature should
Burn itself out. If Edgar live, O, bless him!
Now, fellow, fare thee well. (*He falls forward.*)

EDGAR: Gone, sir, farewell—
And yet I know not how conceit[3] may rob
The treasury of life when life itself
Yields to the theft. Had he been where he thought,
By this had thought been past.—Alive or dead?
Ho you, sir! friend! Hear you, sir? Speak!—
Thus might he pass indeed; yet he revives.
What are you, sir?

GLOUCESTER: Away, and let me die.

EDGAR: Hadst thou been aught but gossamer, feathers, air,
So many fathom down precipitating,
Thou'dst shivered like an egg; but thou dost breathe,
Hast heavy substance, bleed'st not, speak'st, art sound;
Ten masts at each[4] make not the altitude
Which thou hast perpendicularly fell;
Thy life's a miracle. Speak yet again.

GLOUCESTER: But have I fallen, or no?

EDGAR: From the dread summit of this chalky bourn.

[1]Irresistible.
[2]Burnt-out wick.
[3]Imagination.
[4]End to end.

Look up a-height; the shrill-gorged[1] lark so far
Cannot be seen or heard. Do but look up.

GLOUCESTER: Alack, I have no eyes.
Is wretchedness deprived that benefit
To end itself by death? 'Twas yet some comfort
When misery could beguile the tyrant's rage
And frustrate his proud will.

EDGAR: Give me your arm.
Up—so. How is't? Feel you your legs? You stand.

GLOUCESTER: Too well, too well.

EDGAR: This is above all strangeness.
Upon the crown o'th' cliff what thing was that
Which parted from you?

GLOUCESTER: A poor unfortunate beggar.

EDGAR: As I stood here below, methought his eyes
Were two full moons; he had a thousand noses,
Horns whelked[2] and waved like the enridged sea;
It was some fiend. Therefore, thou happy father,
Think that the clearest gods, who make them honors
Of men's impossibilities, have preserved thee.

GLOUCESTER: I do remember now. Henceforth I'll bear
Affliction till it do cry out itself
"Enough, enough," and die. That thing you speak of,
I took it for a man. Often 'twould say
"The fiend, the fiend"—he led me to that place.

EDGAR: Bear free and patient thoughts.
(*Enter* LEAR, *mad.*)
But who comes here?
The safer[3] sense will ne'er accommodate[4]
His master thus.

LEAR: No, they cannot touch me for coining;
I am the King himself.

EDGAR: O thou side-piercing sight!

LEAR: Nature's above art in that respect. There's your press money. That fellow handles his bow like a crow-keeper. Draw me a clothier's yard.[5] Look, look, a mouse! Peace, peace, this piece of toasted cheese will do't. There's my gauntlet; I'll prove it on a giant. Bring up the brown bills.[6] O, well flown, bird! i'th' clout, i'th' clout![7] Hewgh! Give the word.

EDGAR: Sweet marjoram.

[1]Shrill-throated.
[2]Twisted.
[3]Sane.
[4]Equip, clothe.
[5]An arrow a yard long.
[6]Pikes.
[7]Bull's eye of target.

LEAR: Pass.

GLOUCESTER: I know that voice.

LEAR: Ha! Goneril with a white beard? They flattered me like a dog, and told me I had white hairs in my beard ere the black ones were there. To say "ay" and "no" to everything I said! "Ay" and "no" too was no good divinity. When the rain came to wet me once, and the wind to make me chatter, when the thunder would not peace at my bidding, there I found 'em, there I smelt 'em out. Go to, they are not men o' their words! they told me I was everything. 'Tis a lie—I am not ague-proof.

GLOUCESTER: The trick of that voice I do well remember.
Is't not the King?

LEAR: Ay, every inch a king!
When I do stare, see how the subject quakes.
I pardon that man's life. What was thy cause?
Adultery?
Thou shalt not die. Die for adultery? No.
The wren goes to't, and the small gilded fly
Does lecher in my sight.
Let copulation thrive; for Gloucester's bastard son
Was kinder to his father than my daughters
Got 'tween the lawful sheets.
To't, luxury,[1] pell-mell! for I lack soldiers.
Behold yond simpering dame,
Whose face between her forks[2] presages snow,[3]
That minces virtue, and does shake the head
To hear of pleasure's name.
The fitchew[4] now the soiled horse goes to't
With a more riotous appetite.
Down from the waist they are Centaurs,
Though women all above.
But to the girdle do the gods inherit,
Beneath is all the fiend's.
There's hell, there's darkness, there is the sulphurous pit; burning, scalding, stench, consumption. Fie, fie, fie! pah, pah! Give me an ounce of civet, good apothecary, to sweeten my imagination. There's money for thee.

GLOUCESTER: O, let me kiss that hand!

LEAR: Let me wipe it first; it smells of mortality.

GLOUCESTER: O ruined piece of nature! This great world
Shall so wear out to naught. Dost thou know me?

[1]Lust.
[2]Legs.
[3]Chastity.
[4]Polecat.

LEAR: I remember thine eyes well enough. Dost thou squiny[1] at me? No, do thy worst, blind Cupid! I'll not love. Read thou this challenge; mark but the penning of it.

GLOUCESTER: Were all the letters suns, I could not see.

EDGAR: (*aside*): I would not take this from report. It is,
And my heart breaks at it.

LEAR: Read.

GLOUCESTER: What, with the case[2] of eyes?

LEAR: O, ho, are you there with me? No eyes in your head, nor no money in your purse? Your eyes are in a heavy case, your purse in a light. Yet you see how this world goes.

GLOUCESTER: I see it feelingly.

LEAR: What, art mad? A man may see how this world goes with no eyes. Look with thine ears. See how yond justice rails upon yond simple thief. Hark in thine ear; change places and, handy-dandy, which is the justice, which is the thief? Thou hast seen a farmer's dog bark at a beggar?

GLOUCESTER: Ay, sir.

LEAR: And the creature run from the cur? There thou mightst behold the great image of authority: a dog's obeyed in office.
Thou rascal beadle, hold thy bloody hand!
Why dost thou lash that whore? Strip thine own back.
Thou hotly lusts to use her in that kind
For which thou whip'st her. The usurer hangs the cozener.[3]
Through tattered clothes small vices do appear;
Robes and furred gowns hide all. Plate sin with gold,
And the strong lance of justice hurtless breaks;
Arm it in rags, a pygmy's straw does pierce it.
None does offend, none—I say none! I'll able[4] 'em.
Take that of me, my friend, who have the power
To seal th'accuser's lips. Get thee glass eyes
And, like a scurvy politician, seem
To see the things thou dost not. Now, now, now, now!
Pull off my boots. Harder, harder! So.

EDGAR: O, matter and impertinency[5] mixed
Reason in madness!

LEAR: If thou wilt weep my fortunes, take my eyes.
I know thee well enough; thy name is Gloucester.
Thou must be patient. We came crying hither;
Thou knowest, the first time that we smell the air

[1]Squint.
[2]Sockets.
[3]Cheater.
[4]Vouch for.
[5]Nonsense.

We wawl and cry. I will preach to thee. Mark.
GLOUCESTER: Alack, alack the day!
LEAR: When we are born, we cry that we are come
To this great stage of fools. This' a good block.[1]
It were a delicate stratagem to shoe
A troop of horse with felt. I'll put't in proof,
And when I have stolen upon these sons-in-law,
Then kill, kill, kill, kill, kill, kill!
(*Enter a* GENTLEMAN *with* ATTENDANTS.)
GENTLEMAN: O, here he is! Lay hand upon him.—Sir,
Your most dear daughter—
LEAR: No rescue? What, a prisoner? I am even
The natural fool of fortune. Use me well;
You shall have ransom. Let me have a surgeon;
I am cut to th' brains.
GENTLEMAN: You shall have anything.
LEAR: No seconds? All myself?
Why, this would make a man a man of salt,
To use his eyes for garden waterpots,
Ay, and laying autumn's dust.
GENTLEMAN: Good sir—
LEAR: I will die bravely, like a smug bridegroom. What!
I will be jovial. Come, come, I am a king;
My masters, know you that?
GENTLEMAN: You are a royal one, and we obey you.
LEAR: Then there's life in't. Come, an you get it, you shall get it by running. Sa, sa, sa, sa! (*Exit running.* ATTENDANTS *follow.*)
GENTLEMAN: A sight most pitiful in the meanest wretch,
Past speaking of in a king! Thou hast one daughter
Who redeems nature from the general curse
Which twain have brought her to.
EDGAR: Hail, gentle sir.
GENTLEMAN: Sir, speed you. What's your will?
EDGAR: Do you hear aught, sir, of a battle toward?
GENTLEMAN: Most sure and vulgar.[2] Every one hears that
Which can distinguish sound.
EDGAR: But, by your favor,
How near's the other army?
GENTLEMAN: Near and on speedy foot; the main descry
Stands on the hourly thought.[3]
EDGAR: I thank you, sir. That's all.

[1]This is a well-made hat.

[2]Commonly known.

[3]The main body is expected any hour.

GENTLEMAN: Though that the Queen on special cause is here,
Her army is moved on.
EDGAR: I thank you, sir.
(*Exit* GENTLEMAN.)
GLOUCESTER: You ever-gentle gods, take my breath from me;
Let not my worser spirit tempt me again
To die before you please!
EDGAR: Well pray you, father.
GLOUCESTER: Now, good sir, what are you?
EDGAR: A most poor man, made tame to fortune's blows,
Who, by the art[1] of known and feeling sorrows,
Am pregnant[2] to good pity. Give me your hand;
I'll lead you to some biding.[3]
GLOUCESTER: Hearty thanks.
The bounty and the benison of heaven
To boot, and boot!
(*Enter* OSWALD.)
OSWALD: A proclaimed prize! Most happy!
That eyeless head of thine was first framed flesh
To raise my fortunes. Thou old unhappy traitor,
Briefly thyself remember;[4] the sword is out
That must destroy thee.
GLOUCESTER: Now let thy friendly hand
Put strength enough to't.
(EDGAR *interposes.*)
OSWALD: Wherefore, bold peasant,
Darest thou support a published traitor? Hence,
Lest that the infection of his fortune take
Like hold on thee. Let go his arm.
EDGAR: Chill[5] not let go, zir, without vurther 'cagion.
OSWALD: Let go, slave, or thou diest!
EDGAR: Good gentleman, go your gait, and let poor voke pass.
An chud[6] ha' bin zwaggered out of my life, 'twould not ha' bin zo long as 'tis by a vortnight. Nay, come not near the old man. Keep out, che vore ye,[7] or Ise try whether your costard[8] or my ballow[9] be the harder. Chill be plain with you.
OSWALD: Out, dunghill! (*They fight.*)

[1]Experience.
[2]Disposed.
[3]Refuge.
[4]Say your prayers.
[5]I will (Edgar feigns a dialect.)
[6]If I could.
[7]If I warn you.
[8]Head.
[9]Cudgel.

EDGAR: Chill pick your teeth, zir. Come, no matter vor your foins.[1]
(OSWALD *falls.*)

OSWALD: Slave, thou hast slain me. Villain, take my purse.
If ever thou wilt thrive, bury my body,
And give the letters which thou findest about me
To Edmund Earl of Gloucester. Seek him out
Upon the British party. O, untimely death! Death! (*He dies.*)

EDGAR: I know thee well. A serviceable villain,
As duteous to the vices of thy mistress
As badness would desire.

GLOUCESTER: What, is he dead?

EDGAR: Sit you down, father; rest you.
Let's see his pockets; these letters that he speaks of
May be my friends. He's dead; I am only sorry
He had no other deathsman. Let us see.
Leave, gentle wax; and, manners, blame us not.
To know our enemies' minds, we'ld rip their hearts;
Their papers, is more lawful. (*Reads the letter.*)

Let our reciprocal vows be remembered. You have many opportunities to cut him off. If your will want not, time and place will be fruitfully offered. There is nothing done, if he return the conqueror. Then am I the prisoner, and his bed my jail, from the loathed warmth whereof deliver me, and supply the place for your labor.

Your (wife, so I would say) affectionate servant,
GONERIL.

O indistinguished[2] space of woman's will!
A plot upon her virtuous husband's life,
And the exchange my brother! Here in the sands
Thee I'll rake up,[3] the post unsanctified
Of murtherous lechers; and in the mature time
With this ungracious paper strike the sight
Of the death-practised Duke. For him 'tis well
That of thy death and business I can tell.

GLOUCESTER: The King is mad. How stiff is my vile sense,
That I stand up, and have ingenious[4] feeling
Of my huge sorrows! Better I were distract.
So should my thoughts be severed from my griefs,
And woes by wrong imaginations lose

[1]Thrusts.
[2]Unlimited.
[3]Bury.
[4]Sharp.

The knowledge of themselves.
(*A drum afar off.*)
EDGAR: Give me your hand.
Far off methinks I hear the beaten drum.
Come, father, I'll bestow you with a friend. (*Exeunt.*)

SCENE VII

(*A Tent in the French Camp.*)

(*Enter* CORDELIA, KENT, DOCTOR, *and* GENTLEMAN.)

CORDELIA: O thou good Kent, how shall I live and work
To match thy goodness? My life will be too short
And every measure fail me.
KENT: To be acknowledged, madam, is o'erpaid.
All my reports go with the modest truth;
Nor more nor clipped, but so.
CORDELIA: Be better suited;
These weeds[1] are memories of those worser hours.
I prithee put them off.
KENT: Pardon, dear madam,
Yet to be known shortens my made intent.[2]
My boon I make it that you know me not
Till time and I think meet.
CORDELIA: Then be't so, my good lord. (*To the* DOCTOR)
How does the King?
DOCTOR: Madam, sleeps still.
CORDELIA: O you kind gods,
Cure this great breach in his abused nature!
The untuned and jarring senses, O, wind up
Of this child-changed father!
DOCTOR: So please your Majesty
That we may wake the King? He hath slept long.
CORDELIA: Be governed by your knowledge, and proceed
I'th' sway of your own will. Is he arrayed?
(*Enter* LEAR *in a chair carried by* SERVANTS.)
GENTLEMAN: Ay, madam. In the heaviness of sleep
We put fresh garments on him.
DOCTOR: Be by, good madam, when we do awake him.
I doubt not of his temperance.

[1]Garments. [2]Prepared plan.

CORDELIA: Very well.
(*Music.*)
DOCTOR: Please you draw near. Louder the music there!
CORDELIA: O my dear father, restoration hang
Thy medicine on my lips, and let this kiss
Repair those violent harms that my two sisters
Have in thy reverence made!
KENT: Kind and dear princess!
CORDELIA: Had you not been their father, these white flakes
Had challenged pity of them. Was this a face
To be opposed against the warring winds,
To stand against the deep dread-bolted thunder
In the most terrible and nimble stroke
Of quick cross lightning? to watch—poor perdu!—[1]
With this thin helm? Mine enemy's dog,
Though he had bit me, should have stood that night
Against my fire; and wast thou fain, poor father,
To hovel thee with swine and rogues forlorn,
In short and musty straw? Alack, alack!
'Tis wonder that thy life and wits at once
Had not concluded all.—He wakes. Speak to him.
DOCTOR: Madam, do you; 'tis fittest.
CORDELIA: How does my royal lord? How fares your Majesty?
LEAR: You do me wrong to take me out o'th' grave.
Thou art a soul in bliss; but I am bound
Upon a wheel of fire, that mine own tears
Do scald like molten lead.
CORDELIA: Sir, do you know me?
LEAR: You are a spirit, I know. When did you die?
CORDELIA: Still, still, far wide!
DOCTOR: He's scarce awake. Let him alone awhile.
LEAR: Where have I been? Where am I? Fair daylight?
I am mightily abused. I should e'en die with pity,
To see another thus. I know not what to say;
I will not swear these are my hands. Let's see.
I feel this pin prick. Would I were assured
Of my condition!
CORDELIA: O, look upon me, sir,
And hold your hands in benediction o'er me.
No, sir, you must not kneel.
LEAR: Pray, do not mock me.
I am a very foolish fond old man,

[1]Sentinel.

Fourscore and upward, not an hour more nor less;
And, to deal plainly,
I fear I am not in my perfect mind.
Methinks I should know you, and know this man,
Yet I am doubtful, for I am mainly ignorant
What place this is, and all the skill I have
Remembers not these garments; nor I know not
Where I did lodge last night. Do not laugh at me;
For (as I am a man) I think this lady
To be my child Cordelia.

CORDELIA: And so I am! I am!

LEAR: Be your tears wet? Yes, faith. I pray weep not.
If you have poison for me, I will drink it.
I know you do not love me, for your sisters
Have, as I do remember, done me wrong.
You have some cause, they have not.

CORDELIA: No cause, no cause.

LEAR: Am I in France?

KENT: In your own kingdom, sir.

LEAR: Do not abuse me.

DOCTOR: Be comforted, good madam. The great rage
You see is killed in him; and yet it is danger
To make him even o'er[1] the time he has lost.
Desire him to go in. Trouble him no more
Till further settling.

CORDELIA: Will't please your Highness walk?

LEAR: You must bear with me.
Pray you now, forget and forgive. I am old and foolish.
(*Exeunt all but* KENT *and* GENTLEMAN.)

GENTLEMAN: Holds it true, sir, that the Duke of Cornwall was so slain?

KENT: Most certain, sir.

GENTLEMAN: Who is conductor of his people?

KENT: As 'tis said, the bastard son of Gloucester.

GENTLEMAN: They say Edgar, his banished son, is with the Earl of Kent in Germany.

KENT: Report is changeable. 'Tis time to look about; the powers of the kingdom approach apace.

GENTLEMAN: The arbitrement is like to be bloody.
Fare you well, sir. (*Exit.*)

KENT: My point and period will be thoroughly wrought,
Or well or ill, as this day's battle's fought. (*Exit.*)

[1]Catch up with.

ACT V

SCENE I

(The British Camp near Dover.)

(*Enter, with drum and colors,* EDMUND, REGAN, GENTLEMAN, *and* SOLDIERS.)

EDMUND: Know of the Duke if his last purpose hold,
Or whether since he is advised by aught
To change the course. He's full of alteration
And self-reproving. Bring his constant pleasure.[1]
(*Exit an* OFFICER.)
REGAN: Our sister's man is certainly miscarried.
EDMUND: 'Tis to be doubted, madam.
REGAN: Now, sweet lord,
You know the goodness I intend upon you.
Tell me—but truly—but then speak the truth—
Do you not love my sister?
EDMUND: In honored love.
REGAN: But have you never found my brother's way
To the forfended[2] place?
EDMUND: That thought abuses you.
REGAN: I am doubtful that you have been conjunct[3]
And bosomed with her, as far as we call hers.
EDMUND: No, by mine honor, madam.
REGAN: I never shall endure her. Dear my lord,
Be not familiar with her.
EDMUND: Fear me not.
She and the Duke her husband!
(*Enter, with drum and colors,* ALBANY, GONERIL, SOLDIERS.)
GONERIL (*aside*): I had rather lose the battle than that sister
Should loosen him and me.
ALBANY: Our very loving sister, well bemet.
Sir, this I hear: the King is come to his daughter,
With others whom the rigor of our state[4]
Forced to cry out. Where I could not be honest,
I never yet was valiant. For this business,
It touches us as France invades our land,
Not bolds[5] the King, with others whom, I fear,

[1]Final resolve.
[2]Forbidden.
[3]United
[4]Our harsh rule.
[5]Supports.

Most just and heavy causes make oppose.

EDMUND: Sir, you speak nobly.

REGAN: Why is this reasoned?

GONERIL: Combine together 'gainst the enemy;
For these domestic and particular[1] broils
Are not the question here.

ALBANY: Let's then determine
With th'ancient of war[2] on our proceeding.

EDMUND: I shall attend you presently at your tent.

REGAN: Sister, you'll go with us?

GONERIL: No.

REGAN: 'Tis most convenient. Pray you go with us.

GONERIL: (*aside*): O, ho, I know the riddle.—I will go.

(*As they are going out, enter* EDGAR *disguised.*)

EDGAR: If e'er your Grace had speech with man so poor,
Hear me one word.

ALBANY: I'll overtake you.—Speak.

(*Exeunt all but* ALBANY *and* EDGAR.)

EDGAR: Before you fight the battle, ope this letter.
If you have victory, let the trumpet sound
For him that brought it. Wretched though I seem,
I can produce a champion that will prove
What is avouched there. If you miscarry,
Your business of the world hath so an end,
And machination ceases. Fortune love you!

ALBANY: Stay till I have read the letter.

EDGAR: I was forbid it.
When time shall serve, let but the herald cry,
And I'll appear again.

ALBANY: Why, fare thee well. I will o'erlook thy paper.

(*Exit* EDGAR.)

(*Enter* EDMUND.)

EDMUND: The enemy's in view; draw up your powers.
Here is the guess of their true strength and forces
By diligent discovery; but your haste
Is now urged on you.

ALBANY: We will greet the time. (*Exit.*)

EDMUND: To both these sisters have I sworn my love;
Each jealous of the other, as the stung
Are of the adder. Which of them shall I take?
Both? one? or neither? Neither can be enjoyed,
If both remain alive. To take the widow

[1]Private.

[2]Experienced soldiers.

Exasperates, makes mad her sister Goneril,
And hardly shall I carry out my side,[1]
Her husband being alive. Now then, we'll use
His countenance for the battle, which being done,
Let her who would be rid of him devise
His speedy taking off. As for the mercy
Which he intends to Lear and to Cordelia—
The battle done, and they within our power,
Shall never see his pardon; for my state
Stands on[2] me to defend, not to debate. (*Exit.*)

Scene II

(*A Field between the two Camps.*)

(*Alarum within. Enter, with drum and colors,* CORDELIA *and* LEAR *with French forces; and exeunt.*)

(*Enter* EDGAR *and* GLOUCESTER.)

EDGAR: Here, father, take the shadow of this tree
For your good host; pray that the right may thrive.
If ever I return to you again,
I'll bring you comfort.
GLOUCESTER: Grace go with you, sir!
(*Exit* EDGAR.)
(*Alarum and retreat within. Enter* EDGAR.)
EDGAR: Away, old man! give me thy hand, away!
King Lear hath lost, he and his daughter ta'en.
Give me thy hand; come on!
GLOUCESTER: No further, sir. A man may rot even here.
EDGAR: What, in ill thoughts again? Men must endure
Their going hence, even as their coming hither;
Ripeness is all. Come on.
GLOUCESTER: And that's true too. (*Exeunt.*)

[1]Plan. [2]Requires.

SCENE III

(The British Camp near Dover.)

(Enter, in conquest, with drum and colors, EDMUND; LEAR *and* CORDELIA *as prisoners;* SOLDIERS, CAPTAIN.)

EDMUND: Some officers take them away. Good guard
Until their greater pleasures[1] first be known
That are to censure them.

CORDELIA: We are not the first
Who with best meaning have incurred the worst.
For thee, oppressed king, I am cast down;
Myself could else outfrown false Fortune's frown.
Shall we not see these daughters and these sisters?

LEAR: No, no, no, no! Come, let's away to prison.
We too alone will sing like birds i'th' cage.
When thou dost ask me blessing, I'll kneel down
And ask of thee forgiveness. So we'll live,
And pray, and sing, and tell old tales, and laugh
At gilded butterflies, and hear poor rogues
Talk of court news; and we'll talk with them too—
Who loses and who wins; who's in, who's out—
And take upon's the mystery of things,
As if we were gods' spies; and we'll wear out,
In a walled prison, packs and sects of great ones
That ebb and flow by the moon.

EDMUND: Take them away.

LEAR: Upon such sacrifices, my Cordelia,
The gods themselves throw incense. Have I caught thee?
He that parts us shall bring a brand from heaven
And fire us hence[2] like foxes. Wipe thine eyes.
The goodyears[3] shall devour 'em, flesh and fell,[4]
Ere they shall make us weep! We'll see 'em starved first.
Come. (*Exeunt* LEAR *and* CORDELIA, *guarded.*)

EDMUND: Come hither, Captain; hark.
Take thou this note (*gives a paper*). Go follow them to prison.
One step I have advanced thee; if thou dost
As this instructs thee, thou dost make thy way
To noble fortunes. Know thou this, that men
Are as the time is; to be tender-minded

[1]The pleasure (opinion) of greater persons.

[2]Drive us out by fire.

[3]Plagues.

[4]Skin.

Does not become a sword. Thy great employment
Will not bear question. Either say thou'lt do't,
Or thrive by other means.
  CAPTAIN: I'll do't, my lord.
  EDMUND: About it! and write[1] happy when thou hast done.
Mark: I say instantly, and carry it so
As I have set it down.
  CAPTAIN: I cannot draw a cart, nor eat dried oats;
If it be man's work, I'll do't. (*Exit.*)
(*Flourish. Enter* ALBANY, GONERIL, REGAN, SOLDIERS.)
  ALBANY: Sir, you have showed to-day your valiant strain,
And fortune led you well. You have the captives
Who were the opposites of this day's strife;
I do require them of you, so to use them
As we shall find their merits and our safety
May equally determine.
  EDMUND: Sir, I thought it fit
To send the old and miserable King
To some retention and appointed guard;
Whose age has charms in it, whose titles more,
To pluck the common bosom[2] on his side
And turn our impressed lances[3] in our eyes
Which do command them. With him I sent the Queen,
My reason all the same; and they are ready
To-morrow, or at further space, to appear
Where you shall hold your session. At this time
We sweat and bleed; the friend hath lost his friend,
And the best quarrels in the heat are cursed
By those that feel their sharpness.
The question of Cordelia and her father
Requires a fitter place.
  ALBANY: Sir, by your patience,
I hold you but a subject of this war,
Not as a brother.
  REGAN: That's as we list to grace him.
Methinks our pleasure might have been demanded
Ere you had spoke so far. He led our powers,
Bore the commission of my place and person,
The which immediacy[4] may well stand up
And call itself your brother.
  GONERIL: Not so hot!
In his own grace he doth exalt himself

[1]Consider yourself.
[2]Affections of the people.
[3]Soldiers' weapons.
[4]Nearness to my authority.

More than in your addition.
REGAN: In my rights
By me invested, he compeers[1] the best.
GONERIL: That were the most if he should husband you.
REGAN: Jesters do oft prove prophets.
GONERIL: Holla, holla!
That eye that told you so looked but asquint.
REGAN: Lady, I am not well, else I should answer
From a full-flowing stomach. General,
Take thou my soldiers, prisoners, patrimony;
Dispose of them, of me; the walls are thine.
Witness the world that I create thee here
My lord and master.
GONERIL: Mean you to enjoy him?
ALBANY: The let-alone lies not in your good will.
EDMUND: Nor in thine, lord.
ALBANY: Half-blooded[2] fellow, yes.
REGAN (*to* EDMUND): Let the drum strike, prove my title thine.
ALBANY: Stay yet; hear reason. Edmund, I arrest thee
On capital treason; and, in thine attaint,[3]
This gilded serpent (*points to* GONERIL). For your claim, fair sister,
I bar it in the interest of my wife.
'Tis she is subcontracted to this lord,
And I, her husband, contradict your banns.
If you will marry, make your loves to me;
My lady is bespoke.
GONERIL: An interlude![4]
ALBANY: Thou art armed, Gloucester. Let the trumpet sound.
If none appear to prove upon thy person
Thy heinous, manifest, and many treasons,
There is my pledge (*throws down a glove.*) I'll prove it on thy heart,
Ere I taste bread, thou art in nothing less
Than I have here proclaimed thee.
REGAN: Sick, O, sick!
GONERIL (*aside*): If not, I'll ne'er trust medicine.
EDMUND: There's my exchange (*throws down a glove.*) What in the world he is
That names me traitor, villain-like he lies.
Call by thy trumpet. He that dares approach,

[1]Equals.
[2]Base-born (on his mother's side).
[3]Accused with you.
[4]Comedy, farce.

On him, on you, who not? I will maintain
My truth and honor firmly.

ALBANY: A herald, ho!

EDMUND: A herald, ho, a herald!

(*Enter a* HERALD.)

ALBANY: Trust to thy single virtue,[1] for thy soldiers,
All levied in my name, have in my name
Took their discharge.

REGAN: My sickness grows upon me.

ALBANY: She is not well. Convey her to my tent.

(*Exit* REGAN, *led.*)

Come hither, herald. Let the trumpet sound,
And read out this.

CAPTAIN: Sound, trumpet! (*A trumpet sounds.*)

HERALD (*reads*): If any man of quality or degree within the lists of the army will maintain upon Edmund, supposed Earl of Gloucester, that he is a manifold traitor, let him appear by the third sound of the trumpet. He is bold in his defence.

EDMUND: Sound! (*First trumpet.*)
HERALD: Again! (*Second trumpet.*)
HERALD: Again! (*Third trumpet.*)
(*Trumpet answers within.*)

(*Enter* EDGAR, *armed, a trumpet before him.*)

ALBANY: Ask him his purposes, why he appears
Upon this call o'th' trumpet.

HERALD: What are you?
Your name, your quality? and why you answer
This present summons?

EDGAR: Know my name is lost,
By treason's tooth bare-gnawn and canker-bit.[2]
Yet am I noble as the adversary
I come to cope.

ALBANY: Which is that adversary?

EDGAR: What's he that speaks for Edmund Earl of Gloucester?

EDMUND: Himself. What say'st thou to him?

EDGAR: Draw thy sword,
That, if my speech offend a noble heart,
Thy arm may do thee justice. Here is mine.
Behold, it is the privilege of mine honors,
My oath, and my profession. I protest,

[1]Indivual strength. [2]Worm-eaten

Maugre[1] thy strength, place, youth, and eminence,
Despite thy victor sword and fire-new fortune,
Thy valor and thy heart, thou art a traitor,
False to thy gods, thy brother, and thy father,
Conspirant 'gainst this high illustrious prince,
And from th'extremest upward of thy head
To the descent and dust beneath thy foot,
A most toad-spotted traitor. Say thou "no,"
This sword, this arm, and my best spirits are bent
To prove upon thy heart, whereto I speak,
Thou liest.

EDMUND: In wisdom I should ask thy name;
But since thy outside looks so fair and warlike,
And that thy tongue some say[2] of breeding breathes,
What safe and nicely[3] I might well delay
By rule of knighthood, I disdain and spurn.
Back do I toss those treasons to thy head;
With the hell-hated lie o'erwhelm thy heart;
Which, for they yet glance by and scarcely bruise,
This sword of mine shall give them instant way
Where they shall rest for ever. Trumpets, speak!

(*Alarums. Fight.* EDMUND *falls.*)

ALBANY: Save him, save him!

GONERIL: This is mere practice,[4] Gloucester.
By th' law of arms thou wast not bound to answer
An unknown opposite. Thou art not vanquished,
But cozened and beguiled.

ALBANY: Shut your mouth, dame,
Or with this paper shall I stop it. (*Shows her her letter to* EDMUND.) (*To* EDMUND) Hold, sir.
(*To* GONERIL) Thou worse than any name, read thine own evil.
No tearing, lady! I perceive you know it.

GONERIL: Say if I do—the laws are mine, not thine.
Who can arraign me for't?

ALBANY: Most monstrous!
Know'st thou this paper?

GONERIL: Ask me not what I know. (*Exit.*)

ALBANY: Go after her. She's desperate; govern[5] her.
(*Exit an* OFFICER.)

EDMUND: What have you charged me with, that have I done,
And more, much more; the time will bring it out.

[1]In spite of.
[2]Trace.
[3]Technically.
[4]Foul play.
[5]Restrain.

'Tis past, and so am I—But what art thou
That hast this fortune on me? If thou'rt noble,
I do forgive thee.
EDGAR: Let's exchange charity.
I am no less in blood than thou art, Edmund;
If more, the more th'hast wronged me.
My name is Edgar and thy father's son.
The gods are just, and of our pleasant vices
Make instruments to plague us.
The dark and vicious place where thee he got
Cost him his eyes.
EDMUND: Th'hast spoken right, 'tis true;
The wheel[1] is come full circle, I am here.
ALBANY: Methought thy very gait did prophesy
A royal nobleness; I must embrace thee.
Let sorrow split my heart if ever I
Did hate thee, or thy father!
EDGAR: Worthy prince, I know't.
ALBANY: Where have you hid yourself?
How have you known the miseries of your father?
EDGAR: By nursing them, my lord. List a brief tale,
And when 'tis told, O that my heart would burst!
The bloody proclamation to escape
That followed me so near (O, our lives' sweetness!
That we the pain of death would hourly die
Rather than die at once!) taught me to shift
Into a madman's rags, t'assume a semblance
That very dogs disdained, and in this habit
Met I my father with his bleeding rings,
Their precious stones new lost; became his guide,
Led him, begged for him, saved him from despair;
Never (O fault) revealed myself unto him
Until some half hour past, when I was armed,
Not sure, though hoping of this good success,
I asked his blessing, and from first to last
Told him my pilgrimage. But his flawed[2] heart
(Alack, too weak the conflict to support)
'Twixt two extremes of passion, joy and grief,
Burst smilingly.
EDMUND: This speech of yours hath moved me,
And shall perchance do good; but speak you on;
You look as you had something more to say.
ALBANY: If there be more, more woful, hold it in;

[1]Wheel of Fortune. [2]Cracked.

For I am almost ready to dissolve,
Hearing of this.

EDGAR: This would have seemed a period
To such as love not sorrow; but another,
To amplify too much, would make much more,
And top extremity.[1]
Whilst I was big in clamor,[2] came there a man,
Who, having seen me in my worst estate,
Shunned my abhorred society; but then, finding
Who 'twas that so endured, with his strong arms
He fastened on my neck, and bellowed out
As he'd burst heaven; threw him on my father;
Told the most piteous tale of Lear and him
That ever ear received; which in recounting
His grief grew puissant, and the strings of life
Began to crack. Twice then the trumpets sounded,
And there I left him tranced.[3]

ALBANY: But who was this?

EDGAR: Kent, sir, the banished Kent, who in disguise
Followed his enemy king and did him service
Improper for a slave.

(*Enter a* GENTLEMAN *with a bloody knife.*)

GENTLEMAN: Help, help, O, help!

EDGAR: What kind of help?

ALBANY: Speak, man.

EDGAR: What means that bloody knife?

GENTLEMAN: 'Tis hot, it smokes.
It came even from the heart of—O, she's dead!

ALBANY: Who dead? Speak, man.

GENTLEMAN: Your lady, sir, your lady! and her sister
By her is poisoned; she confesses it.

EDMUND: I was contracted to them both. All three
Now marry in an instant.

(*Enter* KENT.)

EDGAR: Here comes Kent.

ALBANY: Produce their bodies, be they alive or dead. (*Exit* GENTLEMAN.)
This judgment of the heavens, that makes us tremble,
Touches us not with pity. Oh, is this he?
The time will not allow the compliment[4]
That very manners urges.

KENT: I am come

[1]Pass the highest possible point.
[2]Loud in grief.
[3]Unconscious.
[4]Ceremony.

To bid my king and master aye good night.
Is he not here?

ALBANY: Great thing of us forgot!
Speak, Edmund, where's the King? and where's Cordelia? (*The bodies of* GONERIL *and* REGAN *are brought in.*)
Seest thou this object, Kent?

KENT: Alack, why thus?

EDMUND: Yet Edmund was beloved.
The one the other poisoned for my sake,
And after slew herself.

ALBANY: Even so. Cover their faces.

EDMUND: I pant for life. Some good I mean to do,
Despite of mine own nature. Quickly send
(Be brief in it) to the castle, for my writ
Is on the life of Lear and on Cordelia.
Nay, send in time.

ALBANY: Run, run, O, run!

EDGAR: To who, my lord? Who has the office? Send
Thy token of reprieve.

EDMUND: Well thought on. Take my sword;
Give it the Captain.

ALBANY: Haste thee for thy life. (*Exit* EDGAR.)

EDMUND: He hath commission from thy wife and me
To hang Cordelia in the prison and
To lay the blame upon her own despair
That she fordid[1] herself.

ALBANY: The gods defend her! Bear him hence awhile.
(EDMUND *is borne off.*)

(*Enter* LEAR, *with* CORDELIA *dead in his arms,* EDGAR, GENTLEMAN, *and others following.*)

LEAR: Howl, howl, howl, howl! O, you are men of stones.
Had I your tongues and eyes, I'ld use them so
That heaven's vault should crack. She's gone for ever!
I know when one is dead, and when one lives;
She's dead as earth. Lend me a looking glass;
If that her breath will mist or stain the stone,[2]
Why, then she lives.

KENT: Is this the promised end?[3]

EDGAR: Or image of that horror?

ALBANY: Fall and cease!

LEAR: This feather stirs; she lives! If it be so,
it is a chance which does redeem all sorrows

[1]Destroyed.

[2]Mirror.

[3]End of the world.

That ever I have felt.

KENT: O my good master!

LEAR: Prithee away!

EDGAR: 'Tis noble Kent, your friend.

LEAR: A plague upon you, murderers, traitors all!
I might have saved her; now she's gone for ever.
Cordelia, Cordelia, stay a little. Ha!
What is't thou say'st? Her voice was ever soft,
Gentle, and low—an excellent thing in woman.
I killed the slave that was a-hanging thee.

CAPTAIN: 'Tis true, my lords, he did.

LEAR: Did I not, fellow?
I have seen the day, with my good biting falchion
I would have made them skip. I am old now,
And these same crosses[1] spoil me. Who are you?
Mine eyes are not o'th' best. I'll tell you straight.

KENT: If fortune brag of two she loved and hated,
One of them we behold.

LEAR: This is a dull sight. Are you not Kent?

KENT: The same—
Your servant Kent. Where is your servant Caius?

LEAR: He's a good fellow, I can tell you that.
He'll strike, and quickly too. He's dead and rotten.

KENT: No, my good lord, I am the very man—

LEAR: I'll see that straight.

KENT: That from your first of difference[2] and decay
Have followed your sad steps.

LEAR: You are welcome hither.

KENT: Nor no man else! All's cheerless, dark, and deadly.
Your eldest daughters have fordone themselves,
And desperately are dead.

LEAR: Ay, so I think.

ALBANY: He knows not what he says, and vain is it
That we present us to him.

EDGAR: Very bootless.

(*Enter a* CAPTAIN.)

CAPTAIN: Edmund is dead, my lord.

ALBANY: That's but a trifle here.
You lords and noble friends, know our intent.
What comfort to this great decay may come
Shall be applied. For us, we will resign,
During the life of this old Majesty,

[1]Sufferings.
[2]Decline.

To him our absolute power; (*to* EDGAR *and* KENT) you to your
rights,
With boot, and such addition as your honors
Have more than merited. All friends shall taste
The wages of their virtue, and all foes
The cup of their deservings.—O, see, see!
LEAR: And my poor fool is hanged! No, no, no life!
Why should a dog, a horse, a rat, have life,
And thou no breath at all? Thou'lt come no more,
Never, never, never, never, never!
Pray you undo this button. Thank you, sir.
Do you see this? Look on her! look! her lips!
Look there, look there! (*He dies.*)
EDGAR: He faints! My lord, my lord!
KENT: Break, heart, I prithee break!
EDGAR: Look up, my lord.
KENT: Vex not his ghost; O let him pass! He hates him
That would upon the rack of this tough world
Stretch him out longer.
EDGAR: He is gone indeed.
KENT: The wonder is, he hath endured so long.
He but usurped his life.
ALBANY: Bear them from hence. Our present business
Is general woe. (*To* KENT *and* EDGAR) Friends of my soul, you
twain
Rule in this realm, and the gored state sustain.
KENT: I have a journey, sir, shortly to go.
My master calls me; I must not say no.
ALBANY: The weight of this sad time we must obey,
Speak what we feel, not what we ought to say.
The oldest hath borne most; we that are young
Shall never see so much, nor live so long.

(*Exeunt with a dead march.*)

Henrik Ibsen:
GHOSTS

For reasons which have been much discussed but never really adequately explained, by the middle of the nineteenth century European drama had reached an appalling depth. Sentimental melodramas chiefly held the stage, and most of the good plays produced were revivals (often shamelessly cut and altered) of older pieces. Clearly a new drama was needed; attempts to imitate the old poetic drama were mostly futile, for although, in England, for example, poets as excellent as Coleridge, Browning, and Tennyson tried their hand, they were hopelessly trying to resuscitate an old, dead theater instead of seeking to create a new vital one. Not Elizabethans, they nevertheless tried to think like men of the Renaissance, and the results are sterile. New important drama had to arise from new ideas.

By the early nineteenth century, science was regarded not only as something dealing with broad general laws but as a method of thinking, of perceiving reality—a method which could not afford to overlook any details. No specimen is too insignificant; every piece of evidence must be collected. In short, where earlier ages had, for the most part, believed that some things are more important than others, the modern scientific age insisted that if we make abstractions and do not concern ourselves with the total creation we falsify reality. Paralleling this development, which turned men's attention to matters previously neglected, was the democratization of Europe. As the merchant class rose, it demanded that it be heeded, and if at first it pretended to enjoy plays about the aristocracy, inevitably it would ultimately see its own image on the stage. Whereas classical and Elizabethan critical theory insisted that tragedy show the fall of a great man, bourgeois tragedy suggests that all men (regardless of birth or rank) are equal in dignity and thus are proper subjects for drama. Implicit in such a theory, it might here be noted, is the idea (which became increasingly dominant) that if all men are equal, an individual is not merely as fine as the best of his species but as low as the worst.

Ibsen's *Ghosts* (1881) reflects not merely Europe's interest in science but its new kind of tragedy. The traditional hero, the king, is dethroned, and the traditional language of drama—poetry—is replaced by a careful (almost scientifically accurate) reproduction of the language we hear around us. Mrs. Alving, a middle-class Norwegian woman, has built an orphanage as a memorial to her late husband, Captain Alving. Her son, Oswald, has returned from Paris. As the drama progresses we learn that Mrs. Alving's marriage was unhappy, for her strict code of morality was opposed to her husband's "joy of life." She once sought to leave him, but on the advice of Pastor Manders she returned to the Captain and later gave birth to Oswald, who inherited the venereal disease which his father had contracted. At the end of the play Oswald's brain has crumbled, and Mrs. Alving, aware that all her plans to expel the Captain from her life are hopeless dreams, stands on the stage, uncertain whether to administer the drug which will end Oswald's pathetic life.

Those who sought a new drama recognized in *Ghosts* a play exactly suited to their hopes. It dealt, they believed, in a realistic manner with a genuine problem, and it cut beneath the surface to see life as it is. André Antoine, acknowledged as having fired the opening shot in the battle for a new kind of drama by founding the Théâtre Libre (Free Theater) in Paris, played Oswald in a French production and, appropriately, instead of acting in a carefully studied or rhetorical way, simply lost himself in the part and *became* the role. In Germany, the Freie Bühne (Free Theater), Berlin's equivalent of the Théâtre Libre, began its career (1889) with *Ghosts,* and in England the Independent Theatre, a similar organization, produced the play for its opening in 1891. The London press was, not unexpectedly, hostile, calling the play "a wicked nightmare" and "a revolting obscenity" by "a gloomy sort of ghoul." Ibsen's plays continued to be reviled in England, one examiner of plays (public drama in England had at that time—and still has—to be officially licensed) stating that Ibsen's men "are all rascals or imbeciles," while his women are all "in a chronic state of rebellion against not only the conditions which nature has imposed on their sex, but against all the duties and obligations of mothers and wives."

Ghosts, however, was not without its defenders, on the Continent and in England. The earliest literary defence justified it on the grounds that its use of syphilis corresponded to the frequent Greek use of a curse on a family, or to the Hebrew assertion that the sins of the fathers are visited upon the children. Similarly, though much of the adverse criticism was based on hostility to the subject matter, some controversy arose about the *scientific accuracy* of Ibsen's picture of syphilis. Darwin's *Origin of Species* had been published in 1859, the air was filled with discussions of the influence of heredity, and Ibsen's play was sometimes regarded as a dramatization of a scientific treatise. (Ibsen incorrectly assumed that syphilis could be genetically inherited.) Moreover, two other themes obtruded between the play and the critics: incestuous marriage and mercy killings are additional provocative, if subsidiary, problems treated.

Actually Ibsen's play is not merely about syphilis, incest, or mercy killing, but about the consequences of human action. Ibsen originally began with the idea that Mrs. Alving is undone because she married the loose-living Captain not out of love but in order to "save" him. He dropped this theme, but continued to focus on Mrs. Alving's behavior rather than on a medical problem. His play is not so much about the facts of syphilis or what to do with a physical degenerate as it is about the *cause* of some kinds of suffering, and its relation to moral responsibility. The fundamental idea of the play, George Bernard Shaw suggests, is that a man of convivial temperament ought to be allowed a suitably free life rather than be forced to catch at his pleasures behind his wife's back. And elsewhere Shaw points out that Mrs. Alving finally perceives that morals are perverted not always by evil intent but sometimes by the very qualities which her upbringing insisted were virtues. The Captain was frustrated by his strait-laced environment, represented by the Pastor and even by Mrs. Alving. Mrs. Alving's temporary break from her husband and her actions in the play mark her as bolder than most of her contemporaries, but she was not bold enough, for she soon yielded to the pressures of Manders' shallow conventional judgment. The deeds were done years ago and the consequences were for a while hidden, but the drama reveals, as Oswald decays, the collapse of Mrs. Alving's world; and at the last she is left terribly aware of the superficiality of her earlier view that she might someday live as though the past had never been.

Ibsen: Biographical Note. Henrik Ibsen (1828–1906) was born in Skien, Norway, of prosperous parents, who, before he was eight, lost their money and social position. In his youth Ibsen achieved a reputation as a local radical, directed a little theater at Bergen, and visited Denmark and Germany to study stage management. His earliest plays are melodramas and romantic historical pieces, but in 1862 a verse satire, *Love's Comedy,* aroused attention. He soon became nationally known, and his realistic dramas of the 1870's and 1880's attracted international attention. His last plays, such as *The Master Builder* and *Rosmersholm,* are more *symbolic* than realistic, and, moving away from social reform, they are psychological explorations of the soul.

Ghosts

Translated by William Archer

Characters

Mrs. Alving (Helen), *widow of Captain Alving, late Chamberlain*[1] *to the King.*

Oswald Alving, *her son, a painter.*

Pastor Manders.

Jacob Engstrand, *a carpenter.*

Regina Engstrand, *Mrs. Alving's maid.*

The action takes place at Mrs. Alving's country-house, beside one of the large fiords in western Norway.

[1]Chamberlain (Kammerherre) is the only title of honour now existing in Norway. It is a distinction conferred by the King on men of wealth and position, and is not hereditary.

ACT I

(A spacious garden-room, with one door to the left, and two doors to the right. In the middle of the room a round table, with chairs about it. On the table lie books, periodicals, and newspapers. In the foreground to the left a window, and by it a small sofa, with a work-table in front of it. In the background, the room is continued into a somewhat narrower conservatory, which is shut in by glass walls with large panes. In the right-hand wall of the conservatory is a door leading down into the garden. Through the glass wall one catches a glimpse of a gloomy fiord-landscape, veiled by steady rain.

ENGSTRAND, *the carpenter, stands by the garden door. His left leg is somewhat bent; he had a clump of wood under the sole of his boot.* REGINA, *with an empty garden syringe in her hand, hinders him from advancing.)*

REGINA (*in a low voice*): What do you want? Stop where you are. You're positively dripping.

ENGSTRAND: It's the Lord's own rain, my girl.

REGINA: It's the devil's rain, *I* say.

ENGSTRAND: Lord! how you talk, Regina. (*Limps a few steps forward into the room.*) What I wanted to say was this—

REGINA: Don't clatter so with that foot of yours, I tell you! The young master's asleep upstairs.

ENGSTRAND: Asleep? In the middle of the day?

REGINA: It's no business of yours.

ENGSTRAND: I was out on the loose last night—

REGINA: I can quite believe that.

ENGSTRAND: Yes, we're weak vessels, we poor mortals, my girl—

REGINA: So it seems.

ENGSTRAND: —and temptations are manifold in this world, you see; but all the same, I was hard at work, God knows, at half-past five this morning.

REGINA: Very well; only be off now. I won't stop here and have *rendezvous.*[1]

ENGSTRAND: What is it you won't have?

[1]This and other French words used by Regina are in that language in the original.

REGINA: I won't have any one find you here; so just you go about your business.

ENGSTRAND (*advances a step or two*): Blest if I go before I've had a talk with you. This afternoon I shall have finished my work at the school-house, and then I shall take to-night's boat and be off home to the town.

REGINA (*mutters*): A pleasant journey to you.

ENGSTRAND: Thank you, my child. To-morrow the Asylum's to be opened, and then there'll be fine doings, no doubt, and plenty of intoxicating drink going, you know. And nobody shall say of Jacob Engstrand that he can't keep out of temptation's way.

REGINA: Oh!

ENGSTRAND: You see, there are to be any number of swells here to-morrow. Pastor Manders is expected from town, too.

REGINA: He's coming to-day.

ENGSTRAND: There, you see! And I should be cursedly sorry if he found out anything to my disadvantage, don't you understand?

REGINA: Oh! is that your game?

ENGSTRAND: Is what my game?

REGINA (*looking hard at him*): What trick are you going to play on Pastor Manders?

ENGSTRAND: Hush! hush! Are you crazy? Do *I* want to play any trick on Pastor Manders? Oh no! Pastor Manders has been far too kind to me for that. But I just wanted to say, you know—that I mean to set off home again to-night.

REGINA: The sooner the better, say I.

ENGSTRAND: Yes, but I want to take you with me, Regina.

REGINA (*open-mouthed*): You want me—? What are you talking about?

ENGSTRAND: I want to take you home, I say.

REGINA (*scornfully*): Never in this world shall you get me home with you.

ENGSTRAND: We'll see about that.

REGINA: Yes, you may be sure we'll see about it! I, who have been brought up by a lady like Mrs. Alving! I, who am treated almost as a daughter here! Is it me you want to go home with you?—to a house like yours? For shame!

ENGSTRAND: What the devil do you mean? Do you set yourself up against your father, girl?

REGINA (*mutters without looking at him*): You've said often enough I was no child of yours.

ENGSTRAND: Stuff! Why should you trouble about that?

REGINA: Haven't you many a time sworn at me and called me a—? *Fi donc!*

ENGSTRAND: Curse me, now, if ever I used such an ugly word.

REGINA: Oh! I know quite well what word you used.

ENGSTRAND: Well, but that was only when I was a bit on, don't you know? Hm! Temptations are manifold in this world, Regina.

REGINA: Ugh!

ENGSTRAND: And besides, it was when your mother rode her high horse. I had to find something to twit her with, my child. She was always setting up for a fine lady. (*Mimics*) "Let me go, Engstrand; let me be. Remember I've been three years in Chamberlain Alving's family at Rosenvold." (*Laughs*) Mercy on us! She could never forget that the Captain was made a Chamberlain while she was in service here.

REGINA: Poor mother! you very soon worried her into her grave.

ENGSTRAND (*turns on his heel*): Oh, of course! I'm to be blamed for everything.

REGINA (*turns away; half aloud*): Ugh! And that leg too!

ENGSTRAND: What do you say, girl?

REGINA: *Pied de mouton.*

ENGSTRAND: Is that English, eh?

REGINA: Yes.

ENGSTRAND: Oh, ah; you've picked up some learning out here; and that may come in useful now, Regina.

REGINA (*after a short silence*): What do you want with me in town?

ENGSTRAND: Can you ask what a father wants with his only child? Am I not a lonely and forsaken widower?

REGINA: Oh! don't try on any nonsense like that! Why do you want me?

ENGSTRAND: Well, let me tell you, I've been thinking of starting a new line of business.

REGINA (*contemptuously*): You've tried that often enough, and never done any good.

ENGSTRAND: Yes, but this time you shall see, Regina! Devil take me—

REGINA (*stamps*): Don't swear!

ENGSTRAND: Hush, hush; you're right enough there, my girl. What I wanted to say was just this—I've laid by a very tidy pile from this Orphanage job.

REGINA: Have you? That's a good thing for you.

ENGSTRAND: What can a man spend his ha'pence on here in the country?

REGINA: Well, what then?

ENGSTRAND: Why, you see, I thought of putting the money into some paying speculation. I thought of a sort of sailors' tavern—

REGINA: Horrid!

ENGSTRAND: A regular high-class affair, of course; not a mere pigsty for common sailors. No! damn it! it would be for captains and mates, and—and—all those swells, you know.

REGINA: And I was to—?

ENGSTRAND: You were to help, to be sure. Only for appearance' sake, you understand. Devil a bit of hard work shall you have, my girl. You shall do exactly what you like.

REGINA: Oh, indeed!

ENGSTRAND: But there must be a petticoat in the house; that's as clear as daylight. For I want to have it a little lively in the evenings, with singing and dancing, and so forth. You must remember they're weary wanderers on the ocean of life. (*Nearer*) Now don't be stupid and stand in your own light, Regina. What can become of you out here? Your mistress has given you a lot of learning; but what good is it to you? You're to look after the children at the new Orphanage, I hear. Is that the sort of thing for you, eh? Are you so desperately bent upon wearing yourself out for the sake of the dirty brats?

REGINA: No; if things go as I want them to, then—well, there's no saying—there's no saying.

ENGSTRAND: What do you mean by "there's no saying"?

REGINA: Never you mind. How much money have you saved up here?

ENGSTRAND: What with one thing and another, a matter of seven or eight hundred crowns.[1]

REGINA: That's not so bad.

ENGSTRAND: It's enough to make a start with, my girl.

REGINA: Aren't you thinking of giving me any?

ENGSTRAND: No, I'm damned if I am!

REGINA: Not even of sending me a scrap of stuff for a new dress?

ENGSTRAND: If you'll come to town with me, you can get dresses enough.

REGINA: Pooh! I can do that on my own account if I want to.

ENGSTRAND: No, a father's guiding hand is what you want, Regina. Now, I've my eye on a capital house in Little Harbour

[1]A "krone" was equal to approximately twenty-seven cents.

Street. It won't need much ready-money, and it could be a sort of sailors' home, you know.

REGINA: But I will *not* live with you. I have nothing whatever to do with you. Be off!

ENGSTRAND: You wouldn't remain long with me, my girl. No such luck! If you knew how to play your cards, such a fine girl as you've grown in the last year or two—

REGINA: Well?

ENGSTRAND: You'd soon get hold of some mate—or perhaps even a captain—

REGINA: I won't marry any one of that sort. Sailors have no *savoir vivre.*

ENGSTRAND: What haven't they got?

REGINA: I know what sailors are, I tell you. They're not the sort of people to marry.

ENGSTRAND: Then never mind about marrying them. You can make it pay all the same. (*More confidentially*) He—the Englishman—the man with the yacht—he gave three hundred dollars, he did; and she wasn't a bit handsomer than you.

REGINA (*going towards him*): Out you go!

ENGSTRAND (*falling back*): Come, come! You're not going to strike me, I hope.

REGINA: Yes, if you begin to talk about mother I shall strike you. Get away with you, I say. (*Drives him back towards the garden door.*) And don't bang the doors. Young Mr. Alving—

ENGSTRAND: He's asleep; I know. It's curious how you're taken up about young Mr. Alving—(*more softly*) Oho! it surely can't be he that—?

REGINA: Be off at once! You're crazy, I tell you! No, not that way. There comes Pastor Manders. Down the kitchen stairs with you.

ENGSTRAND (*towards the right*): Yes, yes, I'm going. But just you talk to him that's coming there. He's the man to tell you what a child owes its father. For I am your father all the same, you know. I can prove it from the church-register.

(*He goes out through the second door to the right, which* REGINA *has opened, and fastens again after him.* REGINA *glances hastily at herself in the mirror, dusts herself with her pocket handkerchief, and settles her collar; then she busies herself with the flowers.* PASTOR MANDERS, *in an overcoat, with an umbrella, and with a small travelling-bag on a strap over his shoulder, comes through the garden door into the conservatory.*)

MANDERS: Good morning, Miss Engstrand.

REGINA (*turning round, surprised and pleased*): No, really! Good morning, Pastor Manders. Is the steamer in already?

MANDERS: It's just in. (*Enters the sitting-room.*) Terrible weather we've been having lately.

REGINA (*follows him*): It's such blessed weather for the country, sir.

MANDERS: Yes, you're quite right. We townspeople think too little about that. (*He begins to take off his overcoat.*)

REGINA: Oh, mayn't I help you? There! Why, how wet it is! I'll just hang it up in the hall. And your umbrella, too—I'll open it and let it dry.

(*She goes out with the things through the second door on the right.* PASTOR MANDERS *takes off his travelling-bag and lays it and his hat on a chair. Meanwhile* REGINA *comes in again.*)

MANDERS: Ah! it's a comfort to get safe under cover. Everything going on well here?

REGINA: Yes, thank you, sir.

MANDERS: You have your hands full, I suppose, in preparation for to-morrow?

REGINA: Yes, there's plenty to do, of course.

MANDERS: And Mrs. Alving is at home, I trust?

REGINA: Oh dear, yes. She's just upstairs looking after the young master's chocolate.

MANDERS: Yes, by-the-bye—I heard down at the pier that Oswald had arrived.

REGINA: Yes, he came the day before yesterday. We didn't expect him before to-day.

MANDERS: Quite strong and well, I hope?

REGINA: Yes, thank you, quite; but dreadfully tired with the journey. He has made one rush all the way from Paris. I believe he came the whole way in one train. He's sleeping a little now, I think; so perhaps we'd better talk a little quietly.

MANDERS: Hush!—as quietly as you please.

REGINA (*arranging an arm-chair beside the table*): Now, do sit down, Pastor Manders, and make yourself comfortable. (*He sits down; she put a footstool under his feet.*) There! are you comfortable now, sir?

MANDERS: Thanks, thanks, I'm most comfortable. (*Looks at her.*) Do you know, Miss Engstrand, I positively believe you've grown since I last saw you.

REGINA: Do you think so, sir? Mrs. Alving says my figure has developed too.

MANDERS: Developed? Well, perhaps a little; just enough. (*Short pause.*)

REGINA: Shall I tell Mrs. Alving you are here?

MANDERS: Thanks, thanks, there's no hurry, my dear child. By-the-bye, Regina, my good girl, just tell me: how is your father getting on out here?

REGINA: Oh, thank you, he's getting on well enough.

MANDERS: He called upon me last time he was in town.

REGINA: Did he, indeed? He's always so glad of a chance of talking to you, sir.

MANDERS: And you often look in upon him at his work, I daresay?

REGINA: I? Oh, of course, when I have time, I—

MANDERS: Your father is not a man of strong character, Miss Engstrand. He stands terribly in need of a guiding hand.

REGINA: Oh, yes; I daresay he does.

MANDERS: He needs to have some one near him whom he cares for, and whose judgment he respects. He frankly admitted that when he last came to see me.

REGINA: Yes, he mentioned something of the sort to me. But I don't know whether Mrs. Alving can spare me; especially now that we've got the new Orphanage to attend to. And then I should be so sorry to leave Mrs. Alving; she has always been so kind to me.

MANDERS: But a daughter's duty, my good girl— Of course we must first get your mistress' consent.

REGINA: But I don't know whether it would be quite proper for me, at my age, to keep house for a single man.

MANDERS: What! My dear Miss Engstrand! When the man is your own father!

REGINA: Yes, that may be; but all the same— Now if it were in a thoroughly respectable house, and with a real gentleman—

MANDERS: But, my dear Regina—

REGINA: —one I could love and respect, and be a daughter to—

MANDERS: Yes, but my dear, good child—

REGINA: Then I should be glad to go to town. It's very lonely out here; you know yourself, sir, what it is to be alone in the world. And I can assure you I'm both quick and willing. Don't you know of any such place for me, sir?

MANDERS: I? No, certainly not.

REGINA: But, dear, dear sir, do remember me if—

MANDERS (*rising*): Yes, yes, certainly, Miss Engstrand.

REGINA: For if I—

MANDERS: Will you be so good as to fetch your mistress?

REGINA: I will, at once, sir. (*She goes out to the left.*)

MANDERS (*paces the room two or three times, stands a moment in the background with his hands behind his back, and looks out over the garden. Then he returns to the table, takes up a book, and looks at the title-page; starts, and looks at several*): Hm—indeed!

(MRS. ALVING *enters by the door on the left; she is followed by* REGINA, *who immediately goes out by the first door on the right.*)

MRS. ALVING (*holds out her hand*): Welcome, my dear Pastor.

MANDERS: How do you do, Mrs. Alving? Here I am as I promised.

MRS. ALVING: Always punctual to the minute.

MANDERS: You may believe it wasn't so easy for me to get away. With all the Boards and Committees I belong to—

MRS. ALVING: That makes it all the kinder of you to come so early. Now we can get through our business before dinner. But where's your luggage?

MANDERS (*quickly*): I left it down at the inn. I shall sleep there to-night.

MRS ALVING (*suppressing a smile*): Are you really not to be persuaded, even now, to pass the night under my roof?

MANDERS: No, no, Mrs. Alving; many thanks. I shall stay down there as usual. It's so convenient for starting again.

MRS. ALVING: Well, you must have your own way. But I really should have thought we two old people—

MANDERS: Now you're making fun of me. Ah! you're naturally in great spirits to-day—what between to-morrow's festival and Oswald's return.

MRS. ALVING: Yes; you can think what a delight it is to me! It's more than two years since he was home last. And now he has promised to stay with me all winter.

MANDERS: Has he really? That's very nice and dutiful of him. For I can well believe that life in Rome and Paris has far more attractions.

MRS. ALVING: True. But here he has his mother, you see. My own darling boy, he hasn't forgotten his old mother!

MANDERS: It would be grievous indeed, if absence and absorption in art and that sort of thing were to blunt his natural feelings.

MRS. ALVING: Yes, you may well say so. But there's nothing of that sort to fear in him. I'm quite curious to see whether you'll know him again. He'll be down presently; he's upstairs just now, resting a little on the sofa. But do sit down, my dear Pastor.

MANDERS: Thank you. Are you quite at liberty—?

MRS. ALVING: Certainly. (*She sits by the table.*)

MANDERS: Very well. Then you shall see—(*He goes to the*

chair where his travelling-bag lies, takes out a packet of papers, sits down on the opposite side of the table, and tries to find a clear space for the papers.) Now, to begin with, here is—(*breaking off*)—Tell me, Mrs. Alving, how do these books come here?

MRS. ALVING: These books? They are books I am reading.

MANDERS: Do you read this sort of literature?

MRS. ALVING: Certainly I do.

MANDERS: Do you feel better or happier for reading of this kind?

MRS. ALVING: I feel, so to speak, more secure.

MANDERS: That's strange. How do you mean?

MRS. ALVING: Well, I seem to find explanation and confirmation of all sorts of things I myself have been thinking. For that's the wonderful part of it, Pastor Manders; there's really nothing new in those books, nothing but what most people think and believe. Only most people either don't formulate it to themselves, or else keep quiet about it.

MANDERS: Great heavens! Do you really believe that most people—?

MRS. ALVING: I do, indeed.

MANDERS: But surely not in this country? Not here, among us?

MRS. ALVING: Yes, certainly, among us too.

MANDERS: Well, I really must say—!

MRS. ALVING: For the rest, what do you object to in these books?

MANDERS: Object to in them? You surely don't suppose that I have nothing to do but study such productions as these?

MRS. ALVING: That is to say, you know nothing of what you are condemning.

MANDERS: I have read enough *about* these writings to disapprove of them.

MRS. ALVING: Yes; but your own opinion—

MANDERS: My dear Mrs. Alving, there are many occasions in life when one must rely upon others. Things are so ordered in this world; and it's well that they are. How could society get on otherwise?

MRS. ALVING: Well, I daresay you're right there.

MANDERS: Besides, I of course don't deny that there may be much that is interesting in such books. Nor can I blame you for wishing to keep up with the intellectual movements that are said to be going on in the great world, where you have let your son pass so much of his life. But—

MRS. ALVING: But?

MANDERS (*lowering his voice*): But one shouldn't talk about it, Mrs. Alving. One is certainly not bound to account to everybody for what one reads and thinks within one's own four walls.

MRS. ALVING: Of course not; I quite think so.

MANDERS: Only think, now, how you are bound to consider the interests of this Orphanage which you decided on founding at a time when you thought very differently on spiritual matters—so far as I can judge.

MRS. ALVING: Oh yes; I quite admit that. But it was about the Orphanage—

MANDERS: It was about the Orphanage we were to speak; yes. All I say is: prudence, my dear lady! And now we'll get to business. (*Opens the packet, and takes out a number of papers.*) Do you see these?

MRS. ALVING: The documents?

MANDERS: All—and in perfect order. I can tell you it was hard work to get them in time. I had to put on strong pressure. The authorities are almost painfully scrupulous when you want them to come to the point. But here they are at last. (*Looks through the bundle.*) See! here is the formal deed of gift of the parcel of ground known as Solvik in the Manor of Rosenvold, with all the newly-constructed buildings, schoolrooms, master's house, and chapel. And here is the legal fiat for the endowment and for the Regulations of the Institution. Will you look at them? (*Reads*) "Regulation for the Children's Home to be known as 'Captain Alving's Foundation.' "

MRS. ALVING (*looks long at the paper*): So there it is.

MANDERS: I have chosen the designation "Captain" rather than "Chamberlain." "Captain" looks less pretentious.

MRS. ALVING: Oh, yes; just as you think best.

MANDERS: And here you have the Bank Account of the capital lying at interest to cover the current expenses of the Orphanage.

MRS. ALVING: Thank you; but please keep it—it will be more convenient.

MANDERS: With pleasure. I think we will leave the money in the Bank for the present. The interest is certainly not what we could wish—four per cent. and six months' notice of withdrawal. If a good mortgage could be found later on—of course it must be a first mortgage and an undoubted security—then we could consider the matter.

MRS. ALVING: Certainly, my dear Pastor Manders. You are the best judge in these things.

MANDERS: I will keep my eyes open at any rate. But now

there's one thing more which I have several times been intending to ask you.

MRS. ALVING: And what's that?

MANDERS: Shall the Orphanage buildings be insured or not?

MRS. ALVING: Of course they must be insured.

MANDERS: Well, stop a minute, Mrs. Alving. Let us look into the matter a little more closely.

MRS. ALVING: I have everything insured; buildings and movables and stock and crops.

MANDERS: Of course you have—on your own estate. And so have I—of course. But here, you see, it's quite another matter. The Orphanage is to be consecrated, as it were, to a higher purpose.

MRS. ALVING: Yes, but that's no reason—

MANDERS: For my own part, I should not see the smallest impropriety in guarding against all contingencies—

MRS. ALVING: No, I should think not.

MANDERS: But what is the general feeling in the neighbourhood? You, of course, know better than I.

MRS. ALVING: Hm—the general feeling—

MANDERS: Is there any considerable number of people—really responsible people—who might be scandalised?

MRS. ALVING: What do you mean by "really responsible people"?

MANDERS: Well, I mean people in such independent and influential positions that one cannot help allowing some weight to their opinions.

MRS. ALVING: There are several people of that sort here, who would very likely be shocked if—

MANDERS: There, you see! In town we have many such people. Think of all my colleague's adherents! People would be only too ready to interpret our action as a sign that neither you nor I had the right faith in a Higher Providence.

MRS. ALVING: But for your own part, my dear Pastor, you can at least tell yourself that—

MANDERS: Yes, I know—I know; my conscience would be quite easy, that is true enough. But nevertheless we should not escape grave misinterpretation; and that might very likely react unfavourably upon the Orphanage.

MRS. ALVING: Well, in that case, then—

MANDERS: Nor can I lose sight of the difficult—I may even say painful—position *I* might perhaps get into. In the leading circles of the town people are much taken up about this Orphanage. It is, of course, founded partly for the benefit of the town, as well; and it is to be hoped it will, to a considerable extent, result in lightening our Poor Rates. Now, as I have been your adviser, and have had the business matters in my hands, I cannot but fear that I may have to bear the brunt of fanaticism.

MRS. ALVING: Oh, you mustn't run the risk of that.

MANDERS: To say nothing of the attacks that would assuredly be made upon me in certain papers and periodicals, which—

MRS. ALVING: Enough, my dear Pastor Manders. That consideration is quite decisive.

MANDERS: Then you do not wish the Orphanage insured?

MRS. ALVING: No. We'll let it alone.

MANDERS (*leaning back in his chair*): But if a disaster were to happen?—one can never tell. Would you be able to make good the damage?

MRS. ALVING: No; I tell you plainly I should do nothing of the kind.

MANDERS: Then I must tell you, Mrs. Alving, we are taking no small responsibility upon ourselves.

MRS. ALVING: Do you think we can do otherwise?

MANDERS: No, that's just the thing; we really cannot do otherwise. We must not expose ourselves to misinterpretation; and we have no right whatever to give offence to our neighbours.

MRS. ALVING: You, as a clergyman, certainly should not.

MANDERS: I really think, too, we may trust that such an institution has fortune on its side; in fact, that it stands under a Special Providence.

MRS. ALVING: Let us hope so, Pastor Manders.

MANDERS: Then we'll let the matter alone.

MRS. ALVING: Yes, certainly.

MANDERS: Very well. Just as you think best. (*Makes a note.*) Then—no insurance.

MRS. ALVING: It's rather curious that you should just happen to mention the matter to-day.

MANDERS: I have often thought of asking you about it—

MRS. ALVING: —for we very nearly had a fire down there yesterday.

MANDERS: You don't say so!

MRS. ALVING: Oh, it was of no importance. A heap of shavings had caught fire in the carpenter's workshop.

MANDERS: Where Engstrand works?

MRS. ALVING: Yes. They say he's often very careless with matches.

MANDERS: He has so many things in his head, that man—so many temptations. Thank God, he's now striving to lead a decent life, I hear.

MRS. ALVING: Indeed! Who says so?

MANDERS: He himself assures me of it. And he's certainly a capital workman.

MRS. ALVING: Oh, yes; so long as he's sober.

MANDERS: Yes, that's a sad weakness. But he's often driven to it by his bad leg, he says. Last time he was in town I was really touched by him. He came and thanked me so warmly for having got him work here, so that he might be near Regina.

MRS. ALVING: He doesn't see much of *her*.

MANDERS: Oh, yes; he has a talk with her every day. He told me so himself.

MRS. ALVING: Well, it may be so.

MANDERS: He feels so acutely that he needs some one to hold him back when temptation comes. That's what I can't help liking about Jacob Engstrand; he comes to you helplessly, accusing himself and confessing his own weakness. The last time he was talking to me— Believe me, Mrs. Alving, supposing it were a real necessity for him to have Regina home again—

MRS. ALVING (*rising hastily*): Regina!

MANDERS: —you must not set yourself against it.

MRS. ALVING: Indeed I shall set myself against it! And besides—Regina is to have a position in the Orphanage.

MANDERS: But, after all, remember he's her father—

MRS. ALVING: Oh! I know best what sort of a father he has been to her. No! she shall never go to him with my goodwill.

MANDERS (*rising*): My dear lady, don't take the matter so warmly. You misjudge Engstrand sadly. You seem to be quite terrified—

MRS. ALVING (*more quietly*): It makes no difference. I have taken Regina into my house, and there she shall stay. (*Listens.*) Hush, my dear Mr. Manders; don't say any more about it. (*Her face lights up with gladness.*) Listen! there's Oswald coming downstairs. Now we'll think of no one but him.

(OSWALD ALVING, *in a light overcoat, hat in hand and smoking a large meerschaum, enters through the door on the left; he stops in the doorway.*)

OSWALD: Oh! I beg your pardon; I thought you were in the study. (*Comes forward.*) Good-morning, Pastor Manders.

MANDERS (*staring*): Ah—! How strange—!

MRS. ALVING: Well now, what do you think of him, Mr. Manders?

MANDERS: I—I—can it really be—?

OSWALD: Yes, it's really the Prodigal Son, sir.

MANDERS (*protesting*): My dear young friend—!

OSWALD: Well, then, the Reclaimed Son.

MRS. ALVING: Oswald remembers how much you were opposed to his becoming a painter.

MANDERS: To our human eyes many a step seems dubious which afterwards proves—(*wrings his hands*). Anyhow, welcome, welcome home. Why, my dear Oswald—I suppose I may call you by your Christian name?

OSWALD: What else should you call me?

MANDERS: Very good. What I wanted to say was this, my dear Oswald—you mustn't believe that I utterly condemn the artist's calling. I have no doubt there are many who can keep their inner self unharmed in that profession, as in any other.

OSWALD: Let us hope so.

MRS. ALVING (*beaming with delight*): I know one who has kept both his inner and outer self unharmed. Just look at him, Mr. Manders.

OSWALD (*moves restlessly about the room*). Yes, yes, my dear mother; let's say no more about it.

MANDERS: Why, certainly—that's undeniable. And you have begun to make a name for yourself already. The newspapers have often spoken of you, most favourably. By-the-bye, just lately they haven't mentioned you so often, I fancy.

OSWALD (*up in the conservatory*): I haven't been able to paint so much lately.

MRS. ALVING: Even a painter needs a little rest now and then.

MANDERS: I can quite believe it. And meanwhile he can be gathering his forces for some great work.

OSWALD: Yes—Mother, will dinner soon be ready?

MRS. ALVING: In less than half-an-hour. He has a capital appetite, thank God.

MANDERS: And a taste for tobacco, too.

OSWALD: I found my father's pipe in my room, and so—

MANDERS: Aha! then that accounts for it.

MRS. ALVING: For what?

MANDERS: When Oswald stood there, in the doorway, with the pipe in his mouth, I could have sworn I saw his father, large as life.

OSWALD: No, really?

MRS. ALVING: Oh! how can you say so? Oswald takes after me.

MANDERS: Yes, but there's an expression about the corners of the mouth—something about the lips that reminds one exactly of Alving; at any rate, now that he's smoking.

MRS. ALVING: Not in the least. Oswald has rather a clerical curve about his mouth, I think.

MANDERS: Yes, yes; some of my colleagues have much the same expression.

MRS. ALVING: But put your pipe away, my dear boy; I won't have smoking in here.

OSWALD (*does so*): By all means. I only wanted to try it; for I once smoked it when I was a child.

MRS. ALVING: You?

OSWALD: Yes. I was quite small at the time. I recollect I came up to father's room one evening when he was in great spirits.

MRS. ALVING: Oh, you can't recollect anything of those times.

OSWALD: Yes, I recollect distinctly. He took me up on his knees, and gave me the pipe. "Smoke, boy," he said; "smoke away, boy." And I smoked as hard as I could, until I felt I was growing quite pale, and the perspiration stood in great drops on my forehead. Then he burst out laughing heartily—

MANDERS: That was most extraordinary.

MRS. ALVING: My dear friend, it's only something Oswald has dreamt.

OSWALD: No, mother, I assure you I didn't dream it. For—don't you remember *this*?—you came and carried me out into the nursery. Then I was sick, and I saw that you were crying.—Did father often play such pranks?

MANDERS: In his youth he overflowed with the joy of life—[1]

OSWALD: And yet he managed to do so much in the world; so much that was good and useful; and he died so young, too.

MANDERS: Yes, you have inherited the name of an active and worthy man, my dear Oswald Alving. No doubt it will be an incentive to you—

OSWALD: It ought to, indeed.

MANDERS: It was good of you to come home for the ceremony in his honour.

OSWALD: I could do no less for my father.

MRS. ALVING: And I am to keep him so long! That's the best of all.

MANDERS: You're going to pass the winter at home, I hear.

OSWALD: My stay is indefinite, sir. But, oh! how delightful it is to be at home again!

MRS. ALVING (*beaming*): Yes, isn't it?

MANDERS (*looking sympathetically at him*): You went out into the world early, my dear Oswald.

[1]"Var en særdeles livsglad mand"—literally, "was a man who took the greatest pleasure in life," *la joie de vivre*—an expression which frequently recurs in this play.

OSWALD: I did. I sometimes wonder whether it wasn't *too* early.

MRS. ALVING: Oh, not at all. A healthy lad is all the better for it; especially when he's an only child. He oughtn't to hang on at home with his mother and father and get spoilt.

MANDERS: It's a very difficult question, Mrs. Alving. A child's proper place is, and must be, the home of his fathers.

OSWALD: There I quite agree with you, Pastor Manders.

MANDERS: Only look at your own son—there's no reason why we shouldn't say it in his presence—what has the consequence been for him? He's six or seven and twenty, and has never had the opportunity of learning what home life really is.

OSWALD: I beg your pardon, Pastor; there you're quite mistaken.

MANDERS: Indeed? I thought you had lived almost exclusively in artistic circles.

OSWALD: So I have.

MANDERS: And chiefly among the younger artists.

OSWALD: Yes, certainly.

MANDERS: But I thought few of these young fellows could afford to set up house and support a family.

OSWALD: There are many who can't afford to marry, sir.

MANDERS: Yes, that's just what I say.

OSWALD: But they can have a home for all that. And several of them have, as a matter of fact; and very pleasant, comfortable homes they are, too.

(MRS ALVING *follows with breathless interest; nods, but says nothing.*)

MANDERS: But I am not talking of bachelors' quarters. By a "home" I understand the home of a family, where a man lives with his wife and children.

OSWALD: Yes; or with his children and his children's mother.

MANDERS (*starts; clasps his hands*): But, good heavens—!

OSWALD: Well?

MANDERS: Lives with—his children's mother!

OSWALD: Yes. Would you have him turn his children's mother out of doors?

MANDERS: Then it's illicit relations you are talking of! Irregular marriages, as people call them!

OSWALD: I have never noticed anything particularly irregular about the life these people lead.

MANDERS: But how is it possible that a—a young man or young woman with any decent principles can endure to live in that way?—in the eyes of all the world!

OSWALD: What are they to do? A poor young artist—a poor girl—it costs a lot to get married. What are they to do?

MANDERS: What are they to do? Let me tell you, Mr. Alving, what they ought to do. They ought to exercise self-restraint from the first; that's what they ought to do.

OSWALD: Such talk won't go far with warm-blooded young people, over head and ears in love.

MRS. ALVING: No, it wouldn't go far.

MANDERS (*continuing*): How can the authorities tolerate such things? Allow them to go on in the light of day? (*To* MRS. ALVING) Had I not cause to be deeply concerned about your son? In circles where open immorality prevails, and has even a sort of prestige—!

OSWALD: Let me tell you, sir, that I have been a constant Sunday-guest in one or two such irregular homes—

MANDERS: On Sunday of all days!

OSWALD: Isn't that the day to enjoy oneself? Well, never have I heard an offensive word, and still less have I witnessed anything that could be called immoral. No; do you know when and where I have come across immorality in artistic circles?

MANDERS: No, thank heaven, I don't!

OSWALD: Well, then, allow me to inform you. I have met with it when one or other of our pattern husbands and fathers has come to Paris to have a look round on his own account, and has done the artists the honour of visiting their humble haunts. *They* knew what was what. These gentlemen could tell us all about places and things we had never dreamt of.

MANDERS: What! Do you mean to say that respectable men from home here would—?

OSWALD: Have you never heard these respectable men, when they got home again, talking about the way in which immorality was running rampant abroad?

MANDERS: Yes, of course.

MRS. ALVING: I have too.

OSWALD: Well, you may take their word for it. They know what they're talking about! (*Presses his hands to his head.*) Oh! that that great, free, glorious life out there should be defiled in such a way!

MRS. ALVING: You mustn't get excited, Oswald. You will do yourself harm.

OSWALD: Yes; you're quite right, mother. It's not good for me. You see, I'm wretchedly worn out. I'll go for a little turn before dinner. Excuse me, Pastor; I know you can't take my point of view; but I couldn't help speaking out.

(*He goes out through the second door to the right.*)

MRS. ALVING: My poor boy!

MANDERS: You may well say so. Then that's what he has come to!

(MRS ALVING *looks at him silently.*)

MANDERS (*walking up and down*): He called himself the Prodigal Son—alas! alas!

(MRS. ALVING *continues looking at him.*)

MANDERS: And what do you say to all this?

MRS. ALVING: I say that Oswald was right in every word.

MANDERS (*stands still*): Right! Right! In such principles?

MRS. ALVING: Here, in my loneliness, I have come to the same way of thinking, Pastor Manders. But I've never dared to say anything. Well! now my boy shall speak for me.

MANDERS: You are much to be pitied, Mrs. Alving. But now I must speak seriously to you. And now it is no longer your business manager and adviser, your own and your late husband's early friend, who stands before you. It is the priest—the priest who stood before you in the moment of your life when you had gone most astray.

MRS. ALVING: And what has the priest to say to me?

MANDERS: I will first stir up your memory a little. The time is well chosen. To-morrow will be the tenth anniversary of your husband's death. To-morrow the memorial in his honour will be unveiled. To-morrow I shall have to speak to the whole assembled multitude. But to-day I will speak to you alone.

MRS. ALVING: Very well, Pastor Manders. Speak.

MANDERS: Do you remember that after less than a year of married life you stood on the verge of an abyss? That you forsook your house and home? That you fled from your husband? Yes, Mrs. Alving—fled, fled, and refused to return to him, however much he begged and prayed you?

MRS. ALVING: Have you forgotten how infinitely miserable I was in that first year?

MANDERS: It is only the spirit of rebellion that craves for happiness in this life. What right have we human beings to happiness? No, we have to do our duty! And your duty was to hold firmly to the man you had once chosen and to whom you were bound by a holy tie.

MRS. ALVING: You know very well what sort of life Alving was leading—what excesses he was guilty of.

MANDERS: I know very well what rumours there were about him, and I am the last to approve the life he led in his young days, if report did not wrong him. But a wife is not to be her husband's judge. It was your duty to bear with humility the cross which a Higher Power had, for your own good, laid upon you. But instead of that you rebelliously throw away the cross, desert the backslider whom you should have supported, go and risk your good name and reputation, and—nearly succeed in ruining other people's reputation into the bargain.

MRS. ALVING: Other people's? One other person's, you mean.

MANDERS: It was incredibly reckless of you to seek refuge with me.

MRS. ALVING: With our clergyman? With our intimate friend?

MANDERS: Just on that account. Yes, you may thank God that I possessed the necessary firmness; that I dissuaded you from your wild designs; and that it was vouchsafed me to lead you back to the path of duty, and home to your lawful husband.

MRS. ALVING: Yes, Pastor Manders, it was certainly your work.

MANDERS: I was but a poor instrument in a Higher Hand. And what a blessing has it not been to you, all the days of your life, that I got you to resume the yoke of duty and obedience! Did not everything happen as I foretold? Did not Alving turn his back on his errors, as a man should? Did he not live with you from that time, lovingly and blamelessly, all his days? Did he not become a benefactor to the whole district? And did he not raise you up to him, so that you little by little became his assistant in all his undertakings? And a capital assistant, too—Oh! I know, Mrs. Alving, that praise is due to you. But now I come to the next great error in your life.

MRS. ALVING: What do you mean?

MANDERS: Just as you once disowned a wife's duty, so you have since disowned a mother's.

MRS. ALVING: Ah!

MANDERS: You have been all your life under the dominion of a pestilent spirit of self-will. All your efforts have been bent towards emancipation and lawlessness. You have never known how to endure any bond. Everything that has weighed upon you in life you have cast away without care or conscience, like a burden you could throw off at will. It did not please you to be a wife any longer, and you left your husband. You found it troublesome to be a mother, and you sent your child forth among strangers.

MRS. ALVING: Yes. That is true. I did so.

MANDERS: And thus you have become a stranger to him.

MRS. ALVING: No! no! I am not.

MANDERS: Yes, you are; you must be. And how have you got him back again? Bethink yourself well, Mrs. Alving. You have sinned greatly against your husband;—that you recognise by raising yonder memorial to him. Recognise now, also, how you have sinned against your son. There may be time to lead him back from the paths of error. Turn back yourself, and save what may yet be saved in him. For (*with uplifted forefinger*) verily, Mrs. Alving, you are a guilt-laden mother!—This I have thought it my duty to say to you. (*Silence.*)

MRS. ALVING (*slowly and with self-control*): You have now spoken out, Pastor Manders; and to-morrow you are to speak publicly in memory of my husband. I shall not speak to-morrow. But now I will speak frankly to you, as you have spoken to me.

MANDERS: To be sure; you will plead excuses for your conduct—

MRS. ALVING: No. I will only narrate.

MANDERS: Well?

MRS. ALVING: All that you have just said about me and my husband and our life after you had brought me back to the path of duty—as you called it—about all that you know nothing from personal observation. From that moment you, who had been our intimate friend, never set foot in our house again.

MANDERS: You and your husband left the town immediately after.

MRS. ALVING: Yes; and in my husband's lifetime you never came to see us. It was business that forced you to visit me when you undertook the affairs of the Orphanage.

MANDERS (*softly and uncertainly*): Helen—if that is meant as a reproach, I would beg you to bear in mind—

MRS. ALVING: —the regard you owed to your position, yes; and that I was a runaway wife. One can never be too careful with such unprincipled creatures.

MANDERS: My dear—Mrs. Alving, you know that is an absurd exaggeration—

MRS. ALVING: Well well, suppose it is. My point is that your judgment as to my married life is founded upon nothing but current gossip.

MANDERS: Well, I admit that. What then?

MRS. ALVING: Well, then, Mr. Manders—I will tell you the truth. I have sworn to myself that one day you should know it—you alone!

MANDERS: What is the truth, then?

MRS. ALVING: The truth is that my husband died just as dissolute as he had lived all his days.

MANDERS (*feeling after a chair*): What do you say?

MRS. ALVING: After nineteen years of marriage, as dissolute—in his desires at any rate—as he was before you married us.

MANDERS: And those—those wild oats, those irregularities, those excesses, if you like, you call "a dissolute life"?

MRS. ALVING: Our doctor used the expression.

MANDERS: I don't understand you.

MRS. ALVING: You need not.

MANDERS: It almost makes me dizzy. Your whole married life, the seeming union of all these years, was nothing more than a hidden abyss!

MRS. ALVING: Nothing more. Now you know it.

MANDERS: This is—it will take me long to accustom myself to the thought. I can't grasp it! I can't realise it! But how was it possible to—? How could such a state of things be kept dark?

MRS. ALVING: That has been my ceaseless struggle, day after day. After Oswald's birth, I thought Alving seemed to be a little better. But it didn't last long. And then I had to struggle twice as hard, fighting for life or death, so that nobody should know what sort of a man my child's father was. And you know what power Alving had of winning people's hearts. Nobody seemed able to believe anything but good of him. He was one of those people whose life does not bite upon their reputation. But at last, Mr. Manders—for you must know the whole story—the most repulsive thing of all happened.

MANDERS: More repulsive than the rest?

MRS. ALVING: I had gone on bearing with him, although I knew very well the secrets of his life out of doors. But when he brought the scandal within our own walls—

MANDERS: Impossible! Here!

MRS. ALVING: Yes; here in our own home. It was there (*pointing towards the first door on the right*), in the dining-room, that I first got to know of it. I was busy with something in there, and the door was standing ajar. I heard our housemaid come up from the garden, with water for those flowers.

MANDERS: Well—?

MRS. ALVING: Soon after I heard Alving come too. I heard him say something softly to her. And then I heard—(*with a short laugh*)—oh! it still sounds in my ears, so hateful and yet so ludicrous—I heard my own servant-maid whisper, "Let me go, Mr. Alving! Let me be."

MANDERS: What unseemly levity on his part! But it cannot have been more then levity, Mrs. Alving; believe me, it cannot.

MRS. ALVING: I soon knew what to believe. Mr. Alving had his way with the girl; and that connection had consequences, Mr. Manders.

MANDERS (*as though petrified*): Such things in this house! in this house!

MRS. ALVING: I had borne a great deal in this house. To keep him at home in the evenings—and at night—I had to make myself his boon companion in his secret orgies up in his room. There I have had to sit alone with him, to clink glasses and drink with him, and to listen to his ribald, silly talk. I have had to fight with him to get him dragged to bed—

MANDERS (*moved*): And you were able to bear all that?

MRS. ALVING: I had to bear it for my little boy's sake. But when the last insult was added; when my own servant-maid—Then I swore to myself: This shall come to an end. And so I took the reins into my own hand—the whole control over him and everything else. For now I had a weapon against him, you see; he dared not oppose me. It was then I sent Oswald from home. He was in his seventh year, and was beginning to observe and ask questions, as children do. That I could not bear. It seemed to me the child must be poisoned by merely breathing the air of this polluted home. That was why I sent him away. And now you can see, too, why he was never allowed to set foot inside his home so long as his father lived. No one knows what it has cost me.

MANDERS: You have indeed had a life of trial.

MRS. ALVING: I could never have borne it if I hadn't had my work. For I may truly say that I have worked! All those additions to the estate—all the improvements—all the useful appliances, that won Alving such general praise—do you suppose *he* had energy for anything of the sort?—he who lay all day on the sofa and read an old court guide! No; this I will tell you too: it was I who urged him on when he had his better intervals; it was I who had to drag the whole load when he relapsed into his evil ways, or sank into querulous wretchedness.

MANDERS: And to that man you raise a memorial?

MRS. ALVING: There you see the power of an evil conscience.

MANDERS: Evil—? What do you mean?

MRS. ALVING: It always seemed to me impossible but that the truth must come out and be believed. So the Asylum was to deaden all rumours and banish doubt.

MANDERS: In that you have certainly not missed your aim, Mrs. Alving.

MRS. ALVING: And besides, I had one other reason. I did not wish that Oswald, my own boy, should inherit anything whatever from his father.

MANDERS: Then it is Alving's fortune that—?

MRS. ALVING: Yes. The sums I have spent upon the Orphanage, year by year, make up the amount—I have reckoned it up precisely—the amount which made Lieutenant Alving a good match in his day.

MANDERS: I don't quite understand—

MRS. ALVING: It was my purchase-money. I do not choose that that money should pass into Oswald's hands. My son shall have everything from me—everything. (OSWALD ALVING *enters through the second door to the right; he has taken off his hat and overcoat in the hall.* MRS. ALVING *goes towards him.*) Are you back again already? my dear, dear boy!

OSWALD: Yes. What can a fellow do out of doors in this eternal rain? But I hear dinner's ready. That's capital!

REGINA (*with a parcel, from the dining-room*): A parcel has come for you, Mrs. Alving. (*Hands it to her.*)

MRS. ALVING (*with a glance at* MR. MANDERS): No doubt copies of the ode for to-morrow's ceremony.

MANDERS: Hm—

REGINA: And dinner is ready.

MRS. ALVING: Very well. We'll come directly. I'll just—(*Begins to open the parcel.*)

REGINA (*to* OSWALD): Would Mr. Alving like red or white wine?

OSWALD: Both, if you please.

REGINA: *Bien.* Very well, sir. (*She goes into the dining-room.*)

OSWALD: I may as well help to uncork it. (*He also goes into the dining-room, the door of which swings half open behind him.*)

MRS. ALVING (*who has opened the parcel*): Yes, as I thought. Here is the Ceremonial Ode, Pastor Manders.

MANDERS (*with folded hands*): With what countenance I'm to deliver my discourse to-morrow—!

MRS. ALVING: Oh! you'll get through it somehow.

MANDERS (*softly, so as not to be heard in the dining-room*): Yes; it would not do to provoke scandal.

MRS. ALVING (*under her breath, but firmly*): No. But then this long, hateful comedy will be ended. From the day after to-morrow it shall be for me as though he who is dead had never lived in this house. No one shall be here but my boy and his mother. (*From within the dining-room comes the noise of a chair overturned, and at the same moment is heard*):

REGINA (*sharply, but whispering*): Oswald! take care! are you mad? Let me go!

MRS. ALVING (*starts in terror*): Ah!

(*She stares wildly towards the half-opened door.* OSWALD *is heard coughing and humming. A bottle is uncorked.*)

MANDERS (*excited*): What in the world is the matter? What is it, Mrs. Alving?

MRS. ALVING (*hoarsely*): Ghosts! The couple from the conservatory—risen again!

MANDERS: What! Is it possible! Regina—? Is she—?

MRS. ALVING: Yes. Come. Not another word!

(*She seizes* MR. MANDERS *by the arm, and walks unsteadily towards the dining-room.*)

ACT II

(*The same room. The mist still lies heavy over the landscape.* MANDERS *and* MRS. ALVING *enter from the dining-room.*)

MRS. ALVING (*still in the doorway*): Hearty appetite, Mr. Manders. (*Turns back towards the dining-room.*) Aren't you coming too, Oswald?

OSWALD (*from within*): No, thank you. I think I shall go out a little.

MRS. ALVING: Yes, do. The weather seems brighter now. (*She shuts the dining-room door, goes to the hall door, and calls:*) Regina!

REGINA (*outside*): Yes, Mrs. Alving.

MRS. ALVING: Go down to the laundry, and help with the garlands.

REGINA: I'll go directly, Mrs. Alving.

(MRS. ALVING *assures herself that* REGINA *goes; then shuts the door.*)

MANDERS: I suppose he can't overhear us in there?

MRS. ALVING: Not when the door is shut. Besides, he's just going out.

MANDERS: I'm still quite upset. I can't think how I could get down a morsel of dinner.

MRS. ALVING (*controlling her nervousness, walks up and down*): No more can I. But what's to be done now?

MANDERS: Yes; what's to be done? Upon my honour, I don't know. I'm so utterly without experience in matters of this sort.

MRS. ALVING: I'm quite convinced that, so far, no mischief has been done.

MANDERS: No; heaven forbid! But it's an unseemly state of things, nevertheless.

MRS. ALVING: The whole thing is an idle fancy of Oswald's; you may be sure of that.

MANDERS: Well, as I say, I'm not accustomed to affairs of the kind. But I should certainly think—

MRS. ALVING: Out of the house she must go, and that immediately. That's as clear as daylight.

MANDERS: Yes, of course she must.

MRS. ALVING: But where to? It would not be right to—

MANDERS: Where to? Home to her father, of course.

MRS. ALVING: To whom did you say?

MANDERS: To her— But then, Engstrand is not—? Good God, Mrs. Alving, it's impossible! You must be mistaken after all.

MRS. ALVING: Alas! I'm mistaken in nothing. Johanna confessed all to me, and Alving could not deny it. So there was nothing to be done but to get the matter hushed up.

MANDERS: No, you could do nothing else.

MRS. ALVING: The girl left our service at once, and got a good sum of money to hold her tongue for the time. The rest she managed for herself when she got into the town. She renewed her old acquaintance with Engstrand, no doubt gave him to understand how much money she had received, and told him some tale about a foreigner who put in here with a yacht that summer. So she and Engstrand got married in hot haste. Why, you married them yourself.

MANDERS: But then how to account for—? I recollect distinctly Engstrand coming to give notice of the marriage. He was broken down with contrition, and reproached himself so bitterly for the misbehaviour he and his sweetheart had been guilty of.

MRS. ALVING: Yes; of course he had to take the blame upon himself.

MANDERS: But such a piece of duplicity on his part! And towards me too! I never could have believed it of Jacob Engstrand. I shan't fail to give him a serious talking to; he may be sure of that. And then the immorality of such a connection! For money! How much did the girl receive?

MRS. ALVING: Three hundred dollars.

MANDERS: There! think of that! for a miserable three hundred dollars to go and marry a fallen woman!

MRS. ALVING: Then what have you to say of me? I went and married a fallen man.

MANDERS: But—good heavens!—what are you talking about? A fallen man?

MRS. ALVING: Do you think Alving was any purer when I

went with him to the altar than Johanna was when Engstrand married her?

MANDERS: Well, but there's a world of difference between the two cases—

MRS. ALVING: Not so much difference after all, except in the price—a wretched three hundred dollars and a whole fortune.

MANDERS: How can you compare the two cases? You had taken counsel with your own heart and with your friends.

MRS. ALVING (*without looking at him*): I thought you understood where what you call my heart had strayed to at the time.

MANDERS (*distantly*): Had I understood anything of the kind, I should not have continued a daily guest in your husband's house.

MRS. ALVING: Well, the fact remains that with myself I took no counsel whatever.

MANDERS: Well then, with your nearest relatives—as your duty bade you—with your mother and both your aunts.

MRS. ALVING: Yes, that's true. Those three cast up the account for me. Oh! it's marvellous how clearly they made out that it would be downright madness to refuse such an offer. If mother could only see me now, and know what all that grandeur has come to!

MANDERS: Nobody can be held responsible for the result. This, at least, remains clear: your marriage was in accordance with law and order.

MRS. ALVING (*at the window*): Oh! that perpetual law and order! I often think that's what does all the mischief here in the world.

MANDERS: Mrs. Alving, that is a sinful way of talking.

MRS. ALVING: Well, I can't help it; I can endure all this constraint and cowardice no longer. It's too much for me. I must work my way out to freedom.

MANDERS: What do you mean by that?

MRS. ALVING (*drumming on the window-sill*): I ought never to have concealed the facts of Alving's life. But at that time I was afraid to do anything else—afraid on my own account. I was such a coward.

MANDERS: A coward?

MRS. ALVING: If people had come to know anything, they would have said—"Poor man! with a runaway wife, no wonder he kicks over the traces."

MANDERS: Such remarks might have been made with a certain show of right.

MRS. ALVING (*looking steadily at him*): If I were what I ought to be, I should go to Oswald and say, "Listen, my boy; your father was self-indulgent and vicious—"

MANDERS: Merciful heavens—!

MRS. ALVING: —and then I should tell him all I have told you—every word of it.

MANDERS: The idea is shocking, Mrs. Alving.

MRS. ALVING: Yes; I know that. I know that very well. I'm shocked at it myself. (*Goes away from the window.*) I'm such a coward.

MANDERS: You call it "cowardice" to do your plain duty? Have you forgotten that a son should love and honour his father and mother?

MRS. ALVING: Don't let us talk in such general terms. Let us ask: should Oswald love and honour Chamberlain Alving?

MANDERS: Is there no voice in your mother's heart that forbids you to destroy your son's ideals?

MRS. ALVING: But what about the truth?

MANDERS: But what about the ideals?

MRS. ALVING: Oh! Ideals! Ideals! If only I weren't such a coward!

MANDERS: Do not despise ideals, Mrs. Alving; they will avenge themselves cruelly. Take Oswald's case; he, unfortunately, seems to have few enough ideals as it is; but I can see that his father stands before him as an ideal.

MRS. ALVING. You're right there.

MANDERS: And this habit of mind you have yourself implanted and fostered by your letters.

MRS. ALVING: Yes; in my superstitious awe for Duty and Decency I lied to my boy, year after year. Oh! what a coward, what a coward I've been!

MANDERS: You have established a happy illusion in your son's heart, Mrs. Alving, and assuredly you ought not to undervalue it.

MRS. ALVING: Hm; who knows whether it's so happy after all—? But, at any rate, I won't have any goings-on with Regina. He shan't go and ruin the poor girl.

MANDERS: No; good God! that would be dreadful!

MRS. ALVING: If I knew he was in earnest, and that it would be for his happiness—

MANDERS: What? What then?

MRS. ALVING: But it couldn't be; for I'm sorry to say Regina is not a girl to make him happy.

MANDERS: Well, what then? What do you mean?

MRS. ALVING: If I weren't such a pitiful coward I would say

to him, "Marry her, or make what arrangement you please, only let us have nothing underhand about it."

MANDERS: Good heavens, would you let them *marry*! Anything so dreadful—! so unheard of—!

MRS. ALVING: Do you really mean "unheard of"? Frankly, Pastor Manders, do you suppose that throughout the country there aren't plenty of married couples as closely akin as they?

MANDERS: I don't in the least understand you.

MRS. ALVING: Oh yes, indeed you do.

MANDERS: Ah, you are thinking of the possibility that—Yes, alas! family life is certainly not always so pure as it ought to be. But in such a case as you point to, one can never know—at least with any certainty. Here, on the other hand—that you, a mother, can think of letting your son—!

MRS. ALVING: But I can't—I wouldn't for anything in the world; that's precisely what I am saying.

MANDERS: No, because you are a "coward," as you put it. But if you were not a "coward," then—? Good God! a connection so shocking.

MRS. ALVING: So far as that goes, they say we're all sprung from connections of that sort. And who is it that arranged the world so, Pastor Manders?

MANDERS: Questions of that kind I must decline to discuss with you, Mrs. Alving; you are far from being in the right frame of mind for them. But that you dare to call your scruples "cowardly"—!

MRS. ALVING: Let me tell you what I mean. I am timid and half-hearted because I cannot get rid of the Ghosts that haunt me.

MANDERS: What do you say haunts you?

MRS. ALVING: Ghosts! When I heard Regina and Oswald in there, I seemed to see Ghosts before me. I almost think we're all of us Ghosts, Pastor Manders. It's not only what we have inherited from our father and mother that "walks" in us. It's all sorts of dead ideas, and lifeless old beliefs, and so forth. They have no vitality, but they cling to us all the same, and we can't get rid of them. Whenever I take up a newspaper, I seem to see Ghosts gliding between the lines. There must be Ghosts all the country over, as thick as the sand of the sea. And then we are, one and all, so pitifully afraid of the light.

MANDERS: Ah! here we have the fruits of your reading! And pretty fruits they are, upon my word! Oh! those horrible, revolutionary, free-thinking books!

MRS. ALVING: You are mistaken, my dear Pastor. It was you

yourself who set me thinking; and I thank you for it with all my heart.

MANDERS: I?

MRS. ALVING: Yes—when you forced me under the yoke you called Duty and Obligation; when you praised as right and proper what my whole soul rebelled against as something loathsome. It was then that I began to look into the seams of your doctrine. I wanted only to pick at a single knot; but when I had got that undone, the whole thing ravelled out. And then I understood that it was all machine-sewn.

MANDERS (*softly, with emotion*): And was that the upshot of my life's hardest battle?

MRS. ALVING: Call it rather your most pitiful defeat.

MANDERS: It was my greatest victory, Helen—the victory over myself.

MRS. ALVING: It was a crime against us both.

MANDERS: When you went astray, and came to me crying, "Here I am; take me!" I commanded you, saying, "Woman, go home to your lawful husband." Was that a crime?

MRS. ALVING: Yes, I think so.

MANDERS: We two do not understand each other.

MRS. ALVING: Not now, at any rate.

MANDERS: Never—never in my most secret thoughts have I regarded you otherwise than as another's wife.

MRS. ALVING: Oh!—indeed?

MANDERS: Helen—!

MRS. ALVING: People so easily forget their past selves.

MANDERS: I do not. I am what I always was.

MRS. ALVING (*changing the subject*): Well, well, well; don't let us talk of old times any longer. You are now over head and ears in Commissions and Boards of Direction, and I am fighting my battle with Ghosts both within me and without.

MANDERS: Those without I shall help you to lay. After all the shocking things I've heard from you today, I cannot in conscience permit an unprotected girl to remain in your house.

MRS. ALVING: Don't you think the best plan would be to get her provided for?—I mean, by a good marriage.

MANDERS: No doubt. I think it would be desirable for her in every respect. Regina is now at the age when— Of course I don't know much about these things, but—

MRS. ALVING: Regina matured very early.

MANDERS: Yes, did she not? I have an impression that she was remarkably well developed, physically, when I prepared her for confirmation. But in the meantime, she must go home, under her father's eye.—Ah! but Engstrand is not— That he—that *he*—could so hide the truth from me!

(*A knock at the door into the hall.*)

MRS. ALVING: Who can that be? Come in!

ENGSTRAND (*in his Sunday clothes, in the doorway*): I beg your pardon humbly, but—

MANDERS: Ah! Hm—

MRS. ALVING: Is that you, Engstrand?

ENGSTRAND: —there was none of the servants about, so I took the great liberty of just knocking.

MRS. ALVING: Oh! very well. Come in. Do you want to speak to me?

ENGSTRAND (*comes in*): No, I'm greatly obliged to you; it was with his Reverence I wanted to have a word or two.

MANDERS (*walking up and down the room*): Hm—indeed! You want to speak to me, do you?

ENGSTRAND: Yes, I should like so much to—

MANDERS (*stops in front of him*): Well; may I ask what you want?

ENGSTRAND: Well, it was just this, your Reverence; we've been paid off down yonder—my grateful thanks to you, ma'am,—and now everything's finished, I've been thinking it would be but right and proper if we, that have been working so honestly together all this time—well, I was thinking we ought to end up with a little prayer-meeting tonight.

MANDERS: A prayer-meeting? Down at the Orphanage?

ENGSTRAND: Oh, if your Reverence doesn't think it proper—

MANDERS: Oh yes! I do; but—hm—

ENGSTRAND: I've been in the habit of offering up a little prayer in the evenings, myself.

MRS. ALVING: Have you?

ENGSTRAND: Yes every now and then—just a little exercise, you might call it. But I'm a poor, common man, and have little enough gift, God help me! and so I thought, as the Reverend Mr. Manders happened to be here, I'd—

MANDERS: Well, you see, Engstrand, I must first ask you a question. Are you in the right frame of mind for such a meeting? Do you feel your conscience clear and at ease?

ENGSTRAND: Oh! God help us, your Reverence! we'd better not talk about conscience.

MANDERS: Yes, that's just what we must talk about. What have you to answer?

ENGSTRAND: Why—one's conscience—it can be bad enough now and then.

MANDERS: Ah, you admit that. Then will you make a clean breast of it, and tell the truth about Regina?

MRS. ALVING (*quickly*): Mr. Manders!

MANDERS (*reassuringly*): Just let me—

ENGSTRAND: About Regina! Lord! how you frighten me! (*Looks at* MRS. ALVING.) There's nothing wrong about Regina, is there?

MANDERS: We'll hope not. But I mean, what is the truth about you and Regina? You pass for her father, eh!

ENGSTRAND (*uncertain*): Well—hm—your Reverence knows all about me and poor Johanna.

MANDERS: Come, no more prevarication! Your wife told Mrs. Alving the whole story before quitting her service.

ENGSTRAND: Well, then, may—! Now, did she really?

MANDERS: So you're found out, Engstrand.

ENGSTRAND: And she swore and took her Bible oath—

MANDERS: Did she take her Bible oath?

ENGSTRAND: No; she only swore; but she did it so earnestly.

MANDERS: And you have hidden the truth from me all these years? Hidden it from me! from me, who have trusted you without reserve, in everything.

ENGSTRAND: Well, I can't deny it.

MANDERS: Have I deserved this of you, Engstrand? Haven't I always been ready to help you in word and deed, so far as it stood in my power? Answer me. Have I not?

ENGSTRAND: It would have been a poor look-out for me many a time but for the Reverend Mr. Manders.

MANDERS: And you reward me thus! You cause me to enter falsehoods in the Church Register, and you withhold from me, year after year, the explanations you owed alike to me and to truth. Your conduct has been wholly inexcusable, Engstrand; and from this time forward all is over between us.

ENGSTRAND (*with a sigh*): Yes! I suppose it must be.

MANDERS: How can you possibly justify yourself?

ENGSTRAND: How could I think she'd gone and made bad worse by talking about it? Will your Reverence just fancy yourself in the same trouble as poor Johanna—

MANDERS: I!

ENGSTRAND: Lord bless you! I don't mean just exactly the same. But I mean, if your Reverence had anything to be ashamed of in the eyes of the world, as the saying is— We men oughtn't to judge a poor woman too hardly, your Reverence.

MANDERS: I am not doing so. It's you I am reproaching.

ENGSTRAND: Might I make so bold as to ask your Reverence a bit of a question?

MANDERS: Yes, ask away.

ENGSTRAND: Isn't it right and proper for a man to raise up the fallen?

MANDERS: Most certainly it is.

ENGSTRAND: And isn't a man bound to keep his sacred word?

MANDERS: Why, of course he is; but—

ENGSTRAND: When Johanna had got into trouble through that Englishman—or it might have been an American or a Russian, as they call them—well, you see, she came down into the town. Poor thing! she'd sent me about my business once or twice before: for she couldn't bear the sight of anything but what was handsome; and I'd got this damaged leg. Your Reverence recollects how I ventured up into a dancing-saloon, where seafaring people carried on with drink and devilry, as the saying goes. And then, when I was for giving them a bit of an admonition to lead a new life—

MRS. ALVING (*at the window*): Hm—

MANDERS: I know all about that, Engstrand; the ruffians threw you downstairs. You've told me of the affair already.

ENGSTRAND: I'm not puffed up about it, your Reverence. But what I wanted to say was, that then she came and confessed all to me, with weeping and gnashing of teeth. I can tell your Reverence I was sore at heart to hear it.

MANDERS: Were you indeed, Engstrand? Well, go on.

ENGSTRAND: So I said to her, "The American, he's sailing about on the boundless sea. And as for you, Johanna," said I, "you've committed a grievous sin and you're a fallen creature. But Jacob Engstrand," said I, "he's got two good legs to stand upon, *he* has—" You know, your Reverence, I was speaking figurative-like.

MANDERS: I understand quite well. Go on.

ENGSTRAND: Well, that was how I raised her up and made an honest woman of her, so that folks shouldn't get to know how she'd gone astray with foreigners.

MANDERS: All that was very good of you. Only I can't approve of your stooping to take money—

ENGSTRAND: Money? I? Not a farthing!

MANDERS (*inquiringly to* MRS. ALVING): But—

ENGSTRAND: Oh, wait a minute!—now I recollect. Johanna had a trifle of money. But I would have nothing to do with it. "No," said I, "that's a mammon; that's the wages of sin. This dirty gold—or notes, or whatever it was—we'll just fling that back to the American," said I. But he was gone and away, over the stormy sea, your Reverence.

MANDERS: Was he really, my good fellow?

ENGSTRAND: Ay, sir. So Johanna and I, we agreed that the money should go to the child's education; and so it did, and I can account for every blessed farthing of it.

MANDERS: Why, this alters the case considerably.

ENGSTRAND: That's just how it stands, your Reverence. And I make so bold as to say I've been an honest father to Regina, so far as my poor strength went; for I'm but a poor creature, worse luck!

MANDERS: Well, well, my good fellow—

ENGSTRAND: But I may make bold to say that I've brought up the child, and lived kindly with poor Johanna, and ruled over my own house, as the Scripture has it. But I could never think of going up to your Reverence and puffing myself up and boasting because I too had done some good in the world. No, sir; when anything of that sort happens to Jacob Engstrand, he holds his tongue about it. It doesn't happen so very often, I daresay. And when I do come to see your Reverence, I find a mortal deal to say about what's wicked and weak. For I do say—as I was saying just now—one's conscience isn't always as clean as it might be.

MANDERS: Give me your hand, Jacob Engstrand.

ENGSTRAND: Oh, Lord! your Reverence—

MANDERS: Come, no nonsense (*wrings his hand*). There we are!

ENGSTRAND: And if I might humbly beg your Reverence's pardon—

MANDERS: You? On the contrary, it's I who ought to beg your pardon—

ENGSTRAND: Lord, no, sir!

MANDERS: Yes, certainly. And I do it with all my heart. Forgive me for misunderstanding you. And I wish I could give you some proof of my hearty regret, and of my good-will towards you—

ENGSTRAND: Would your Reverence?

MANDERS: With the greatest pleasure.

ENGSTRAND: Well then, there's the very opportunity now. With the money I've saved here, I was thinking I might set up at Sailors Home down in the town.

MRS. ALVING: *You?*

ENGSTRAND: Yes; it too might be a sort of Orphanage, in a manner of speaking. There are many temptations for seafaring folk ashore. But in this Home of mine, a man might feel as under a father's eye, I was thinking.

MANDERS: What do you say to this, Mrs. Alving?

ENGSTRAND: It isn't much I've got to start with, the Lord help me! But if I could only find a helping hand, why—

MANDERS: Yes, yes; we'll look into the matter. I entirely approve of your plan. But now, go before me and make everything ready, and get the candles lighted, so as to give the place an air of festivity. And then we'll pass an edifying hour together, my good fellow; for now I quite believe you're in the right frame of mind.

ENGSTRAND: Yes, I trust I am. And so I'll say good-bye, ma'am, and thank you kindly; and take good care of Regina for me—(*wipes a tear from his eye*)—poor Johanna's child; hm, it's an odd thing, now; but it's just as if she'd grown into the very apple of my eye. It is indeed.

(*He bows and goes out through the hall.*)

MANDERS: Well, what do you say of that man now, Mrs. Alving? That threw a totally different light on matters, didn't it?

MRS. ALVING: Yes, it certainly did.

MANDERS: It only shows how excessively careful one must be in judging one's fellow-creatures. But it's a great joy to ascertain that one has been mistaken. Don't you think so?

MRS. ALVING: I think you are, and will always be, a great baby, Manders.

MANDERS: I?

MRS. ALVING (*laying her two hands upon his shoulders*): And I say that I've half a mind to put my arms round your neck, and kiss you.

MANDERS (*stepping hastily back*): No, no! God bless me! What an idea!

MRS. ALVING (*with a smile*): Oh! you needn't be afraid of me.

MANDERS (*by the table*): You have sometimes such an exaggerated way of expressing yourself. Now, I'll just collect all the documents, and put them in my bag. (*He does so.*) There, now. And now, good-bye for the present. Keep your eyes open when Oswald comes back. I shall look in again later.

(*He takes his hat and goes out through the hall door.*)

MRS. ALVING (*sighs, looks for a moment out the window, sets the room in order a little, and is about to go into the dining-*

room, but stops at the door with a half-suppressed cry): Oswald, are you still at table?

OSWALD (*in the dining-room*): I'm only finishing my cigar.

MRS. ALVING: I thought you'd gone for a little walk.

OSWALD: In such weather as this? (*A glass clinks.* MRS. ALVING *leaves the door open, and sits down with her knitting on the sofa by the window.*) Wasn't that Pastor Manders that went out just now?

MRS. ALVING: Yes; he went down to the Orphanage.

OSWALD: Hm. (*The glass and decanter clink again.*)

MRS. ALVING (*with a troubled glance*): Dear Oswald, you should take care of that liqueur. It's strong.

OSWALD: It keeps out the damp.

MRS. ALVING: Wouldn't you rather come in to me?

OSWALD: I mayn't smoke in there.

MRS. ALVING: You know quite well you may smoke cigars.

OSWALD: Oh! all right then; I'll come in. Just a tiny drop more first! There! (*He comes into the room with his cigar, and shuts the door after him. A short silence.*) Where's Manders gone to?

MRS. ALVING: I've just told you; he went down to the Orphanage.

OSWALD: Oh, ah; so you did.

MRS. ALVING: You shouldn't sit so long at table after dinner, Oswald.

OSWALD (*holding his cigar behind him*): But I find it so pleasant, mother. (*Strokes and pets her.*) Just think what it is for me to come home and sit at mother's own table, in mother's room, and eat mother's delicious dinners.

MRS. ALVING: My dear, dear boy!

OSWALD: (*somewhat impatiently walks about and smokes*): And what else can I do with myself here? I can't set to work at anything.

MRS. ALVING: Why can't you?

OSWALD: In such weather as this? Without a single ray of sunlight the whole day? (*Walks up the room.*) Oh! not to be able to work!

MRS. ALVING: Perhaps it was not quite wise of you to come home?

OSWALD: Oh, yes, mother; I had to.

MRS. ALVING: Why? I would ten times rather forgo the joy of having you here than—

OSWALD (*stops beside the table*): Now just tell me, mother: does it really make you so very happy to have me home again?

MRS. ALVING: *Does* it make me happy!

OSWALD (*crumpling up a newspaper*): I should have thought it must be pretty much the same to you whether I was in existence or not.

MRS. ALVING: Have you the heart to say that to your mother, Oswald?

OSWALD: But you've got on very well without me all this time.

MRS. ALVING: Yes; I've got on without you. That's true.

(*A silence. Twilight gradually falls.* OSWALD *walks to and fro across the room. He has laid his cigar down.*)

OSWALD (*stops beside* MRS. ALVING): Mother, may I sit on the sofa beside you?

MRS. ALVING (*makes room for him*): Yes do, my dear boy.

OSWALD (*sits down*): Now I'm going to tell you something, mother.

MRS. ALVING (*anxiously*): Well?

OSWALD (*looks fixedly before him*): For I can't go on hiding it any longer.

MRS. ALVING: Hiding what. What is it?

OSWALD (*as before*): I could never bring myself to write to you about it; and since I've come home—

MRS. ALVING (*seizes him by the arm*): Oswald, what *is* the matter?

OSWALD (*as before*): Both yesterday and to-day I've tried to put the thoughts away from me—to get free from them; but it won't do.

MRS. ALVING (*rising*): Now you must speak out, Oswald.

OSWALD (*draws her down to the sofa again*): Sit still; and then I'll try to tell you. I complained of fatigue after my journey—

MRS. ALVING: Well, what then?

OSWALD: But it isn't that that's the matter with me; it isn't any ordinary fatigue—

MRS. ALVING (*tries to jump up*): You're not ill, Oswald?

OSWALD (*draws her down again*): Do sit still, mother. Only take it quietly. I'm not downright ill, either; not what's commonly called "ill." (*Clasps his hands above his head.*) Mother, my mind is broken down—ruined—I shall never be able to work again. (*With his hands before his face, he buries his head in her lap, and breaks into bitter sobbing.*)

MRS. ALVING (*white and trembling*): Oswald! Look at me! No, no; it isn't true.

OSWALD (*looks up with despair in his eyes*): Never to be able to work again! Never! never! It will be like living death! Mother, can you imagine anything so horrible?

MRS. ALVING: My poor boy! How has this horrible thing come over you?

OSWALD (*sits upright*): That's just what I can't possibly grasp or understand. I've never led a dissipated life—never, in any respect. You mustn't believe that of me, mother. I've never done that.

MRS. ALVING: I'm sure you haven't, Oswald.

OSWALD: And yet this has come over me just the same—this awful misfortune!

MRS. ALVING: Oh, but it will pass away, my dear, blessed boy. It's nothing but over-work. Trust me, I am right.

OSWALD (*sadly*): I thought so too at first; but it isn't so.

MRS. ALVING: Tell me the whole story from beginning to end.

OSWALD: Well, I will.

MRS. ALVING: When did you first notice it?

OSWALD: It was directly after I had been home last time, and had got back to Paris again. I began to feel the most violent pains in my head—chiefly in the back of my head, I thought. It was as though a tight iron ring was being screwed round my neck and upwards.

MRS. ALVING: Well, and then?

OSWALD: At first I thought it was nothing but the ordinary headache I had been so plagued with when I was growing up—

MRS. ALVING: Yes, yes—

OSWALD: But it wasn't that. I soon found that out. I couldn't work. I wanted to begin upon a big new picture, but my powers seemed to fail me; all my strength was crippled; I couldn't form any definite images; everything swam before me—whirling round and round. Oh! it was an awful state! At last I sent for a doctor, and from him I learned the truth.

MRS. ALVING: How do you mean?

OSWALD: He was one of the first doctors in Paris. I told him my symptoms, and then he set to work asking me a heap of questions which I thought had nothing to do with the matter. I couldn't imagine what the man was after—

MRS. ALVING: Well?

OSWALD: At last he said: "You have been worm-eaten from your birth." He used that very word—*vermoulu.*

MRS. ALVING (*breathlessly*): What did he mean by that?

OSWALD: I didn't understand either, and begged him to explain himself more clearly. And then the old cynic said—(*clenching his fist*) Oh—!

MRS. ALVING: What did he say?

OSWALD: He said, "The sins of the fathers are visited upon the children."

MRS. ALVING (*rising slowly*): The sins of the fathers—!

OSWALD: I very nearly struck him in the face—

MRS. ALVING (*walks away across the floor*): The sins of the fathers—

OSWALD (*smiles sadly*): Yes; what do you think of that? Of course I assured him that such a thing was out of the question. But do you think he gave in? No, he stuck to it; and it was only when I produced your letters and translated the passages relating to father—

MRS. ALVING: But then?

OSWALD: Then of course he was bound to admit that he was on the wrong track; and so I got to know the truth—the incomprehensible truth! I ought to have held aloof from my bright and happy life among my comrades. It had been too much for my strength. So I had brought it upon myself!

MRS. ALVING: Oswald! Oh no, don't believe it!

OSWALD: No other explanation was possible, he said. That's the awful part of it. Incurably ruined for life—by my own heedlessness! All that I meant to have done in the world—I never dare think of again—I'm not *able* to think of it. Oh! if I could but live over again, and undo all I've done! (*He buries his face in the sofa.* MRS. ALVING *wrings her hands and walks, in silent struggle, backwards and forwards.* OSWALD, *after a while, looks up and remains resting upon his elbow.*) If it had only been something inherited, something one wasn't responsible for! But this! To have thrown away so shamefully, thoughtlessly, recklessly, one's own happiness, one's own health, everything in the world—one's future, one's very life!

MRS. ALVING: No, no, my dear, darling boy! It's impossible. (*Bends over him.*) Things are not so desperate as you think.

OSWALD: Oh! you don't know— (*Springs up.*) And then, mother, to cause you all this sorrow! Many a time I've almost wished and hoped that at bottom you didn't care so very much about me.

MRS. ALVING: I, Oswald? My only boy! You are all I have in the world! The only thing I care about!

OSWALD (*seizes both her hands and kisses them*): Yes, mother dear, I see it well enough. When I'm at home, I see it, of course; and that's the hardest part for me. But now you know the whole story, and now we won't talk any more about it to-day. I daren't think of it for long together. (*Goes up the room.*) Get me something to drink, mother.

MRS. ALVING: Drink? What do you want to drink now?

OSWALD: Oh! anything you like. You have some cold punch in the house.

MRS. ALVING: Yes, but my dear Oswald—

OSWALD: Don't refuse me, mother. Do be nice, now! I must have something to wash down all these gnawing thoughts. (*Goes into the conservatory.*) And then—it's so dark here! (MRS. ALVING *pulls a bell-rope on the right.*) And this ceaseless rain! It may go on week after week for months together. Never to get a glimpse of the sun! I can't recollect ever having seen the sun shine all the times I've been at home.

MRS. ALVING: Oswald, you're thinking of going away from me.

OSWALD: Hm—(*drawing a deep breath*)—I'm not thinking of anything. I can't think of anything. (*In a low voice.*) I let thinking alone.

REGINA (*from the dining-room.*): Did you ring, ma'am?

MRS. ALVING: Yes; let us have the lamp in.

REGINA: I will, directly. It's ready lighted. (*Goes out.*)

MRS. ALVING (*goes across to* OSWALD): Oswald, be frank with me.

OSWALD: Well, so I am, mother. (*Goes to the table.*) I think I've told you enough.

(REGINA *brings the lamp and sets it upon the table.*)

MRS. ALVING: Regina, you might fetch us a half-bottle of champagne.

REGINA: Very well, ma'am. (*Goes out.*)

OSWALD (*puts his arm round* MRS. ALVING'S *neck*): That's just what I wanted. I knew mother wouldn't let her boy be thirsty.

MRS. ALVING: My own, poor, darling Oswald, how could I deny you anything now?

OSWALD (*eagerly*): Is that true, mother? Do you mean it?

MRS. ALVING: How? What?

OSWALD: That you couldn't deny me anything.

MRS. ALVING: My dear Oswald—

OSWALD: Hush!

REGINA (*brings a tray with a half-bottle of champagne and two glasses, which she sets on the table*): Shall I open it?

OSWALD: No, thanks, I'll do it myself.

(REGINA *goes out again.*)

MRS. ALVING (*sits down by the table*): What was it you meant, I mustn't deny you?

OSWALD (*busy opening the bottle*): First let's have a glass—or two.

(*The cork pops; he pours wine into one glass, and is about to pour it into the other.*)

MRS. ALVING (*holding her hand over it*): Thanks; not for me.
OSWALD: Oh! won't you? Then I will!

(*He empties the glass, fills, and empties it again; then he sits down by the table.*)

MRS. ALVING (*in expectation*): Well?

OSWALD (*without looking at her*): Tell me—I thought you and Pastor Manders seemed so odd—so quiet—at dinner today.

MRS. ALVING: Did you notice it?

OSWALD: Yes. Hm— (*After a short silence.*) Tell me: what do you think of Regina?

MRS. ALVING: What I think?

OSWALD: Yes; isn't she splendid?

MRS. ALVING: My dear Oswald, you don't know her as I do—

OSWALD: Well?

MRS. ALVING: Regina, unfortunately, was allowed to stay at home too long. I ought to have taken her earlier into my house.

OSWALD: Yes, but isn't she splendid to look at, mother?

(*He fills his glass.*)

MRS. ALVING: Regina has many serious faults.

OSWALD: Oh, what does it matter?

(*He drinks again.*)

MRS. ALVING: But I'm fond of her, nevertheless, and I'm responsible for her. I wouldn't for all the world have any harm happen to her.

OSWALD (*springs up*): Mother! Regina is my only salvation.

MRS. ALVING (*rising*): What do you mean by that?

OSWALD: I can't go on bearing all this anguish of mind alone.

MRS. ALVING: Haven't you got your mother to share it with you?

OSWALD: Yes, that's what I thought; and so I came home to you. But that won't do. I see it won't do. I can't endure my life here.

MRS. ALVING: Oswald!

OSWALD: I must live differently, mother. That's why I must leave you. I won't have you looking on at it.

MRS. ALVING: My unhappy boy! But, Oswald, while you're so ill as this—

OSWALD: If it were only the illness, I should stay with you, mother, you may be sure; for you are the best friend I have in the world.

MRS. ALVING: Yes, indeed I am, Oswald; am I not?

OSWALD (*wanders restlessly about*): But it's all the torment, the remorse; and besides that, the great, killing dread. Oh! that awful dread!

MRS. ALVING (*walking after him*): Dread? What dread? What do you mean?

OSWALD: Oh, you mustn't ask me any more! I don't know. I can't describe it. (MRS. ALVING *goes over to the right and pulls the bell.*) What is it you want?

MRS. ALVING: I want my boy to be happy—that's what I want. He shan't go on racking his brains. (*To* REGINA, *who comes in at the door:*) More champagne—a whole bottle. (REGINA *goes.*)

OSWALD: Mother!

MRS. ALVING: Do you think we don't know how to live here at home?

OSWALD: Isn't she splendid to look at? How beautifully she's built! And so thoroughly healthy!

MRS. ALVING (*sits by the table*): Sit down, Oswald; let us talk quietly together.

OSWALD (*sits*): I daresay you don't know, mother, that I owe Regina some reparation.

MRS. ALVING: You?

OSWALD: For a bit of thoughtlessness, or whatever you like to call it—very innocent, anyhow. When I was home last time—

MRS. ALVING: Well?

OSWALD: She used often to ask me about Paris, and I used to tell her one thing and another. Then I recollect I happened to say to her one day, "Wouldn't you like to go there yourself?"

MRS. ALVING: Well?

OSWALD: I saw her face flush, and then she said, "Yes, I should like it of all things." "Ah, well," I replied, "it might perhaps be managed"—or something like that.

MRS. ALVING: And then?

OSWALD: Of course I'd forgotten the whole thing; but the day before yesterday I happened to ask her whether she was glad I was to stay at home so long—

MRS. ALVING: Yes?

OSWALD: And then she looked so strangely at me and asked, "But what's to become of my trip to Paris?"

MRS. ALVING: Her trip!

OSWALD: And so I got out of her that she had taken the thing seriously; that she had been thinking of me the whole time, and had set to work to learn French—

MRS. ALVING: So that was why she did it!

OSWALD: Mother! when I saw that fresh, lovely, splendid girl standing there before me—till then I had hardly noticed her—but when she stood there as though with open arms ready to receive me—

MRS. ALVING: Oswald!

OSWALD: —then it flashed upon me that my salvation lay in her; for I saw that she was full of the joy of life.[1]

MRS. ALVING (*starts*): The joy of life? Can there be salvation in that?

REGINA (*from the dining-room, with a bottle of champagne*): I'm sorry to have been so long, but I had to go to the cellar. (*Puts the bottle on the table.*)

OSWALD: And now fetch another glass.

REGINA (*looks at him in surprise*): There is Mrs. Alving's glass, Mr. Alving.

OSWALD: Yes, fetch one for yourself, Regina. (REGINA *starts and gives a lightning-like side glance at* MRS. ALVING.) Why do you wait?

REGINA (*softly and hesitatingly*): Is it Mrs. Alving's wish?

MRS. ALVING: Fetch the glass, Regina.

(REGINA *goes out into the dining-room.*)

OSWALD (*follows her with his eyes*): Have you noticed how she walks?—so firmly and lightly!

MRS. ALVING: It can never be, Oswald!

OSWALD: It's a settled thing. Can't you see that? It's no use saying anything against it. (REGINA *enters with an empty glass, which she keeps in her hand.*) Sit down, Regina.

(REGINA *looks inquiringly at* MRS. ALVING.)

MRS. ALVING: Sit down. (REGINA *sits on a chair by the dining-room door, still holding the empty glass in her hand.*) Oswald, what were you saying, about the joy of life?

OSWALD: Ah! the joy of life, mother—that's a thing you don't know much about in these parts. I've never felt it here.

MRS. ALVING: Not when you're with me?

OSWALD: Not when I'm at home. But you don't understand that.

MRS. ALVING: Yes, yes; I think I almost understand it—now.

OSWALD: And then, too, the joy of work! At bottom, it's the same thing. But that, too, you know nothing about.

MRS. ALVING: Perhaps you're right, Oswald; tell me more about it.

OSWALD: Well, I only mean that here people are brought up to believe that work is a curse and a punishment for sin, and

[1]Livsglæde—"la joie de vivre."

that life is something miserable, something we want to be done with, the sooner the better.

MRS. ALVING: "A vale of tears," yes; and we take care to make it one.

OSWALD: But in the great world people won't hear of such things. There, nobody really believes such doctrines any longer. There, you feel it bliss and ecstasy merely to draw the breath of life. Mother, have you noticed that everything I've painted has turned upon the joy of life?—always, always upon the joy of life?—light and sunshine and glorious air and faces radiant with happiness. That's why I'm afraid of remaining at home with you.

MRS. ALVING: Afraid? What are you afraid of here, with me?

OSWALD: I'm afraid lest all my instincts should be warped into ugliness.

MRS. ALVING (*looks steadily at him*): Do you think that would be the way of it?

OSWALD: I know it. You may live the same life here as there, and yet it won't be the same life.

MRS. ALVING (*who has been listening eagerly, rises, her eyes big with thought, and says*): Now I see the connection.

OSWALD: What is it you see?

MRS. ALVING: I see it now for the first time. And now I can speak.

OSWALD: (*rising*): Mother, I don't understand you.

REGINA (*who has also risen*): Perhaps I ought to go?

MRS. ALVING: No. Stay here. Now I can speak. Now, my boy, you shall know the whole truth. And then you can choose. Oswald! Regina!

OSWALD: Hush! Here's Manders—

MANDERS (*comes in by the hall door*): There! We've had a most edifying time down there.

OSWALD: So have we.

MANDERS: We must stand by Engstrand and his Sailors' Home. Regina must go to him and help him—

REGINA: No thank you, sir.

MANDERS (*noticing her for the first time*): What? You here? and with a glass in your hand!

REGINA (*hastily putting the glass down): Pardon!*

OSWALD: Regina is going with me, Mr. Manders.

MANDERS: Going with you!

OSWALD: Yes; as my wife—if she wishes it.

MANDERS: But, good God—

REGINA: I can't help it, sir.

OSWALD: Or she'll stay here, if I stay.

REGINA (*involuntarily*): Here!

MANDERS: I am thunderstruck at your conduct, Mrs. Alving.

MRS. ALVING: They will do neither one thing nor the other; for now I can speak out plainly.

MANDERS: You surely won't do that. No, no, no!

MRS. ALVING: Yes, I can speak and I will. And no ideal shall suffer after all.

OSWALD: Mother! What on earth are you hiding from me?

REGINA (*listening*): Oh, ma'am! listen! Don't you hear shouts outside?

(*She goes into the conservatory and looks out.*)

OSWALD (*at the window on the left*): What's going on? Where does that light come from?

REGINA (*cries out*): The Orphanage is on fire!

MRS. ALVING (*rushing to the window*): On fire?

MANDERS: On fire! Impossible! I've just come from there.

OSWALD: Where's my hat? Oh, never mind it—Father's Orphanage!

(*He rushes out through the garden door.*)

MRS. ALVING: My shawl, Regina! It's blazing!

MANDERS: Terrible! Mrs. Alving, it's a judgment upon his abode of sin.

MRS. ALVING: Yes, of course. Come, Regina.

(*She and* REGINA *hasten out through the hall.*)

MANDERS (*clasps his hands together*): And uninsured, too!

(*He goes out the same way.*)

ACT III

(The room as before. All the doors stand open. The lamp is still burning on the table. It is dark out of doors; there is only a faint glow from the conflagration in the background to the left.

MRS. ALVING, *with a shawl over her head, stands in the conservatory and looks out.* REGINA, *also with a shawl on, stands a little behind her.*)

MRS. ALVING: All burnt!—burnt to the ground!

REGINA: The basement is still burning.

MRS. ALVING: How is it Oswald doesn't come home? There's nothing to be saved.

REGINA: Would you like me to take down his hat to him?

MRS. ALVING: Hasn't he even got his hat on?

REGINA (*pointing to the hall*): No; there it hangs.

MRS. ALVING: Let it be. He must come up now. I'll go and look for him myself.

(*She goes out through the garden door.*)

MANDERS (*comes in from the hall*): Isn't Mrs. Alving here?

REGINA: She's just gone down the garden.

MANDERS: This is the most terrible night I ever went through.

REGINA: Yes; isn't it a dreadful misfortune, sir?

MANDERS: Oh, don't talk about it! I can hardly bear to think of it.

REGINA: How *can* it have happened?

MANDERS: Don't ask me, Regina! How should *I* know? Do *you,* too—? Isn't it enough that your father—?

REGINA: What about him?

MANDERS: Oh! he has driven me clean out of my mind—

ENGSTRAND (*comes through the hall*): Your Reverence!

MANDERS (*turns round in terror*): Are you after me here, too?

ENGSTRAND: Yes, strike me dead, but I must—Oh, Lord! what am I saying? It's an awfully ugly business, your Reverence.

MANDERS (*walks to and fro*): Alas! alas!

REGINA: What's the matter?

ENGSTRAND: Why, it all came of that prayer-meeting, you see. (*Softly*) The bird's limed, my girl. (*Aloud*) And to think that it's my fault that it's his Reverence's fault!

MANDERS: But I assure you, Engstrand—

ENGSTRAND: There wasn't another soul except your Reverence that ever touched the candles down there.

MANDERS (*stops*): Ah! so you declare. But I certainly can't recollect that I ever had a candle in my hand.

ENGSTRAND: And I saw as clear as daylight how your Reverence took the candle and snuffed it with your fingers, and threw away the snuff among the shavings.

MANDERS: And you stood and looked on?

ENGSTRAND: Yes; I saw it as plain as a pikestaff.

MANDERS: It's quite beyond my comprehension. Besides, it's never been my habit to snuff candles with my fingers.

ENGSTRAND: And very risky it looked, that it did! But is there so much harm done after all, your Reverence?

MANDERS (*walks restlessly to and fro*): Oh, don't ask me!

ENGSTRAND (*walks with him*): And your Reverence hadn't insured it, neither?

MANDERS (*continuing to walk up and down*): No, no, no; you've heard that already.

ENGSTRAND (*following him*): Not insured! And then to go right down and set light to the whole thing. Lord! Lord! what a misfortune!

MANDERS (*wipes the sweat from his forehead*): Ay, you may well say that, Engstrand.

ENGSTRAND: And to think that such a thing should happen to a benevolent Institution, that was to have been a blessing both to town and country, as the saying is! The newspapers won't handle your Reverence very gently, I expect.

MANDERS: No; that's just what I'm thinking of. That's almost the worst of it. All the malignant attacks and accusations—! Oh! it's terrible only to imagine it.

MRS. ALVING (*comes in from the garden*): He can't be got away from the fire.

MANDERS: Ah! there you are, Mrs. Alving!

MRS. ALVING: So you've escaped your Inaugural Address, Pastor Manders.

MANDERS: Oh! I should so gladly—

MRS. ALVING (*in an undertone*): It's all for the best. That Orphanage would have done no good to anybody.

MANDERS: Do you think not?

MRS. ALVING: Do you think it would?

MANDERS: It's a terrible misfortune, all the same.

MRS. ALVING: Let us speak plainly of it, as a piece of business. Are you waiting for Mr. Manders, Engstrand?

ENGSTRAND (*at the hall door*): Ay, ma'am; indeed I am.

MRS. ALVING: Then sit down meanwhile.

ENGSTRAND: Thank you, ma'am; I'd rather stand.

MRS. ALVING (*to* MANDERS): I suppose you're going by the steamer?

MANDERS: Yes; it starts in an hour.

MRS. ALVING: Be so good as to take all the papers with you. I won't hear another word about this affair. I have other things to think about.

MANDERS: Mrs. Alving—

MRS. ALVING: Later on I shall send you a Power of Attorney to settle everything as you please.

MANDERS: That I shall very readily undertake. The original destination of the endowment must now be completely changed, alas!

MRS. ALVING: Of course it must.

MANDERS: I think, first of all, I shall arrange that the Solvik property shall pass to the parish. The land is by no means without value. It can always be turned to account for some purpose or other. And the interest of the money in the Bank I could, perhaps, best apply for the benefit of some undertaking that has proved itself a blessing to the town

MRS. ALVING: Do just as you please. The whole matter is now completely indifferent to me.

ENGSTRAND: Give a thought to my Sailors' Home, your Reverence.

MANDERS: Yes, that's not a bad suggestion. That must be considered.

ENGSTRAND: Oh, devil take considering—I beg your pardon!

MANDERS (*with a sigh*): And I'm sorry to say I don't know how long I shall be able to retain control of these things—whether public opinion may not compel me to retire. It entirely depends upon the result of the official inquiry into the fire—

MRS. ALVING: What are you talking about?

MANDERS: And the result can by no means be foretold.

ENGSTRAND (*comes close to him*): Ay, but it can though. For here stands Jacob Engstrand.

MANDERS: Well, well, but—?

ENGSTRAND (*more softly*): And Jacob Engstrand isn't the man to desert a noble benefactor in the hour of need, as the saying is.

MANDERS: Yes, but my good fellow—how—?

ENGSTRAND: Jacob Engstrand may be likened to a guardian angel, he may, your Reverence.

MANDERS: No, no; I can't accept that.

ENGSTRAND: Oh! you will though, all the same. I know a man that's taken others' sins upon himself before now, I do.

MANDERS: Jacob! (*Wrings his hand.*) You are a rare character. Well, you shall be helped with your Sailors' Home. That you may rely upon. (ENGSTRAND *tries to thank him, but cannot for emotion.* MR. MANDERS *hangs his travelling-bag over his shoulder.*) And now let's be off. We two go together.

ENGSTRAND (*at the dining-room door, softly to* REGINA): You come along too, girl. You shall live as snug as the yolk in an egg.

REGINA (*tosses her head*): *Merci!*

(*She goes out into the hall and fetches* MANDERS'S *overcoat.*)

MANDERS: Good-bye, Mrs. Alving! and may the spirit of Law and Order descend upon this house, and that quickly.

MRS. ALVING: Good-bye, Manders.

(*See goes up toward the conservatory, as she sees* OSWALD *coming in through the garden door.*)

ENGSTRAND (*while he and* REGINA *help* MANDERS *to get his coat on*): Good-bye, my child. And if any trouble should come to you, you know where Jacob Engstrand is to be found.

(*Softly*) Little Harbour Street, hm—! (*To* MRS. ALVING *and* OSWALD.) And the refuge for wandering mariners shall be called "Captain Alving's Home," that it shall! And if I'm spared to carry on that house in my own way, I venture to promise that it shall be worthy of his memory.

MANDERS (*in the doorway*): Hm-hm!—Now come, my dear Engstrand. Good-bye! Good-bye!

(*He and* ENGSTRAND *go out through the hall.*)

OSWALD (*goes towards the table*): What house was he talking about?

MRS. ALVING: Oh, a kind of Home that he and Manders want to set up.

OSWALD: It will burn down like the other.

MRS. ALVING: What makes you think so?

OSWALD: Everything will burn. All that recalls father's memory is doomed. Here am I, too, burning down.

(REGINA *starts and looks at him.*)

MRS. ALVING: Oswald! you oughtn't to have remained so long down there, my poor boy!

OSWALD (*sits down by the table*): I almost think you're right.

MRS. ALVING: Let me dry your face, Oswald; you're quite wet.

(*She dries his face with her pocket-handkerchief.*)

OSWALD (*stares indifferently in front of him*): Thanks, mother.

MRS. ALVING: Aren't you tired, Oswald? Would you like to sleep?

OSWALD (*nervously*): No, no—I can't sleep. I never sleep. I only pretend to. (*Sadly.*) That will come soon enough.

MRS. ALVING (*looking sorrowfully at him*): Yes, you really are ill, my blessed boy.

REGINA (*eagerly*): Is Mr. Alving ill?

OSWALD (*impatiently*): Oh, do shut all the doors! This killing dread—

MRS. ALVING: Shut the doors, Regina.

(REGINA *shuts them and remains standing by the hall door.* MRS. ALVING *takes her shawl off.* REGINA *does the same.* MRS. ALVING *draws a chair across to* OSWALD'S, *and sits by him.*)

MRS. ALVING: There now! I'm going to sit beside you—

OSWALD: Ah! do. And Regina shall stay here, too. Regina shall be with me always. You'll come to the rescue, Regina, won't you?

REGINA: I don't understand—

MRS. ALVING: To the rescue?

OSWALD: Yes—in the hour of need.

MRS. ALVING: Oswald, have you not your mother to come to the rescue?

OSWALD: You? (*Smiles.*) No. Matter; *that* rescue you will never bring me. (*Laughs sadly.*) You! ha ha! (*Looks earnestly at her.*) Though, after all, it lies nearest to you. (*Impetuously*) Why don't you say "thou"[1] to me, Regina? Why don't you call me "Oswald"?

REGINA (*softly*): I don't think Mrs. Alving would like it.

MRS. ALVING: You shall soon have leave to do it. And sit over here beside us, won't you?

(REGINA *sits down quietly and hesitatingly at the other side of the table.*)

MRS. ALVING: And now, my poor suffering boy, I'm going to take the burden off your mind—

OSWALD: You, mother?

MRS. ALVING: —all the gnawing remorse and self-reproach you speak of.

OSWALD: And you think you can do that?

MRS. ALVING: Yes, now I can, Oswald. You spoke of the joy of life; and at that word a new light burst for me over my life and all it has contained.

OSWALD (*shakes his head*): I don't understand you.

MRS. ALVING: You ought to have known your father when he was a young lieutenant. He was brimming over with the joy of life!

OSWALD: Yes, I know he was.

MRS. ALVING: It was like a breezy day only to look at him. And what exuberant strength and vitality there was in him!

OSWALD: Well—?

MRS. ALVING: Well then, child of joy as he was—for he *was* like a child at that time—he had to live here at home in a half-grown town, which had no joys to offer him—only dissipations. He had no object in life—only an official position. He had no work into which he could throw himself heart and soul; he had only business. He had not a single comrade that knew what the joy of life meant—only loungers and boon-companions—

OSWALD: Mother!

MRS. ALVING: So the inevitable happened.

OSWALD: The inevitable?

MRS. ALVING: You said yourself, this evening, what would happen to you if you stayed at home.

OSWALD: Do you mean to say that father—?

[1]"Sige du"=Fr. *tutoyer.*

MRS. ALVING: Your poor father found no outlet for the overpowering joy of life that was in him. And I brought no brightness into his home.

OSWALD: Not even you?

MRS. ALVING: They had taught me a lot about duties and so on, which I had taken to be true. Everything was marked out into duties—into my duties, and his duties, and—I'm afraid I made home intolerable for your poor father, Oswald.

OSWALD: Why did you never write me anything about all this?

MRS. ALVING: I have never before seen it in such a light that I could speak of it to you, his son.

OSWALD: In what light did you see it then?

MRS. ALVING (*slowly*): I saw only this one thing, that your father was a broken-down man before you were born.

OSWALD (*softly*): Ah!

(*He rises and walks away to the window.*)

MRS. ALVING: And then, day after day, I dwelt on the one thought that by rights Regina should be at home in this house—just like my own boy.

OSWALD (*turning round quickly*): Regina!

REGINA (*springs up and asks, with bated breath*): I?

MRS. ALVING: Yes, now you know it, both of you.

OSWALD: Regina!

REGINA (*to herself*): So mother was that kind of woman, after all.

MRS. ALVING: Your mother had many good qualities, Regina.

REGINA: Yes, but she was one of that sort, all the same. Oh! I've often suspected it; but— And now, if you please, ma'am, may I be allowed to go away at once?

MRS. ALVING: Do you really wish it, Regina?

REGINA: Yes, indeed I do.

MRS. ALVING: Of course you can do as you like; but—

OSWALD (*goes toward* REGINA): Go away now? Isn't this your home?

REGINA: *Merci,* Mr. Alving!—or now, I suppose, I may say Oswald. But I can tell you this wasn't what I expected.

MRS. ALVING: Regina, I have not been frank with you—

REGINA: No, that you haven't, indeed. If I'd known that Oswald was ill, why— And now, too, that it can never come to anything serious between us— I really can't stop out here in the country and wear myself out nursing sick people.

OSWALD: Not even one who is so near to you?

REGINA: No, that I can't. A poor girl must make the best of her young days, or she'll be left out in the cold before she knows where she is. And I, too, have the joy of life in me, Mrs. Alving.

MRS. ALVING: Yes, I see you have. But don't throw yourself away, Regina.

REGINA: Oh! what must be, must be. If Oswald takes after his father, I take after my mother, I daresay. May I ask, ma'am, if Mr. Manders knows all this about me?

MRS. ALVING: Mr. Manders knows all about it.

REGINA (*puts on her shawl hastily*): Well then, I'd better make haste and get away by this steamer. Pastor Manders is so nice to deal with; and I certainly think I've as much right to a little of that money as he has—that brute of a carpenter.

MRS. ALVING: You're heartily welcome to it, Regina.

REGINA (*looks hard at her*): I think you might have brought me up as a gentleman's daughter, ma'am; it would have suited me better. (*Tosses her head.*) But it's done now—it doesn't matter! (*With a bitter side glance at the corked bottle*) All the same, I may come to drink champagne with gentlefolks yet.

MRS. ALVING: And if you ever need a home, Regina, come to me.

REGINA: No, thank you, ma'am. Mr. Manders will look after me, I know. And if the worse comes to the worst, I know of one house where I've every right to a place.

MRS. ALVING: Where is that?

REGINA: "Captain Alving's Home."

MRS. ALVING: Regina—now I see it—you're going to your ruin.

REGINA: Oh, stuff! Good-bye.

(*She nods and goes out through the hall.*)

OSWALD (*stands at the window and looks out*): Is she gone?

MRS. ALVING: Yes.

OSWALD (*murmuring aside to himself*): I think it's a great mistake, all this.

MRS. ALVING (*goes behind him and lays her hands on his shoulders*): Oswald, my dear boy; has it shaken you very much?

OSWALD (*turn his face towards her*): All that about father, do you mean?

MRS. ALVING: Yes, about your unhappy father. I'm so afraid it may have been too much for you.

OSWALD: Why should you fancy that? Of course it came upon me as a great surprise; but, after all, it can't matter much to me.

MRS. ALVING (*draws her hands away*): Can't matter! That your father was so infinitely miserable!

OSWALD: Of course I can pity him as I would anybody else; but—

MRS. ALVING: Nothing more? Your own father!

OSWALD (*impatiently*): Oh, there! "father," "father"! I never knew anything of father. I don't remember anything about him except that he once made me sick.

MRS. ALVING: That's a terrible way to speak! Should a son not love his father, all the same?

OSWALD: When a son has nothing to thank his father for? has never known him? Do you really cling to that old superstition?—you who are so enlightened in other ways?

MRS. ALVING: Is it only a superstition—?

OSWALD: Yes; can't you see it, mother? It's one of those notions that are current in the world, and so—

MRS. ALVING (*deeply moved*): Ghosts!

OSWALD (*crossing the room*): Yes; you may well call them Ghosts.

MRS. ALVING (*wildly*): Oswald!—then you don't love me, either!

OSWALD: You I know, at any rate.

MRS. ALVING: Yes, you know me; but is that all?

OSWALD: And of course I know how fond you are of me, and I can't but be grateful to you. And you can be so very useful to me, now that I'm ill.

MRS. ALVING: Yes, can't I, Oswald? Oh! I could almost bless the illness that has driven you home to me. For I can see very plainly you are not mine; I have to win you.

OSWALD (*impatiently*): Yes, yes, yes; all these are just so many phrases. You must recollect I'm a sick man, mother. I can't be much taken up with other people; I have enough to do thinking about myself.

MRS. ALVING (*in a low voice*): I shall be patient and easily satisfied.

OSWALD: And cheerful too, mother.

MRS. ALVING: Yes, my dear boy, you're quite right. (*Goes towards him.*) Have I relieved you of all remorse and self-reproach now?

OSWALD: Yes, you have. But who's to relieve me of the dread?

MRS. ALVING: The dread?

OSWALD (*walks across the room*): Regina could have been got to do it.

MRS. ALVING: I don't understand you. What is all this about dread—and Regina?

OSWALD: Is it very late, mother?

MRS. ALVING: It's early morning. (*She looks out through the conservatory.*) The day is dawning over the hills; and the weather is fine, Oswald. In a little while you shall see the sun.

OSWALD: I'm glad of that. Oh! I may still have much to rejoice in and live for—

MRS. ALVING: Yes, much—much, indeed!

OSWALD: Even if I can't work—

MRS. ALVING: Oh! You'll soon be able to work again, my dear boy, now that you haven't got all those gnawing and depressing thoughts to brood over any longer.

OSWALD: Yes, I'm glad you were able to rid me of all those fancies; and when I've got one thing more arranged— (*Sits on the sofa.*) Now we'll have a little talk, mother.

MR. ALVING: Yes, let us.

(*She pushes an arm-chair towards the sofa, and sits down close to him.*)

OSWALD: And meantime the sun will be rising. And then you'll know all. And then I shan't have that dread any longer.

MRS. ALVING: What am I to know?

OSWALD (*not listening to her*): Mother, didn't you say, a little while ago, that there was nothing in the world you wouldn't do for me, if I asked you?

MRS. ALVING: Yes, to be sure I said it.

OSWALD: And you'll stick to it, mother?

MRS. ALVING: You may rely on that, my dear and only boy! I have nothing in the world to live for but you alone.

OSWALD: All right, then; now you shall hear. Mother, you have a strong, steadfast mind, I know. Now you're to sit quite still when you hear it.

MRS. ALVING: What dreadful thing can it be—?

OSWALD: You're not to scream out. Do you hear? Do you promise me that? We'll sit and talk about it quite quietly. Promise me, mother?

MRS. ALVING: Yes, yes; I promise. Only speak.

OSWALD: Well, you must know that all this fatigue, and my inability to think of work—all that is not the illness itself—

MRS. ALVING: Then what is the illness itself?

OSWALD: The disease I have as my birthright (*he points to his forehead and adds very softly*)—is seated here.

MRS. ALVING (*almost voiceless*): Oswald! No, no!

OSWALD: Don't scream. I can't bear it. Yes, it's seated here—waiting. And it may break out any day—at any moment.

MRS. ALVING: Oh! What horror!

OSWALD: Now, do be quiet. That's how it stands with me—

MRS. ALVING (*jumps up*): It's not true, Oswald. It's impossible. It can't be so.

OSWALD: I have had one attack down there already. It was soon over. But when I got to know what had been the matter with me, then the dread came upon me raging and tearing; and so I set off home to you as fast as I could.

MRS. ALVING: Then this is the dread—?

OSWALD: Yes, for it's so indescribably loathsome, you know. Oh! if it had only been an ordinary mortal disease—! For I'm not so afraid of death—though I should like to live as long as I can.

MRS. ALVING: Yes, yes, Oswald, you must!

OSWALD: But this is so unutterably loathsome! To become a little baby again. To have to be fed! To have to— Oh, it's not to be spoken of!

MRS. ALVING: The child has his mother to nurse him.

OSWALD (*jumps up*): No, never; that's just what I won't have. I can't endure to think that perhaps I should lie in that state for many years—get old and grey. And in the meantime you might die and leave me. (*Sits in* MRS. ALVING's *chair.*) For the doctor said it wouldn't necessarily prove fatal at once. He called it a sort of softening of the brain—or something of the kind. (*Smiles sadly.*) I think that expression sounds so nice. It always sets me thinking of cherry-coloured velvet—something soft and delicate to stroke.

MRS. ALVING (*screams*): Oswald!

OSWALD (*springs up and paces the room*): And now you have taken Regina from me. If I'd only had her! She would come to the rescue, I know.

MRS. ALVING (*goes to him*): What do you mean by that, my darling boy? Is there any help in the world that I wouldn't give you?

OSWALD: When I got over my attack in Paris, the doctor told me that when it came again—and it will come again—there would be no more hope.

MRS. ALVING: He was heartless enough to—

OSWALD: I demanded it of him. I told him I had preparations to make. (*He smiles cunningly.*) And so I had. (*He takes a little box from his inner breast pocket and opens it.*) Mother, do you see this?

MRS. ALVING: What is that?

OSWALD: Morphia.

MRS. ALVING (*looks horrified at him*): Oswald—my boy!

OSWALD: I've scraped together twelve pilules—

MRS. ALVING (*snatches at it*): Give me the box, Oswald.

OSWALD: Not yet, mother.

(*He hides the box again in his pocket.*)

MRS. ALVING: I shall never survive this!

OSWALD: It must be survived. Now if I'd had Regina here, I should have told her how things stood with me, and begged her to come to the rescue at the last. She would have done it. I'm certain she would.

MRS. ALVING: Never!

OSWALD: When the horror had come upon me, and she saw me lying there helpless, like a little new-born baby, impotent, lost, hopeless, past all saving—

MRS. ALVING: Never in all the world would Regina have done this.

OSWALD: Regina would have done it. Regina was so splendidly light-hearted. And she would soon have wearied of nursing an invalid like me—

MRS. ALVING: Then heaven be praised that Regina is not here.

OSWALD: Well then, it's you that must come to the rescue, mother.

MRS. ALVING (*screams aloud*): I!

OSWALD: Who is nearer to it than you?

MRS. ALVING: I! your mother!

OSWALD: For that very reason.

MRS. ALVING: I, who gave you life!

OSWALD: I never asked you for life. And what sort of a life have you given me? I won't have it. You shall take it back again.

MRS. ALVING: Help! Help!

(*She runs out into the hall.*)

OSWALD (*going after her*): Don't leave me. Where are you going?

MRS. ALVING (*in the hall*): To fetch the doctor, Oswald. Let me go.

OSWALD (*also outside*): You shall not go. And no one shall come in. (*The locking of a door is heard.*)

MRS. ALVING (*comes in again*): Oswald—Oswald!—my child!

OSWALD (*follows her*): Have you a mother's heart for me, and yet can see me suffer from this unutterable dread?

MRS. ALVING (*after a moment's silence, commands herself, and says*): Here's my hand upon it.

OSWALD: Will you—?

MRS. ALVING: If it's ever necessary. But it will never be necessary. No, no; it's impossible.

OSWALD: Well, let us hope so, and let us live together as long as we can. Thank you, mother.

(*He seats himself in the arm-chair which* MRS. ALVING *has moved to the sofa. Day is breaking. The lamp is still burning on the table.*)

MRS. ALVING (*drawing near cautiously*): Do you feel calm now?

OSWALD: Yes.

MRS. ALVING (*bending over him*): It has been a dreadful fancy of yours, Oswald—nothing but a fancy. All this excitement has been too much for you. But now you shall have a long rest; at home with your mother, my own blessed boy. Everything you point to you shall have, just as when you were a little child. There now. That crisis is over now. You see how easily it passed. Oh! I was sure it would— And do you see, Oswald, what a lovely day we're going to have? Brilliant sunshine! Now you'll really be able to see your home.

(*She goes to the table and puts the lamp out. Sunrise. The glacier and the snow-peaks in the background glow in the morning light.*)

OSWALD (*sits in the arm-chair with his back towards the landscape, without moving. Suddenly he says*): Mother, give me the sun.

MRS. ALVING (*by the table, starts and looks at him*): What do you say?

OSWALD (*repeats, in a dull, toneless voice*): The sun. The sun.

MRS. ALVING (*goes to him*): Oswald, what's the matter with you? (OSWALD *seems to shrink together in the chair; all his muscles relax; his face is expressionless, his eyes have a glassy stare.* MRS. ALVING *is quivering with terror.*) What is this? (*Shrieks*) Oswald, what's the matter with you? (*Falls on her knees beside him and shakes him.*) Oswald, Oswald! Look at me! Don't you know me?

OSWALD (*tonelessly as before*): The sun. The sun.

MRS. ALVING (*springs up in despair, entwines her hands in her hair and shrieks*): I can't bear it (*whispers, as though petrified);* I can't bear it! Never! (*Suddenly*) Where has he got them? (*Fumbles hastily in his breast.*) Here! (*Shrinks back a few steps and screams*) No; no; no! Yes!—No; no!

(*She stands a few steps from him with her hands twisted in her hair, and stares at him in speechless terror.*)

OSWALD (*sits motionless as before and says*): The sun. The sun.

August Strindberg:
MISS JULIE

Realism, as practiced by Ibsen, insists that the drama ought to be a close copy of life, but it does not insist that life has a particular characteristic. That is, realism is not allied to any particular philosophy, but rather devotes its efforts to setting the stage with props that do not look like props and to writing plays about people of the period rather than of ancient Greece or of a never-never land where the country squire weds the fair village maiden. Closely related to realism—yet fundamentally different—is naturalism, an artistic movement characterized not merely by an attempt to imitate life and life's dialogue, but by a basic assumption about the nature of existence. Heavily influenced by scientific—especially biological—research, the naturalists believed that human actions are less free than had generally been supposed, and are in fact the results of influences exerted by heredity and environment. In the first half of the nineteenth century, for example, Balzac sought in his novels to examine man partly by examining his environment, working on the biological assumption that the creature's nature is partly determined by his surroundings. But, as Strindberg points out in his rambling preface to *Miss Julie,* though naturalism has, by appealing to factors outside of man's control, abolished guilt, the consequences of man's actions nevertheless remain.

Naturalism, then, aims not merely at presenting "a slice of life" *(tranche de vie),* but, assuming that men are motivated by their biological inheritance and their milieu, it has a definite attitude as to what life is like. It thus dethrones reason, and for free will it substitutes biological drives, notably hunger and sex, and, sometimes, economic pressures. In 1881 Zola published a collection of essays demanding that the drama take account of scientific research, and in 1887 André Antoine, founder of the Théâtre Libre (see p. 240), staged a dramatization of one of Zola's naturalistic stories. Because it emphasizes environment, naturalism tends to concentrate on the lower classes, where basic drives and economic pressures are most obviously manifested in actions. Zola, in his novel, *L'Assommoir (The Tavern),* for example, using the appropriate slang, describes the influence of a lazy drunkard (who ultimately dies in an asylum) on his mistress (who ultimately dies of starvation). But Zola, despite the protests he evoked, was basically moral, and though he depicted the influence of environment, he nevertheless held his characters morally responsible for their actions. In twentieth-century America, Theodore Dreiser ranges, in a series of novels, from frightened young men to ruthless financiers, but excuses their crimes and lies by assuming that, given their "chemistry" and their situation, they could do nothing else.

Because naturalism generally explores an environment, and in addition often traces actions back to one's ancestors, the novel, by virtue of its breadth, is more suited to its needs than is the drama. Strindberg, however, found its philosophy congenial to his own obviously irrational nature and sought to write plays for the naturalistic theater. He succeeded admirably, and Eugene O'Neill called him "the greatest interpreter in the theater of the characteristic spiritual conflicts which constitute the drama—the blood—of our lives today." *Miss Julie* (1888), characterized by Strindberg in a letter to his publisher as "the Swedish drama's first naturalistic tragedy," is among the finest products of naturalism, though it has not had its deserved success on the stage. A Swedish motion picture version, however, has recently brought *Miss Julie* to a wider public than ever before. The germ of the play, Strindberg claimed, was a real story of which he had heard, though he admitted altering the ending. Incidentally, if his account is accurate, by reworking the facts he violated one of the tenets of naturalism.

Technically, the play (which lasts about an hour and a half) has no intermission, for Strindberg, in his attempt to imitate life exactly, did not want to destroy the dramatic illusion by a break which would allow the spectators to be reminded that they are watching a play, not life itself. Equally naturalistic, and more important, is the tragic outcome of the conflict of wills, a conflict equivalent to the Darwinian struggle for existence. Furthermore, the actions are not the outcome of this or that obvious motive but are the products of a number of forces, some almost invisible, uniting with a particular circumstance to produce deeds not rationally willed. In his preface Strindberg suggests that Julie's motives are deliberately complex, for whereas (he claims) older drama falsely suggests that a character is motivated by one trait, such as pride, or love, or hate, his figures have all the complexity of life itself. Jean, the count's valet, on Midsummer Eve (a night, when the sun does not set, devoted to festive dancing and celebration) seduces Julie, his master's daughter, and then drives her to suicide. Why did Julie yield? As a matter of fact, a reading of the play will show that this summary is misleading, for Jean is seduced by Julie as much as she is by him. Strindberg states that she was undone by many causes: her nature, which she derived from her mother; her father's faulty care of her; his absence; the aphrodisiacal influence of flowers; the excitement of the dance; and chance, which happened to bring her into proximity with an excited, aggressive man.

Coupled with this picture of man as a victim of heredity, environment, and chance, is Strindberg's assumption that, in addition to the conflict between individuals and more especially between the male and the female, there is a larger battle, the class struggle. Thus, Julie and Jean represent not only the struggle between the sexes but also the clash between a decaying aristocracy and a rising working class. Strindberg himself reports in one of his autobiographies how delighted he was by the thought that he, the son of poor parents, had married—conquered—a daughter of the aristocracy, Baron Wrangel's former wife. But whether the conflict be sexual or economic, behind the struggle of the individual looms Fate, now composed of heredity and environment, absolving man from moral responsibility. Furthermore, Strindberg assumes that the conflicts are irreconcilable, for no compromise can be worked out in these struggles which must be to the death. Drawing on his own unhappy marital experiences, he assumed that each individual is propelled by a desire to dominate, and though life is ghastly, we irrationally desire to prolong it. In a letter to a friend, however, Strindberg said that Julie's suicide is properly (i.e., complexly) motivated: she is ashamed, depressed, under the influence of a will stronger than her own, and near a razor. Her tragedy, Strindberg implies, is pathetic as she struggles against a destiny which cannot be averted, and at last yields, semi-voluntarily.

Strindberg: Biographical Note: August Strindberg (1849–1912) was born in Sweden, two months after the marriage of his parents (who already had three children). After a desperately unhappy childhood and youth, he turned to playwriting; King Charles XV of Sweden was impressed by one drama and granted Strindberg a small scholarship to the university. The king, however, soon died, and Strindberg found employment in the Royal Library, where he studied Chinese. He married a divorced baroness, but they separated in 1891; he then married an Austrian girl and again separated, and lastly, after a period in a sanatorium, he married and separated for a third time. During and between marriages he worked fiercely at Chinese, dramaturgy, and, for a while, chemistry. His early plays are mostly either historical or realistic; his later ones, wherein he tries to dramatize the conflict of the soul, are symbolic and expressionistic; that is, they present not life as we all see it but life as the artist passionately feels it to be. In his third autobiography Strindberg said he had searched for God and found the Devil.

Miss Julie

TRANSLATED BY C. D. LOCOCK

Characters

MISS JULIE, *aged 25.*

JEAN, *a valet, aged 30.*

KRISTIN, *a cook, aged 35.*

The action takes place in the count's kitchen on Midsummer Eve.

(*A large kitchen. The ceiling and side walls are concealed by hangings and draperies. The wall at the back runs obliquely up the stage from the left. On it, to the left, are two shelves with utensils of copper, brass, iron, and tin. The shelves are fringed with crinkled paper. A little to the right, three-fourths of the great arched doorway, with two glass doors, through which are seen a fountain with a Cupid, lilac shrubs in flower, and the tops of some Italian poplars.*

To the left of the stage is the corner of a large tiled range and a part of the chimney-hood.

On the right protrudes one end of the servants' dinner table of white pine, with some chairs beside it.

The stove is decorated with birch boughs: the floor strewn with twigs of juniper.

On the end of the table is a large Japanese spice-jar filled with lilac blossoms.

A refrigerator, a scullery table, and a washstand.

A large, old-fashioned bell above the door, and on the left of the door a speaking-tube.

KRISTIN *is standing by the stove, frying something in a frying pan. She is wearing a light cotton dress and a cook's apron.* JEAN *comes in, dressed in livery and carrying a pair of large riding boots, with spurs, which he puts down on a conspicuous part of the floor.*)

JEAN: Miss Julie's mad again to-night: absolutely mad!

KRISTIN: So you're back again, are you?

JEAN: I took the Count to the station, and as I passed the barn on my way home I went in and danced, and who should I see but the young lady leading the dance with the game-keeper. But the moment she catches sight of me she rushes straight up to me and asks me to dance the ladies' waltz. And then she danced like—well, I've never seen the like of it. She's mad!

KRISTIN: That she's always been, but never like this last fort-night since the engagement was broken off.

JEAN: I wonder what really was at the bottom of that affair! A fine fellow, wasn't he, though not well off. Oh, but they're so full of whims! (*Sits down at the end of the table.*) Anyhow, it's curious that a young lady—ahem!—should prefer to stay at home with the servants—eh?—rather than go with her father to see her relations?

KRISTIN: I expect she feels a bit shy after that set-to with her young man.

JEAN: Very likely! Anyhow, he could hold his own—that young fellow! Do you know how it happened, Kristin? I saw it myself, though I didn't want to let them see I did.

KRISTIN: You saw it, did you?

JEAN: I did. They were in the stable-yard one evening and our young lady was "training" him, as she called it. D'you know what that was? Why, she was making him jump over her riding-whip the way you teach a dog to jump. Twice he jumped, and got a cut with the whip each time; but the third time he snatched the whip from her and broke it into a thousand pieces. And then he went off.

KRISTIN: So that's how it was! Well, I never!

JEAN: Yes, that's how that was! But what have you got for me there, Kristin?

KRISTIN (*putting what she has cooked on a plate and placing it in front of* JEAN): Oh, just a little kidney that I cut from the veal!

JEAN (*smelling the food*): Splendid! My great *délice*! (*Feeling the plate*) But you might have warmed the plate!

KRISTIN: Well, if you aren't more fussy than the Count himself—when you give your mind to it! (*Pulls his hair gently.*)

JEAN (*annoyed*): Don't go pulling my hair! You know how sensitive I am.

KRISTIN: There, there now! It was only love, you know!

(JEAN *begins to eat.* KRISTIN *opens a bottle of beer.*)

JEAN: Beer? On Midsummer Eve? No, thank you! *I*'ve got something better than that! (*Opens a drawer in the table and takes out a bottle of red wine with yellow seal.*) Yellow seal, you observe! Now give me a glass. A wineglass, of course, when one drinks *neat*!

KRISTIN (*goes back to the stove and puts a small saucepan on it*): Lord help the woman who gets *you* for a husband! Such an old fusser!

JEAN: Oh nonsense! You'd be glad enough to get such a smart fellow as I am! I don't think it's done you much harm *my* being known as your sweetheart! (*Tastes the wine.*) Fine! Remarkably fine! Might be just a shade warmer! (*Warms the glass in his hands.*) We bought this at Dijon, four francs the litre—without the bottle; and then there was the duty!—What are you cooking there—making that infernal smell?

KRISTIN: Oh, some devil's stuff Miss Julie wants for Diana.

JEAN: You should be more refined in your language, Kristin!

But why should you have to cook for that cur on the eve of a holiday? Is the dog ill then?

KRISTIN: Yes, she's ill! She's been sneaking about with the pug at the lodge—and now things have gone wrong—and that, you see, the young lady won't hear of.

JEAN: The young lady is too stuck up in some ways and not enough in others—just like the Countess was while she was alive. She was at home in the kitchen and the cowsheds, yet she would never go out driving with one horse only; she went about with dirty cuffs, but she would have the coronet on the buttons. Our young lady—to come back to her—doesn't take any care about herself or her person. I might almost say that she's not refined. When she was dancing in the barn just now she snatched away the gamekeeper from Anna's side and actually asked him to dance with her. We shouldn't do that sort of thing ourselves; but that's what happens when the gentry try to behave like common people: they *become* common. But she's a fine woman! Magnificent! Ah, what shoulders! And—and so on!

KRISTIN: Now then, don't overdo it! Clara has dressed her, and I know what she says.

JEAN: Oh, Clara! You're always jealous of each other! But I've been out riding with her. . . . And look at her dancing!

KRISTIN: Now then, Jean! Won't you dance with me when I'm ready?

JEAN: Of course I will.

KRISTIN: Promise?

JEAN: Promise? If I say I will, of course I will! Well, thanks for the supper. It was very nice! (*Replaces the cork in the bottle.*)

JULIE (*in the doorway, speaking to someone outside*): Go on. I'll join you in a minute.

(JEAN *slips the bottle into the drawer and rises respectfully.* JULIE *comes in and goes up to* KRISTIN *by the looking-glass.*) Well, have you finished it?

(KRISTIN *makes a sign that* JEAN *is present.*)

JEAN (*gallantly*): Have the ladies some secret between them?

JULIE (*striking him in the face with her handkerchief*): Don't be inquisitive!

JEAN: Oh, what a lovely smell of violets!

JULIE (*coquettishly*): What impudence! So you're an expert in scents too, are you? Dancing you're certainly good at. . . . There now, don't peep! Go away!

JEAN (*pertly, but politely*): Is it some witches' broth for Midsummer Eve you ladies are brewing? Something to tell one's fortune by in the star of fate, and so behold one's future love?

JULIE (*sharply*): You'd want good eyes to see *that*! (*To* KRISTIN) Put it into a pint bottle and cork it well. Now come and dance a schottische with me, Jean.

JEAN (*hesitating*): I don't want to be rude to anybody, but I'd promised Kristin this dance—

JULIE: Well, but she can have another instead—can't you, Kristin? Won't you lend me Jean?

KRISTIN: That's not for me to say. Since the young lady is so condescending it isn't for him to say no. Be off, now! And be thankful for the honour.

JEAN: Speaking frankly—no offence meant of course—I'm wondering if it's wise of Miss Julie to dance twice running with the same partner, especially as people here are only too ready to put their own construction on—

JULIE (*flaring up*): What do you mean? What sort of construction? What are you hinting at?

JEAN (*submissively*): As you won't understand I must speak more plainly. It doesn't look well to prefer one of your dependents to others who are expecting the same unusual honour—

JULIE: Prefer! What an idea! I'm surprised at you! I, the mistress of the house, honour the servants' ball with my presence, and now that I really do want to dance I intend to dance with someone who can guide and not make me look ridiculous.

JEAN: Just as you wish, Miss Julie! I am at your service.

JULIE (*gently*): Don't take it as a command! To-night we're happy people enjoying a holiday, and all questions of rank are set aside! Now give me your arm. Don't worry, Kristin! I shan't take your sweetheart away from you!

(JEAN *offers her his arm and leads her out.*)

PANTOMIME. *Played as though the actress were really alone. When desirable she turns her back on the audience. Does not look towards the spectators. Does not hurry, as though she were afraid the audience might become impatient.*

KRISTIN *alone. Soft violin music in the distance, in schottische time.* KRISTIN, *humming the tune, clears the table where* JEAN *has been sitting, washes the plate at the scullery board, dries it, and puts it into a cupboard.*

After that she removes her apron, takes out a small looking-glass from a table drawer, and leans it against the jar of lilac on the table. Lights a candle and heats a hairpin, with which she curls her front hair.

Then she goes to the door and listens. Comes back to the table. Discovers the handkerchief which MISS JULIE *has left behind; picks it up and smells it. Then she spreads it out abstractedly, pulls it straight, smooths it and folds it in four, and so on.*)

JEAN (*coming in alone*): Well, she really *is* mad! The way she danced! With everybody standing behind the doors grinning at her. What do you think about it, Kristin?

KRISTIN: Oh, she's not very well just now. And that always makes her a bit queer. But won't you come and dance with me now?

JEAN: You aren't angry with me for throwing you over—

KRISTIN: Of course not—not for a little thing like that. Besides, I know my place—

JEAN (*putting his arm around her waist*): You're a sensible girl, Kristin, and you ought to make a good wife—

JULIE (*comes in, unpleasantly surprised; with assumed jocularity*): Well, you *are* a nice cavalier, running away from your lady!

JEAN: On the contrary, Miss Julie; I have, as you see, hurried back to find the one I deserted!

JULIE (*changing her note*): Do you know there's not a man that can dance like you!—But why are you in livery on a holiday evening? Take it off at once!

JEAN: Then I must ask you to go away for a moment; my black coat is hanging up here. (*Indicates the place and goes towards the right.*)

JULIE: Are you shy because of me? Just changing your coat? Go into your room then, and come back. Or you can stay here, and I'll turn my back.

JEAN: With your permission, Miss Julie! (*Goes towards the right. One of his arms is visible while he changes his coat.*)

JULIE (*to* KRISTIN): Tell me, Kristin: is Jean engaged to you that he's so intimate?

KRISTIN: Engaged? Yes, if you like! We call it that.

JULIE: Call?

KRISTIN: But you've been engaged yourself, my lady, and—

JULIE: Yes, we were properly engaged—

KRISTIN: But it didn't come to anything for all that—

(JEAN *comes in, in a black frock-coat and black bowler.*)

JULIE: *Très gentil, monsieur Jean! Très gentil!*

JEAN: *Vous voulez plaisanter, madame!*

JULIE: *Et vous voulez parler français!* Where did you learn that?

JEAN: In Switzerland, while I was acting as *sommelier* at one of the largest hotels in Lucerne.

JULIE: But you look like a gentleman in that frock-coat! *Charmant!* (*Sits down at the table.*)

JEAN: Oh, you flatter me!

JULIE (*offended*): Flatter you?

JEAN: My natural modesty does not permit me to think that you are paying genuine compliments to one in my position. Consequently I take the liberty of assuming that you were exaggerating, or, in other words, flattering.

JULIE: Where did you learn to make speeches like that? I suppose you've been to the theatre a great deal?

JEAN: I have indeed! I've been about a lot, I have!

JULIE: But you were born in this neighbourhood?

JEAN: My father was a labourer on the district attorney's estate close by. I must have seen you as a child, though you never took any notice of me!

JULIE: Well really!

JEAN: Yes, I remember one occasion especially. . . . No, I can't tell you about that!

JULIE: Oh, but do! Yes, just for once!

JEAN: No, I really cannot now! Another time, perhaps.

JULIE: Another time means no time. Is it so risky now?

JEAN: Not risky at all; but I'd rather not. Look at her there! (*Points to* KRISTIN, *who has fallen asleep on a chair by the stove.*)

JULIE: She'll make a nice sort of wife! Perhaps she snores too?

JEAN: No, but she talks in her sleep.

JULIE: (*sarcastically*): How do you know she talks in her sleep?

JEAN (*impudently*): I've heard her!

(*A pause during which they look at each other.*)

JULIE: Why don't you sit down?

JEAN: I cannot take that liberty in your presence!

JULIE: But if I order you to?

JEAN: Then I obey.

JULIE: Sit down, then! No, wait! Can you give me something to drink first?

JEAN: I don't know what we've got here in the refrigerator. I fancy it's only beer.

JULIE: Don't say *only* beer! My tastes are simple and I prefer it to wine.

JEAN (*takes a bottle of beer from the refrigerator and opens it; fetches a glass and a plate from the cupboard and serves the beer*): Allow me!

JULIE: Thank you! Won't you have some yourself?

JEAN: I am not very fond of beer, but if your ladyship commands—

JULIE: Commands? I imagine that a polite cavalier would keep his lady company.

JEAN: Very true! (*Opens a bottle and fetches a glass.*)

JULIE: Drink my health now!

(JEAN *hesitates.*)

I really believe the fellow's shy!

JEAN (*kneeling, and raising his glass with mock solemnity*): To the health of my lady!

JULIE: Bravo! Now you must kiss my shoe too, and then everything will be quite perfect.

(JEAN *hesitates. Then he takes hold of her foot boldly and kisses it lightly.*)

Splendid! You ought to have been an actor.

JEAN (*getting up*): This can't go on any longer, my lady! Somebody may come in and see us.

JULIE: What would that matter?

JEAN: People would talk—that's all! If you only knew how their tongues went, up there just now, you—

JULIE: What sort of things did they say? Tell me! Sit down, please.

JEAN (*sitting down*): I don't want to hurt you, but they made use of expressions—which threw suspicions of a kind which . . . well, you can imagine that for yourself. You are no longer a child, and when a lady is seen drinking alone with a man—not to say a servant—at night—well—

JULIE: Well, what? Besides, we're not alone. Kristin is here.

JEAN: Yes, asleep!

JULIE: Then I'll wake her up. (*Gets up.*) Kristin! Are you asleep?

KRISTIN (*in her sleep*): Bla-bla-bla-bla!

JULIE: Kristin!—What a sleeper!

KRISTIN (*in her sleep*): The Count's boots are clean—put the coffee on—in one moment—heigh-ho—pouff!

JULIE (*taking her by the nose*): Do wake up!

JEAN (*sternly*): One shouldn't disturb a sleeper!

JULIE (*sharply*): What?

JEAN: A woman who has stood by the stove all day long may well be tired at night. Besides, one ought to respect sleep. . . .

JULIE (*changing her tone*): A pretty thought: it does you credit! Thank you. (*Gives* JEAN *her hand.*) Now come out and pick a few lilacs for me.

(*During the following scene* KRISTIN *wakes up and walks sleepily to the right on her way to bed.*)

JEAN: With you, my lady?

JULIE: With me.

JEAN: That won't do! It simply won't!

JULIE: I can't understand your ideas. Is it possible that you're imagining something?

JEAN: Not I: the people.

JULIE: What? That I'm in love with my valet?

JEAN: I'm not a conceited man, but one has seen such cases—and to the people nothing is sacred!

JULIE: You're an aristocrat, I suppose!

JEAN: Yes, I am.

JULIE: I'm stepping down—

JEAN: Take my advice, my lady, and don't step down! No one will believe that you step down of your own accord. People will always say that you're falling down.

JULIE: I have a higher opinion of the people than you have. Come and put it to the test! Come! (*She holds him fast with her eye.*)

JEAN: You're very strange, you know!

JULIE: Perhaps, but so are you! Besides, everything is strange! Life, humanity, everything—slush that is whirled, whirled along the water, till it sinks, sinks! There's a dream of mine which comes back to me now and then; I remember it now. I have climbed to the top of a pillar, and am sitting there without seeing any possibility of getting down. When I look down I get dizzy, and yet get down I must, though I haven't the courage to throw myself down. I can't hold on, and I long to be able to fall; but I don't fall. And yet I have no peace till I am down, no rest till I am down, down, on the ground! And if I did reach the ground I should want to be down in the earth. . . . Have you ever felt like that?

JEAN: No. I usually dream that I'm lying under a tall tree in a dark wood. I want to be up, up at the top, to look out over the bright landscape where the sun is shining, and plunder the bird's nest where the golden eggs lie. So I climb and climb, but the stem of the tree is so thick and so smooth, and it's such a long way to the first branch. But I know that if I could only reach the first branch I should get to the top as easily as if I were on a ladder. I have never reached it yet; but reach it I shall, if only in my dreams!

JULIE: Here I am, chattering to you about dreams! Come now. Just into the park.

(*She offers him her arm and they go towards the door.*)

JEAN: We must sleep on nine midsummer flowers to-night: then our dreams will come true. Miss Julie!

(JULIE *and* JEAN *turn round at the door.* JEAN *puts his hand up to one eye.*)

JULIE: Let me see what you've got in your eye!

JEAN: Oh, it's nothing—just a speck of dust; it'll soon be gone.

JULIE: My sleeve must have brushed against it. Sit down and I'll help you. (*She takes him by the arm and makes him sit down; takes hold of his head and bends it backward; tries to remove the dust with the corner of her handkerchief.*) Sit still now, quite still! (*Slaps him on the hand.*) Do what I tell you now! I do believe he's trembling, the great big fellow! (*Feels his biceps.*) And such arms too!

JEAN (*warningly*): Miss Julie!

JULIE: Yes, *Monsieur* Jean!

JEAN: *Attention! Je ne suis qu'un homme!*

JULIE: *Will* you sit still!—There! Now it's out! Kiss my hand and say thank you!

JEAN (*getting up*): Miss Julie, listen to me. Kristin has gone to bed now. Will you listen to me!

JULIE: Kiss my hand first!

JEAN: Listen to me!

JULIE: Kiss my hand first!

JEAN: Very well: but you'll have only yourself to blame!

JULIE: For what?

JEAN: For what? Are you a child at twenty-five? Don't you know it's dangerous to play with fire?

JULIE: Not for me; I'm insured!

JEAN (*bluntly*): No, that you're not! And even if you are, there are inflammable stores close by!

JULIE: Yourself, I suppose?

JEAN: Yes. Not because it is I, but because I'm a young man—

JULIE: Of prepossessing appearance—what incredible conceit! A Don Juan perhaps? Or a Joseph? On my soul, I think you must be a Joseph!

JEAN: Do you think so?

JULIE: I almost fear it!

(JEAN *goes boldly up to her and tries to clasp her round the waist to kiss her.*)

(*Boxing his ears.*) Impudence!

JEAN: Is that serious or a joke?

JULIE: Serious!

JEAN: Then what happened just before was also serious! Your play is much too serious, and that's the danger of it! Now I'm tired of play and I beg to leave to return to my work. The Count's boots must be ready in time, and it's long past midnight.

JULIE: Put those boots away!

JEAN: No. This is my work and I must do it. I never undertook to be your playfellow, and I never can be that. I consider myself too good for it!

JULIE: You are proud!

JEAN: In some ways; in other ways not.

JULIE: Have you ever been in love?

JEAN: We don't use that word, but I've been fond of several girls, and once I got ill because I couldn't have the one I wanted: ill, mark you, like the princes in the *Thousand and One Nights* who couldn't eat or drink from sheer love!

JULIE: Who was it?

(JEAN *is silent.*)

Who was it.

JEAN: You can't make me say that.

JULIE: If I ask you as an equal, as a—friend! Who was it?

JEAN: It was you!

JULIE (*sitting down*): How priceless! . . .

JEAN: Yes, if you like! It was ridiculous! That, you see, was the story which I wouldn't tell you just now, but now I will.

Do you know how the world looks from below? You don't. Like hawks and falcons, whose backs one rarely sees because they usually hover above us! I used to live in the labourer's cottage with seven brothers and sisters and a pig, out in the grey fields where there wasn't a single tree! But from the windows I could see the Count's park wall with apple trees above it. It was the Garden of Eden; and a multitude of frowning angels with flaming swords stood there keeping watch over it.

But none the less I and some other boys found the way to the Tree of Life.—You despise me now?

JULIE: Oh, all boys steal apples.

JEAN: You may say that now, but you despise me all the same. No matter! One day I went into the Paradise with my mother to weed the onion beds. Close to the garden stood a Turkish pavilion, shaded by jasmine and overgrown with honeysuckle. I had no idea what it might be used for, but I had never seen such a beautiful building. People went in and out of it, and one day the door was left open. I crept up and saw the walls covered with pictures of kings and emperors, and there were red curtains on the windows, with fringes on them—now you understand what I mean. I— (*Breaks off a lilac blossom and holds it under* JULIE's *nose*)—I had never been inside the castle, never seen anything but the church—but this was more beautiful; and whatever course my thoughts took they always went back—to that. Then gradually arose the desire to taste, just for once, the full pleasure of—*enfin,* I crept in, saw, and admired. Then I heard someone coming! There was only one exit for members of the family, but for me there was another and I had to choose that.

(JULIE, *who has taken up the lilac blossom, lets it drop on the table.*)

So I took to my heels, plunged through a raspberry bed, darted across some strawberry beds, and came up on to the rose terrace. There I caught sight of a pink dress and a pair of white stockings—that was you. I lay down under a heap of weeds—right under it, I tell you—under prickly thistles and damp, evil-smelling earth. And I watched you going about among the roses, and I thought to myself: "If it's true that a thief may enter into heaven and dwell with the angels, it's curious that a labourer's child here on God's earth cannot come into the castle park and play with the Count's daughter!"

JULIE (*sentimentally*): Do you think all poor children think the same as you did then?

JEAN (*doubtfully at first, then with conviction*): *All* poor—yes—of course! Of course!

JULIE: It must be terrible to be poor!

JEAN (*with deep distress, much exaggerated*): Oh, Miss Julie! Oh!—A dog may lie on the Countess's sofa, a horse be stroked on the nose by a young lady; but a servant—(*Changes his tone.*) Well, now and then you find a man with enough stuff in him to pull himself up into the world; but how often does that happen? However, do you know what I did next? I jumped into the millstream with my clothes on, was pulled out, and got a thrashing. But the following Sunday, when my father and all the others went off to my grandmother's, I contrived to stay at home. So I washed with soap and hot water, put on my best clothes, and went to church in order to see you! I saw you and went home, determined to die; but I wanted to die beautifully and comfortably, without pain. And then I remembered that it was dangerous to sleep under an elder bush. We had a large one, just then in bloom. I robbed it of all it had, and then made my bed in the oats-chest. Have you noticed how smooth oats are? Soft to the touch as the human skin! . . . Well, I shut the lid and closed my eyes; then fell asleep, and woke up feeling really ill. But I didn't die, as you see.

What I wanted—I really don't know! There was no hope of winning you—but you were a sign to me of the hopelessness of getting out of the circle in which I was born.

JULIE: You tell stories charmingly, you know! Did you ever go to school?

JEAN: Only for a short time. But I've read a good many novels, and gone to theatres. Besides that, I've listened to the conversation of refined people; and I've learnt most from them.

JULIE: So you stand about listening to what we say!

JEAN: Certainly! And I've heard a lot, I have, sitting on the coach-box or rowing the boat. Once I heard your ladyship and a girl friend . . .

JULIE: Oh? And what did you hear?

JEAN: Well, it's not very easy to tell you; but I must say I was rather surprised; I couldn't think where you'd learnt all those words. Perhaps, at bottom, there isn't so much difference as one thinks between one human being and another.

JULIE: For shame! We don't behave like you when we're engaged.

JEAN (*looking hard at her*): Is that a fact? Really, I shouldn't bother to make yourself out so innocent. . . .

JULIE: The man I gave my love to was a scoundrel.

JEAN: That's what you always say—afterwards.

JULIE: Always?

JEAN: Always, I believe—since I've heard the expression several times before on similar occasions.

JULIE: What sort of occasions?

JEAN: Like the one in question! The last time—

JULIE (*getting up*): Stop! I won't hear any more!

JEAN: *She* didn't want to either—strange to say. Now may I go to bed?

JULIE (*gently*): Go to bed on Midsummer Eve?

JEAN: Yes? Dancing with the riff-raff up there doesn't really amuse me.

JULIE: Get the key to the boat-house and take me out for a row on the lake; I want to see the sunrise!

JEAN: Is that prudent?

JULIE: That sounds as if you were anxious about your reputation!

JEAN: Why not? I don't want to be ridiculous. I don't want to be discharged without a character when I want to settle down. Moreover, I feel that I am more or less under an obligation to Kristin.

JULIE: Oh, so it's Kristin then. . . .

JEAN: Yes, but you too. Take my advice and go to bed!

JULIE: Am I to obey you?

JEAN: For once, for your own sake! I implore you! The night is far gone, sleepiness intoxicates, and one's head grows hot! Go to bed! Besides, if I'm not mistaken, I hear the people coming this way to look for me. If they find us here you're lost!

(*The Chorus approaches singing:*)

Two wives from the woods came walking,
  Tridiridi-ralla tridiridi-ra.
And one had a hole in her stocking,
  Tridiridi-ralla-la.

Their talk was of hundreds of dalers,
  Tridiridi-ralla tridiridi-ra.
Yet between them they'd hardly a daler,
  Tridiridi-ralla-ra.

No garland need I give you,
  Tridiridi-ralla tridiridi-ra.
For another, alas, I must leave you,
  Tridiridi-ralla, ra!

JULIE: I know my people and I love them, as they love me. Let them come and you'll see!

JEAN: No, Miss Julie, they don't love you. They accept your food, but they spit at it! Believe me! Listen to them: just listen to what they're singing! No, don't listen to them!

JULIE: What are they singing?

JEAN: Some scurrilous verses! About you and me!

JULIE: Abominable! How disgraceful! And how sneaking!

JEAN: The rabble are always cowardly. In this sort of fight one can only run away!

JULIE: Run away? But where? We can't go out by the door! And we can't get into Kristin's room!

JEAN: Very well! Into mine then! Necessity knows no law. Besides, you can trust me, your true, sincere, and respectful friend!

JULIE: But think—think if they should look for you there!

JEAN: I shall bolt the door, and if they try to break in I shall shoot! Come! (*On his knees.*) Come!

JULIE (*meaningly*): Will you promise? . . .

JEAN: I swear it!

(JULIE *goes out quickly to the right,* JEAN *follows her excitedly.*)

(BALLET. *The peasants enter, in holiday attire, with flowers in their hats. A fiddler leads the procession. A barrel of small beer and a keg of spirits, decorated with greenery, are placed on the table. Glasses are fetched and drinking begins. Then they form a circle and sing and dance to the tune "Two wives from the woods came walking."*

When this is finished they leave the room, singing.

JULIE *comes in alone; gazes on the havoc made of the kitchen; claps her hands together. Then she takes her powderpuff and powders her face.*)

JEAN (*comes in excitedly*): There, you see! And you heard too! Do you think it possible to remain here?

JULIE: No, I do not. But what are we to do?

JEAN: Run away, travel, far away from here!

JULIE: Travel? Yes, but where?

JEAN: To Switzerland, to the Italian lakes; you've never been there, have you?

JULIE: No. Is it nice there?

JEAN: Ah! It's eternal summer—orange trees, laurels! Glorious!

JULIE: But what are we to do when we get there?

JEAN: I'll start a hotel: first-class accommodations and first-class customers.

JULIE: A hotel?

JEAN: Yes, there's life for you! New faces continually, and new languages; not a minute's leisure for brooding or nerves; no worrying about something to do—the work makes itself: bells that ring night and day, whistling trains and 'buses coming and going; and gold pieces rolling along the counter. There's life for you!

JULIE: Yes, that is life. And what about me?

JEAN: Mistress of the house, chief ornament of the firm. With your looks ... and your style—oh—success is a certainty! Magnificent! You sit like a queen in the office and set your slaves in motion by pressing an electric button; the guests file past your throne and shyly place their treasures on your table—you can't imagine how people tremble when they get a bill in their hands—I'll salt the accounts and you shall sugar them with your prettiest smiles—ah, let's get away from here. (*Takes a time-table out of his pocket.*) At once, by the next train! We're in Malmö at six-thirty; Hamburg eight-forty in the morning; Frankfort-Basle in a day, and Como, by the St. Gothard line, in—let me see—three days. Three days!

JULIE: That's all very well! But, Jean—you must give me courage—tell me that you love me! Come and put your arms around me!

JEAN (*hesitating*): I should like to—but I dare not! Not again in this house. I love you, Miss Julie! Without doubt—can you doubt it?

JULIE (*shyly, with true womanly feeling*): Miss Julie! Call me Julie! There are no longer any barriers between us two!—Call me Julie!

JEAN (*uneasily*): I cannot! There are barriers still between us, as long as we stay in this house. There is the past, there is the Count—I have never met any one for whom I felt such respect: I've only to see his gloves lying on a chair and I feel small: I've only to hear his bell upstairs and I start like a shying horse: and now when I see his boots standing there so stiff and proud, I feel my back beginning to bend! (*Kicks the boots.*) Superstition, prejudice, taught us from childhood—but as easily forgotten again. Only come to another country, a republic, and they'll bow to the earth before my porter's livery. Bow to the earth, I tell you! But *I* shall not! I am not born to bow to the earth; for there's stuff in me—there is character; and if only I can set my foot on the first branch you shall see me climb! To-day I'm a valet, but next year I shall be a man of property: in ten years I shall be living on my own dividends: and then I shall got to Roumania, get myself an order, and may—mark you. I say *may*—end my days as a Count!

JULIE: Splendid! Splendid!

JEAN: Oh, in Roumania one can buy the title, so you'll be a Countess after all! My Countess!

JULIE: What does all that matter to me? I'm putting it all behind me now! Say that you love me, or—if you don't—what am I?

JEAN: I'll say it, a thousand times—later on! But not here! And above all, no sentiment, if everything is not to be lost! We must take the matter coolly like sensible people. (*Takes a cigar, cuts it and lights it.*) Now you sit there, and I'll sit here; then we can talk as if nothing had happened.

JULIE (*in despair*): My god! Have you no feelings, then?

JEAN: I? No man is more full of feeling than I am; but I'm able to control myself.

JULIE: Just now you could kiss my shoe—and now?

JEAN (*hardly*): Yes, then! Now we've got something else to think of.

JULIE: Don't speak cruelly to me!

JEAN: No, but sensibly. One folly has been committed—don't commit more! The Count may be here any moment, and before he comes our fates must be settled. What do you think of my plans for the future? Do you approve of them?

JULIE: They seem to me quite reasonable; but just one question: so large an undertaking requires considerable capital; have you got that?

JEAN (*chewing his cigar*): Have I? Certainly I have! I have my professional skill, my unrivalled experience, my knowledge of languages! That's the sort of capital that counts, I should think!

JULIE: But you can't even buy a railway ticket with that.

JEAN: No doubt; that's why I'm looking for a partner—one who can advance the capital required!

JULIE: Where can you find one at a moment's notice?

JEAN: It's for you to find one, if you want to be my partner.

JULIE: I can't do that, and I've nothing of my own. (*A pause.*)

JEAN: Then the whole thing falls to the ground—

JULIE: And—

JEAN: All remains as before!

JULIE: Do you think I'm going to remain under this roof as your mistress? Do you think I'll have the people pointing their fingers at me? Do you think I can look my father in the face after this? No! Take me away from here—away from this humiliation and disgrace! O God, God, what have I done? (*Weeps.*)

JEAN: So that's the tune now—what have you done? What many have done before you!

JULIE (*screaming hysterically*): And now you despise me! I'm falling, I'm falling!

JEAN: Fall down to my level, and I'll lift you up again!

JULIE: What dreadful power drew me towards you? The attraction of the weak to the strong? Of the falling to the rising? Or was it love? *This* love? Do you know what love is?

JEAN: Do I? You bet I do! Do you think I've never been with a girl before?

JULIE: What a way to speak! What thoughts to have!

JEAN: That's how I've been brought up and that's what I am! Now don't be hysterical, and don't give yourself airs, for we're both in the same boat now! There, little girl, let me give you a glass of something special!

(*Opens the table drawer and takes out the bottle of wine; fills the two glasses which had been used before.*)

JULIE: Where did you get that wine from?

JEAN: The wine-cellar!

JULIE: My father's burgundy!

JEAN: Isn't it good enough for his son-in-law?

JULIE: And I drink beer myself!

JEAN: That merely shows your tastes are worse than mine.

JULIE: Thief!

JEAN: Are you going to give me away?

JULIE: Oh, oh! The accomplice of a house-thief! Have I been drunk, have I been walking in dreams to-night? Midsummer Eve! The feast of innocent pleasures. . . .

JEAN: Innocent; h'm!

JULIE (*pacing backwards and forwards*): Is there a human being on earth so wretched as I am now?

JEAN: Why should you be? After such a conquest! Think of Kristin in there! Can't you imagine that she has her feelings too?

JULIE: I thought so just now, but I no longer think so! No, a menial is a menial—

JEAN: And a whore's a whore!

JULIE (*on her knees, with hands clasped together*): O God in heaven, put an end to my miserable life! Take me away from this filth in which I am sinking! Save me! Save me!

JEAN: I can't deny that I feel sorry for you! When I lay in the onion bed and saw you in the rose-garden, I . . . I can tell you now . . . I had the same ugly thoughts as other boys.

JULIE: You, who wanted to die because of me!

JEAN: In the oats-chest? That was all humbug.

JULIE: In other words, a lie!

JEAN (*beginning to feel sleepy*): Next door to it! Probably I read the story in some paper—about a chimney-sweep who shut himself up in a woodchest full of lilac blossoms because he was sued in some maintenance case. . . .

JULIE: So that's the sort of man you are. . . .

JEAN: I had to invent something; it's always the pretty speeches that capture women!

JULIE: Scoundrel!

JEAN: Filth!

JULIE: And now you've seen the hawk's back!

JEAN: Not exactly its *back*!

JULIE: And I was to be the first branch . . .

JEAN: But the branch was rotten . . .

JULIE: I was to be the signboard at the hotel . . .

JEAN: And I the hotel . . .

JULIE: Sit inside your office, lure your customers, falsify their accounts . . .

JEAN: *I* was to do that.

JULIE: To think that a human soul could be so steeped in filth!

JEAN: Wash it then!

JULIE: You lackey, you menial, stand up when I'm speaking!

JEAN: You mistress of a menial, you lackey's wench, hold your jaw and get out! Are you the one to come and lecture me on my coarseness? No one in my class has ever behaved so coarsely as you have to-night. Do you think any servant girl attacks a man as you did? Have you ever seen a girl of my class throw herself at a man like that? I have only seen that sort of thing among beasts and fallen women!

JULIE (*crushed*): That's right; strike me; trample on me; I deserve it all. I'm a vile creature; but help me! Help me out of this, if there *is* any way out!

JEAN (*more gently*): I've no wish to lower myself by denying my own share in the honour of being the seducer. But do you imagine that any one in my position would have dared to look at you if you hadn't invited it yourself? Even now I am astounded . . .

JULIE: And proud . . .

JEAN: Why not? Though I must confess the conquest was too easy to carry me off my feet.

JULIE: Go on striking me!

JEAN (*getting up*): No! Rather forgive me for what I have said! I don't strike the defenceless—least of all a woman. I can't deny that in one way I am glad to have discovered that what dazzled us below was merely tinsel: to have discovered that the hawk's back, too, was only grey, that the delicate complexion was mere powder, that the polished nails might have black edges, that the handkerchief was dirty, scented though it was! . . . On the other hand, it pains me to find that what I myself was striving to reach was not something higher, something more substantial; it pains me to see you sunk to a level far below that of your own cook; it pains me like the sight of autumn flowers lashed to pieces by the rain and turned into mud.

JULIE: You speak as if you already stood above me?

JEAN: And so I do. I could make you a Countess, you see, but you could never make me a Count.

JULIE: But I am the child of a Count; you can never be that!

JEAN: True, but I might be the father of Counts—if . . .

JULIE: But you are a thief. I am not that.

JEAN: There are worse things than being a thief! There are lower levels than that! Besides, when I serve in a house I regard myself to some extent as a member of the family, or one of the children; one doesn't count it theft when children filch a berry from loaded bushes! (*His passion wakens again.*) Miss Julie, you're a splendid woman, far too good for a man like me! You've been the prey of an intoxication, and you want to conceal the mistake by persuading yourself that you love me! That you do not do, unless possibly my outward appearance attracts you—in which case your love is no higher than mine—but I could never be content with being a mere animal for you, and your love I can never awaken.

JULIE: Are you sure of that?

JEAN: You mean that it might be possible!—My ability to love you, yes, without doubt! You are beautiful, you are refined—(*goes up to her and takes her hand*)—cultivated, amiable when you like, and the flame that is roused by you in a man will probably never be quenched. (*Puts his arm round her waist.*) You're like mulled wine with strong spices in it, and a kiss from you . . . (*He tries to lead her out; but she frees herself gently.*)

JULIE: Leave me! You won't win me in that fashion!

JEAN: *How* then?—Not in that fashion! Not by caresses and pretty speeches; not by thought for the future, by saving you from disgrace! *How* then?

JULIE: How? How? I don't know. Not in any way! I loathe you as I loathe rats, but I can't escape you!

JEAN: Escape with me!

JULIE (*drawing herself up*): Escape? Yes, we must escape! But I'm so tired! Give me a glass of wine.

(JEAN *fills her glass.*)

(*Looking at her watch*) But we must talk first; we've still a little time left. (*Drinks the wine and holds out her glass for more.*)

JEAN: Don't drink so immoderately—it will go to your head!

JULIE: What if it does?

JEAN: What if it does? It's vulgar to get drunk! What was it you wanted to say?

JULIE: We must fly! But we must talk first; that is, I must talk; so far you have done all the talking. You've told me the story of your life; now I want to tell you mine; then we shall know each other thoroughly before we begin our travels together.

JEAN: One moment! Pardon me! Consider whether you won't regret it afterwards when you've laid bare the secrets of your life.

JULIE: Aren't you my friend?

JEAN: Yes, sometimes. But don't rely on me.

JULIE: You don't really mean that. Besides, my secrets are already common property. You see, my mother was of plebeian birth, the daughter of quite simple people. She was brought up according to the theories of her time as regards equality, woman's liberty, and all that sort of thing; and she had a decided objection to marriage. So when my father made love to her she said she could never marry him, but . . . she did marry him all the same. I came into the world—against my mother's wishes, so far as I can make out. My mother wanted to bring me up as a child of nature: I was even to learn everything a boy learns, to become a proof that a woman is as good as a man. I had to go about dressed as a boy and learn how to handle a horse; but I wasn't allowed in the cowshed, I was made to groom and harness and go out hunting; I even had to try and learn farming! On our estate men were given women's work to do, and women men's—the result being that the property was on the verge of ruin and we became the laughing-stock of the neighbourhood. In the end my father must have wakened from the spell; he rebelled, and everything was altered to suit his wishes. My mother was taken ill—what it was I don't know—but she frequently had convulsive attacks, used to hide in the attic or in the garden, and sometimes stayed out all night. Then came the great fire which you have heard about. The house, the stables, and the farm-buildings were burnt down, and in circumstances which led one to suspect that the fire was no accident; for the disaster occurred the very day after the quarterly insurance premium had expired, and the new premium sent by my father was delayed by the messenger's carelessness, so that it arrived too late. (*She fills her glass and drinks.*)

JEAN: Don't drink any more!

JULIE: Oh, what does it matter? We have absolutely nowhere to go, and had to sleep in the carriages. My father didn't know where to get money for rebuilding the house. Then my mother advised him to try and borrow from a friend whom she had known in her youth, a brick-manufacturer near here. My father borrowed the money, without having to pay any interest, which surprised him. And so the estate was rebuilt. (*Drinks again.*) Do you know who burnt it down?

JEAN: The Countess, your mother!

JULIE: Do you know who the brick-manufacturer was?

JEAN: Your mother's lover?

JULIE: Do you know who the money belonged to?

JEAN: Wait a little—no, I don't know!

JULIE: It was my mother's!

JEAN: The Count's, then—if there was no settlement?

JULIE: There was no settlement. My mother had a little money of her own, which she didn't want to be under my father's control, so she deposited it with—her friend!

JEAN: Who pinched it!

JULIE: Quite so! He kept it! All this comes to my father's knowledge; he can't bring an action; nor pay his wife's lover; nor prove that the money was hers! That was my mother's revenge on him for assuming control over the household. At that time he was on the point of shooting himself! Rumour said that he tried and failed. But he took a new lease of life, and my mother had to pay dearly for her conduct! You can imagine what those five years were for me! I sympathized with my father, but I took my mother's side nevertheless, because I didn't know the circumstances. From her I had learnt to mistrust and hate men—for she hated men, as you know—and I swore to her that I would never be the slave of a man.

JEAN: So you became engaged to the district attorney!

JULIE: Merely that he should be my slave.

JEAN: And that he wouldn't be?

JULIE: Oh, he wanted it all right, but he didn't get the chance. I got bored with him!

JEAN: I saw that—in the stable-yard!

JULIE: What did you see?

JEAN: What I did!—How he broke off the engagement.

JULIE: That is a lie! It was I who broke it off! Has he been saying that he did it—the scoundrel?

JEAN: Oh, I don't think he was a scoundrel! You hate men, Miss Julie?

JULIE: Yes, for the most part! But sometimes—when weakness comes—oh, the shame of it!

JEAN: You hate me too?

JULIE: Beyond words! I should like to have you killed like a wild beast.

JEAN: Just as one shoots a mad dog. Is that what you mean?

JULIE: Yes, just that!

JEAN: But now there's nothing here to shoot with—and no dog! What are we to do then?

JULIE: Travel!

JEAN: And plague each other to death?

JULIE: No—enjoy ourselves, for a day or two, for a week, for as long as one can enjoy oneself, and then—die—

JEAN: Die? How stupid! In that case I think it's better to start a hotel—

JULIE (*paying no attention*):—by Lake Como, where the sun is always shining, where the laurels are green at Christmas and the oranges glow.

JEAN: Lake Como is a rainy hole, and I never saw any oranges there except at the grocer's. But it's a good place for strangers, as there are lots of villas to be let to loving couples, a most paying industry—do you know why? Why, because the contract is for six months and they leave after three weeks!

JULIE: Why after three weeks?

JEAN: They quarrel, of course! But the rent has to be paid just the same! Then one lets again. So it goes on and on, for there's love enough—even if it doesn't last very long!

JULIE: You don't want to die with me?

JEAN: I don't want to die at all! Not only because I am fond of life, but because I regard self-murder as a crime against the Providence which has given us life.

JULIE: You believe in God—you?

JEAN: Certainly I do! And I go to church every other Sunday.—And now, to tell the truth, I'm tired of all this and I'm going to bed.

JULIE: Indeed! And you think I shall be content with that? Do you know what a man owes the woman he has brought to shame?

JEAN (*takes out his purse and throws a silver coin on the table*): There you are! I don't want to have any debts!

JULIE (*pretending not to notice the insult*): Do you know what the law lays down?

JEAN: Unfortunately the law lays down no penalty for the woman who seduces a man!

JULIE: Do you see any way out other than going abroad, marrying, and then getting a divorce?

JEAN: And suppose I refuse to enter into this *mésalliance*?

JULIE: *Mésalliance* . . .

JEAN: Yes, for me! For, mark you! I'm better bred than you are; my pedigree contains no woman guilty of arson!

JULIE: Can you be sure of that?

JEAN: You can't be sure of the opposite, since we have no family records—except at the police-station! But your family records I have seen in a book on the drawing-room table. Do you know who the founder of your family was? A miller who let the king sleep with his wife one night during the Danish war. I have no ancestors of that sort! I haven't any ancestors at all, but I can become one myself!

JULIE: That's what I get for opening my heart to one who is unworthy of it, for sacrificing the honour of my family.

JEAN: Dishonour!—Now what did I tell you? People shouldn't drink—it makes them garrulous! And one must *not* be garrulous!

JULIE: Oh, how I regret what has happened!—how bitterly I regret it!—And if you had only loved me!

JEAN: For the last time—what do you mean? Do you want me to weep, to jump over your riding-whip, to kiss you? Do you want me to lure you away to Lake Como for three weeks, and then? . . . What am I to do? What do you want? This is getting rather painful! It always does when one goes and sticks one's nose into women's affairs! Miss Julie! I can see that you're unhappy: I know that you're suffering: but I cannot understand you. *We* don't have any of these whims; *we* don't hate one another! We make love for fun when our work gives us time; but we don't have time all day and all night, as you do! I think you're ill; I'm sure you're ill.

JULIE: Then you must be kind to me; and now you *are* talking like a human being.

JEAN: Yes, but be human yourself! You spit on me, and then forbid me to wipe it off—on you!

JULIE: Help me, help me! Only tell me what to do—where to go!

JEAN: O Lord! if I only knew myself!

JULIE: I've been mad—raving mad! But is there no possible escape?

JEAN: Keep still and be calm! Nobody knows anything.

JULIE: Impossible! The people know, and Kristin knows!

JEAN: They don't know: they could never believe such a thing!

JULIE (*hesitating*): But—it might happen again!

JEAN: That is true!

JULIE: And the consequences?

JEAN (*frightened*): The consequences!—Where *were* my wits, that I never thought of that? Yes, there's only one thing to do—you must go! At once! I shan't go with you or all would be lost. You must travel alone—abroad—anywhere!

JULIE: Alone? Where?—I can't do that!

JEAN: You must! And before the Count comes back! If you stay here you know what will happen! Once one has done wrong one wants to go on with it, since the harm is already done. . . . So one gets more and more reckless and—at last one is found out! So you must go! Afterwards you can write to the Count and confess everything, except that it was me! And that I don't think he'd guess! Nor do I think he'd be very pleased to know it!

JULIE: I'll go if you come with me!

JEAN: Are you mad, woman? Miss Julie running away with her valet! It would be in the papers the next day, and the Count would never survive it!

JULIE: I can't go! I can't stay here! Help me! I am so tired, so unutterably tired. Order me! Set me in motion! I can no longer think, nor act! . . .

JEAN: There, now! What a wretched creature you are! Why do you give yourselves airs and turn up your noses as if you were the lords of creation? Very well then—I'll give you your orders! Go upstairs and dress; provide yourself with money for the journey, and then come down again!

JULIE (*half whispering*): Come upstairs with me!

JEAN: To your room?—Now you're mad again! (*Hesitates a moment.*) No! Go, at once! (*Takes her hand and leads her out.*)

JULIE (*on her way out*): Do speak kindly to me, Jean!

JEAN: An order always sounds unkind; you can feel that yourself now!

(JEAN *alone; he gives a sigh of relief; sits down at the table; takes out a note-book and pencil; adds up figures aloud now and then. Dumb show, till* KRISTIN *comes in dressed for church, carrying a dicky and a white tie.*)

KRISTIN: Good Lord, what a state the room's in! What have you been up to?

JEAN: Oh, it's the young lady been bringing the people in. Were you so sound asleep you couldn't hear anything?

KRISTIN: I've slept like a log.

JEAN: And dressed for church already!

KRISTIN: Ye-es! Why, you promised to come to communion with me to-day!

JEAN: Why, so I did!—And I see you've got the vestments there! Come along then!

(*Sits down.* KRISTIN *begins putting on his dicky and white tie. A pause.*)

(*Sleepily*): What's the gospel for the day?

KRISTIN: Something about the beheading of John the Baptist, I expect!

JEAN: Awfully long affair that's sure to be!—Look out, you're choking me!—Oh, I'm so sleepy, so sleepy!

KRISTIN: Yes: what have you been doing, sitting up all night? Why, you're quite green in the face!

JEAN: I've been sitting here talking to Miss Julie.

KRISTIN: She doesn't know what's proper, that creature! (*A pause.*)

JEAN: I say, Kristin!

KRISTIN: Well?

JEAN: It's queer anyhow, when one comes to think of it! She!

KRISTIN: What is so queer?

JEAN: Everything! (*A pause.*)

KRISTIN (*looking at the glasses standing half empty on the table*): Have you been drinking together too?

JEAN: Yes!

KRISTIN: For shame!—Look me in the face!

JEAN: Yes!

KRISTIN: Is it possible? *Is* it possible?

JEAN (*after consideration*): Yes! It is!

KRISTIN: Faugh! I could never have believed it! Shame! Shame!

JEAN: Surely you're not jealous of her?

KRISTIN: No, not of her! If it had been Clara or Sophy I'd have scratched your eyes out!—Yes, that's how it is: why, I don't know! Oh, but it really was disgusting!

JEAN: Are you angry with her then?

KRISTIN: No, with you! It was wrong, very wrong! Poor girl! No, I tell you I won't stop in this house any longer—where one can't feel any respect for the people in it.

JEAN: Why should one feel respect for them?

KRISTIN: Yes, tell me that, my artful young fellow! But you wouldn't like to be in the service of people who don't live decently, would you? Eh! It lowers one, I think.

JEAN Yes, but isn't it some consolation to find that the others aren't one scrap better than we are?

KRISTIN: No, I don't think so; for unless they *are* better

there's no standard for us to aim at, so as to better ourselves. And think of the Count! Think of all the sorrow he's had in his life! No, I won't stay here any longer! With a fellow like you too! If it had been the district attorney: if it had been somebody a little higher.

JEAN: What's that you say?

KRISTIN: Yes, yes! You may be all right in your own way, but there *is* a difference between one class and another all the same. No, this is a thing I can never get over. To think that a young lady who was so proud, so bitter against men, should go and give herself—and to such a man! She who almost had poor Diana shot for running after the lodge-keeper's pug!—Just fancy! But I won't stay here any longer; on the twenty-fourth of October I quit.

JEAN: And then?

KRISTIN: Well, talking of that, it's about time you looked round for a job, if we are going to marry after all.

JEAN: Yes, but what sort of job? I can't get a place like this when I'm married.

KRISTIN: Of course not! But I suppose you could take a hall-porter's job, or try for a place as commissionaire in some institution. Government rations are scanty, but they're safe, and there's a pension for the widow and children . . .

JEAN (*with a grimace*): That's all very fine, but it isn't in my line to start thinking so soon abut dying for the sake of wife and children. I must admit that I really had slightly higher views.

KRISTIN: Your views indeed! Yes, and your duties too! Don't you forget them!

JEAN: Don't you go irritating me, talking about duties! I know well enough what I ought to do, without your telling me! (*Listens to some sound outside.*) However, we've plenty of time to think over that. Now go and get ready and we'll go to church.

KRISTIN: Who's that walking about upstairs?

JEAN: I don't know, unless it's Clara.

KRISTIN (*going out*): Surely it can't be the Count's come home without anybody hearing him?

JEAN (*frightened*): The Count? No it can't be him, or he'd have rung.

KRISTIN (*going out*): God help us! I've never seen the like.

(*The sun has now risen and is shining on the tree-tops in the park; the light moves slowly till it falls obliquely through the windows.* JEAN *goes to the doorway and makes a sign.*

JULIE *comes in in travelling dress, carrying a small birdcage covered with a towel. She places it on a chair.*)

JULIE: I'm ready now.

JEAN: Hush! Kristin's awake.

JULIE (*extremely nervous during the following scene):* Did she suspect anything?

JEAN: She knows absolutely nothing! But, good heavens, what a sight you are!

JULIE: A sight? In what way?

JEAN: You're as pale as a corpse, and—pardon me, but your face is dirty.

JULIE: Let me wash then!—There! (*Goes to the basin and washes her hands and face.*) Give me a towel! Oh—there's the sun rising!

JEAN: And then the troll bursts!

JULIE: Yes, there've been trolls about to-night! Now, Jean! Come with me: I've got the money.

JEAN (*doubtfully*): Enough?

JULIE: Enough to begin with! Come with me! I can't travel alone to-day. Think of it—Midsummer Day, in a stuffy train, crowded with masses of people all staring at one; standing at stations when one wants to fly. No, I can't do it, I can't do it! And then memories will rise: childhood's memories of midsummer days with the church decked in green—birch leaves and lilac: dinner at the table spread for relations and friends: after dinner the park, with dancing, music, flowers, and games! Ah, one may fly and fly, but one's memories follow in the luggage van and remorse, and the pangs of conscience.

JEAN: I'll come with you—but at once, before it's too late. This moment!

JULIE: Go and get ready then! (*Takes up the cage.*)

JEAN: No luggage though! That would betray us!

JULIE: No, nothing at all! Only what we can take in the carriage with us.

JEAN (*who has got his hat*): What on earth have you got there? What is it?

JULIE: Only my greenfinch. I don't want to leave her behind!

JEAN: Well, I'm blowed! So we're to take a bird-cage with us, are we? You must be mad! Drop that cage!

JULIE: The only thing of mine I'm taking with me from my home: the only living creature that loves me since Diana proved faithless! Don't be cruel! Let me take her with me!

JEAN: Drop that cage, I tell you—and don't talk so loud! Kristin can hear us!

JULIE: No, I can't leave her in strange hands! I'd rather you killed her!

JEAN: Give me the little beast, then, and I'll wring its neck!

JULIE: Very well, but don't hurt her! Don't—no, I cannot!

JEAN: Bring it here; I can!

JULIE (*takes the bird out of the cage and kisses it*): Oh, my little Serine, must you die then and leave your mistress?

JEAN: Please don't let's have any scenes; your life, your whole future is at stake! Quick now! (*Snatches the bird from her; carries it to the chopping-block, and picks up the kitchen chopper.* MISS JULIE *turns her head away.*) You should have learnt how to kill chickens instead of revolver-shooting. (*Brings down the chopper.*) Then you wouldn't faint at the sight of a drop of blood!

JULIE (*screaming*): Kill me too! Kill me! You who can butcher an innocent creature without a quiver! Oh, how I hate you, how I loathe you! There is blood between us! I curse the hour when I first saw you; I curse the hour when I was conceived in my mother's womb!

JEAN: Oh, what's the good of your cursing? Let's go!

JULIE (*goes to the chopping-block, as though she were dragged there against her will*): No, I won't go yet; I cannot . . . I must see . . . Hush! There's a carriage outside. (*Listens to the sounds outside, without taking her eyes off the block and the chopper.*) So you think I can't bear the sight of blood! You think I'm so weak. . . . Oh, how I should love to see your blood, your brains on a chopping-block—to see your whole sex swimming in a sea of blood, like that poor creature. . . . I believe I could drink out of your skull; I would gladly bathe my feet in your breast; I could eat your heart roasted whole! You think I am weak; you think I love you because the fruit of my womb thirsted for your seed; you think I want to carry your offspring beneath my heart, to nourish it with my blood—to bear your child and take your name. By the way, what *is* your name! I've never heard your surname—probably you haven't got one. I should be "Mrs. Gatekeeper," or "Madam Dunghill"—you dog who wear my collar; you lackey with my crest on your buttons! I to share you with my own cook, to be the rival of my own servant! Oh! Oh! Oh! You think I'm a coward and want to run away! No, now I'm going to stay—blow wind, come wrack! My father will come home . . . find his desk broken open . . . his money gone! Then he'll ring—that bell there . . . twice for the valet—and then he'll send for the police . . . and I shall tell everything! Everything! Oh, how lovely to have an end to it all—if only it could be the end!—And then he'll get a stroke and die! And that will be the end of all of us . . . and then there will be quiet . . . peace! . . . eternal rest! . . . And then the coat of arms will be broken on the coffin—the Count's line is extinct—but the valet's line will continue, in an orphan asylum . . . win laurels in a gutter, and end in a prison!

JEAN: There speaks the royal blood! Bravo, Miss Julie! Now cram the miller into his sack!

(KRISTIN *comes in, dressed for church, with a hymn-book in her hand.*

JULIE *hastens up to her and throws herself into her arms, as though seeking protection.*)

JULIE: Help me, Kristin! Help me against this man!

KRISTIN (*coldly and unmoved*): What a sight for a holiday morning! (*Looks at the chopping-block.*) And what a filthy mess! What does it all mean? And all this shrieking and hullabaloo!

JULIE: Kristin! You're a woman, and you're my friend! Beware of that scoundrel!

JEAN (*rather awkward and embarrassed*): While the ladies are discussing things I'll go and shave. (*Slips out to the right.*)

JULIE: *You* will understand me; *you* will listen to me!

KRISTIN: No, I really don't understand this sort of underhand business! Where are you off to, dressed up for a journey like that? And he with his hat on! What is it? What is it?

JULIE: Listen, Kristin; listen to me and I'll tell you everything . . .

KRISTIN: I don't want to know anything . . .

JULIE: You *shall* hear me . . .

KRISTIN: What is it about? Is it about your folly with Jean? Well, I don't worry about that at all; I've nothing to do with all that. But if you're thinking of fooling him into running off with you, why, we'll soon put a stopper on that!

JULIE (*extremely nervous*): Now try to be calm, Kristin, and listen to me! I can't stay here, and Jean can't stay here—so we must go abroad. . . .

KRISTIN: H'm, h'm!

JULIE (*brightening up*): I've just got an idea, though—suppose we all three went off—abroad—to Switzerland, and started a hotel together. . . . I've got money, you see, and Jean and I would be responsible for everything—and you, I thought, could look after the kitchen. . . . Won't that be splendid? . . . Say yes, now! And come with us; then everything will be settled! . . . Now do say yes! (*Embraces* KRISTIN *and pats her on the shoulder.*)

KRISTIN (*coldly and thoughtfully*): H'm, h'm!

JULIE (*presto tempo*): You've never been abroad, Kristin—you must have a look round the world. You can't imagine what fun it is travelling by train—new people continually—new countries—and then we'll go to Hamburg and have a look at the Zoological Gardens on our way—you'll like that—and go to the theatre and hear the opera—and when we get to Munich we shall have the picture galleries! There are Rubenses and Raphaels there—the great painters, you know. You've heard of Munich, where King Ludwig lived—the king who went mad, you know.—And then we'll see his castle—he still has castles furnished just like they are in fairy tales—and from there it's not far to Switzerland—and the Alps! Think of the Alps covered with snow in the middle of summer—and oranges growing there, and laurels that are green all year round . . .

(JEAN *is seen in the right wing, stropping his razor on a strop which he holds between his teeth and his left hand; he listens amused to the conversation and nods approval now and then.*)

(*Tempo prestissimo*). And then we'll take a hotel—and I shall sit in the office while Jean stands and receives the guests . . . goes out shopping . . . writes letters.—There's life for you! Whistling trains, omnibuses driving up, bells ringing in the bedrooms and the restaurant—and I shall make out the bills—and I know how to salt them too. . . . You can't imagine how timid travellers are when it comes to paying bills! And you—you will sit in the kitchen as housekeeper in chief. Of course you won't do any cooking yourself—and you'll have to dress neatly and stylishly when you see people—and you, with your looks—no, I'm not flattering you—why, you'll be able to catch a husband one fine day! A rich Englishman, I shouldn't wonder—they're the easy ones to—(*slackens her pace*) catch—and then we'll get rich—and build ourselves a villa on Lake Como—of course it rains there a little occasionally—but—(*slower*) I suppose the sun shines sometimes—however gloomy it seems—and—then—otherwise we can come home again—and come back—(*a pause*) here—or somewhere else——

KRISTIN: Now do you believe all that yourself?

JULIE (*crushed*): Do I believe it myself?

KRISTIN: Yes!

JULIE (*wearily*): I don't know; I don't believe anything now. (*Sinks down on the bench; puts her head between her arms on the table.*) I believe in nothing! Nothing whatever!

KRISTIN (*turning towards the right, where* JEAN *is standing*): Aha, so you were going to run away!

JEAN (*disconcerted, putting the razor on the table*): Run away? That's putting it rather strong! You've heard the young lady's plan, and though she's tired now after being up all night, the plan can quite well be carried out!

KRISTIN: Listen to me now! Did you think I was going to be cook to that——

JEAN (*sharply*): Kindly use decent language when you're speaking to your mistress! Do you understand?

KRISTIN: Mistress!

JEAN: Yes!

KRISTIN: Listen! Just listen to the man!

JEAN: Yes, listen yourself—it would do you good—and talk a little less! Miss Julie *is* your mistress; you ought to despise yourself for the same reason that you despise her now!

KRISTIN: I've always had so much self-respect——

JEAN: That you were able to despise other people!——

KRISTIN: That I have never sunk below my station. You can't say that the Count's cook has had any dealings with the groom or the swineherd! You can't say that!

JEAN: No, you've had to do with a fine fellow—luckily for you!

KRISTIN: Yes, he must be a fine fellow to sell the oats from the Count's stable——

JEAN: You're a nice one to talk about that—getting a commission on the groceries and accepting bribes from the butcher!

KRISTIN: What do you mean?

JEAN: So you can't feel any respect for your mistress now! *You* indeed!

KRISTIN: Are you coming to church now? A good sermon on your fine deeds might do you good!

JEAN: No, I'm not going to church to-day; you can go alone and confess your own misdeeds.

KRISTIN: Yes, I shall; and I shall come back with enough forgiveness to cover yours too! Our Redeemer suffered and died on the Cross for our sins, and if we draw nigh to Him in faith and with a penitent heart He will take all our guilt upon Himself.

JEAN: Including grocery peculations?

JULIE: Do you believe that, Kristin?

KRISTIN: That is my living faith, as sure as I'm standing here; It's the faith which I learnt as a child, which I have kept from my youth upwards, Miss Julie. Moreover, where sin aboundeth, grace aboundeth also!

JULIE: Oh, if I only had your faith! Oh, if—

KRISTIN: Ah, but you see one can't get that without God's especial grace, and it is not given to all men to obtain that.

JULIE: Who do obtain it then?

KRISTIN: That is the great secret of the operation of grace, Miss Julie. God is no respecter of persons, but the last there shall be first. . . .

JULIE: Well, but in that case He must have respect for the last?

KRISTIN (*continuing*): And it is easier for a camel to go through the eye of a needle than for a rich man to enter the kingdom of heaven! Yes, there you have it, Miss Julie! However, I'm going now—by myself, and on my way I shall tell the groom not to let anybody have the horses, just in case they should want to get away before the Count comes back! Goodbye! (*Goes.*)

JEAN: What a little devil! And all this because of a greenfinch!

JULIE (*wearily*): Never mind the greenfinch!—Can you see any way out of this? Any end to it?

JEAN (*after consideration*): No!

JULIE: What would you do in my place?

JEAN: In your place? Let me think!—A woman, of noble birth, fallen! I don't know—yes, now I know!

JULIE (*takes the razor and makes a gesture*): Like this?

JEAN: Yes. But I shouldn't myself—not that! There's a difference between us!

JULIE: Because you're a man and I'm a woman? What difference does that make?

JEAN: The same difference—as—between a man and a woman!

JULIE (*still holding the razor*): I should like to! But I can't! My father couldn't either, that time when he should have done it.

JEAN: No, he should *not* have done it! He had to get his revenge first.

JULIE: And now my mother gets her revenge, through me.

JEAN: Have you never loved your father, Miss Julie?

JULIE: Yes, most dearly, but I think I must have hated him too! I must have done so without being aware of it! But it was he who brought me up to despise my own sex, as half a woman and half a man! Whose fault is it—what has happened? My father's, my mother's, or my own? My own? But I *have* no own? I haven't a thought that I didn't get from my father, one passion that I didn't get from my mother, and this last idea—about all men being equal—that I got from *him,* my affianced husband—for that reason I call him a scoundrel! How can it be my own fault? To put the blame on Jesus, as Kristin did—no, I'm too proud to do that, and—thanks to my father's teaching—too sensible. And as to a rich man not being able to go to heaven—that is a lie; anyhow Kristin, who has money in the savings-bank, will certainly never get there! Whose fault is it?—What does it matter whose fault it is? After all, it is I who have to bear the blame, to bear the consequences. . . .

JEAN: Yes, but—

(*Two sharp rings on the bell,* JULIE *starts to her feet;* JEAN *changes his coat.*)

The Count is back! Suppose Kristin—(*Goes to the speaking-tube, taps it and listens.*)

JULIE: Has he been to his desk yet?

JEAN: It's Jean, my Lord! (*Listens. The audience cannot hear what the* COUNT *says.*) Yes, my Lord! (*Listens.*) Yes, my Lord! In one moment! (*Listens.*) At once, my Lord! (*Listens.*) Very good! In half an hour!

JULIE (*extremely anxious*): What did he say? My God! What *did* he say?

JEAN: He wants his boots and his coffee in half an hour.

JULIE: In half an hour then! Oh, I'm so tired; I haven't the strength to do anything: I can't repent, can't run away, can't stay, can't live—can't die! Help me now! Order me, and I'll obey you like a dog! Do me this last service, save my honour, save his name! You know what I *ought* to will, but cannot. . . . Will it yourself, and command me to carry it out!

JEAN: I don't know—but now *I* can't either—I don't understand—it's just as if this coat made me—I cannot order you—and now, since the Count spoke to me—why—I can't really explain it—but—oh, it's that devil the lackey working in my backbone!—I really believe if the Count came down now and ordered me to cut my throat I'd do it on the spot.

JULIE: Then pretend you're he, and I you!—You showed me how well you could act just now, when you were on your knees—you were the aristocrat then—or—have you never been to the theatre and seen the mesmerist? (JEAN *nods.*) He says to his subject: Fetch the broom, and he fetches it. Then he says: sweep, and the man sweeps—

JEAN: The other man has to be asleep, though!

JULIE (*as if in a trance*): I am asleep already—the whole room seems like smoke to me . . . and you look like an iron stove . . . a stove like a man in black clothes and a tall hat—and your eyes are shining like coals when the fire is going out—and your face is a white patch like the ashes—(*the sunlight has now reached the floor and is shining upon* JEAN) it's so warm and lovely—(*she rubs her hands as if she were warming them before a fire*) and so light—and so peaceful!

JEAN (*takes the razor and puts it into her hand*): There is the broom! Now go, while it's light—out to the barn—and . . . (*Whispers in her ear.*)

JULIE (*waking up*): Thank you! Now I am going, to rest! But just say—that the first can also obtain the gift of grace. Say it, even if you don't believe it.

JEAN: The first? No, I can't say that!—But stay—Miss Julie—now I know! You're no longer among the first—you're among the—last!

JULIE: That is true.—I'm among the very last; I *am* the last! Oh!—But now I can't go—tell me once more that I'm to go!

JEAN: No, now I can't either! I can't!

JULIE: And the first shall be last!

JEAN: Don't think! Don't think! Why, you're taking away all my strength too, and making me a coward—What! I fancied I saw the bell move!—No! Shall we stuff it up with paper?—Fancy being so afraid of a bell!—Yes, but it isn't only a bell—there's someone behind it—a hand that sets it in motion—and something else that sets the hand in motion—but just stop your ears—stop your ears! Yes, and then it rings worse! Just goes on ringing till you answer it—and then it's too late! and then the police come—and then—(*The bell rings twice violently.* JEAN *shrinks at the sound; then straightens himself.*) It's horrible! But there's no other possible end to it!—Go! (JULIE *walks out firmly through the door.*)

William Butler Yeats:
ON BAILE'S STRAND

Although such major British poets as Shelley, Tennyson, and Browning had tried to continue the Shakespearean tradition, the finest poetic dramas in English since Shakespeare came not from England but from Ireland in the early twentieth century. The fact is the more remarkable when one realizes that although Ireland has had a theater for hundreds of years, until the late nineteenth century the Irish playhouses generally staged English plays and were used by touring English companies, and most of Ireland's talented dramatists and actors left their native country for London. But in the 1890's Ireland, weakened and yet in a way strengthened by domestic and foreign quarrels, saw the rise of a theater which was to make significant contributions to the world.

William Butler Yeats rejected the melodramatic claptrap that Dublin audiences (like London audiences) had demanded, and was even dissatisfied with the achievements of Ibsen, though he recognized him as a master of plot construction and of realism. Ibsen was concerned with imitating life as sensible people perceive it, and with the problems of life which had been ignored by prudes and sentimentalists; but Yeats, repudiating the realistic tradition, demanded yet another kind of drama. A poet, he called for enchanting language, for an increased use of music, and for plays whose stories would captivate audiences not by melodramatic sentiment of good triumphing over all adversity, or by a mere accurate reproduction of the life about us, but by stirring our long-dormant sensitivity to beauty.

In the folk tales of Ireland's heroes—tales older than Christianity in Ireland—Yeats found the materials for his dramas. Art, he insisted, ought to depict a world or reality *greater* than our trivial lives. It ought to transcend our experience—indeed, he said, it must transcend our experience if it is to crowd into a few minutes the knowledge of a lifetime. Yet the stories of great warriors are not utterly removed from us, first, because of their language, and second, because of their nature. These heroic folk tales are not in the flat language of passionless people weakened by reason or civilization, but in the rich language of the people who have treasured them. It is not surprising, then, that Yeats advised John Millington Synge, one of Ireland's greatest dramatists, to live among the peasantry and to borrow their language. And Synge himself, after following Yeats's advice, records in the preface to his best drama, *The Playboy of the Western World,* that he listened to Irish servant girls in the kitchen, and therefore was able to write speeches "as fully flavored as a nut or an apple." The second point, that the dramas with their mythical plots are not as removed from life as we might think, but are the distillation or essence of life, is less obvious but even more important.

Myth, Yeats believed, was the means by which the poet communicated his intense feelings to an audience. Fanciful stories are the symbols which express the poet's perceptions, and these perceptions thus communicate the essence rather than the surface of life. The Greek dramatists, too, saw in myth suitable symbols for eternal truths and not merely the accidental happenings we now so carefully treasure in history books. The fable of Oedipus, say, may not indeed be based on the life of a king named Oedipus, but the tale nevertheless gives as true a view of life as any piece of history can. Similarly, Aeschylus' *Persians,* the one complete extant Greek play on a historical theme, is not a representation of what a historian would see in the battle of Marathon and Salamis, but, like the other Greek tragedies, a picture of divine powers working through man. For the Greeks and for Yeats myths were not fixed stories or pieces of history but poetic perceptions of essential human experiences. And because men have not fundamentally changed, the poet can take the old myths and see in them truths still true, and he can add to them the truths which his predecessors did not perceive. Myth, then, for Yeats, as for the Greeks, is the means or language whereby the poet conveys his intuitions to a public. Myth presents an insight into life, and life is far more exciting than our weak eyes looking on the scenes about us can discern.

The myth which Yeats uses in *On Baile's Strand*[1] is his ad-

[1]The pronunciation of old Irish names can only be approximated, and it differs both from modern Irish and from Yeats's pronunciations. The editors wish to thank Professor John Kelleher of Harvard for the following suggestions. Baile: disyllabic, the first syllable accented and rhyming with "Hal"; Aoife: accented on the first syllable, Ee-fe; Cuchulain: Coo-chu-len, accented on first two syllables, the "ch" heavily guttural; Conchubar: Con-a-choor, accented on the first syllable, the "ch" heavily guttural.

aptation of one version of the death of the great Irish warrior Cuchulain. Yeats believed that a tragic hero, though destroyed, expires in a moment of intense joy not known to the everyday world. The hero is usually at first uncertain or halfhearted, but finally achieves a passionate wholeness of mind which lifts his spirit yet brings his body to destruction. Yeats fully approved of his friend Lady Gregory's opinion that every tragedy is a joy to him who dies, and if this epigram does not apply fully to all the plays we call tragedies, especially to the Greek dramas, we nevertheless feel that *On Baile's Strand* is a fit example and, inconsistently, that Yeats's play is, as he himself described it, "Greek tragedy, spoken with a Dublin accent." Cuchulain, at first hostile to the High King Conchubar, maintains that he will "dance or hunt, or quarrel or make love,/ Wherever and whenever I've a mind to," but he finally yields to Conchubar, pledges an oath of submission, is forced (despite inner promptings) to kill a young man who threatens Conchubar's realm, and finally, after perceiving that it is his son whom he has killed, bursts the bonds of our understanding and is totally taken up in his mad fight with the sea. This last struggle, apparently insane, is Cuchulain's final exaltation—the moment when, undefeated by men and combatting the wild sea, he is completely unified in his passion. It is his moment of tragic greatness, for as Yeats put it in a letter, Cuchulain is "joy separated from fear."

Cuchulain is paired with the Fool, and Conchubar with the Blind Man. Cuchulain represents passion or action, and Conchubar represents intellect or thought. The Fool is the singing, passionate (active) man—the man who hunts, or who steals a chicken—while the Blind Man is crafty and uses the Fool as his pawn. Conchubar and the Blind Man know how to make the most of passionate, daring, and unthinking fools such as Cuchulain. But Yeats's passionate men, though lacking in rational ability, have a wisdom which transcends reason.

Yeats's drama of the death of the hero may possibly have autobiographical relevance, and Yeats himself said the play contained "heart-mysteries." The first of two common theories proposes that this drama of father versus son reflects Yeats's hostility (for which there is little convincing evidence) toward his father. The second suggests that Yeats, in his portrayal of the two kings, is depicting himself: Cuchulain's longing for a son, and his destruction by Conchubar's craftiness or intellect may reflect Yeats's bitterness with himself for not pursuing Maud Gonne, the beautiful Irish revolutionary whom Yeats loved but whom (he may have felt) he did not win because he had restrained himself. But however interesting biographical conjectures may be, they are irrelevant to the aesthetic value of the play. The tragedy of the drama is not merely Yeats's, but man's, in his inability to perceive until too late, and the consequent self-destruction which somehow is more passionate and more glorious than what has come before.

Yeats: Biographical Note. William Butler Yeats (1865-1939) was born near Dublin, and along with Lady Gregory can be said to have created the Irish Dramatic Movement at the end of the nineteenth century. Yeats, the son of the painter John B. Yeats, had already achieved a reputation as a lyric poet before he turned to the theater, and though he continued to write plays all his life, he is best known for his nondramatic poems. Although Protestant, he was an ardent supporter of Irish independence, a conscientious senator, and a lover of Irish traditions. He was awarded the Nobel Prize in 1923. He died in France in 1939, but his body was not returned to Ireland until nine years later.

On Baile's Strand, first published in 1903 and the first play ever produced at the Abbey Theatre (December 27, 1904) although several times revised, remains a relatively early play. Yeats had already written a few dramas, and was later to write many more, some slightly influenced by the aristocratic Japanese Noh drama, but *On Baile's Strand,* always his favorite play, remains Yeats's greatest achievement in drama and ranks with his finest nondramatic poems.

On Baile's Strand

TO WILLIAM FAY
because of the beautiful fantasy of his playing in the character of the Fool

---

Persons in the Play

A FOOL.

A BLIND MAN.

CUCHULAIN, *King of Muirthemne.*

CONCHUBAR, *High King of Uladh.*

A YOUNG MAN, *son of Cuchulain.*

KINGS *and* SINGING WOMEN.

*(A great hall at Dundealgan, not "*CHUCHULAIN'S *great ancient house" but an assembly-house nearer to the sea. A big door at the back, and through the door misty light as of sea-mist. There are many chairs and one long bench. One of these chairs, which is towards the front of the stage, is bigger than the others. Somewhere at the back there is a table with flagons of ale upon it and drinking-horns. There is a small door at one side of the hall. A* FOOL *and* BLIND MAN, *both ragged, and their features made grotesque and extravagant by masks, come in through the door at the back. The* BLIND MAN *leans upon a staff.)*

FOOL: What a clever man you are though you are blind! There's nobody with two eyes in his head that is as clever as you are. Who but you could have thought that the henwife sleeps every day a little at noon? I would never be able to steal anything if you didn't tell me where to look for it. And what a good cook you are! You take the fowl out of my hands after I have stolen it and plucked it, and you put it into the big pot at the fire there, and I can go out and run races with the witches at the edge of the waves and get an appetite, and when I've got it, there's the hen waiting inside for me, done to the turn.

BLIND MAN (*who is feeling about with his stick*): Done to the turn.

FOOL (*putting his arm round* BLIND MAN'S *neck*): Come now, I'll have a leg and you'll have a leg, and we'll draw lots for the wish-bone. I'll be praising you, I'll be praising you while we're eating it, for your good plans and for your good cooking. There's nobody in the world like you, Blind Man. Come, come. Wait a minute. I shouldn't have closed the door. There are some that look for me, and I wouldn't like them not to find me. Don't tell it to anybody, Blind Man. There are some that follow me. Boann herself out of the river and Fand out of the deep sea. Witches they are, and they come by in the wind, and they cry, "Give a kiss, Fool, give a kiss," that's what they cry. That's wide enough. All the witches can come in now. I wouldn't have them beat at the door and say, "Where is the Fool? Why has he put a lock on the door?" Maybe they'll hear the bubbling of the pot and come in and sit on the ground. But we won't give them any of the fowl. Let them go back to the sea, let them go back to the sea.

BLIND MAN (*feeling legs of big chair with his hands*): Ah! (*Then, in a louder voice as he feels the back of it*) Ah—ah—

FOOL: Why do you say "Ah-ah"?

BLIND MAN: I know the big chair. It is to-day the High King Conchubar is coming. They have brought out his chair. He is going to be Cuchulain's master in earnest from this day out. It is that he's coming for.

FOOL: He must be a great man to be Cuchulain's master.

BLIND MAN: So he is. He is a great man. He is over all the rest of the kings of Ireland.

FOOL: Cuchulain's master! I thought Cuchulain could do anything he liked.

BLIND MAN: So he did, so he did. But he ran too wild, and Conchubar is coming to-day to put an oath upon him that will stop his rambling and make him as biddable as a house-dog and keep him always at his hand. He will sit in this chair and put the oath upon him.

FOOL: How will he do that?

BLIND MAN: You have no wits to understand such things. (*The* BLIND MAN *has got into the chair.*) He will sit up in this chair and he'll say: "Take the oath, Cuchulain. I bid you take the oath. Do as I tell you. What are your wits compared with mine, and what are your riches compared with mine? And what sons have you to pay your debts and to put a stone over you when you die? Take the oath, I tell you. Take a strong oath."

FOOL (*crumpling himself up and whining*): I will not. I'll take no oath. I want my dinner.

BLIND MAN: Hush, hush! It is not done yet.

FOOL: You said it was done to a turn.

BLIND MAN: Did I, now? Well, it might be done, and not done. The wings might be white, but the legs might be red. The flesh might stick hard to the bones and not come away in the teeth. But, believe me, Fool, it will be well done before you put your teeth in it.

FOOL: My teeth are growing long with the hunger.

BLIND MAN: I'll tell you a story—the kings have story-tellers while they are waiting for their dinner—I will tell you a story with a fight in it, a story with a champion in it, and a ship and a queen's son that has his mind set on killing somebody that you and I know.

FOOL: Who is that? Who is he coming to kill?

BLIND MAN: Wait, now, till you hear. When you were stealing the fowl, I was lying in a hole in the sand, and I heard three men coming with a shuffling sort of noise. They were wounded and groaning.

FOOL: Go on. Tell me about the fight.

BLIND MAN: There had been a fight, a great fight, a tremendous fight. A young man had landed on the shore, the guardians of the shore had asked his name, and he had refused to tell it, and he had killed one, and others had run away.

FOOL: That's enough. Come on now to the fowl. I wish it was bigger. I wish it was as big as a goose.

BLIND MAN: Hush! I haven't told you all. I know who that young man is. I heard the men who were running away say he had red hair, that he had come from Aoife's country, that he was coming to kill Cuchulain.

FOOL: Nobody can do that.

(To a tune)
Cuchulain has killed kings,
Kings and sons of kings,
Dragons out of the water,
And witches out of the air,
Banachas and Bonachas and people of the woods.

BLIND MAN. Hush! hush!

FOOL *(still singing)*:
Witches that steal the milk,
Fomor that steal the children,
Hags that have heads like hares,
Hares that have claws like witches,
All riding a-cock-horse
(Spoken)
Out of the very bottom of the bitter black North.

BLIND MAN: Hush, I say!

FOOL: Does Cuchulain know that he is coming to kill him?

BLIND MAN. How would he know that with his head in the clouds? He doesn't care for common fighting. Why would he put himself out, and nobody in it but that young man? Now if it were a white fawn that might turn into a queen before morning—

FOOL: Come to the fowl. I wish it was as big as a pig; a fowl with goose grease and pig's crackling.

BLIND MAN: No hurry, no hurry. I know whose son it is. I wouldn't tell anybody else, but I will tell you,—a secret is better to you than your dinner. You like being told secrets.

FOOL: Tell me the secret.

BLIND MAN: That young man is Aoife's son. I am sure it is Aoife's son, it flows in upon me that it is Aoife's son. You have often heard me talking of Aoife, the great woman-fighter Cuchulain got the mastery over in the North?

FOOL: I know, I know. She is one of those cross queens that lives in hungry Scotland.

BLIND MAN: I am sure it is her son. I was in Aoife's country for a long time.

FOOL: That was before you were blinded for putting a curse upon the wind.

BLIND MAN: There was a boy in her house that had her own red colour on him, and everybody said he was to be brought up to kill Cuchulain, that she hated Cuchulain. She used to put a helmet on a pillar-stone and call it Cuchulain and set him casting at it. There is a step outside—Cuchulain's step.

(CUCHULAIN *passes by in the mist outside the big door.*)

FOOL: Where is Cuchulain going?

BLIND MAN: He is going to meet Conchubar that has bidden him to take the oath.

FOOL: Ah, an oath, Blind Man. How can I remember so many things at once? Who is going to take an oath?

BLIND MAN: Cuchulain is going to take an oath to Conchubar who is High King.

FOOL: What a mix-up you make of everything, Blind Man! You were telling me one story, and now you are telling me another story. . . . How can I get the hang of it at the end if you mix everything at the beginning? Wait till I settle it out. There now, there's Cuchulain (*he points to one foot*), and there is the young man (*he points to the other foot*) that is coming to kill him, and Cuchulain doesn't know. But where's Conchubar? (*Takes bag from side.*) That's Conchubar with all his riches—Cuchulain, young man, Conchubar.—And where's Aoife? (*Throws up cap.*) There is Aoife, high up on the mountains in high hungry Scotland. Maybe it is not true after all. Maybe it was your own making up. It's many a time you cheated me before with your lies. Come to the cooking-pot, my stomach is pinched and rusty. Would you have it to be creaking like a gate?

BLIND MAN: I tell you it's true. And more than that is true. If you listen to what I say, you'll forget your stomach.

FOOL: I won't.

BLIND MAN: Listen. I know who the young man's father is, but I won't say. I would be afraid to say. Ah, Fool, you would forget everything if you could know who the young man's father is.

FOOL: Who is it? Tell me now quick, or I'll shake you. Come, out with, or I'll shake you.

(*A murmur of voices in the distance.*)

BLIND MAN: Wait, wait. There's somebody coming. . . . It is Cuchulain is coming. He's coming back with the High King. Go and ask Cuchulain. He'll tell you. It's little you'll care about the cooking-pot when you have asked Cuchulain that . . .

(BLIND MAN *goes out by side door.*)

FOOL: I'll ask him. Cuchulain will know. He was in Aoife's country. (*Goes up stage.*) I'll ask him. (*Turns and goes down stage.*) But, no, I won't ask him, I would be afraid. (*Going up again*) Yes, I will ask him. What harm in asking? The Blind Man said I was to ask him. (*Going down*) No, no. I'll not ask him. He might kill me. I have but killed hens and geese and pigs. He has killed kings. (*Goes up again almost to big door.*) Who says I'm afraid? I'm not afraid. I'm no coward. I'll ask him. No, no, Cuchulain, I'm not going to ask you.

He has killed kings,
Kings and the sons of kings,
Dragons out of the water,
And witches out of the air,
Banachas and Bonachas and people of the woods.

(FOOL *goes out by the side door, the last words being heard outside.* CUCUHLAIN *and* CONCHUBAR *enter through the big door at the back. While they are still outside,* CUCHULAIN'S *voice is heard raised in anger. He is a dark man, something over forty years of age.* CONCHUBAR *is much older and carries a long staff, elaborately carved or with an elaborate gold handle.*)

CUCHULAIN: Because I have killed men without your bidding
And have rewarded others at my own pleasure,
Because of half a score of trifling things,
You'd lay this oath upon me, and now—and now
You add another pebble to the heap,
And I must be your man, well-nigh your bondsman,
Because a youngster out of Aoife's country
Has found the shore ill-guarded.
CONCHUBAR: He came to land
While you were somewhere out of sight and hearing,
Hunting or dancing with your wild companions.
CUCHULAIN: He can be driven out. I'll not be bound.
I'll dance or hunt, or quarrel or make love,

Wherever and whenever I've a mind to.
If time had not put water in your blood,
You never would have thought it.

CONCHUBAR: I would leave
A strong and settled country to my children.

CUCHULAIN: And I must be obedient in all things;
Give up my will to yours; go where you please;
Come when you call; sit at the council-board
Among the unshapely bodies of old men;
I whose mere name has kept this country safe,
I that in early days have driven out
Maeve of Cruachan and the northern pirates,
The hundred kings of Sorcha, and the kings
Out of the Garden in the East of the World.
Must I, that held you on the throne when all
Had pulled you from it, swear obedience
As if I were some cattle-raising king?
Are my shins speckled with the heat of the fire,
Or have my hands no skill but to make figures
Upon the ashes with a stick? Am I
So slack and idle that I need a whip
Before I serve you?

CONCHUBAR: No, no whip, Cuchulain,
But every day my children come and say:
"This man is growing harder to endure.
How can we be at safety with this man
That nobody can buy or bid or bind?
We shall be at his mercy when you are gone;
He burns the earth as if he were a fire,
And time can never touch him."

CUCHULAIN: And so the tale
Grows finer yet; and I am to obey
Whatever child you set upon the throne,
As if it were yourself!

CONCHUBAR: Most certainly.
I am High King, my son shall be High King;
And you for all the wildness of your blood,
And though your father came out of the sun,
Are but a little king and weigh but light
In anything that touches government,
If put into the balance with my children.

CUCHULAIN: It's well that we should speak our minds out plainly,
For when we die we shall be spoken of
In many countries. We in our young days

Have seen the heavens like a burning cloud
Brooding upon the world, and being more
Than men can be now that cloud's lifted up,
We should be the more truthful. Conchubar,
I do not like your children—they have no pith,
No marrow in their bones, and will lie soft
Where you and I lie hard.
CONCHUBAR: You rail at them
Because you have no children of your own.
CUCHULAIN: I think myself most lucky that I leave
No pallid ghost or mockery of a man
To drift and mutter in the corridors
Where I have laughed and sung.
CONCHUBAR: That is not true,
For all your boasting of the truth between us;
For there is no man having house and lands,
That have been in the one family, called
By that one family's name for centuries,
But is made miserable if he know
They are to pass into a stranger's keeping,
As yours will pass.
CUCHULAIN: The most of men feel that,
But you and I leave names upon the harp.
CONCHUBAR: You play with arguments as lawyers do,
And put no heart in them. I know your thoughts,
For we have slept under the one cloak and drunk
From the one wine-cup. I know you to the bone,
I have heard you cry, aye, in your very sleep,
"I have no son," and with such bitterness
That I have gone upon my knees and prayed
That it might be amended.
CUCHULAIN: For you thought
That I should be as biddable as others
Had I their reason for it; but that's not true;
For I would need a weightier argument
Than one that marred me in the copying,
As I have that clean hawk out of the air
That, as men say, begot this body of mine
Upon a mortal woman.
CONCHUBAR: Now as ever
You mock at every reasonable hope,
And would have nothing, or impossible things.
What eye has ever looked upon the child
Would satisfy a mind like that?
CUCHULAIN: I would leave

My house and name to none that would not face
Even myself in battle.
CONCHUBAR: Being swift of foot,
And making light of every common chance,
You should have overtaken on the hills
Some daughter of the air, or on the shore
A daughter of the Country-under-Wave.
CUCHULAIN: I am not blasphemous.
CONCHUBAR: Yet you despise
Our queens, and would not call a child your own,
If one of them had borne him.
CONCHULAIN: I have not said it.
CONCHUBAR: Ah! I remember I have heard you boast,
When the ale was in your blood, that there was one
In Scotland, where you had learnt the trade of war,
That had a stone-pale cheek and red-brown hair;
And that although you had loved other women,
You'd sooner that fierce woman of the camp
Bore you a son than any queen among them.
CUCHULAIN: You call her a "fierce woman of the camp,"
For, having lived among the spinning-wheels,
You'd have no woman near that would not say,
"Ah! how wise!" "What will you have for supper?"
"What shall I wear that I may please you, sir?"
And keep that humming through the day and night
For ever. A fierce woman of the camp!
But I am getting angry about nothing.
You have never seen her. Ah! Conchubar, had you seen her
With that high, laughing, turbulent head of hers
Thrown backward, and the bowstring at her ear,
Or sitting at the fire with those grave eyes
Full of good counsel as it were with wine,
Or when love ran through all the lineaments
Of her wild body—although she had no child,
None other had all beauty, queen or lover,
Or was so fitted to give birth to kings.
CONCHUBAR: There's nothing I can say but drifts you farther
From the one weighty matter. That very woman—
For I know well that you are praising Aoife—
Now hates you and will leave no subtlety
Unknotted that might run into a noose
About your throat, no army in idleness
That might bring ruin on this land you serve.
CUCHULAIN: No wonder in that, no wonder at all in that.
I never have known love but as a kiss

In the mid-battle, and a difficult truce
Of oil and water, candles and dark night,
Hillside and hollow, the hot-footed sun
And the cold, sliding, slippery-footed moon—
A brief forgiveness between opposites
That have been hatreds for three times the age
Of this long-'stablished ground.

CONCHUBAR: Listen to me.
Aoife makes war on us, and every day
Our enemies grow greater and beat the walls
More bitterly, and you within the walls
Are every day more turbulent; and yet,
When I would speak about these things, your fancy
Runs as it were a swallow on the wind.

(*Outside the door in the blue light of the sea-mist are many old and young* KINGS; *amongst them are three* WOMEN, *two of whom carry a bowl of fire. The third, in what follows, puts from time to time fragrant herbs into the fire so that it flickers up into brighter flame.*)

Look at the door and what men gather there—
Old counsellors that steer the land with me,
And younger kings, the dancers and harp-players
That follow in your tumults, and all these
Are held there by the one anxiety.
Will you be bound into obedience
And so make this land safe for them and theirs?
You are but half a king and I but half;
I need your might of hand and burning heart,
And you my wisdom.

CUCHULAIN (*going near to door*): Nestlings of a high nest,
Hawks that have followed me into the air
And looked upon the sun, we'll out of this
And sail upon the wind once more. This king
Would have me take an oath to do his will,
And having listened to his tune from morning,
I will no more of it. Run to the stable
And set the horses to the chariot-pole,
And send a messenger to the harp-players.
We'll find a level place among the woods,
And dance awhile.

A YOUNG KING: Cuchulain, take the oath.
There is none here that would not have you take it.

CUCHULAIN: You'd have me take it? Are you of one mind?

THE KINGS: All, all, all, all!
A YOUNG KING: Do what the Head King bids you.
CONCHUBAR: There is not one but dreads this turbulence
Now that they're settled men.
CUCHULAIN: Are you so changed,
Or have I grown more dangerous of late?
But that's not it. I understand it all.
It's you that have changed. You've wives and children now,
And for that reason cannot follow one
That lives like a bird's flight from tree to tree.—
It's time the years put water in my blood
And drowned the wildness of it, for all's changed,
But that unchanged.—I'll take what oath you will:
The moon, the sun, the water, light, or air,
I do not care how binding.
CONCHUBAR: On this fire
That has been lighted from your hearth and mine;
The older men shall be my witnesses,
The younger, yours. The holders of the fire
Shall purify the thresholds of the house
With waving fire, and shut the outer door,
According to the custom; and sing rhyme
That has come down from the old law-makers
To blow the witches out. Considering
That the wild will of man could be oath-bound,
But that a woman's could not, they bid us sing
Against the will of woman at its wildest
In the Shape-Changers that run upon the wind.

(CONCHUBAR *has gone on to his throne.*)

THE WOMEN (*They sing in a very low voice after the first few words so that the others all but drown their words*):
May this fire have driven out
The Shape-Changers that can put
Ruin on a great king's house
Until all be ruinous.
Names whereby a man has known
The threshold and the hearthstone,
Gather on the wind and drive
The women none can kiss and thrive,
For they are but whirling wind,
Out of memory and mind.
They would make a prince decay

With light images of clay
Planted in the running wave;
Or, for many shapes they have,
They would change them into hounds
Until he had died of his wounds,
Though the change were but a whim;
Or they'd hurl a spell at him,
That he follow with desire
Bodies that can never tire
Or grow kind, for they anoint
All their bodies, joint by joint,
With a miracle-working juice
That is made out of the grease
Of the ungoverned unicorn.
But the man is thrice forlorn,
Emptied, ruined, wracked, and lost,
That they followed, for at most
They will give him kiss for kiss
While they murmur, "After this
Hatred may be sweet to the taste."
Those wild hands that have embraced
All his body can but shove
At the burning wheel of love
Till the side of hate comes up.
Therefore in this ancient cup
May the sword-blades drink their fill
Of the home-brew there, until
They will have for masters none
But the threshold and hearthstone.

CUCHULAIN (*speaking, while they are singing*): I'll take and keep this oath, and from this day
I shall be what you please, my chicks, my nestlings.
Yet I had thought you were of those that praised
Whatever life could make the pulse run quickly,
Even though it were brief, and that you held
That a free gift was better than a forced.—
But that's all over.—I will keep it, too;
I never gave a gift and took it again.
If the wild horse should break the chariot-pole,
It would be punished. Should that be in the oath?

(*Two of the* WOMEN, *still singing, crouch in front of him holding the bowl over their heads. He spreads his hands over the flame.*)

I swear to be obedient in all things
To Conchubar, and to uphold his children.
CONCHUBAR: We are one being, as these flames are one:
I give my wisdom, and I take your strength.
Now thrust the swords into the flame, and pray
That they may serve the threshold and the hearthstone
With faithful service.

(*The* KINGS *kneel in a semicircle before the two* WOMEN *and* CUCHULAIN, *who thrusts his sword into the flame. They all put the points of their swords into the flame. The third* WOMAN *is at the back near the big door.*)

CUCHULAIN: O pure, glittering ones
That should be more than wife or friend or mistress,
Give us the enduring will, the unquenchable hope,
The friendliness of the sword!—

(*The song grows louder, and the last words ring out clearly. There is a loud knocking at the door, and a cry of* "Open! open!")

CONCHUBAR: Some king that has been loitering on the way.
Open the door, for I would have all know
That the oath's finished and Cuchulain bound,
And that the swords are drinking up the flame.

(*The door is opened by the third* WOMAN, *and a* YOUNG MAN *with a drawn sword enters.*)

YOUNG MAN: I am of Aoife's country.

(*The* KINGS *rush towards him.* CUCHULAIN *throws himself between.*)

CUCHULAIN: Put up your swords.
He is but one. Aoife is far away.
YOUNG MAN: I have come alone into the midst of you
To weigh this sword against Cuchulain's sword.
CONCHUBAR: And are you noble? for if of common seed,
You cannot weigh your sword against his sword
But in mixed battle.
YOUNG MAN: I am under bonds
To tell my name to no man; but it's noble.
CONCHUBAR: But I would know your name and not your bonds.
You cannot speak in the Assembly House,
If you are not noble.

FIRST OLD KING: Answer the High King!
YOUNG MAN: I will give no other proof than the hawk gives
That it's no sparrow!

(*He is silent for a moment, then speaks to all.*)

Yet look upon me, kings.
I, too, am of that ancient seed, and carry
The signs about this body and in these bones.
CUCHULAIN: To have shown the hawk's grey feather is enough,
And you speak highly, too. Give me that helmet.
I'd thought they had grown weary sending champions.
That sword and belt will do. This fighting's welcome.
The High King there has promised me his wisdom;
But the hawk's sleepy till its well-beloved
Cries out amid the acorns, or it has seen
Its enemy like a speck upon the sun.
What's wisdom to the hawk, when that clear eye
Is burning nearer up in the high air?

(*Looks hard at* YOUNG MAN; *then comes down steps and grasps* YOUNG MAN *by shoulder.*)

Hither into the light.
(*To* CONCHUBAR) The very tint
Of her that I was speaking of but now.
Not a pin's difference.
(*To* YOUNG MAN) You are from the North,
Where there are many that have that tint of hair—
Red-brown, the light red-brown. Come nearer, boy,
For I would have another look at you.
There's more likeness—a pale, a stone-pale cheek.
What brought you, boy? Have you no fear of death?
YOUNG MAN: Whether I live or die is in the gods' hands.
CUCHULAIN: That is all words, all words; a young man's talk.
I am their plough, their harrow, their very strength;
For he that's in the sun begot this body
Upon a mortal woman, and I have heard tell
It seemed as if he had outrun the moon
That he must follow always through waste heaven,
He loved so happily. He'll be but slow
To break a tree that was so sweetly planted.
Let's see that arm. I'll see it if I choose.
That arm had a good father and a good mother,
But it is not like this.

YOUNG MAN: You are mocking me;
You think I am not worthy to be fought.
But I'll not wrangle but with this talkative knife.
CUCHULAIN: Put up your sword; I am not mocking you.
I'd have you for my friend, but if it's not
Because you have a hot heart and a cold eye,
I cannot tell the reason.
(*To* CONCHUBAR) He has got her fierceness,
And nobody is as fierce as those pale women.
But I will keep him with me, Conchubar,
That he may set my memory upon her
When the day's fading.—You will stop with us,
And we will hunt the deer and the wild bulls;
And, when we have grown weary, light our fires
Between the wood and water, or on some mountain
Where the Shape-Changers of the morning come.
The High King there would make a mock of me
Because I did not take a wife among them.
Why do you hang your head? It's a good life:
The head grows prouder in the light of the dawn,
And friendship thickens in the murmuring dark
Where the spare hazels meet the wool-white foam.
But I can see there's no more need for words
And that you'll be my friend from this day out.
CONCHUBAR: He has come hither not in his own name
But in Queen Aoife's, and has challenged us
In challenging the foremost man of us all.
CUCHULAIN: Well, well, what matter?
CONCHUBAR: You think it does not matter,
And that a fancy lighter than the air,
A whim of the moment, has more matter in it.
For, having none that shall reign after you,
You cannot think as I do, who would leave
A throne too high for insult.
CUCHULAIN: Let your children
Re-mortar their inheritance, as we have,
And put more muscle on.—I'll give you gifts,
But I'd have something too—that arm-ring, boy.
We'll have this quarrel out when you are older.
YOUNG MAN: There is no man I'd sooner have my friend
Than you, whose name has gone about the world
As if it had been the wind; but Aoife'd say
I had turned coward.
CUCHULAIN: I will give you gifts
That Aoife'll know, and all her people know,

To have come from me. (*Showing cloak*) My father gave me this.
He came to try me, rising up at dawn
Out of the cold dark of the rich sea.
He challenged me to battle, but before
My sword had touched his sword, told me his name,
Gave me this cloak, and vanished. It was woven
By women of the Country-under-Wave
Out of the fleeces of the sea. O! tell her
I was afraid, or tell her what you will.
No; tell her that I heard a raven croak
On the north side of the house, and was afraid.

CONCHUBAR: Some witch of the air has troubled Cuchulain's mind.

CUCHULAIN: No witchcraft. His head is like a woman's head
I had a fancy for.

CONCHUBAR: A witch of the air
Can make a leaf confound us with memories.
They run upon the wind and hurl the spells
That makes us nothing, out of the invisible wind.
They have gone to school to learn the trick of it.

CUCHULAIN: No, no—there's nothing out of common here;
The winds are innocent.—That arm-ring, boy.

A KING: If I've your leave I'll take this challenge up.

ANOTHER KING: No, give it me, High King, for this wild Aoife
Has carried off my slaves.

ANOTHER KING: No, give it me,
For she has harried me in house and herd.

ANOTHER KING: I claim this fight.

OTHER KINGS (*together*): And I! And I! And I!

CUCHULAIN: Back! back! Put up your swords! Put up your swords!
There's none alive that shall accept a challenge I have refused.
Laegaire, put up your sword!

YOUNG MAN: No, let them come. If they've a mind for it,
I'll try it out with any two together.

CUCHULAIN: That's spoken as I'd have spoken it at your age.
But you are in my house. Whatever man
Would fight with you shall fight it out with me.
They're dumb, they're dumb. How many of you would meet (*Draws sword*)
This mutterer, this old whistler, this sand-piper,
This edge that's greyer than the tide, this mouse

That's gnawing at the timbers of the world,
This, this—Boy, I would meet them all in arms
If I'd a son like you. He would avenge me
When I have withstood for the last time the men
Whose fathers, brothers, sons, and friends I have killed
Upholding Conchubar, when the four provinces
Have gathered with the ravens over them.
But I'd need no avenger. You and I
Would scatter them like water from a dish.

YOUNG MAN: We'll stand by one another from this out.
Here is the ring.

CUCHULAIN: No, turn and turn about.
But my turn's first because I am older.
(*spreading out cloak*)
Nine queens out of the Country-under-Wave
Have woven it with the fleeces of the sea
And they were long embroidering at it.—Boy,
If I had fought my father, he'd have killed me,
As certainly as if I had a son
And fought with him, I should be deadly to him;
For the old fiery fountains are far off
And every day there is less heat o' the blood.

CONCHUBAR (*in a loud voice*): No more of this. I will not have this friendship.
Cuchulain is my man, and I forbid it.
He shall not go unfought, for I myself—

CUCHULAIN: I will not have it.

CONCHUBAR: You lay commands on me?

CUCHULAIN (*seizing* CONCHUBAR): You shall not stir, High King. I'll hold you there.

CONCHUBAR: Witchcraft has maddened you.

THE KINGS (*shouting*): Yes, witchcraft! witchcraft!

FIRST OLD KING: Some witch has worked upon your mind, Cuchulain.
The head of that young man seemed like a woman's
You'd had a fancy for. Then of a sudden
You laid your hands on the High King himself!

CUCHULAIN: And laid my hands on the High King himself?

CONCHUBAR: Some witch is floating in the air above us.

CUCHULAIN: Yes, witchcraft! witchcraft! Witches of the air!
(*To* YOUNG MAN): Why did you? Who was it set you to this work?
Out, out! I say, for now it's sword on sword!

YOUNG MAN: But . . . but I did not.
CUCHULAIN: Out I say, out, out!

(YOUNG MAN *goes out followed by* CUCHULAIN. *The* KINGS *follow them out with confused cries, and words one can hardly hear because of the noise. Some cry,* "Quicker, quicker!" "Why are you so long at the door?" "We'll be too late!" "Have they begun to fight?" "Can you see if they are fighting?" *and so on. Their voices drown each other. The three* WOMEN *are left alone.*)

FIRST WOMAN: I have seen, I have seen!
SECOND WOMAN: What do you cry aloud?
FIRST WOMAN: The Ever-living have shown me what's to come.
THIRD WOMAN: How? Where?
FIRST WOMAN: In the ashes of the bowl.
SECOND WOMAN: While you were holding it between your hands?
THIRD WOMAN: Speak quickly!
FIRST WOMAN: I have seen Cuchulain's roof-tree
Leap into fire, and the walls split and blacken.
SECOND WOMAN: Cuchulain has gone out to die.
THIRD WOMAN: O! O!
SECOND WOMAN: Who could have thought that one so great as he
Should meet his end at this unnoted sword!
FIRST WOMAN: Life drifts between a fool and a blind man
To the end, and nobody can know his end.
SECOND WOMAN: Come, look upon the quenching of this greatness.

(*The other two go to the door, but they stop for a moment upon the threshold and wail.*)

FIRST WOMAN: No crying out, for there'll be need of cries
And rending of the hair when it's all finished.

(*The* WOMEN *go out There is the sound of clashing swords from time to time during what follows.*)
(*Enter the* FOOL, *dragging the* BLIND MAN.)

FOOL: You have eaten it, you have eaten it! You have left me nothing but the bones. (*He throws* BLIND MAN *down by big chair.*)

BLIND MAN: O, that I should have to endure such a plague! O, I ache all over! O, I am pulled to pieces! This is the way you pay me all the good I have done you.

FOOL: You have eaten it! Your have told me lies. I might have known you had eaten it when I saw your slow, sleepy walk. Lie there till the kings come. O, I will tell Conchubar and Cuchulain and all the kings about you!

BLIND MAN: What would have happened to you but for me, and you without your wits? If I did not take care of you, what would you do for food and warmth?

FOOL: You take care of me? You stay safe, and send me into every kind of danger. You sent me down the cliff for gulls' eggs while you warmed your blind eyes in the sun; and then you ate all that were good for food. You left me the eggs that were neither egg nor bird. (BLIND MAN *tries to rise;* FOOL *makes him lie down again.*) Keep quiet now, till I shut the door. There is some noise outside—a high vexing noise, so that I can't be listening to myself. (*Shuts the big door.*) Why can't they be quiet? Why can't they be quiet? (BLIND MAN *tries to get away.*) Ah! you would get away, would you? (*Follows* BLIND MAN *and brings him back.*) Lie there! lie there! No, you won't get away! Lie there till the kings come. I'll tell them all about you. I will tell it all. How you sit warming yourself, when you have made me light a fire of sticks, while I sit blowing it with my mouth. Do you not always make me take the windy side of the bush when it blows, and the rainy side when it rains?

BLIND MAN: O, good Fool! listen to me. Think of the care I have taken of you. I have brought you to many a warm hearth, where there was a good welcome for you, but you would not stay there; you were always wandering about.

FOOL: The last time you brought me in, it was not I who wandered away, but you that got put out because you took the crubeen out of the pot when nobody was looking. Keep quiet, now!

CUCHULAIN (*rushing in*): Witchcraft! There is no witchcraft on the earth, or among the witches of the air, that these hands cannot break.

FOOL: Listen to me, Cuchulain. I left him turning the fowl at the fire. He ate it all, though I had stolen it. He left me nothing but the feathers.

CUCHULAIN: Fill me a horn of ale!

BLIND MAN: I gave him what he likes best. You do not know how vain this Fool is. He likes nothing so well as a feather.

FOOL: He left me nothing but bones and feathers. Nothing but the feathers, though I had stolen it.

CUCHULAIN: Give me that horn. Quarrels here, too! (*Drinks.*) What is there between you two that is worth a quarrel? Out with it!

BLIND MAN: Where would he be but for me? I must be always thinking—thinking to get food for the two of us, and when we've got it, if the moon is at the full or the tide on the turn, he'll leave the rabbit in the snare till it is full of maggots, or let the trout slip back through his hands into the stream.

(*The* FOOL *has begun singing while the* BLIND MAN *is speaking.*)

FOOL (*singing*):

When you were an acorn on the tree-top,
  Then was I an eagle-cock;
Now that you are a withered old block,
  Still am I an eagle-cock.

BLIND MAN: Listen to him, now. That's the sort of talk I have to put up with day out, day in.

(*The* FOOL *is putting the feathers into his hair.* CUCHULAIN *takes a handful of feathers out of a heap the* FOOL *has on the bench beside him, and out of the* FOOL'S *hair, begins to wipe the blood from his sword with them.*)

FOOL: He has taken my feathers to wipe his sword. It is blood that he is wiping from his sword.

CUCHULAIN (*goes up to door at back and throws away feathers*): They are standing about his body. They will not awaken him, for all his witchcraft.

BLIND MAN: It is that young champion that he has killed. He that came out of Aoife's country.

CUCHULAIN: He thought to have saved himself with witchcraft.

FOOL: That Blind Man there said he would kill you. He came from Aoife's country to kill you. That Blind Man said they had taught him every kind of weapon that he might do it. But I always knew that you would kill him.

CUCHULAIN (*to the* BLIND MAN): You knew him, then?

BLIND MAN: I saw him, when I had my eyes, in Aoife's country.

CUCHULAIN: You were in Aoife's country?

BLIND MAN: I knew him and his mother there.

CUCHULAIN: He was about to speak of her when he died.

BLIND MAN: He was a queen's son.

CUCHULAIN: What queen? what queen? (*Seizes* BLIND MAN, *who is now sitting upon the bench.*) Was it Scathach? There were many queens. All the rulers there were queens.

BLIND MAN: No, not Scathach.

CUCHULAIN: It was Uathach, then? Speak! speak!

BLIND MAN: I cannot speak; you are clutching me too tightly. (CUCHULAIN *lets him go.*) I cannot remember who it was. I am not certain. It was some queen.

FOOL: He said a while ago that the young man was Aoife's son.

CUCHULAIN: She? No, no! She had no son when I was there.

FOOL: That Blind Man there said that she owned him for her son.

CUCHULAIN: I had rather he had been some other woman's son. What father had he? A soldier out of Alba? She was an amorous woman—a proud, pale, amorous woman.

BLIND MAN: None knew whose son he was.

CUCHULAIN: None knew! Did you know, old listener at doors?

BLIND MAN: No, no; I knew nothing.

FOOL: He said a while ago that he heard Aoife boast that she'd never but the one lover, and he the only man that had overcome her in battle. (*Pause.*)

BLIND MAN: Somebody is trembling, Fool! The bench is shaking. Why are you trembling? Is Cuchulain going to hurt us? It was not I who told you, Cuchulain.

FOOL: It is Cuchulain who is trembling. It is Cuchulain who is shaking the bench.

BLIND MAN: It is his own son he has slain.

CUCHULAIN: 'Twas they that did it, the pale windy people.
Where? where? where? My sword against the thunder!
But no, for they have always been my friends;
And though they love to blow a smoking coal
Till it's all flame, the wars they blow aflame
Are full of glory, and heart-uplifting pride,
And not like this. The wars they love awaken
Old fingers and the sleepy strings of harps.
Who did it then? Are you afraid? Speak out!
For I have put you under my protection,
And will reward you well. Dubthach the Chafer?
He'd an old grudge. No, for he is with Maeve.
Laegaire did it! Why do you not speak?

What is this house? (*Pause.*) Now I remember all.

(*Comes before* CONCHUBAR'S *chair, and strikes out with his sword, as if* CONCHUBAR *was sitting upon it.*)

'Twas you who did it—you who sat upon there
With your old rod of kingship, like a magpie
Nursing a stolen spoon. No, not a magpie,
A maggot that is eating up the earth!
Yes, but a magpie, for he's flown away.
Where did he fly to?

BLIND MAN: He is outside the door.

CUCHULAIN: Outside the door?

BLIND MAN: Between the door and the sea.

CUCHULAIN: Conchubar, Conchubar! the sword into your heart!

(*He rushes out. Pause.* FOOL *creeps up to the big door and looks after him.*)

FOOL: He is going up to King Conchubar. They are all about the young man. No, no, he is standing still. There is a great wave going to break, and he is looking at it. Ah! now he is running down to the sea, but he is holding up his sword as if he were going into a fight. (*Pause.*) Well struck! well struck!

BLIND MAN: What is he doing now?

FOOL: O! he is fighting the waves!

BLIND MAN: He sees King Conchubar's crown on every one of them.

FOOL: There, he has struck at a big one! He has struck the crown off it; he has made the foam fly. There again, another big one!

BLIND MAN: Where are the kings? What are the kings doing?

FOOL: They are shouting and running down to the shore, and the people are running out of the houses. They are all running.

BLIND MAN: You say they are running out of the houses? There will be nobody left in the houses. Listen, Fool!

FOOL: There, he is down! He is up again. He is going out in the deep water. There is a big wave. It has gone over him. I cannot see him now. He has killed kings and giants, but the waves have mastered him, the waves have mastered him!

BLIND MAN: Come here, Fool!

FOOL: The waves have mastered him.

BLIND MAN: Come here!

FOOL: The waves have mastered him.

BLIND MAN: Come here, I say.

FOOL (*coming towards him, but looking backwards towards the door*): What is it?

BLIND MAN: There will be nobody in the houses. Come this way; quickly! The ovens will be full. We will put our hands into the ovens. (*They go out.*)

Eugene O'Neill:
DESIRE UNDER THE ELMS

Although tragic drama traditionally depicted the fall of kings and princes, as early as the sixteenth century there were tragedies with middle-class protagonists. Playwrights, of course, sought to justify their new tragedies against conservative critical theory. The standard argument in favor of the old heroic tragedy is that only the fall of a great man can excite pity and fear, whereas the fall of an ordinary man—a man like ourselves—is not awe-inspiring but merely pathetic. Great passions, the argument runs, are found only in great men; a king, for example, can avenge his honor, but a shopkeeper has no honor to avenge. More specifically, the fall of a great hero is more tragic than the fall of an ordinary citizen because it is a bigger fall, and because it necessarily has greater reverberations. When a king crashes, a kingdom trembles:

> The cease of majesty
> Dies not alone, but, like a gulf doth draw
> What's near it with it. (*Hamlet,* III, iii. 15-17)

On the other hand, advocates of bourgeois tragedy generally insist that tragic drama derives much of its impact from our sympathy for (or identification with) the tragic hero, and this identification is, presumably, more likely to be achieved when the hero resembles us. Furthermore, democratic supporters of middle-class tragedy say, all men are potentially great, and rank is irrelevant to largeness of spirit.

The emotions which we feel at a tragedy are so complex that even if we sense we are witnessing a drama which we can only call tragic, we can hardly communicate our precise sensations to our neighbor. Tragedy, then, is most easily (though perhaps inadequately) defined by pointing to certain obvious characteristics of dramas which are generally acknowledged (though on no particular basis) as being tragic: a noble hero, and an unhappy ending. The chief alternative to this obviously crude definition seeks to define tragedy in terms of the emotions it arouses in us, but this second method is so highly personal that it allows every spectator to erect his own standard. X can never say to Y that a particular play is untragic. He can only say that the play failed to arouse in him a particular sensation, a sensation which Y might think (if he could experience it) irrelevant to true tragedy. The two theories can be related if we agree that only certain kinds of characters can arouse certain emotions. That is, the critic who demands regal characters may really be doing so not because he is undemocratic but because he has found that he experiences the tragic emotion only when he looks at the fall of great power.

The tragic emotion, according to the vast majority of those who have written on the subject, is a curious combination of pleasure and pain, or rather, is a pleasure which somehow derives its pleasurableness from being based on pain. Plato suggests in the *Philebus* that an itch (pain) affords a special pleasure when it is scratched, and the anticipation of a drink is pleasurable to a thirsty man. So tragedy, which depicts a sight in some respects painful, affords a special pleasure—but unfortunately Plato does not analyze this emotion. Some theorists, however, interestingly suggest that we assert ourselves with the tragic hero, and suffer his punishment (and ours) along with him; thus we sin and atone, and the atonement is partly derived from the fact that the hero has died for us. But if we are to feel that we have purged ourselves by sympathetically suffering with the hero and by the hero's sacrifice, the tragic figure must be a fit representative of fallible man, and a small hero may not fill the role.

In several plays, notably *Ghosts,* Henrik Ibsen demonstrated the power which middle-class tragedy could achieve. But it is worth noting that the tragedy of Mrs. Alving, the upper-middle-class heroine in *Ghosts,* is party reinforced by the tragic or at least pathetic ruin of her son. The play, that is, might be said not to have a single tragic hero, for the spectator almost feels that Ibsen is trying to add a cubit to the stature of his heroine by standing her on the ruin of her son.

In Eugene O'Neill's *Desire under the Elms* (1924) we descend even further down the social scale, and perhaps to compensate for a lack in social stature we now have no less than three tragic heroes. The characters on his New England farm are earthy, primitive people, not much above the beasts they tend. Eben, for example, is described as having the eyes of a caged beast, and he later describes himself as "the prize rooster o' this roost." But such animalism is not, in O'Neill's view, a disqualification for the tragic hero. The play seeks to confer a heroic tragic dignity on motives and deeds usually thought base, and O'Neill attempts to turn his tale of adultery and infanticide into something of a modern *Oedipus,* where strong passions gain a kind of glory. The son rebels against the father and covets the father's wife. And the father, wife, and son who dwell on this rocky farm are all seen not as unimportant little people but as human beings endowed with monumental passions whose depth is their justification. At the close of the play, a play which might seem superficially depressing, O'Neill's New England farmers have acquired a strength, a knowledge, and perhaps a tragic dignity which brings them close to the traditional heroic figures of Greece and the Renaissance. Eben, the son, has matured, proved his manhood, and—more important—experienced a love so great that he accepts suffering rather than renounce it. Abbie, the stepmother whom he comes to love, courageously accepts the consequences of both adulterous love and murder: she repents the latter ("I got t' take my punishment—t' pay fur my sin"), but she will not renounce her love for Eben. Like Job, she insists she will maintain her own ways before God; like Prometheus, she refuses to admit that her passionate assertion is wicked. And the third hero is the father, who at the end renounces them both. Surrounded by betrayals, he shakes off adversity and rises above the rest as he sets out to put his farm in order. He is no king banished from his land, but he is bereft of human companionship on the farm which he has built among the rocks. He accepts his lot, accepts it so fully that we feel there is something "heroic" in his ascetic triumph over the loneliness around him. "God's lonesome, hain't He? God's hard an' lonesome!"

O'Neill has often been accused of being not a tragic but a merely depressing dramatist. Two years before he wrote *Desire under the Elms* he replied to this charge and attempted to set forth his conception of tragedy. "Happiness," he said, "is a word. What does it mean? Exaltation; an intensified feeling of the significant worth of a man's being and becoming? Well, if it means that—and not a mere smirking contentment with one's lot—I know there is more of it in one real tragedy than in all the happy-ending plays ever written. It's mere present-day judgment to think of tragedy as unhappy! The Greeks and the Elizabethans knew better. They felt the tremendous lift to it. It roused them spiritually to a deeper understanding of life. Through it they found release from the petty considerations of everyday existence. They saw their lives ennobled by it. A work of art is always happy; all else is unhappy."

O'Neill: Biographical Note. Eugene O'Neill (1888-1953), the son of a noted American actor, was born on Broadway in 1888, but his road back to the theater was a devious one. He entered Princeton in 1906, but withdrew the following year. In 1909 he shipped to Honduras, then to Buenos Aires and South Africa. In 1912 he had to spend five months in a sanatorium, recuperating from tuberculosis, and here he began to meditate on life, especially as depicted by the dramatists. (Incidentally, readers of Strindberg's *Miss Julie,* included in this volume, may want to look at O'Neill's *Diff'rent,* a play certainly influenced by Strindberg's.) He then wrote a trunkful of plays, studied dramaturgy with George Pierce Baker at Harvard, and saw his first play produced in Provincetown, Massachusetts, in 1916. Fame came quickly, and when he died in 1953 he had won three Pulitzer Prizes and the Nobel Prize for Literature.

Desire under the Elms

CHARACTERS

EPHRAIM CABOT.

SIMEON }
PETER } his sons.
EBEN }

ABBIE PUTNAM.

Young GIRL, *two* FARMERS, *the* FIDDLER, *a* SHERIFF, *and other folk from the neighboring farms.*

(The action of the entire play takes place in, and immediately outside of, the Cabot Farmhouse in New England, in the year 1850. The south end of the house faces front to a stone wall with a wooden gate at center opening on a country road. The house is in good condition but in need of paint. Its walls are a sickly grayish, the green of the shutters faded. Two enormous elms are on each side of the house. They bend their trailing branches down over the roof. They appear to protect and at the same time subdue. There is a sinister maternity in their aspect, a crushing, jealous absorption. They have developed from their intimate contact with the life of man in the house an appalling humaneness. They brood oppressively over the house. They are like exhausted women resting their sagging breasts and hands and hair on its roof, and when it rains their tears trickle down monotonously and rot on the shingles.

There is a path running from the gate around the right corner of the house to the front door. A narrow porch is on this side. The end wall facing us has two windows in its upper story, two larger ones on the floor below. The two upper are those of the father's bedroom and that of the brothers. On the left, ground floor, is the kitchen—on the right, the parlor, the shades of which are always drawn down.)

PART I

SCENE I

(Exterior of the farmhouse. It is sunset of a day at the beginning of summer in the year 1850. There is no wind and everything is still. The sky above the roof is suffused with deep colors, the green of the elms glows, but the house is in shadow, seeming pale and washed out by contrast.

A door opens and EBEN CABOT *comes to the end of the porch and stands looking down the road to the right. He has a large bell in his hand and this he swings mechanically, awakening a deafening clangor. Then he puts his hands on his hips and stares up at the sky. He sighs with a puzzled awe and blurts out with halting appreciation.)*

EBEN: God! Purty! (*His eyes fall and he stares about him frowningly. He is twenty-five, tall and sinewy. His face is well-formed, good-looking, but its expression is resentful and defensive. His defiant, dark eyes remind one of a wild animal's in captivity. Each day is a cage in which he finds himself trapped but inwardly unsubdued. There is a fierce repressed vitality about him. He has black hair, mustache, a thin curly trace of beard. He is dressed in rough farm clothes.*

He spits on the ground with intense disgust, turns and goes back into the house.

SIMEON *and* PETER *come in from their work in the fields. They are tall men, much older than their half-brother* [SIMEON *is thirty-nine and* PETER *thirty-seven*], *built on a squarer, simpler model, fleshier in body, more bovine and homelier in face, shrewder and more practical. Their shoulders stoop a bit from years of farm work. They clump heavily along in their clumsy thick-soled boots caked with earth. Their clothes, their faces, hands, bare arms and throats are earth-stained. They smell of earth. They stand together for a moment in front of the house and, as if with the one impulse, stare dumbly up at the sky, leaning on their hoes. Their faces have a compressed, unresigned expression. As they look upward, this softens.)*

SIMEON (*grudgingly*): Purty.

PETER: Ay-eh.

SIMEON (*suddenly*): Eighteen year ago.

PETER: What?

SIMEON: Jenn. My woman. She died.

PETER: I'd fergot.

SIMEON: I rec'lect—now an' agin. Makes it lonesome. She'd hair long's a hoss' tail—an' yaller like gold!

PETER: Waal—she's gone. (*This with indifferent finality—then after a pause*) They's gold in the West, Sim.

SIMEON (*still under the influence of sunset—vaguely*): In the sky?

PETER: Waal—in a manner o' speakin'—thar's the promise. (*Growing excited*) Gold in the sky—in the West—Golden Gate—Californi-a!—Goldest West!—fields o' gold!

SIMEON (*excited in his turn*): Fortunes layin' just atop o' the ground waitin' t' be picked! Solomon's mines, they says! (*For a moment they continue looking up at the sky—then their eyes drop.*)

PETER (*with sardonic bitterness*): Here—it's stones atop o' the ground—stones atop o' stones—makin' stone walls—year atop o' year—him 'n' yew 'n' me 'n' then Eben—makin' stone walls fur him to fence us in!

SIMEON: We've wuked. Give our strength. Give our years. Plowed 'em under in the ground—(*he stamps rebelliously*)—rottin'—makin' soil for his crops! (*A pause.*) Waal—the farm pays good for hereabouts.

PETER: If we plowed in Californi-a, they'd be lumps o' gold in the furrow!

SIMEON: Californi-a's t'other side o' earth, a'most. We got t' calc'late—

PETER (*after a pause*): 'Twould be hard fur me, too, to give up what we've 'arned here by our sweat. (*A pause,* EBEN *sticks his head out of the dining-room window, listening.*)

SIMEON: Ay-eh. (*A pause.*) Mebbe—he'll die soon.

PETER (*doubtfully*): Mebbe.

SIMEON: Mebbe—fur all we knows—he's dead now.

PETER: Ye'd need proof.

SIMEON: He's been gone two months—with no word.

PETER: Left us in the fields an evenin' like this. Hitched up an' druv off into the West. That's plum onnateral. He hain't never been off this farm 'ceptin' t' the village in thirty year or more, not since he married Eben's maw. (*A pause. Shrewdly*) I calc'late we might git him declared crazy by the court.

SIMEON: He skinned 'em too slick. He got the best o' all on 'em. They'd never b'lieve him crazy. (*A pause*) We got t' wait—till he's under ground.

EBEN (*with a sardonic chuckle*): Honor thy father! (*They

turn, startled, and stare at him. He grins, then scowls.) I pray he's died. (*They stare at him. He continues matter-of-factly*) Supper's ready.

SIMEON *and* PETER (*together*): Ay-eh.

EBEN (*gazing up at the sky*): Sun's downin' purty.

SIMEON *and* PETER (*together*): Ay-eh. They's gold in the West.

EBEN: Ay-eh. (*Pointing*) Yonder atop o' the hill pasture, ye mean?

SIMEON *and* PETER (*together*): In Californi-a!

EBEN: Hunh! (*Stares at them indifferently for a second, then drawls*) Waal—supper's gittin' cold. (*He turns back into kitchen.*)

SIMEON (*startled—smacks his lips*): I air hungry!

PETER (*sniffing*): I smells bacon!

SIMEON (*with hungry appreciation*): Bacon's good!

PETER (*in same tone*): Bacon's bacon! (*They turn, shouldering each other, their bodies bumping and rubbing together as they hurry clumsily to their food, like two friendly oxen toward their evening meal. They disappear around the right corner of house and can be heard entering the door.*)

(*Curtain.*)

Scene II

(*The color fades from the sky. Twilight begins. The interior of the kitchen is now visible. A pine table is at center, a cookstove in the right rear corner, four rough wooden chairs, a tallow candle on the table. In the middle of the rear wall is fastened a big advertising poster with a ship in full sail and the word "California" in big letters. Kitchen utensils hang from nails. Everything is neat and in order but the atmosphere is of a men's camp kitchen rather than that of a home.*

Places for three are laid. EBEN *takes boiled potatoes and bacon from the stove and puts them on the table, also a loaf of bread and a crock of water.* SIMEON *and* PETER *shoulder in, slump down in their chairs without a word.* EBEN *joins them. The three eat in silence for a moment, the two elder as naturally unrestrained as beasts of the field,* EBEN *picking at his food without appetite, glancing at them with a tolerant dislike.*)

SIMEON (*suddenly turns to* EBEN): Looky here! Ye'd oughtn't t' said that, Eben.

PETER: 'Twa'n't righteous.

EBEN: What?

SIMEON: Ye prayed he'd died.

EBEN: Waal—don't yew pray it? (*A pause.*)

PETER: He's our Paw.

EBEN (*violently*): Not mine!

SIMEON (*dryly*): Ye'd not let no one else say that about yer Maw! Ha! (*He gives one abrupt sardonic guffaw.* PETER *grins.*)

EBEN (*very pale*): I meant—I hain't his'n—I hain't like him—he hain't me!

PETER (*dryly*): Wait till ye've growed his age!

EBEN (*intensely*): I'm Maw—every drop o' blood! (*A pause. They stare at him with indifferent curiosity.*)

PETER (*reminiscently*): She was good t' Sim 'n' me. A good Stepmaw's scurse.

SIMEON: She was good t' everyone.

EBEN (*greatly moved, gets to his feet and makes an awkward bow to each of them—stammering*): I be thankful t' ye. I'm her—her heir. (*He sits down in confusion.*)

PETER (*after a pause—judicially*): She was good even t' him.

EBEN (*fiercely*): An' fur thanks he killed her!

SIMEON (*after a pause*): No one never kills nobody. It's allus somethin'. That's the murderer.

EBEN: Didn't he slave Maw t' death?

PETER: He's slaved himself t' death. He's slaved Sim 'n' me 'n' yew t' death—on'y none o' us hain't died—yit.

SIMEON: It's somethin'—drivin' him—t' drive us!

EBEN (*vengefully*): Waal—I hold him t' jedgment! (*Then scornfully*) Somethin'! What's somethin'?

SIMEON: Dunno.

EBEN (*sardonically*): What's drivin' yew to Californi-a, mebbe? (*They look at him in surprise.*) Oh, I've heerd ye! (*Then, after a pause*) But ye'll never go t' the gold fields!

PETER (*assertively*): Mebbe!

EBEN: Whar'll ye git the money?

PETER: We kin walk. It's an a'mighty ways—Californi-a—but if yew was t' put all the steps we've walked on this farm end t' end we'd be in the moon!

EBEN: The Injuns'll skulp ye on the plains.

SIMEON (*with grim humor*): We'll mebbe make 'em pay a hair fur a hair!

EBEN (*decisively*): But t'ain't that. Ye won't never go because ye'll wait here fur yer share o' the farm, thinkin' allus he'll die soon.

SIMEON (*after a pause*): We've a right.

PETER: Two-thirds belongs t'us.

EBEN (*jumping to his feet*): Ye've no right! She wa'n't yewr Maw! It was her farm! Didn't he steal it from her? She's dead. It's my farm.

SIMEON (*sardonically*): Tell that t' Paw—when he comes! I'll bet ye a dollar he'll laugh—fur once in his life. Ha! (*He laughs himself in one single mirthless bark.*)

PETER (*amused in turn, echoes his brother*): Ha!

SIMEON (*after a pause*): What've ye got held agin us, Eben? Year arter year it's skulked in yer eye—somethin'.

PETER: Ay-eh.

EBEN: Ay-eh. They's somethin'. (*Suddenly exploding*) Why didn't ye never stand between him 'n' my Maw when he was slavin' her to her grave—t' pay her back fur the kindness she done t' yew? (*There is a long pause. They stare at him in surprise.*)

SIMEON: Waal—the stock'd got t' be watered.

PETER: 'R they was woodin' t' do.

SIMEON: 'R plowin'.

PETER: 'R hayin'.

SIMEON: 'R spreadin' manure.

PETER: 'R weedin'.

SIMEON: 'R prunin'.

PETER: 'R milkin'.

EBEN (*breaking in harshly*): An' makin' walls—the stone atop o' stone—makin' walls till yer heart's a stone ye heft up out o' the way o' growth onto a stone wall t' wall in yer heart!

SIMEON (*matter-of-factly*): We never had no time t' meddle.

PETER (*to* EBEN): Yew was fifteen afore yer Maw died—an' big fur yer age. Why didn't ye never do nothin'?

EBEN (*harshly*): They was chores t' do, wa'n't they? (*A pause—then slowly*) It was on'y arter she died I come to think o' it. Me cookin'—doin' her work—that made me know her, suffer her sufferin'—she'd come back t' help—come back t' bile potatoes—come back t' fry bacon—come back t' bake biscuits—come back all cramped up t' shake the fire, an' carry ashes, her eyes weepin' an' bloody with smoke an' cinders same's they used t' be. She still comes back—stands by the stove thar in the evenin'—she can't find it nateral sleepin' an' restin' in peace. She can't git used t' bein' free—even in her grave.

SIMEON: She never complained none.

EBEN: She'd got too tired. She'd got too used t' bein' too tired. That was what he done. (*With vengeful passion*) An' sooner'r later, I'll meddle. I'll say the thin's I didn't say then t' him! I'll yell 'em at the top o' my lungs. I'll see t' it my

Maw gits some rest an' sleep in her grave! (*He sits down again, relapsing into a brooding silence. They look at him with a queer indifferent curiosity.*)

PETER (*after a pause*): Whar in tarnation d'ye s'pose he went, Sim?

SIMEON: Dunno. He druv off in the buggy, all spick an' span, with the mare all breshed an' shiny, druv off clackin' his tongue an' wavin' his whip. I remember it right well. I was finishin' plowin', it was spring an' May an' sunset, an' gold in the West, an' he druv off into it. I yells "Whar ye goin', Paw?" an' he hauls up by the stone wall a jiffy. His old snake's eyes was glitterin' in the sun like he'd been drinkin' a jugful an' he says with a mule's grin: "Don't ye run away till I come back!"

PETER: Wonder if he knowed we was wantin' fur Californi-a?

SIMEON: Mebbe. I didn't say nothin' and he says, lookin' kinder queer an' sick: "I been hearin' the hens cluckin' an' the roosters crowin' all the durn day. I been listenin' t' the cows lowin' an' everythin' else kickin' up till I can't stand it no more. It's spring an' I'm feelin' damned," he says. "Damned like an old bare hickory tree fit on'y fur burnin'," he says. An' then I calc'late I must've looked a mite hopeful, fur he adds real spry and vicious: "But don't git no fool idee I'm dead. I've sworn t' live a hundred an' I'll do it, if on'y t' spite yer sinful greed! An' now I'm ridin' out t' learn God's message t' me in the spring, like the prophets done. An' yew git back t' yer plowin'," he says. An' he druv off singin' a hymn. I thought he was drunk—'r I'd stopped him goin'.

EBEN (*scornfully*): No, ye wouldn't! Ye're scared o' him. He's stronger—inside—than both o' ye put together!

PETER (*sardonically*): An' yew—be yew Samson?

EBEN: I'm gittin' stronger. I kin feel it growin' in me—growin' an' growin'—till it'll burst out—! (*He gets up and puts on his coat and a hat. They watch him, gradually breaking into grins.* EBEN *avoids their eyes sheepishly.*) I'm goin' out fur a spell—up the road.

PETER: T' the village?

SIMEON: T' see Minnie?

EBEN (*defiantly*): Ay-eh!

PETER (*jeeringly*): The Scarlet Woman!

SIMEON: Lust—that's what's growin' in ye!

EBEN: Waal—she's purty!

PETER: She's been purty fur twenty year!

SIMEON: A new coat o' paint'll make a heifer out of forty.

EBEN: She hain't forty!

PETER: If she hain't, she's teeterin' on the edge.

EBEN (*desperately*): What d'yew know—

PETER: All they is . . . Sim knew her—an' then me arter—

SIMEON: An' Paw kin tell yew somethin' too! He was fust!

EBEN: D'ye mean t' say he . . . ?

SIMEON (*with a grin*): Ay-eh! We air his heirs in everythin'!

EBEN (*intensely*): That's more to it! That grows on it! It'll bust soon! (*Then violently*) I'll go smash my fist in her face! (*He pulls open the door in rear violently.*)

SIMEON (*with a wink at* PETER*—drawlingly*): Mebbe—but the night's wa'm—purty—by the time ye git thar mebbe ye'll kiss her instead!

PETER: Sart'n he will! (*They both roar with coarse laughter.* EBEN *rushes out and slams the door—then the outside front door—comes around the corner of the house and stands still by the gate, staring up at the sky.*)

SIMEON (*looking after him*): Like his Paw.

PETER: Dead spit an' image!

SIMEON: Dog'll eat dog!

PETER: Ay-eh. (*Pause. With yearning*) Mebbe a year from now we'll be in Californi-a.

SIMEON: Ay-eh. (*A pause. Both yawn.*) Let's git t'bed. (*He blows out the candle. They go out door in rear.* EBEN *stretches his arms up to the sky—rebelliously.*)

EBEN: Waal—thar's a star, an' somewhar's they's him, an' here's me, an' thar's Min up the road—in the same night. What if I does kiss her? She's like t'night, she's soft 'n' wa'm, her eyes kin wink like a star, her mouth's wa'm, her arms're wa'm, she smells like a wa'm plowed field, she's purty . . . Ay-eh! By God A'mighty she's purty, an' I don't give a damn how many sins she's sinned afore mine or who she's sinned 'em with, my sin's as purty as any one on 'em! (*He strides off down the road to the left.*)

SCENE III

(*It is the pitch darkness just before dawn.* EBEN *comes in from the left and goes around to the porch, feeling his way, chuckling bitterly and cursing half-aloud to himself.*)

EBEN: The cussed old miser! (*He can be heard going in the front door. There is a pause as he goes upstairs, then a loud knock on the bedroom door of the brothers.*) Wake up!

SIMEON (*startledly*): Who's thar?

EBEN (*pushing open the door and coming in, a lighted candle in his hand. The bedroom of the brothers is revealed. Its ceiling is the sloping roof. They can stand upright only close to the center dividing wall of the upstairs.* SIMEON *and* PETER *are in a double bed, front.* EBEN'S *cot is to the rear.* EBEN *has a mixture of silly grin and vicious scowl on his face*): I be!

PETER (*angrily*): What in hell's-fire . . . ?

EBEN: I got news fur ye! Ha! (*He gives one abrupt sardonic guffaw.*)

SIMEON (*angrily*): Couldn't ye hold it 'til we'd got our sleep?

EBEN: It's nigh sunup. (*Then explosively*) He's gone an' married agen!

SIMEON *and* PETER (*explosively*): Paw?

EBEN: Got himself hitched to a female 'bout thirty-five—an' purty, they says . . .

SIMEON (*aghast*): It's a durn lie!

PETER: Who says?

SIMEON: They been stringin' ye!

EBEN: Think I'm a dunce, do ye? The hull village says. The preacher from New Dover, he brung the news—told it t'our preacher—New Dover, that's whar the old loon got himself hitched—that's whar the woman lived—

PETER (*no longer doubting—stunned*): Waal . . . !

SIMEON (*the same*): Waal . . . !

EBEN (*sitting down on a bed—with vicious hatred*): Ain't he a devil out o' hell? It's jest t' spite us—the damned old mule!

PETER (*after a pause*): Everythin'll go t' her now.

SIMEON: Ay-eh. (*A pause—dully*) Waal—if it's done—

PETER: It's done us. (*Pause—then persuasively*) They's gold in the fields o' Californi-a, Sim. No good a-stayin' here now.

SIMEON: Jest what I was a-thinkin'. (*Then with decision*) S'well fust's last! Let's light out and git this mornin'.

PETER: Suits me.

EBEN: Ye must like walkin'.

SIMEON (*sardonically*): If ye'd grow wings on us we'd fly thar!

EBEN: Ye'd like ridin' better—on a boat, wouldn't ye? (*Fumbles in his pocket and takes out a crumpled sheet of foolscap.*) Waal, if ye sign this ye kin ride on a boat. I've had it writ out an' ready in case ye'd ever go. It says fur three hundred dollars t' each ye agree yewr shares o' the farm is sold t' me. (*They look suspiciously at the paper. A pause.*)

SIMEON (*wonderingly*): But if he's hitched agen—

PETER: An' whar'd yew git that sum o' money, anyways?

EBEN (*cunningly*): I know whar it's hid. I been waitin'—

Maw told me. She knew whar it lay fur years, but she was waitin' . . . It's her'n—the money he hoarded from her farm an' hid from Maw. It's my money by rights now.

PETER: Whar's it hid?

EBEN (*cunningly*): Whar yew won't never find it without me. Maw spied on him—'r she'd never knowed. (*A pause. They look at him suspiciously, and he at them.*) Waal, is it fa'r trade?

SIMEON: Dunno.

PETER: Dunno.

SIMEON (*looking at window*): Sky's grayin'.

PETER: Ye better start the fire, Eben.

SIMEON: An' fix some vittles.

EBEN: Ay-eh. (*Then with a forced jocular heartiness*) I'll git ye a good one. If ye're startin' t' hoof it t' Californi-a ye'll need somethin' that'll stick t' yer ribs. (*He turns to the door, adding meaningly*) But ye kin ride on a boat if ye'll swap. (*He stops at the door and pauses. They stare at him.*)

SIMEON (*suspiciously*): Whar was ye all night?

EBEN (*defiantly*): Up t' Min's. (*Then slowly*) Walkin' thar, fust I felt 's if I'd kiss her; then I got a-thinkin' o' what ye'd said o' him an' her an' I says, I'll bust her nose fur that! Then I got t' the village an' heerd the news an' I got madder'n hell an' run all the way t' Min's not knowin' what I'd do— (*He pauses—then sheepishly but more defiantly*) Waal—when I seen her, I didn't hit her—nor I didn't kiss her nuther—I begun t' beller like a calf an' cuss at the same time, I was so durn mad—an' she got scared—an' I jest grabbed holt an' tuk her! (*Proudly*) Yes, sirree! I tuk her. She may've been his'n—an' your'n, too—but she's mine now!

SIMEON (*dryly*): In love, air yew?

EBEN (*with lofty scorn*): Love! I don't take no stock in sech slop!

PETER (*winking* at SIMEON): Mebbe Eben's aimin' t' marry, too.

SIMEON: Min'd make a true faithful he'pmeet! (*They snicker.*)

EBEN: What do I care fur her—'ceptin' she's round an' wa'm? The p'int is she was his'n—an' now she belongs t' me! (*He goes to the door—then turns—rebelliously.*) An' Min hain't sech a bad un. They's worse'n Min in the world, I'll bet ye! Wait'll we see this cow the Old Man's hitched t'! She'll beat Min, I got a notion! (*He starts to go out.*)

SIMEON (*suddenly*): Mebbe ye'll try t' make her your'n, too?

PETER: Ha! (*He gives a sardonic laugh of relish at this idea.*)

EBEN (*spitting with disgust*): Her—here—sleepin' with

him—stealin' my Maw's farm! I'd as soon pet a skunk 'r kiss a snake! (*He goes out. The two stare after him suspiciously. A pause. They listen to his steps receding.*)

PETER: He's startin' the fire.

SIMEON: I'd like t' ride t' Californi-a—but—

PETER: Min might o' put some scheme in his head.

SIMEON: Mebbe it's all a lie 'bout Paw marryin'. We'd best wait an' see the bride.

PETER: An' don't sign nothin' till we does!

SIMEON: Nor till we've tested it's good money! (*Then with a grin*) But if Paw's hitched we'd be sellin' Eben somethin' we'd never git nohow!

PETER: We'll wait an' see. (*Then with sudden vindictive anger*) An' till he comes, let's yew 'n' me not wuk a lick, let Eben tend to thin's if he's a mind t', let's us jest sleep an' eat an' drink likker, an' let the hull damned farm go t' blazes!

SIMEON (*excitedly*): By God, we've 'arned a rest! We'll play rich fur a change. I hain't a-going to stir outa bed till breakfast's ready.

PETER: An' on the table!

SIMEON (*after a pause—thoughtfully*): What d'ye calc'late she'll be like—our new Maw? Like Eben thinks?

PETER: More'n likely.

SIMEON (*vindictively*): Waal—I hope she's a she-devil that'll make him wish he was dead an' livin' in the pit o' hell fur comfort!

PETER (*fervently*): Amen!

SIMEON (*imitating his father's voice*): "I'm ridin' out t' learn God's message t' me in the spring like the prophets done," he says. I'll bet right then an' thar he knew plumb well he was goin' whorin', the stinkin' old hypocrite!

SCENE IV

(*Same as Scene II—shows the interior of the kitchen with a lighted candle on table. It is gray dawn outside.* SIMEON *and* PETER *are just finishing their breakfast.* EBEN *sits before his plate of untouched food, brooding frowningly.*)

PETER (*glancing at him rather irritably*): Lookin' glum don't help none.

SIMEON (*sarcastically*): Sorrowin' over his lust o' the flesh!

PETER (*with a grin*): Was she yer fust?

EBEN (*angrily*): None o' yer business. (*A pause.*) I was

thinkin' o' him. I got a notion he's gittin' near—I kin feel him comin' on like yew kin feel malaria chill afore it takes ye.

PETER: It's too early yet.

SIMEON: Dunno. He'd like t' catch us nappin'—jest t' have somethin' t' hoss us 'round over.

PETER (*mechanically gets to his feet.* SIMEON *does the same*): Waal—let's git t' wuk. (*They both plod mechanically toward the door before they realize. Then they stop short.*)

SIMEON (*grinning*): Ye're a cussed fool, Pete—and I be wuss! Let him see we hain't wukin'! We don't give a durn!

PETER (*as they go back to the table*): Not a damned durn! It'll serve t' show him we're done with him. (*They sit down again.* EBEN *stares from one to the other with surprise.*)

SIMEON (*grins at him*): We're aimin' t' start bein' lilies o' the field.

PETER: Nary a toil 'r spin 'r lick o' wuk do we put in!

SIMEON: Ye're sole owner—till he comes—that's what ye wanted. Waal, ye got t' be sole hand, too.

PETER: The cows air bellerin'. Ye better hustle at the milkin'.

EBEN (*with excited joy*): Ye mean ye'll sign the paper?

SIMEON (*dryly*): Mebbe.

PETER: Mebbe.

SIMEON: We're considerin'. (*Peremptorily*) Ye better git t' wuk.

EBEN (*with queer excitement*): It's Maw's farm agen! It's my farm! Them's my cows! I'll milk my durn fingers off fur cows o' mine! (*He goes out door in rear, they stare after him indifferently.*)

SIMEON: Like his Paw.

PETER: Dead spit 'n' image!

SIMEON: Waal—let dog eat dog! (EBEN *comes out of front door and around the corner of the house. The sky is beginning to grow flushed with sunrise.* EBEN *stops by the gate and stares around him with glowing, possessive eyes. He takes in the whole farm with his embracing glance of desire.*)

EBEN: It's purty! It's damned purty! It's mine! (*He suddenly throws his head back boldly and glares with hard, defiant eyes at the sky.*) Mine, d'ye hear? Mine! (*He turns and walks quickly off left, rear, toward the barn. The two brothers light their pipes.*)

SIMEON (*putting his muddy boots up on the table, tilting back his chair, and puffing defiantly*): Waal—this air solid comfort—fur once.

PETER: Ay-eh. (*He follows suit. A pause. Unconsciously they both sigh.*)

SIMEON (*suddenly*): He never was much o' hand at milkin', Eben wa'n't.

PETER (*with a snort*): His hands air like hoofs! (*A pause.*)

SIMEON: Reach down the jug thar! Let's take a swaller. I'm feelin' kind o' low.

PETER: Good idee! (*He does so—gets two glasses—they pour out drinks of whisky.*) Here's t' the gold in Californi-a!

SIMEON: An' luck t' find it! (*They drink—puff resolutely—sigh—take their feet down from the table.*)

PETER: Likker don't pear t' sot right.

SIMEON: We hain't used t' it this early. (*A pause. They become very restless.*)

PETER: Gittin' close in this kitchen.

SIMEON (*with immense relief*): Let's git a breath o' air. (*They arise briskly and go out rear—appear around house and stop by the gate. They stare up at the sky with a numbed appreciation.*)

PETER: Purty!

SIMEON: Ay-eh. Gold's t' the East now.

PETER: Sun's startin' with us fur the Golden West.

SIMEON (*staring around the farm, his compressed face tightened, unable to conceal his emotion*): Waal—it's our last mornin'—mebbe.

PETER (*the same*): Ay-eh.

SIMEON (*stamps his foot on the earth and addresses it desperately*): Waal—ye've thirty year o' me buried in ye—spread out over ye—blood an' bone an' sweat—rotted away—fertilizin' ye—richin' yer soul—prime manure, by God, that's what I been t' ye!

PETER: Ay-eh! An' me!

SIMEON: An' yew, Peter. (*He sighs—then spits.*) Waal—no use'n cryin' over spilt milk.

PETER: They's gold in the West—an' freedom, mebbe. We been slaves t' stone walls here.

SIMEON (*defiantly*): We hain't nobody's slaves from this out—nor no thin's slaves nuther. (*A pause—restlessly*) Speakin' o' milk, wonder how Eben's managin'?

PETER: I s'pose he's managin'.

SIMEON: Mebbe we'd ought t' help—this once.

PETER: Mebbe. The cows knows us.

SIMEON: An' likes us. They don't know him much.

PETER: An' the hosses, an' pigs, an' chickens. They don't know him much.

SIMEON: They knows us like brothers—an' likes us!

(*Proudly*) Hain't we raised 'em t' be fust-rate, number one prize stock?

PETER: We hain't—not no more.

SIMEON (*dully*): I was fergittin'. (*Then resignedly*) Waal, let's go help Eben a spell an' git waked up.

PETER: Suits me. (*They are starting off down left, rear, for the barn when* EBEN *appears from there hurrying toward them, his face excited.*)

EBEN (*breathlessly*): Waal—har they be! The old mule an' the bride! I seen 'em from the barn down below at the turnin'.

PETER: How could ye tell that far?

EBEN: Hain't I as far-sight as he's near-sight? Don't I know the mare 'n' buggy, an' two people settin' in it? Who else . . . ? An' I tell ye I kin feel 'em a-comin', too! (*He squirms as if he had the itch.*)

PETER (*beginning to be angry*): Waal—let him do his own unhitchin'!

SIMEON (*angry in his turn*): Let's hustle in an' git our bundles an' be a-goin' as he's a-comin'. I don't want never t' step inside the door agen arter he's back. (*They both start back around the corner of the house.* EBEN *follows them.*)

EBEN (*anxiously*): Will ye sign it afore ye go?

PETER: Let's see the color o' the old skinflint's money an' we'll sign. (*They disappear left. The two brothers clump upstairs to get their bundles.* EBEN *appears in the kitchen, runs to the window, peers out, comes back and pulls up a strip of flooring in under stove, takes out a canvas bag and puts it on table, then sets the floorboard back in place. The two brothers appear a moment after. They carry old carpet bags.*)

EBEN (*puts his hand on bag guardingly*): Have ye signed?

SIMEON (*shows paper in his hand*): Ay-eh. (*Greedily*) Be that the money?

EBEN (*opens bag and pours out pile of twenty-dollar gold pieces*): Twenty-dollar pieces—thirty on 'em. Count 'em. (PETER *does so, arranging them in stacks of five, biting one or two to test them.*)

PETER: Six hundred. (*He puts them in bag and puts it inside his shirt carefully.*)

SIMEON (*handing paper to* EBEN): Har ye be.

EBEN (*after a glance, folds it carefully and hides it under his shirt—gratefully*): Thank yew.

PETER: Thank yew fur the ride.

SIMEON: We'll send ye a lump o' gold fur Christmas. (*A pause.* EBEN *stares at them and they at him.*)

PETER (*awkwardly*): Waal—we're a-goin'.

SIMEON: Comin' out t' the yard?

EBEN: No. I'm waitin' in here a spell. (*Another silence. The brothers edge awkwardly to door in rear—then turn and stand.*)

SIMEON: Waal—good-by.

PETER: Good-by.

EBEN: Good-by. (*They go out. He sits down at the table, faces the stove and pulls out the paper. He looks from it to the stove. His face, lighted up by the shaft of sunlight from the window, has an expression of trance. His lips move. The two brothers come out to the gate.*)

PETER (*looking off toward barn*): Thar he be—unhitchin'.

SIMEON (*with a chuckle*): I'll bet ye he's riled!

PETER: An' thar she be.

SIMEON: Let's wait 'n' see what our new Maw looks like.

PETER (*with a grin*): An' give him our partin' cuss!

SIMEON (*grinning*): I feel like raisin' fun. I feel light in my head an' feet.

PETER: Me, too. I feel like laffin' till I'd split up the middle.

SIMEON: Reckon it's the likker?

PETER: No. My feet feel itchin' t' walk an' walk—an' jump high over thin's—an'. . . .

SIMEON: Dance? (*A pause.*)

PETER (*puzzled*): It's plumb onnateral.

SIMEON (*a light coming over his face*): I calc'late it's 'cause school's out. It's holiday. Fur once we're free!

PETER (*dazedly*): Free?

SIMEON: The halter's broke—the harness is busted—the fence bars is down—the stone walls air crumblin' an' tumblin'! We'll be kickin' up an' tearin' away down the road!

PETER (*drawing a deep breath—oratorically*): Anybody that wants this stinkin' old rock-pile of a farm kin hev it. 'Tain't our'n, no siree!

SIMEON (*takes the gate off its hinges and puts it under his arm*): We harby 'bolishes shet gates an' open gates, an' all gates, by thunder!

PETER: We'll take it with us fur luck an' let 'er sail free down some river.

SIMEON (*as a sound of voices comes from left, rear*): Har they comes! (*The two brothers congeal into two stiff, grim-visaged statues.* EPHRAIM CABOT *and* ABBIE PUTNAM *come in.* CABOT *is seventy-five, tall and gaunt, with great, wiry, concentrated power, but stoop-shouldered from toil. His face is as hard as if it were hewn out of a boulder, yet there is a weakness in it, a petty pride in its own narrow strength. His eyes are small, close together, and extremely near-sighted, blinking continually in the effort to focus on objects, their stare having a straining, ingrowing quality. He is dressed in his dismal black Sunday suit.* ABBIE *is thirty-five, buxom, full of vitality. Her round face is pretty but marred by its rather gross sensuality. There is strength and obstinacy in her jaw, a hard determination in her eyes, and about her whole personality the same unsettled, untamed, desperate quality which is so apparent in* EBEN.)

CABOT (*as they enter—a queer strangled emotion in his dry cracking voice*): Har we be t'hum, Abbie.

ABBIE (*with lust for the word*): Hum! (*Her eyes gloating on the house without seeming to see the two stiff figures at the gate.*) It's purty—purty! I can't b'lieve it's r'ally mine.

CABOT (*sharply*): Yewr'n? Mine! (*He stares at her penetratingly. She stares back. He adds relentingly.*) Our'n—mebbe! It was lonesome too long. I was growin' old in the spring. A hum's got t' hev a woman.

ABBIE (*her voice taking possession*): A woman's got t' hev a hum!

CABOT (*nodding uncertainly*): Ay-eh. (*Then irritably*) Whar be they? Ain't thar nobody about—'r wukin'—r' nothin'?

ABBIE (*sees the brothers. She returns their stare of cold appraising contempt with interest—slowly*): Thar's two men loafin' at the gate an' starin' at me like a couple o' strayed hogs.

CABOT (*straining his eyes*): I kin see 'em—but I can't make out. . . .

SIMEON: It's Simeon.

PETER: It's Peter.

CABOT (*exploding*): Why hain't ye wukin'?

SIMEON (*dryly*): We're wantin' t' welcome ye hum—yew an' the bride!

CABOT (*confusedly*): Huh? Waal—this be yer new Maw, boys. (*She stares at them and they at her.*)

SIMEON (*turns away and spits contemptuously*): I see her!

PETER (*spits also*): An' I see her!

ABBIE (*with the conqueror's conscious superiority*): I'll go in an' look at *my* house. (*She goes slowly around to porch.*)

SIMEON (*with a snort*): *Her* house!

PETER (*calls after her*): Ye'll find Eben inside. Ye better not tell him it's *yewr* house.

ABBIE (*mouthing the name*): Eben. (*Then quietly*) I'll tell Eben.

CABOT (*with a contemptuous sneer*): Ye needn't heed Eben. Eben's a dumb fool—like his Maw—soft an' simple!

SIMEON (*with his sardonic burst of laughter*): Ha! Eben's a chip o' yew—spit 'n' image—hard 'n' bitter's a hickory tree! Dog'll eat dog. He'll eat ye yet, old man!

CABOT (*commandingly*): Ye git t' wuk!

SIMEON (*as* ABBIE *disappears in house—winks at* PETER *and says tauntingly*): So that thar's our new Maw, be it? Whar in hell did ye dig her up? (*He and* PETER *laugh.*)

PETER: Ha! Ye'd better turn her in the pen with the other sows. (*They laugh uproariously, slapping their thighs.*)

CABOT (*so amazed at their effrontery that he stutters in confusion*): Simeon! Peter! What's come over ye? Air ye drunk?

SIMEON: We're free, old man—free o' yew an' the hull damned farm! (*They grow more and more hilarious and excited.*)

PETER: An' we're startin' out fur the gold fields o' Californi-a!

SIMEON: Ye kin take this place an' burn it!

PETER: An' bury it—fur all we cares!

SIMEON: We're free, old man! (*He cuts a caper.*)

PETER: Free! (*He gives a kick in the air.*)

SIMEON (*in a frenzy*): Whoop!

PETER: Whoop! (*They do an absurd Indian war dance about the old man who is petrified between rage and the fear that they are insane.*)

SIMEON: We're free as Injuns! Lucky we don't sculp ye!

PETER: An' burn yer barn an' kill the stock!

SIMEON: An' rape yer new woman! Whoop! (*He and* PETER *stop their dance, holding their sides, rocking with wild laughter.*)

CABOT (*edging away*): Lust fur gold—fur the sinful, easy gold o' Californi-a! It's made ye mad!

SIMEON (*tauntingly*): Wouldn't ye like us to send ye back some sinful gold, ye old sinner?

PETER: They's gold besides what's in Californi-a! (*He retreats back beyond the vision of the old man and takes the bag of money and flaunts it in the air above his head, laughing.*)

SIMEON: And sinfuller, too!

PETER: We'll be voyagin' on the sea! Whoop! (*He leaps up and down.*)

SIMEON: Livin' free! Whoop! (*He leaps in turn.*)

CABOT (*suddenly roaring with rage*): My cuss on ye!

SIMEON: Take our'n in trade fur it! Whoop!

CABOT: I'll hev ye both chained up in the asylum!

PETER: Ye old skinflint! Good-by!

SIMEON: Ye old blood sucker! Good-by!

CABOT: Go afore I . . . !

PETER: Whoop! (*He picks a stone from the road.* SIMEON *does the same.*)

SIMEON: Maw'll be in the parlor.

PETER: Ay-eh! One! Two!

CABOT (*frightened*): What air ye . . . ?

PETER: Three! (*They both throw, the stones hitting the parlor window with a crash of glass, tearing the shade.*)

SIMEON: Whoop!

PETER: Whoop!

CABOT (*in a fury now, rushing toward them*): If I kin lay hands on ye—I'll break yer bones fur ye! (*But they beat a capering retreat before him,* SIMEON *with the gate still under his arm.* CABOT *comes back, panting with impotent rage. Their voices as they go off take up the song of the gold-seekers to the old tune of "Oh, Susannah!"*)

"I jumped aboard the Liza ship,
And traveled on the sea,
And every time I thought of home
I wished it wasn't me!
Oh! Californi-a,
That's the land fur me!
I'm off to Californi-a!
With my wash bowl on my knee."

(*In the meantime, the window of the upper bedroom on right is raised and* ABBIE *sticks her head out. She looks down at* CABOT*—with a sigh of relief.*)

ABBIE: Waal—that's the last o' them two, hain't it? (*He doesn't answer. Then in possessive tones*) This here's a nice bedroom, Ephraim. It's a r'al nice bed. Is it my room, Ephraim?

CABOT (*grimly—without looking up*): Our'n! (*She cannot control a grimace of aversion and pulls back her head slowly and shuts the window. A sudden horrible thought seems to enter* CABOT'*s head.*) They been up to somethin'! Mebbe—mebbe they've pizened the stock—'r somethin'! (*He almost runs off down toward the barn. A moment later the kitchen door is slowly pushed open and* ABBIE *enters. For a moment she stands looking at* EBEN. *He does not notice her at first. Her eyes take him in penetratingly with a calculating appraisal of his strength as against hers. But under this her desire is dimly awakened by his youth and good looks. Suddenly he becomes conscious of her presence and looks up. Their eyes meet. He leaps to his feet, glowering at her speechlessly.*)

ABBIE (*in her most seductive tones which she uses all through this scene*): Be you—Eben? I'm Abbie— (*She laughs.*) I mean, I'm yer new Maw.

EBEN (*viciously*): No, damn ye!

ABBIE (*as if she hadn't heard—with a queer smile*): Yer Paw's spoke a lot o' yew. . . .

EBEN: Ha!

ABBIE: Ye mustn't mind him. He's an old man. (*A long pause. They stare at each other.*) I don't want t' pretend playin' Maw t' ye, Eben. (*Admiringly*) Ye're too big an' too strong fur that. I want t' be frens with ye. Mebbe with me fur a fren ye'd find ye'd like livin' here better. I kin make it easy fur ye with him, mebbe. (*With a scornful sense of power*) I calc'late I kin git him t' do most anythin' fur me.

EBEN (*with bitter scorn*): Ha! (*They stare again,* EBEN *obscurely moved, physically attracted to her—in forced stilted tones*) Yew kin go t' the devil!

ABBIE (*calmly*): If cussin' me does ye good, cuss all ye've a mind t'. I'm all prepared t' have ye agin me—at fust. I don't blame ye nuther. I'd feel the same at any stranger comin' t' take my Maw's place. (*He shudders. She is watching him carefully.*) Yew must've cared a lot fur yewr Maw, didn't ye? My Maw died before I'd growed. I don't remember her none. (*A pause.*) But yew won't hate me long, Eben. I'm not the wust in the world—an' yew an' me've got a lot in common. I kin tell that by lookin' at ye. Waal—I've had a hard life, too—oceans o' trouble an' nuthin' but wuk fur reward. I was a orphan early an' had t' wuk fur others in other folks' hums. Then I married an' he turned out a drunken spreer an' so he had to wuk fur others an' me too agen in other folks' hums, an' the baby died, an' my husband got sick an' died too, an' I was glad sayin' now I'm free fur once, on'y I diskivered right away all I was free fur was t' wuk agen in other folks' hums, doin' other folks' wuk till I'd most give up hope o' ever doin' my own wuk in my own hum, an' then your Paw come. . . . (CABOT *appears returning from the barn. He comes to the gate and looks down the road the brothers have gone. A faint strain of their retreating voices is heard: "Oh, Californi-a! That's the place for me." He stands glowering, his fist clenched, his face grim with rage.*)

EBEN (*fighting against his growing attraction and sympathy—harshly*): An' bought yew—like a harlot! (*She is stung and flushes angrily. She has been sincerely moved by the recital of her troubles. He adds furiously:*) An' the price he's payin' ye—this farm—was my Maw's, damn ye!—an' mine now!

ABBIE (*with a cool laugh of confidence*): Yewr'n? We'll see 'bout that! (*Then strongly*) Waal—what if I did need a hum? What else'd I marry an old man like him fur?

EBEN (*maliciously*): I'll tell him ye said that!

ABBIE (*smiling*): I'll say ye're lyin' a-purpose—an' he'll drive ye off the place!

EBEN: Ye devil!

ABBIE (*defying him*): This be my farm—this be my hum—this be my kitchen—!

EBEN (*furiously, as if he were going to attack her*): Shut up, damn ye!

ABBIE (*walks up to him—a queer coarse expression of desire in her face and body—slowly*): An' upstairs—that be my bedroom—an' my bed! (*He stares into her eyes, terribly confused and torn. She adds softly:*) I hain't bad nor mean—'cept-in' fur an enemy—but I got t' fight fur what's due me out o' life, if I ever 'spect t' git it. (*Then putting her hand on his arm—seductively*) Let's yew 'n' me be frens, Eben.

EBEN (*stupidly—as if hypnotized*): Ay-eh. (*Then furiously flinging off her arm*) No, ye durned old witch! I hate ye! (*He rushes out the door.*)

ABBIE (*looks after him smiling satisfiedly—then half to herself, mouthing the word*): Eben's nice. (*She looks at the table, proudly.*) I'll wash up *my* dishes now. (EBEN *appears outside, slamming the door behind him. He comes around corner, stops on seeing his father, and stands staring at him with hate.*)

CABOT (*raising his arms to heaven in the fury he can no longer control*): Lord God o' Hosts, smite the undutiful sons with Thy wust cuss!

EBEN (*breaking in violently*): Yew 'n' yewr God! Allus cussin' folks—allus naggin' 'em!

CABOT (*oblivious to him—summoningly*): God o' the old! God o' the lonesome!

EBEN (*mockingly*): Naggin' His sheep t' sin! T' hell with yewr God! (CABOT *turns. He and* EBEN *glower at each other.*)

CABOT (*harshly*): So it's yew. I might've knowed it. (*Shaking his finger threatening at him*) Blasphemin' fool! (*Then quickly*) Why hain't ye t' wuk?

EBEN: Why hain't yew? They've went. I can't wuk it all alone.

CABOT (*contemptuously*): Nor noways! I'm wuth ten o' ye

yit, old's I be! Ye'll never be more'n half a man! (*Then, matter-of-factly*) Waal—let's git t' the barn. (*They go. A last faint note of the "Californi-a" song is heard from the distance.* ABBIE *is washing her dishes.*)

PART II

Scene I

(*The exterior of the farmhouse, as in Part I—a hot Sunday afternoon two months later.* ABBIE, *dressed in her best, is discovered sitting in a rocker at the end of the porch. She rocks listlessly, enervated by the heat, staring in front of her with bored, half-closed eyes.*

EBEN *sticks his head out of his bedroom window. He looks around furtively and tries to see—or hear—if anyone is on the porch, but although he has been careful to make no noise,* ABBIE *has sensed his movement. She stops rocking, her face grows animated and eager, she waits attentively.* EBEN *seems to feel her presence, he scowls back his thoughts of her and spits with exaggerated disdain—then withdraws back into the room.* ABBIE *waits, holding her breath as she listens with passionate eagerness for every sound within the house.*

EBEN *comes out. Their eyes meet. His falter, he is confused, he turns away and slams the door resentfully. At this gesture,* ABBIE *laughs tantalizingly, amused but at the same time piqued and irritated. He scowls, strides off the porch to the path and starts to walk past her to the road with a grand swagger of ignoring her existence. He is dressed in his store suit, spruced up, his face shines from soap and water.* ABBIE *leans forward on her chair, her eyes hard and angry now, and, as he passes her, gives a sneering, taunting chuckle.*)

EBEN (*stung—turns on her furiously*): What air yew cacklin' 'bout?

ABBIE (*triumphant*): Yew!

EBEN: What about me?

ABBIE: Ye look all slicked up like a prize bull.

EBEN (*with a sneer*): Waal—ye hain't so durned purty yerself, be ye? (*They stare into each other's eyes, his held by hers in spite of himself, hers glowingly possessive. Their physical attraction becomes a palpable force quivering in the hot air.*)

ABBIE (*softly*): Ye don't mean that, Eben. Ye may think ye mean it, mebbe, but ye don't. Ye can't. It's agin nature, Eben. Ye been fightin' yer nature ever since the day I come—tryin' t' tell yerself I hain't purty t'ye. (*She laughs a low humid laugh without taking her eyes from his. A pause—her body squirms desirously—she murmurs languorously.*) Hain't the sun strong an' hot? Ye kin feel it burnin' into the earth—Nature—makin' thin's grow—bigger 'n 'bigger—burnin' inside ye—makin' ye want t' grow—into somethin' else—till ye're jined with it—an' it's your'n—but it owns ye, too—an' makes ye grow bigger—like a tree—like them elums— (*She laughs again softly, holding his eyes. He takes a step toward her, compelled against his will.*) Nature'll beat ye, Eben. Ye might's well own up t' it fust 's last.

EBEN (*trying to break from her spell—confusedly*): If Paw'd hear ye goin' on. . . . (*Resentfully*) But ye've made such a damned idjit out o' the old devil . . . ! (ABBIE *laughs.*)

ABBIE: Waal—hain't it easier fur yew with him changed softer?

EBEN (*defiantly*): No. I'm fightin' him—fightin' yew—fightin' fur Maw's rights t' her hum! (*This breaks her spell for him. He glowers at her.*) An' I'm onto ye. Ye hain't foolin' me a mite. Ye're aimin' t' swaller up everythin' an' make it your'n. Waal, you'll find I'm a heap sight bigger hunk nor yew kin chew! (*He turns from her with a sneer.*)

ABBIE (*trying to regain her ascendancy—seductively*): Eben!

EBEN: Leave me be! (*He starts to walk away.*)

ABBIE (*more commandingly*): Eben!

EBEN (*stops—resentfully*): What d'ye want?

ABBIE (*trying to conceal a growing excitement*): Whar air ye goin'?

EBEN (*with malicious nonchalance*): Oh—up the road a spell.

ABBIE: T' the village?

EBEN (*airily*): Mebbe.

ABBIE (*excitedly*): T' see that Min, I s'pose?

EBEN: Mebbe.

ABBIE (*weakly*): What d'ye want t' waste time on her fur?

EBEN (*revenging himself now—grinning at her*): Ye can't beat Nature, didn't ye say? (*He laughs and again starts to walk away.*)

ABBIE (*bursting out*): An ugly old hake!

EBEN (*with a tantalizing sneer*): She's purtier'n yew be!

ABBIE: That every wuthless drunk in the country has. . . .

EBEN (*tauntingly*): Mebbe—but she's better'n yew. She owns up fa'r 'n' squar' t' her doin's.

ABBIE (*furiously*): Don't ye dare compare. . . .

EBEN: She don't go sneakin' an' stealin'—what's mine.

ABBIE (*savagely seizing on his weak point*): Your'n? Yew mean—my farm?

EBEN: I mean the farm yew sold yerself fur like any other old whore—my farm!

ABBIE (*stung—fiercely*): Ye'll never live t' see the day when even a stinkin' weed on it 'll belong t' ye! (*Then in a scream*) Git out o' my sight! Go on t' yer slut—disgracin' yer Paw 'n' me! I'll git yer Paw t' horsewhip ye off the place if I want t'! Ye're only livin' here 'cause I tolerate ye! Git along! I hate the sight o' ye! (*She stops, panting and glaring at him.*)

EBEN (*returning her glance in kind*): An' I hate the sight o' yew! (*He turns and strides off up the road. She follows his retreating figure with concentrated hate. Old* CABOT *appears coming up from the barn. The hard, grim expression of his face has changed. He seems in some queer way softened, mellowed. His eyes have taken on a strange, incongruous dreamy quality. Yet there is no hint of physical weakness about him—rather he looks more robust and younger.* ABBIE *sees him and turns away quickly with unconcealed aversion. He comes slowly up to her.*)

CABOT (*mildly*): War yew an' Eben quarrelin' agen?

ABBIE (*shortly*): No.

CABOT: Ye was talkin' a'mighty loud. (*He sits down on the edge of porch.*)

ABBIE (*snappishly*): If ye heerd us they hain't no need askin' questions.

CABOT: I didn't hear what ye said.

ABBIE (*relieved*): Waal—it wa'n't nothin' t' speak on.

CABOT (*after a pause*): Eben's queer.

ABBIE (*bitterly*): He's the dead spit 'n' image o' yew!

CABOT (*queerly interested*): D'ye think so, Abbie? (*After a pause, ruminatingly*) Me 'n' Eben's allus fit 'n' fit. I never could b'ar him noways. He's so thunderin' soft—like his Maw.

ABBIE (*scornfully*): Ay-eh! 'Bout as soft as yew be!

CABOT (*as if he hadn't heard*): Mebbe I been too hard on him.

ABBIE (*jeeringly*): Waal—ye're gittin' soft now—soft as slop! That's what Eben was sayin'.

CABOT (*his face instantly grim and ominous*): Eben was sayin'? Waal, he'd best not do nothin' t' try me 'r he'll soon diskiver. . . . (*A pause. She keeps her face turned away. His gradually softens. He stares up at the sky.*) Purty, hain't it?

ABBIE (*crossly*): I don't see nothin' purty.

CABOT: The sky. Feels like a wa'm field up thar.

ABBIE (*sarcastically*): Air yew aimin' t' buy up over the farm too? (*She snickers contemptuously.*)

CABOT (*strangely*): I'd like t' own my place up thar. (*A pause.*) I'm gittin' old, Abbie. I'm gittin' ripe on the bough. (*A pause. She stares at him mystified. He goes on.*) It's allus lonesome cold in the house—even when it's bilin' hot outside. Hain't yew noticed?

ABBIE: No.

CABOT: It's wa'm down t' the barn—nice smellin' an' warm—with the cows. (*A pause.*) Cows is queer.

ABBIE: Like yew?

CABOT: Like Eben. (*A pause.*) I'm gittin t' feel resigned t' Eben—jest as I got t' feel 'bout his Maw. I'm gittin' t' learn to b'ar his softness—jest like her'n. I calc'late I c'd a'most take t' him—if he wa'n't sech a dumb fool! (*A pause.*) I s'pose it's old age a-creepin' in my bones.

ABBIE (*indifferently*): Waal—ye hain't dead yet.

CABOT (*roused*): No, I hain't, yew bet—not by a hell of a sight—I'm sound 'n' tough as hickory! (*Then moodily*) But arter three score and ten the Lord warns ye t' prepare. (*A pause.*) That's why Eben's come in my head. Now that his cussed sinful brothers is gone their path t' hell, they's no one left but Eben.

ABBIE (*resentfully*): They's me, hain't they? (*Agitatedly*) What's all this sudden likin' ye tuk to Eben? Why don't ye say nothin' 'bout me? Hain't I yer lawful wife?

CABOT (*simply*): Ay-eh. Ye be. (*A pause—he stares at her desirously—his eyes grow avid—then with a sudden movement he seizes her hands and squeezes them, declaiming in a queer camp meeting preacher's tempo:*) Yew air my Rose o' Sharon! Behold, yew air fair; yer eyes air doves; yer lips air like scarlet; yer two breasts air like two fawns; yer navel be like a round goblet; yer belly be like a heap o' wheat. . . . (*He covers her hand with kisses. She does not seem to notice. She stares before her with hard angry eyes.*)

ABBIE (*jerking her hands away—harshly*): So ye're plannin' t' leave the farm t' Eben, air ye?

CABOT (*dazedly*): Leave . . . ? (*Then with resentful obstinacy*) I hain't a-givin' it t' no one!

ABBIE (*remorselessly*): Ye can't take it with ye.

CABOT (*thinks a moment—then reluctantly*): No, I calc'late not. (*After a pause—with a strange passion*) But if I could, I would, by the Etarnal! 'R if I could, in my dyin' hour, I'd set it afire an' watch it burn—this house an' every ear o' corn an' every tree down t' the last blade o' hay! I'd sit an' know it was all a-dying with me an' no one else'd ever own what was mine, what I'd made out o' nothin' with my own sweat 'n' blood! (*A pause—then he adds with a queer affection.*) 'Ceptin' the cows. Them I'd turn free.

ABBIE (*harshly*): An' me?

CABOT (*with a queer smile*): Ye'd be turned free, too.

ABBIE (*furiously*): So that's the thanks I git fur marryin' ye—t' have ye change kind to Eben who hates ye, an' talk o' turnin' me out in the road.

CABOT (*hastily*): Abbie! Ye know I wa'n't. . . .

ABBIE (*vengefully*): Just let me tell ye a thing or two 'bout Eben! Whar's he gone? T' see that harlot, Min! I tried fur t' stop him. Disgracin' yew an' me—on the Sabbath, too!

CABOT (*rather guiltily*): He's a sinner—nateral-born. It's lust eatin' his heart.

ABBIE (*enraged beyond endurance—wildly vindictive*): An' his lust fur me! Kin ye find excuses fur that?

CABOT (*stares at her—after a dead pause*): Lust—fur yew?

ABBIE (*defiantly*): He was tryin' t' make love t' me—when ye heerd us quarrelin'.

CABOT (*stares at her—then a terrible expression of rage comes over his face—he springs to his feet shaking all over*): By the A'mighty God—I'll end him!

ABBIE (*frightened now for* EBEN): No! Don't ye!

CABOT (*violently*): I'll git the shotgun an' blow his soft brains t' the top o' them elums!

ABBIE (*throwing her arms around him*): No, Ephraim!

CABOT (*pushing her away violently*): I will, by God!

ABBIE (*in a quieting tone*): Listen, Ephraim. 'Twa'n't nothin' bad—on'y a boy's foolin'—'twa'n't meant serious—jest jokin' an' teasin'. . . .

CABOT: Then why did ye say—lust?

ABBIE: It must hev sounded wusser'n I meant. An' I was mad at thinkin'—ye'd leave him the farm.

CABOT (*quieter but still grim and cruel*): Waal then, I'll horsewhip him off the place if that much'll content ye.

ABBIE (*reaching out and taking his hand*): No. Don't think o' me! Ye mustn't drive him off. 'Tain't sensible. Who'll ye get to help ye on the farm? They's no one hereabouts.

CABOT (*considers this—then nodding his appreciation*): Ye got a head on ye. (*Then irritably:*) Waal, let him stay. (*He sits down on the edge of the porch. She sits beside him. He murmurs contemptuously:*) I oughtn't t' git riled so—at that 'ere fool calf. (*A pause.*) But har's the p'int. What son o' mine'll keep on here t' the farm—when the Lord does call me? Simeon an' Peter air gone t' hell—an' Eben's follerin' 'em.

ABBIE: They's me.

CABOT: Ye're on'y a woman.

ABBIE: I'm yewr wife.

CABOT: That hain't me. A son is me—my blood—mine. Mine ought t' git mine. An' then it's still mine—even though I be six foot under. D'ye see?

ABBIE (*giving him a look of hatred*): Ay-eh. I see. (*She becomes very thoughtful, her face growing shrewd, her eyes studying* CABOT *craftily.*)

CABOT: I'm gettin' old—ripe on the bough. (*Then with a sudden forced reassurance*) Not but what I hain't a hard nut t' crack even yet—an' fur many a year t' come! By the Etarnal, I kin break most o' the young fellers' backs at any kind o' work any day o' the year!

ABBIE (*suddenly*): Mebbe the Lord'll give *us* a son.

CABOT (*turns and stares at her eagerly*): Ye mean—a son—t' me 'n' yew?

ABBIE (*with a cajoling smile*): Ye're a strong man yet, hain't ye? 'Tain't noways impossible, be it? We know that. Why d'ye stare so? Hain't ye never thought o' that afore? I been thinkin' o' it all along. Ay-eh—an' I been prayin' it'd happen, too.

CABOT (*his face growing full of joyous pride and a sort of religious ecstasy*): Ye been prayin', Abbie?—fur a son?—t' us?

ABBIE: Ay-eh. (*With a grim resolution*) I want a son now.

CABOT (*excitedly clutching both of her hands in his*): It'd be the blessin' o' God, Abbie—the blessin' o' God A'mighty on me—in my old age—in my lonesomeness! They hain't nothin' I wouldn't do fur ye then, Abbie. Ye'd hev on'y t' ask it—anythin' ye'd a mind t'!

ABBIE (*interrupting*): Would ye will the farm t' me then—t' me an' it . . .?

CABOT (*vehemently*): I'd do anythin' ye axed, I tell ye! I swar it! May I be everlastin' damned t' hell if I wouldn't! (*He sinks to his knees pulling her down with him. He trembles all over with the fervor of his hopes.*) Pray t' the Lord agen, Abbie. It's the Sabbath! I'll jine ye! Two prayers air better nor one. "An' God hearkened unto Rachel"! An' God hearkened unto Abbie! Pray, Abbie! Pray for him to hearken! (*He bows his head, mumbling. She pretends to do likewise but gives him a side glance of scorn and triumph.*)

SCENE II

*(About eight in the evening. The interior of the two bedrooms on the top floor is shown—*EBEN *is sitting on the side of his bed in the room on the left. On account of the heat he has taken off everything but his undershirt and pants. His feet are bare. He faces front, brooding moodily, his chin propped on his hands, a desperate expression on his face.*

In the other room CABOT *and* ABBIE *are sitting side by side on the edge of their bed, an old four-poster with feather mattress. He is in his night shirt, she in her nightdress. He is still in the queer, excited mood into which the notion of a son has thrown him. Both rooms are lighted dimly and flickeringly by tallow candles.)*

CABOT: The farm needs a son.

ABBIE: I need a son.

CABOT: Ay-eh. Sometimes ye air the farm an' sometimes the farm be yew. That's why I clove t' ye in my lonesomeness. (*A pause. He pounds his knee with his fist.*) Me an' the farm has got t' beget a son!

ABBIE: Ye'd best go t' sleep. Ye're gittin' thin's all mixed.

CABOT: (*with an impatient gesture*): No, I hain't. My mind's clear's a well. Ye don't know me, that's it. (*He stares hopelessly at the floor.*)

ABBIE (*indifferently*): Mebbe. (*In the next room* EBEN gets up and paces up and down distractedly. ABBIE *hears him. Her eyes fasten on the intervening wall with concentrated attention.* EBEN *stops and stares. Their hot glances seem to meet through the wall. Unconsciously he stretches out his arms for her and she half rises. Then aware, he mutters a curse at himself and flings himself face downward on the bed, his clenched fists above his head, his face buried in the pillow.* ABBIE *relaxes with a faint sigh but her eyes remain fixed on the wall; she listens with all her attention for some movement from* EBEN.)

CABOT (*suddenly raises his head and looks at her—scornfully*): Will ye ever know me—'r will any man 'r woman? (*Shaking his head*) No. I calc'late 't wa'n't t' be. (*He turns away.* ABBIE *looks at the wall. Then, evidently unable to keep silent about his thoughts, without looking at his wife, he puts out his hand and clutches her knee. She starts violently, looks at him, sees he is not watching her, concentrates again on the wall and pays no attention to what he says.*) Listen, Abbie. When I come here fifty odd years ago—I was jest twenty an' the strongest an' hardest ye ever seen—ten times as strong an' fifty times as hard as Eben. Waal—this place was nothin' but fields o' stones. Folks laughed when I tuk it. They couldn't know what I knowed. When ye kin make corn sprout out o' stones, God's livin' in yew! They wa'n't strong enuf fur that! They reckoned God was easy. They laughed. They don't laugh no more. Some died hereabouts. Some went West an' died. They're all under ground—fur follerin' arter an easy God. God hain't easy. (*He shakes his head slowly.*) An' I growed hard. Folks kept allus sayin' he's a hard man like 'twas sinful t' be hard, so's at last I said back at 'em: Waal then, by thunder, ye'll git me hard an' see how ye like it! (*Then suddenly*) But I give in t' weakness once. 'Twas arter I'd been here two year. I got weak—despairful—they was so many stones. They was a party leavin', givin' up, goin' West. I jined 'em. We tracked on 'n' on. We come t' broad medders, plains, whar the soil was black an' rich as gold. Nary a stone. Easy. Ye'd on'y to plow an' sow an' then set an' smoke yer pipe an' watch thin's grow. I could o' been a rich man—but somethin' in me fit me an' fit me—the voice o' God sayin': "This hain't wuth nothin' t' Me. Get ye back t' hum!" I got afeerd o' that voice an' I lit out back t' hum here, leavin' my claim an' crops t' whoever'd a mind t' take 'em. Ay-eh. I actoolly give up what was rightful mine! God's hard, not easy! God's in the stones! Build my church on a rock—out o' stones an' I'll be in them! That's what He meant t' Peter! (*He sighs heavily—a pause.*) Stones. I picked 'em up an' piled 'em into walls. Ye kin read the years o' my life in them walls, every day a hefted stone, climbin' over the hills up and down, fencin' in the fields that was mine, whar I'd made thin's grow out o' nothin'—like the will o' God, like the servant o' His hand. It wa'n't easy. It was hard an' He made me hard fur it. (*He pauses.*) All the time I kept gittin' lonesomer. I tuk a wife. She bore Simeon an' Peter. She was a good woman. She wuked hard. We was married twenty year. She never knowed me. She helped but she never knowed what she was helpin'. I was allus lonesome. She died. After that it wa'n't so lonesome fur a spell. (*A pause.*) I lost count o' the years. I had no time t' fool away countin' 'em. Sim an' Peter helped. The farm growed. It was all mine! When I thought o' that I didn't feel lonesome. (*A pause.*) But ye can't hitch yer mind t' one thin' day an' night. I tuk another wife—Eben's Maw. Her folks was contestin' me at law over my deeds t' the farm—my farm! That's why Eben keeps a-talkin' his fool talk o' this bein' his Maw's farm. She bore Eben. She was purty—but soft. She tried t' be hard. She couldn't. She never knowed me nor nothin'. It was lonesomer 'n hell with her. After a matter o' sixteen odd years, she died. (*A pause.*) I lived with the boys. They hated me 'cause I was hard. I hated them 'cause they was soft. They coveted the farm without knowin' what it meant. It made me bitter 'n wormwood. It aged me—them coveting what I'd made fur mine. Then this spring the call come—the voice o' God cryin' in my wilderness, in my lonesomeness—t' go out an' seek an' find! (*Turning to her with strange passion*) I sought ye an' I found ye! Yew air my Rose o' Sharon! Yer eyes air like. . . . (*She has turned a blank face, resentful eyes to his. He stares at her for a moment—then harshly*) Air ye any the wiser fur all I've told ye?

ABBIE (*confusedly*): Mebbe.

CABOT (*pushing her away from him—angrily*): Ye don't know nothin'—nor never will. If ye don't hev a son t' redeem ye . . . (*This in a tone of cold threat.*)

ABBIE (*resentfully*): I've prayed, hain't I?

CABOT (*bitterly*): Pray agen—fur understandin'!

ABBIE (*a veiled threat in her tone*): Ye'll have a son out o' me, I promise ye.

CABOT: How kin ye promise?

ABBIE: I got second-sight mebbe. I kin foretell. (*She gives a queer smile.*)

CABOT: I believe ye have. Ye give me the chills sometimes. (*He shivers.*) It's cold in this house. It's oneasy. They's thin's pokin' about in the dark—in the corners. (*He pulls on his trousers, tucking in his night shirt, and pulls on his boots.*)

ABBIE (*surprised*): Whar are ye goin'?

CABOT (*queerly*): Down whar it's restful—whar it's warm—down t' the barn. (*Bitterly*) I kin talk t' the cows. They know. They know the farm an' me. They'll give me peace. (*He turns to go out the door.*)

ABBIE (*a bit frighteningly*): Air ye ailin' tonight, Ephraim?

CABOT: Growin'. Growin' ripe on the bough. (*He turns and goes, his boots clumping down the stairs.* EBEN *sits up with a start, listening.* ABBIE *is conscious of his movement and stares at the wall.* CABOT *comes out of the house around the corner and stands by the gate, blinking at the sky. He stretches up his hands in a tortured gesture*) God A'mighty, call from the dark! (*He listens as if expecting an answer. Then his arms drop, he shakes his head and plods off toward the barn.* EBEN *and* ABBIE *stare at each other through the wall.* EBEN *sighs heavily and* ABBIE *echoes it. Both become terribly nervous, uneasy. Finally* ABBIE *gets up and listens, her ear to the wall. He acts as if he saw every move she was making, he becomes resolutely still.*

She seems driven into a decision—goes out the door in rear determinedly. His eyes follow her. Then as the door of his room is opened softly, he turns away, waits in an attitude of strained fixity. ABBIE *stands for a second staring at him, her eyes burning with desire. Then with a little cry she runs over and throws her arms about his neck, she pulls his head back and covers his mouth with kisses. At first, he submits dumbly; then he puts his arms about her neck and returns her kisses, but finally, suddenly aware of his hatred, he hurls her away from him, springing to his feet. They stand speechless and breathless, panting like two animals.*)

ABBIE (*at last—painfully*): Ye shouldn't, Eben—ye shouldn't—I'd make ye happy!

EBEN (*harshly*): I don't want t' be happy—from yew!

ABBIE (*helplessly*): Ye do, Eben! Ye do! Why d'ye lie?

EBEN (*viciously*): I don't take t' ye, I tell ye! I hate the sight o' ye!

ABBIE (*with an uncertain troubled laugh*): Waal, I kissed ye anyways—an' ye kissed back—yer lips was burnin'—ye can't lie 'bout that! (*Intensely*) If ye don't care, why did ye kiss me back—why was yer lips burnin'?

EBEN (*wiping his mouth*): It was like pizen on 'em (*Then tauntingly*) When I kissed ye back, mebbe I thought 'twas someone else.

ABBIE (*wildly*): Min?

EBEN: Mebbe.

ABBIE (*torturedly*): Did ye go t' see her? Did ye r'ally go? I thought ye mightn't. Is that why ye throwed me off jest now?

EBEN (*sneeringly*): What if it be?

ABBIE (*raging*): Then ye're a dog, Eben Cabot!

EBEN (*threateningly*): Ye can't talk that way t' me!

ABBIE (*with a shrill laugh*): Can't I? Did ye think I was in love with ye—a weak thin' like yew? Not much! I on'y wanted ye fur a purpose o' my own—an' I'll hev ye fur it yet 'cause I'm stronger'n yew be!

EBEN (*resentfully*): I knowed well it was on'y part o' yer plan t' swaller everythin'!

ABBIE (*tauntingly*): Mebbe!

EBEN (*furious*): Git out o' my room!

ABBIE: This air my room an' ye're on'y hired help!

EBEN (*threateningly*): Git out afore I murder ye!

ABBIE (*quite confident now*): I hain't a mite afeerd. Ye want me, don't ye? Yes, ye do! An' yer Paw's son'll never kill what he wants! Look at yer eyes! They's lust fur me in 'em, burnin' 'em up! Look at yer lips now! They're tremblin' an' longin' t' kiss me, an' yer teeth t' bite! (*He is watching her now with a horrible fascination. She laughs a crazy triumphant laugh.*) I'm a-goin' t' make all o' this hum my hum! They's one room hain't mine yet, but it's a-goin' t' be tonight. I'm a-goin' down now an light up! (*She makes him a mocking bow.*) Won't ye come courtin' me in the best parlor, Mister Cabot?

EBEN (*staring at her—horribly confused—dully*): Don't ye dare! It hain't been opened since Maw died an' was laid out thar! Don't ye . . . ! (*But her eyes are fixed on his so burningly that his will seems to wither before hers. He stands swaying toward her helplessly.*)

ABBIE (*holding his eyes and putting all her will into her words as she backs out the door*): I'll expect ye afore long, Eben.

EBEN (*stares after her for a while, walking toward the door. A light appears in the parlor window. He murmurs*): In the parlor? (*This seems to arouse connotations for he comes back and puts on his white shirt, collar, half ties the tie mechanically, puts on coat, takes his hat, stands barefooted looking about him in bewilderment, mutters wonderingly:*) Maw! Whar air yew? (*Then goes slowly toward the door in rear.*)

SCENE III

(*A few minutes later. The interior of the parlor is shown. A grim, repressed room like a tomb in which the family has been interred alive.* ABBIE *sits on the edge of the horsehair sofa. She has lighted all the candles and the room is revealed in all its preserved ugliness. A change has come over the woman. She looks awed and frightened now, ready to run away.*

The door is opened and EBEN *appears. His face wears an expression of obsessed confusion. He stands staring at her, his arms hanging disjointedly from his shoulders, his feet bare, his hat in his hand.*)

ABBIE (*after a pause—with a nervous, formal politeness*): Won't ye set?

EBEN (*dully*): Ay-eh. (*Mechanically he places his hat carefully on the floor near the door and sits stiffly beside her on the edge of the sofa. A pause. They both remain rigid, looking straight ahead with eyes full of fear.*)

ABBIE: When I fust came in—in the dark—they seemed somethin' here.

EBEN (*simply*): Maw.

ABBIE: I kin still feel—somethin'. . . .

EBEN: It's Maw.

ABBIE: At fust I was feered o' it. I wanted t' yell an' run. Now—since yew come—seems like it's growin' soft an' kind t' me. (*Addressing the air—queerly*) Thank yew.

EBEN: Maw allus loved me.

ABBIE: Mebbe it knows I love yew too. Mebbe that makes it kind t' me.

EBEN (*dully*): I dunno. I should think she'd hate ye.

ABBIE (*with certainty*): No, I kin feel it don't—not no more.

EBEN: Hate ye fur stealin' her place—here in her hum—settin' in her parlor whar she was laid— (*He suddenly stops, staring stupidly before him.*)

ABBIE: What is it, Eben?

EBEN (*in a whisper*): Seems like Maw didn't want me t' remind ye.

ABBIE (*excitedly*): I knowed, Eben! It's kind t' me! It don't b'ar me no grudges fur what I never knowed an' couldn't help!

EBEN: Maw b'ars him a grudge.

ABBIE: Waal, so does all o' us.

EBEN: Ay-eh. (*With passion*) I does, by God!

ABBIE (*taking one of his hands in hers and patting it*): Thar! Don't git riled thinkin' o' him. Think o' yer Maw who's kind t' us. Tell me about yer Maw, Eben.

EBEN: They hain't nothin' much. She was kind. She was good.

ABBIE (*putting one arm over his shoulder. He does not seem to notice—passionately*): I'll be kind an' good t' ye!

EBEN: Sometimes she used t' sing fur me.

ABBIE: I'll sing fur ye!

EBEN: This was her hum. This was her farm.

ABBIE: This is my hum! This is my farm!

EBEN: He married her t' steal 'em. She was soft an' easy. He couldn't 'preciate her.

ABBIE: He can't 'preciate me!

EBEN: He murdered her with his hardness.

ABBIE: He's murderin' me!

EBEN: She died. (*A pause.*) Sometimes she used to sing fur me. (*He bursts into a fit of sobbing.*)

ABBIE (*both her arms around him—with wild passion*): I'll sing fur ye! I'll die fur ye! (*In spite of her overwhelming desire for him, there is a sincere maternal love in her manner and voice—a horribly frank mixture of lust and mother love.*) Don't cry, Eben! I'll take yer Maw's place! I'll be everythin' she was t' ye! Let me kiss ye, Eben! (*She pulls his head around. He makes a bewildered pretense of resistance. She is tender.*) Don't be afeered! I'll kiss ye pure, Eben—same 's if I was a Maw t' ye—an' ye kin kiss me back 's if yew was my son—my boy—sayin' good-night t' me! Kiss me, Eben. (*They kiss in restrained fashion. Then suddenly wild passion overcomes her. She kisses him lustfully again and again and he flings his arms about her and returns her kisses. Suddenly, as in the bedroom, he frees himself from her violently and springs to his feet. He is trembling all over, in a strange state of terror.* ABBIE *strains her arms toward him with fierce pleading.*) Don't ye leave me, Eben! Can't ye see it hain't enuf—lovin' ye like a Maw—can't ye see it's got t' be that an' more—much more—a hundred times more—fur me t' be happy—fur yew t' be happy?

EBEN (*to the presence he feels in the room*): Maw! Maw! What d'ye want? What air ye tellin' me?

ABBIE: She's tellin' ye t' love me. She knows I love ye an' I'll be good t' ye. Can't ye feel it? Don't ye know? She's tellin' ye t' love me, Eben!

EBEN: Ay-eh. I feel—mebbe she—but—I can't figger out—why—when ye've stole her place—here in her hum—in the parlor whar she was—

ABBIE (*fiercely*): She knows I love ye!

EBEN (*his face suddenly lighting up with a fierce triumphant grin*): I see it! I sees why. It's her vengeance on him—so's she kin rest quiet in her grave!

ABBIE (*wildly*): Vengeance o' God on the hull o' us! What d'we give a durn? I love ye, Eben! God knows I love ye! (*She stretches out her arms for him.*)

EBEN (*throws himself on his knees beside the sofa and grabs her in his arms—releasing all his pent-up passion*): An' I love yew, Abbie!—now I kin say it! I been dyin' fur want o' ye—every hour since ye come! I love ye! (*Their lips meet in a fierce, bruising kiss.*)

SCENE IV

(*Exterior of the farmhouse. It is just dawn. The front door at right is opened and* EBEN *comes out and walks around to the gate. He is dressed in his working clothes. He seems changed. His face wears a bold and confident expression, he is grinning to himself with evident satisfaction. As he gets near the gate, the window of the parlor is heard opening and the shutters are flung back and* ABBIE *sticks her head out. Her hair tumbles over her shoulders in disarray, her face is flushed, she looks at* EBEN *with tender, languorous eyes and calls softly.*)

ABBIE: Eben. (*As he turns—playfully*) Jest one more kiss afore ye go. I'm goin' to miss ye fearful all day.

EBEN: An' me yew, ye kin bet! (*He goes to her. They kiss several times. He draws away, laughingly.*) Thar. That's enuf, hain't it? Ye won't hev none left fur next time.

ABBIE: I got a million o' 'em left fur yew! (*Then a bit anxiously*) D'ye r'ally love me, Eben?

EBEN (*emphatically*): I like ye better'n any gal I ever knowed! That's gospel!

ABBIE: Likin' hain't lovin'.

EBEN: Waal then—I love ye. Now air yew satisfied?

ABBIE: Ay-eh, I be. (*She smiles at him adoringly.*)

EBEN: I better git t' the barn. The old critter's liable t' suspicion an' come sneakin' up.

ABBIE (*with a confident laugh*): Let him! I kin allus pull the wool over his eyes. I'm goin' t' leave the shutters open and let in the sun 'n' air. This room's been dead long enuf. Now it's goin' t' be my room!

EBEN (*frowning*): Ay-eh.

ABBIE (*hastily*): I meant—our room.

EBEN: Ay-eh.

ABBIE: We made it our'n last night, didn't we? We give it life—our lovin' did. (*A pause.*)

EBEN (*with a strange look*): Maw's gone back t' her grave. She kin sleep now.

ABBIE: May she rest in peace! (*Then tenderly rebuking*) Ye oughtn't t' talk o' sad thin's—this mornin'.

EBEN: It jest come up in my mind o' itself.

ABBIE: Don't let it. (*He doesn't answer. She yawns*) Waal, I'm a-going' t' steal a wink o' sleep. I'll tell the Old Man I hain't feelin' pert. Let him git his own vittles.

EBEN: I see him comin' from the barn. Ye better look smart an' git upstairs.

ABBIE: Ay-eh. Good-by. Don't fergit me. (*She throws him a kiss. he grins—then squares his shoulders and awaits his father confidently.* CABOT *walks slowly up from the left, staring up at the sky with a vague face.*)

EBEN (*jovially*): Mornin', Paw. Star-gazin' in daylight?

CABOT: Purty, hain't it?

EBEN (*looking around him possessively*): It's a durned purty farm.

CABOT: I mean the sky.

EBEN (*grinning*): How d'ye know? Them eyes o' your'n can't see that fur. (*This tickles his humor and he slaps his thigh and laughs.*) Ho-ho! That's a good un!

CABOT (*grimly sarcastic*): Ye're feelin' right chipper, hain't ye? Whar'd ye steal the likker?

EBEN (*good-naturedly*): 'Tain't likker. Jest life. (*Suddenly holding out his hand—soberly*) Yew 'n' me is quits. Let's shake hands.

CABOT (*suspiciously*): What's come over ye?

EBEN: Then don't. Mebbe it's jest as well. (*A moment's pause.*) What's come over me? (*Queerly*) Didn't ye feel her passin'—goin' back t' her grave?

CABOT (*dully*): Who?

EBEN: Maw. She kin rest now an' sleep content. She's quits with ye.

CABOT (*confusedly*) I rested. I slept good—down with the cows. They know how t' sleep. They're teachin' me.

EBEN (*suddenly jovial again*): Good fur the cows! Waal—ye better git t' work.

CABOT (*grimly amused*): Air yew bossin' me, ye calf?

EBEN (*beginning to laugh*): Ay-eh! I'm bossin' yew! Ha-ha-ha! see how ye like it! Ha-ha-ha! I'm the prize rooster o' this roost. Ha-ha-ha! (*he goes off toward the barn laughing.*)

CABOT (*looks after him with scornful pity*): Soft-headed. Like his Maw. Dead spit 'n' image. No hope in him! (*He spits with contemptuous disgust.*) A born fool! (*Then matter-of-factly*) Waal—I'm gettin' peckish. (*He goes toward door.*)

(*Curtain.*)

PART III

Scene I

(*A night in late spring the following year. The kitchen and the two bedrooms upstairs are shown. The two bedrooms are dimly lighted by a tallow candle in each.* EBEN *is sitting on the side of the bed in his room, his chin propped on his fists, his face a study of the struggle he is making to understand his conflicting emotions. The noisy laughter and music from below where a kitchen dance is in progress annoy and distract him. He scowls at the floor.*

In the next room a cradle stands beside the double bed.

In the kitchen all is festivity. The stove has been taken down to give more room to the dancers. The chairs, with wooden benches added, have been pushed back against the walls. On these are seated, squeezed in tight against one another, farmers and their wives and their young folks of both sexes from the neighboring farms. They are all chattering and laughing loudly. They evidently have some secret joke in common. There is no end of winking, of nudging, of meaning nods of the head toward CABOT *who, in a state of extreme hilarious excitement increased by the amount he has drunk, is standing near the rear door where there is a small keg of whisky and serving drinks to all the men. In the left corner, front, dividing the attention with her husband,* ABBIE *is sitting in a rocking chair, a shawl wrapped about her shoulders. She is very pale, her face is thin and drawn, her eyes are fixed anxiously on the open door in rear as if waiting for someone.*

The musician is tuning up his fiddle, seated in the far right corner. He is a lanky young fellow with a long, weak face. His pale eyes blink incessantly and he grins about him slyly with a greedy malice.)

ABBIE (*suddenly turning to a young girl on her right*): Whar's Eben?

YOUNG GIRL (*eying her scornfully*): I dunno, Mrs. Cabot. I hain't seen Eben in ages. (*Meaningly*) Seems like he's spent most o' his time t' hum since yew come.

ABBIE (*vaguely*): I tuk his Maw's place.

YOUNG GIRL: Ay-eh. So I've heerd. (*She turns away to retail this bit of gossip to her mother sitting next to her.* ABBIE *turns to her left to a big stoutish middle-aged man whose flushed face and staring eyes show the amount of "likker" he has consumed.*)

ABBIE: Ye hain't seen Eben, hev ye?

MAN: No, I hain't. (*Then he adds with a wink*) If yew hain't, who would?

ABBIE: He's the best dancer in the county. He'd ought t' come an' dance.

MAN (*with a wink*): Mebbe he's doin' the dutiful an' walkin' the kid t' sleep. It's a boy, hain't it?

ABBIE (*nodding vaguely*): Ay-eh—born two weeks back—purty's a picter.

MAN: They all is—t' their Maws. (*Then in a whisper, with a nudge and a leer*) Listen, Abbie—if ye ever git tired o' Eben, remember me! Don't fergit now! (*He looks at her uncomprehending face for a second—then grunts disgustedly.*) Waal—

guess I'll likker agin. (*He goes over and joins* CABOT *who is arguing noisily with an old farmer over cows. They all drink.*)

ABBIE (*this time appealing to nobody in particular*): Wonder what Eben's a-doin'? (*Her remark is repeated down the line with many a guffaw and titter until it reaches the fiddler. He fastens his blinking eyes on* ABBIE.)

FIDDLER (*raising his voice*): Bet I kin tell ye, Abbie, what Eben's doin'! He's down t' the church offerin' up prayers o' thanksgivin'. (*They all titter expectantly.*)

MAN: What fur? (*Another titter.*)

FIDDLER: 'Cause unto him a—(*he hesitates just long enough*)—brother is born! (*A roar of laughter. They all look from* ABBIE *to* CABOT. *She is oblivious, staring at the door.* CABOT, *although he hasn't heard the words, is irritated by the laughter and steps forward, glaring about him. There is an immediate silence.*)

CABOT: What're ye all bleatin' about—like a flock o' goats? Why don't ye dance, damn ye? I axed ye here t' dance—t' eat, drink an' be merry—an' thar ye set cacklin' like a lot o' wet hens with the pip! Ye've swilled my likker an' guzzled my vittles like hogs, hain't ye? Then dance fur me, can't ye? That's fa'r an' squar', hain't it? (*A grumble of resentment goes around but they are all evidently in too much awe of him to express it openly.*)

FIDDLER (*slyly*): We're waitin' fur Eben. (*A suppressed laugh.*)

CABOT (*with a fierce exultation*): T'hell with Eben! Eben's done fur now! I got a new son! (*His mood switching with drunken suddenness*) But ye needn't t' laugh at Eben, none o' ye! He's my blood, if he be a dumb fool. He's better nor any o' yew! He kin do a day's work a'most up t' what I kin—an' that'd put any o' yew pore critters t' shame!

FIDDLER: An' he kin do a good night's work, too! (*A roar of laughter.*)

CABOT: Laugh, ye damn fools! Ye're right jist the same, Fiddler. He kin work day an' night too, like I kin, if need be!

OLD FARMER (*from behind the keg where he is weaving drunkenly back and forth—with great simplicity*): They hain't many t' touch ye, Ephraim—a son at seventy-six. That's a hard man fur ye! I be on'y sixty-eight an' I couldn't do it. (*A roar of laughter in which* CABOT *joins uproariously.*)

CABOT (*slapping him on the back*): I'm sorry fur ye, Hi. I'd never suspicion sech weakness from a boy like yew!

OLD FARMER: An' I never reckoned yew had it in ye nuther, Ephraim. (*There is another laugh.*)

CABOT (*suddenly grim*): I got a lot in me—a hell of a lot—folks don't know on. (*Turning to the* FIDDLER) Fiddle 'er up, durn ye! Give 'em somethin' t' dance t'! What air ye, an ornament? Hain't this a celebration? Then grease yer elbow an' go it!

FIDDLER (*seizes a drink which the* OLD FARMER *holds out to him and downs it*): Here goes! (*He starts to fiddle "Lady of the Lake." Four young fellows and four girls form in two lines and dance a square dance. The* FIDDLER *shouts directions for the different movements, keeping his words in the rhythm of the music and interspersing them with jocular personal remarks to the dancers themselves. The people seated along the walls stamp their feet and clap their hands in unison.* CABOT *is especially active in this respect. Only* ABBIE *remains apathetic, staring at the door as if she were alone in a silent room.*)

FIDDLER: Swing your partner t' the right! That's it, Jim! Give her a b'ar hug! Her Maw hain't lookin'. (*Laughter.*) Change partners! That suits ye, don't it, Essie, now ye got Reub afore ye? Look at her redden up, will ye! Waal, life is short an' so's love, as the feller says. (*Laughter.*)

CABOT (*excitedly, stamping his foot*): Go it, boys! Go it, gals!

FIDDLER (*with a wink at the others*): Ye're the spryest seventy-six ever I sees, Ephraim! Now if ye'd on'y good eyesight . . . ! (*Suppressed laughter. He gives* CABOT *no chance to retort but roars.*) Promenade! Ye're walkin' like a bride down the aisle, Sarah! Waal, while they's life they's allus hope, I've heerd tell. Swing your partner to the left! Gosh A'mighty, look at Johnny Cook high-steppin'! They hain't goin' t'be much strength left fur howin' in the corn lot t'morrow. (*Laughter.*)

CABOT: Go it! Go it! (*Then suddenly, unable to restrain himself any longer, he prances into the midst of the dancers, scattering them, waving his arms about wildly.*) Ye're all hoofs! Git out o' my road! Give me room! I'll show ye dancin'. Ye're all too soft! (*He pushes them roughly away. They crowd back toward the walls, muttering, looking at him resentfully.*)

FIDDLER (*jeeringly*): Go it, Ephraim! Go it! (*He starts "Pop Goes the Weasel," increasing the tempo with every verse until at the end he is fiddling crazily as fast as he can go.*)

CABOT (*starts to dance, which he does very well and with tremendous vigor. Then he begins to improvise, cuts incredibly grotesque capers, leaping up and cracking his heels together, prancing around in a circle with body bent in an Indian war dance, then suddenly straightening up and kicking as high as he can with both legs. He is like a monkey on a string. And all the while he intersperses his antics with shouts and derisive comments*): Whoop! Here's dancin' fur ye! Whoop! See that! Seventy-six, if I'm a day! Hard as iron yet! Beatin' the young 'uns like I allus done! Look at me! I'd invite ye t' dance on my hundredth birthday on'y ye'll all be dead by then. Ye're a sickly generation! Yer hearts air pink, not red! Yer veins is full o' mud an' water! I be the on'y man in the county! Whoop! See that! I'm a Injun! I've killed Injuns in the West afore ye was born—an' skulped 'em too! They's a arrer wound on my backside I c'd show ye! The hull tribe chased me. I outrun 'em all—with the arrer stuck in me! An' I tuk vengeance on 'em. Ten eyes fur an eye, that was my motter! Whoop! Look at me! I kin kick the ceilin' off the room! Whoop!

FIDDLER (*stops playing—exhaustedly*): God A'mighty, I got enuf. Ye got the devil's strength in ye.

CABOT (*delightedly*): Did I beat yew, too? Wa'al, ye played smart. Hev a swig. (*He pours whisky for himself and* FIDDLER. *They drink. The others watch* CABOT *silently with cold, hostile eyes. There is a dead pause. The* FIDDLER *rests.* CABOT *leans against the keg, panting, glaring around him confusedly. In the room above,* EBEN *gets to his feet and tiptoes out the door in rear, appearing a moment later in the other bedroom. He moves silently, even frighteneedly, toward the cradle and stands there looking down at the baby. His face is as vague as his reactions are confused, but there is a trace of tenderness, of interested discovery. At the same moment that he reaches the cradle,* ABBIE *seems to sense something. She gets up weakly and goes to* CABOT.)

ABBIE: I'm goin' up t' the baby.

CABOT (*with real solicitude*): Air ye able fur the stairs? D'ye want me t' help ye, Abbie?

ABBIE: No. I'm able. I'll be down agen soon.

CABOT: Don't ye git wore out! He needs ye, remember—our son does! (*He grins affectionately, patting her on the back. She shrinks from his touch.*)

ABBIE (*dully*): Don't—tech me. I'm goin'—up. (*She goes.* CABOT *looks after her. A whisper goes around the room.* CABOT *turns. It ceases. He wipes his forehead streaming with sweat. He is breathing pantingly.*)

CABOT: I'm a-goin' out t' git fresh air. I'm feelin' a mite dizzy. Fiddle up thar! Dance, all o' ye! Here's likker fur them as wants it. Enjoy yerselves. I'll be back. (*He goes, closing the door behind him.*)

FIDDLER (*sarcastically*): Don't hurry none on our account! (*A suppressed laugh. He imitates* ABBIE.) Whar's Eben? (*More laughter.*)

A WOMAN (*loudly*): What's happened in this house is plain as the nose on yer face! (ABBIE *appears in the doorway upstairs and stands looking in surprise and adoration at* EBEN *who does not see her.*)

A MAN: Ssshh! He's li'ble t' be listenin' at the door. That'd be like him. (*Their voices die to an intensive whispering. Their faces are concentrated on this gossip. A noise as of dead leaves in the wind comes from the room.* CABOT *has come out from the porch and stands by the gate, leaning on it, staring at the sky blinkingly.* ABBIE *comes across the room silently.* EBEN *does not notice her until quite near.*)

EBEN (*starting*): Abbie!

ABBIE: Ssshh! (*She throws her arms around him. They kiss—then bend over the cradle together.*) Ain't he purty?—dead spit 'n' image o' yew!

EBEN (*pleased*): Air he? I can't tell none.

ABBIE: E-zactly like!

EBEN (*frowningly*): I don't like this. I don't like lettin' on what's mine's his'n. I been doin' that all my life. I'm gittin' t' the end o' b'arin' it!

ABBIE (*putting her finger on his lips*): We're doin' the best we kin. We got t' wait. Somethin's bound t' happen. (*She puts her arms around him.*) I got t' go back.

EBEN: I'm goin' out. I can't b'ar it with the fiddle playin' an' the laughin'.

ABBIE: Don't git feelin' low. I love ye, Eben. Kiss me. (*He kisses her. They remain in each other's arms.*)

CABOT (*at the gate, confusedly*): Even the music can't drive it out—somethin'. Ye kin feel it droppin' off the elums, climbin' up the roof, sneakin' down the chimney, pokin' in the corners! They's no peace in houses, they's no rest livin' with folks. Somethin's always livin' with ye. (*With a deep sigh*) I'll go t' the barn an' rest a spell. (*He goes wearily toward the barn.*)

FIDDLER (*tuning up*): Let's celebrate the old skunk gittin' fooled! We kin have some fun now he's went. (*He starts to fiddle "Turkey in the Straw." There is real merriment now. The young folks get up to dance.*)

SCENE II

(*A half hour later—exterior—*EBEN *is standing by the gate looking up at the sky, an expression of dumb pain bewildered by itself on his face.* CABOT appears, returning from the barn, walking wearily, his eyes on the ground. He sees EBEN *and his whole mood immediately changes. He becomes excited, a cruel, triumphant grin comes to his lips, he strides up and slaps* EBEN *on the back. From within comes the whining of the fiddle and the noise of stamping feet and laughing voices.*)

CABOT: So har ye be!

EBEN (*startled, stares at him with hatred for a moment—then dully*): Ay-eh.

CABOT (*surveying him jeeringly*): Why hain't ye been in t' dance? They was all axin' fur ye.

EBEN: Let 'em ax!

CABOT: They's a hull passel o' purty gals.

EBEN: T' hell with 'em!

CABOT: Ye'd ought t' be marryin' one o' 'em soon.

EBEN: I hain't marryin' no one.

CABOT: Ye might 'arn a share o' a farm that way.

EBEN (*with a sneer*): Like yew did, ye mean? I hain't that kind.

CABOT (*stung*): Ye lie! 'Twas yer Maw's folks aimed t' steal my farm from me.

EBEN: Other folks don't say so. (*After a pause—defiantly*) An' I got a farm, anyways!

CABOT (*derisively*): Whar?

EBEN (*stamps a foot on the ground*): Har!

CABOT (*throws his head back and laughs coarsely*): Ho-ho! Ye hev, hev ye? Waal, that's a good un!

EBEN (*controlling himself—grimly*): Ye'll see

CABOT (*stares at him suspiciously, trying to make him out—a pause—then with scornful confidence*): Ay-eh. I'll see. So'll ye. It's ye that's blind—blind as a mole underground. (EBEN *suddenly laughs, one short sardonic bark: "Ha." A pause.* CABOT *peers at him with renewed suspicion.*) Whar air ye hawin' 'bout? (EBEN *turns away without answering.* CABOT *grows angry.*) God A'mighty, yew air a dumb dunce! They's nothin' in that thick skull o' yourn' but noise—like a empty keg it be! (EBEN *doesn't seem to hear*—CABOT'S *rage grows.*) Yewr farm! God A'mighty! If ye wa'n't a born donkey ye'd know ye'll never own stick nor stone on it, specially now arter him bein' born. It's his'n, I tell ye—his'n arter I die—but I'll live a hundred jest t' fool ye all—an' he'll be growed then—yewr age a'most! (EBEN *laughs again his sardonic "Ha." This drives* CABOT *into a fury.*) Ha? Ye think ye kin git 'round that someways, do ye? Waal, it'll be her'n, too—Abbie's—ye won't git 'round her—she knows yer tricks—she'll be too much fur ye—she wants the farm her'n—she was afeerd o' ye—she told me ye was sneakin' 'round tryin' t' make love t' her t' git her on yer side . . . ye . . . ye mad fool, ye! (*He raises his clenched fists threateningly.*)

EBEN (*is confronting him choking with rage*): Ye lie, ye old skunk! Abbie never said no sech thing!

CABOT (*suddenly triumphant when he sees how shaken* EBEN *is*): She did. An' I says, I'll blow his brains t' the top o' them elums—an' she says no, that hain't sense, who'll ye git t' help ye on the farm in his place—an' then she says yewn' me ought t' have a son—I know we kin, she says—an' I says, if we do, ye kin have anythin' I've got ye've a mind t'. An' she says, I wants Eben cut off so's this farm'll be mine when ye die! (*With terrible gloating*) An' that's what's happened, hain't it? An' the farm's her'n! An' the dust o' the road—that's you'rn! Ha! Now who's hawin'?

EBEN (*has been listening, petrified with grief and rage—suddenly laughs wildly and brokenly*): Ha-ha-ha! So that's her sneakin' game—all along!—like I suspicioned at fust—t' swaller it all—an' me, too . . . ! (*Madly*) I'll murder her! (*He springs toward the porch but* CABOT *is quicker and gets in between.*)

CABOT: No, ye don't!

EBEN: Git out o' my road! (*He tries to throw* CABOT *aside. They grapple in what becomes immediately a murderous struggle. The old man's concentrated strength is too much for* EBEN. CABOT *gets one hand on his throat and presses him back across the stone wall. At the same moment,* ABBIE *comes out on the porch. With a stifled cry she runs toward them.*)

ABBIE: Eben! Ephraim! (*She tugs at the hands on* EBEN'S *throat.*) Let go, Ephraim! Ye're chokin' him!

CABOT (*removes his hand and flings* EBEN *sideways full length on the grass, gasping and choking. With a cry,* ABBIE *kneels beside him, trying to take his head on her lap, but he pushes her away.* CABOT *stands looking down with fierce triumph*): Ye needn't t've fret, Abbie, I wa'n't aimin' t' kill him. He hain't wuth hangin' fur—not by a hell of a sight! (*More and more triumphantly*) Seventy-six an' him not thirty yit—an' look whar he be fur thinkin' his Paw was easy! No, by God, I hain't easy! An' him upstairs, I'll raise him t' be like me! (*He turns to leave them.*) I'm goin' in an' dance!—sing an' celebrate! (*He walks to the porch—then turns with a great grin.*) I don't calc'late it's left in him, but if he gits pesky, Abbie, ye jest sing out. I'll come a-runnin' an' by the Etarnal, I'll put him across my knee an' birch him! Ha-ha-ha! (*He goes into the house laughing. A moment later his loud "whoop" is heard.*)

ABBIE (*tenderly*): Eben. Air ye hurt? (*She tries to kiss him but he pushes her violently away and struggles to a sitting position.*)

EBEN (*gaspingly*): T'hell—with ye!

ABBIE (*not believing her ears*): It's me, Eben—Abbie—don't ye know me?

EBEN (*glowering at her with hatred*): Ay-eh—I know ye—now! (*He suddenly breaks down, sobbing weakly.*)

ABBIE (*fearfully*): Eben—what's happened t' ye—why did ye look at me 's if ye hated me?

EBEN (*violently, between sobs and gasps*): I do hate ye! Ye're a whore—a damn trickin' whore!

ABBIE (*shrinking back horrified*): Eben! Ye don't know what ye're sayin'!

EBEN (*scrambling to his feet and following her—accusingly*): Ye'r nothin' but a stinkin' passel o' lies! Ye've been lyin' t' me every word ye spoke, day an' night, since we fust—done it. Ye've kept sayin' ye loved me. . . .

ABBIE (*frantically*): I do love ye! (*She takes his hand but he flings hers away.*)

EBEN (*unheeding*): Ye've made a fool o' me—a sick, dumb fool—a-purpose! Ye've been on'y playin' yer sneakin', stealin' game all along—gittin' me t' lie with ye so's ye'd hev a son he'd think was his'n, an' makin' him promise he'd give ye the farm and let me eat dust, if ye did git him a son! (*Staring at her with anguished, bewildered eyes*) They must be a devil livin' in ye! 'Tain't human t' be as bad as that be!

ABBIE (*stunned—dully*): He told yew . . .?

EBEN: Hain't it true? It hain't no good in yew lyin'.

ABBIE (*pleadingly*): Eben, listen—ye must listen—it was long ago—afore we done nothin'—yew was scornin' me—goin' t' see Min—when I was lovin' ye—an' I said it t' him t' git vengeance on ye!

EBEN (*unheedingly. With tortured passion*): I wish ye was dead! I wish I was dead along with ye afore this come! (*Ragingly*) But I'll git my vengeance too! I'll pray Maw t' come back t' help me—t' put her cuss on yew an' him!

ABBIE (*brokenly*): Don't ye, Eben! Don't ye! (*She throws herself on her knees before him, weeping.*) I didn't mean t' do bad t'ye! Fergive me, won't ye?

EBEN (*not seeming to hear her—fiercely*): I'll git squar' with the old skunk—an' yew! I'll tell him the truth 'bout the son he's so proud o'! Then I'll leave ye here t' pizen each other—

with Maw comin' out o' her grave at nights—an' I'll go t' the gold fields o' Californi-a whar Sim an' Peter be!

ABBIE (*terrified*): Ye won't—leave me? Ye can't!

EBEN (*with fierce determination*): I'm a-goin', I tell ye! I'll git rich thar an' come back an' fight him fur the farm he stole—an' I'll kick ye both out in the road—t' beg an' sleep in the woods—an' yer son along with ye—t' starve an' die! (*He is hysterical at the end.*)

ABBIE (*with a shudder—humbly*): He's yewr son, too, Eben.

EBEN (*torturedly*): I wish he never was born! I wish he'd die this minit! I wish I'd never sot eyes on him! It's him—yew havin' him—a-purpose t' steal—that's changed everythin'!

ABBIE (*gently*): Did ye believe I loved ye—afore he come?

EBEN: Ay-eh—like a dumb ox!

ABBIE: An' ye don't believe no more?

EBEN: B'lieve a lyin' thief! Ha!

ABBIE (*shudders—then humbly*): An did ye r'ally love me afore?

EBEN (*brokenly*): Ay-eh—an' ye was trickin' me!

ABBIE: An' ye don't love me now!

EBEN (*violently*): I hate ye, I tell ye!

ABBIE: An' ye're truly goin' West—goin' t' leave me—all account o' him being born?

EBEN: I'm a-goin' in the mornin'—or may God strike me t' hell!

ABBIE (*after a pause—with a dreadful cold intensity—slowly*): If that's what his comin's done t' me—killin' yewr love—takin' yew away—my on'y joy—the on'y joy I've ever knowed—like heaven t' me—purtier'n heaven—then I hate him, too, even if I be his Maw.

EBEN (*bitterly*): lies! Ye love him! He'll steal the farm fur ye! (*Brokenly*) But 'tain't the farm so much—not no more—it's yew foolin' me—gittin' me t' love ye—lyin' yew loved me—jest t' git a son t' steal!

ABBIE (*distractedly*): He won't steal! I'd kill him fust! I do love ye! I'll prove t' ye . . . !

EBEN (*harshly*): 'Tain't no use lyin' no more. I'm deaf t' ye! (*He turns away.*) I hain't seein' ye agen. Good-by!

ABBIE (*pale with anguish*): Hain't ye even goin' t' kiss me—not once—arter all we loved?

EBEN (*in a hard voice*): I hain't wantin' t' kiss ye never agen! I'm wantin' t' forgit I ever sot eyes on ye!

ABBIE: Eben!—ye mustn't—wait a spell—I want t' tell ye. . . .

EBEN: I'm a-goin' in t' git drunk. I'm a-goin' t' dance.

ABBIE (*clinging to his arm—with passionate earnestness*): If I could make it—'s if he'd never come up between us—if I could prove t' ye I wa'n't schemin' t' steal from ye—so's everythin' could be jest the same with us, lovin' each other jest the same, kissin' an' happy the same's we've been happy afore he come—if I could do it—ye'd love me agen, wouldn't ye? Ye'd kiss me agen? Ye wouldn't never leave me, would ye?

EBEN (*moved*): I calc'late not. (*Then shaking her hand off his arm—with a bitter smile*) But ye hain't God, be ye?

ABBIE (*exultantly*): Remember ye've promised! (*Then with strange intensity*) Mebbe I kin take back one thin' God does!

EBEN (*peering at her*): Ye're gittin' cracked, hain't ye? (*Then going towards door*) I'm a-goin' t' dance.

ABBIE (*calls after him intensely*): I'll prove t' ye! I'll prove I love ye better'n. . . . (*He goes in the door, not seeming to hear. She remains standing where she is, looking after him—then she finishes desperately:*) Better'n everythin' else in the world.

SCENE III

(JUST *before dawn in the morning—shows the kitchen and* CABOT'S *bedroom. In the kitchen, by the light of a tallow candle on the table,* EBEN *is sitting, his chin propped on his hands, his drawn face blank and expressionless. His carpetbag is on the floor beside him. In the bedroom, dimly lighted by a small whale-oil lamp,* CABOT *lies asleep.* ABBIE *is bending over the cradle, listening, her face full of terror yet with an undercurrent of desperate triumph. Suddenly, she breaks down and sobs, appears about to throw herself on her knees beside the cradle; but the old man turns restlessly, groaning in his sleep, and she controls herself, and shrinking away from the cradle with a gesture of horror, backs swiftly toward the door in rear and goes out. A moment later she comes into the kitchen and, running to* EBEN *flings her arms about his neck and kisses him wildly. He hardens himself, he remains unmoved and cold, he keeps his eyes straight ahead.*)

ABBIE (*hysterically*): I done it, Eben! I told ye I'd do it! I've proved I love ye—better'n everythin'—so's ye can't never doubt me no more!

EBEN (*dully*): Whatever ye done, it hain't no good now.

ABBIE (*wildly*): Don't ye say that! Kiss me, Eben, won't ye?

I need ye t' kiss me arter what I done! I need ye t' say ye love me!

EBEN (*kisses her without emotion—dully*): That's fur good-by. I'm a-goin' soon.

ABBIE: No! No! Ye won't go—not now!

EBEN (*going on with his own thoughts*): I been a-thinkin'—an' I hain't goin' t' tell Paw nothin'. I'll leave Maw t' take vengeance on ye. If I told him, the old skunk'd jest be stinkin' mean enuf to take it out on that baby. (*His voice showing emotion in spite of him*) An' I don't want nothin' bad t' happen t' him. He hain't t' blame fur yew. (*He adds with a certain queer pride:*) An' he looks like me! An' by God, he's mine! An' some day I'll be a-comin' back an' . . .!

ABBIE (*too absorbed in her own thoughts to listen to him—pleadingly*): They's no cause fur ye t' go now—they's no sense—it's all the same's it was—they's nothin' come b'tween us now—arter what I done!

EBEN (*something in her voice arouses him. He stares at her a bit frightenedly*): Ye look mad, Abbie. What did ye do?

ABBIE: I—I killed him, Eben.

EBEN (*amazed*): Ye killed him?

ABBIE (*dully*): Ay-eh.

EBEN (*recovering from his astonishment—savagely*): An' serves him right! But we got t' do somethin' quick t' make it look 'sif the old skunk'd killed himself when he was drunk. We kin prove by 'em all how drunk he got.

ABBIE (*wildly*): No! No! Not him! (*Laughing distractedly*) But that's what I ought t' done, hain't it? I oughter killed him instead! Why didn't ye tell me?

EBEN (*appalled*): Instead? What d'ye mean?

ABBIE: Not him.

EBEN (*his face grown ghastly*): Not—not that baby!

ABBIE (*dully*): Ay-eh!

EBEN (*falls to his knees as if he'd been struck—his voice trembling with horror*): Oh, God A'mighty! A'mighty God! Maw, whar was ye, why didn't ye stop her?

ABBIE (*simply*): She went back t'her grave that night we fust done it, remember? I hain't felt her about since. (*A pause.* EBEN *hides his face in his hands, trembling all over as if he had the ague. She goes on dully:*) I left the piller over his little face. Then he killed himself. He stopped breathin'. (*She begins to weep softly.*)

EBEN (*rage beginning to mingle with grief*): He looked like me. He was mine, damn ye!

ABBIE (*slowly and brokenly*): I didn't want t' do it. I hated myself fur doin' it. I loved him. He was so purty—dead spit 'n' image o' yew. But I loved yew more—an' yew was goin' away—far off whar I'd never see ye agen, never kiss ye, never feel ye pressed agin me agen—an' ye said ye hated me fur havin' him—ye said ye hated him an' wished he was dead—ye said if it hadn't been fur him comin' it'd be the same's afore between us.

EBEN (*unable to endure this, springs to his feet in a fury, threatening her, his twitching fingers seeming to reach out for her throat*): Ye lie! I never said—I never dreamed ye'd—I'd cut off my head afore I'd hurt his finger!

ABBIE (*piteously, sinking on her knees*): Eben, don't ye look at me like that—hatin' me—not after what I done fur ye—fur us—so's we could be happy agen—

EBEN (*furiously now*): Shut up, or I'll kill ye! I see yer game now—the same old sneakin' trick—ye're aimin' t' blame me fur the murder ye done!

ABBIE (*moaning—putting her hands over her ears*): Don't ye, Eben! Don't ye! (*She grasps his legs.*)

EBEN (*his mood suddenly changing to horror, shrinks away from her*): Don't ye tech me! Ye're pizen! how could ye—t' murder a pore little critter— Ye must've swapped yer soul t' hell! (*Suddenly raging*) Ha! I kin see why ye done it! Not the lies ye jest told—but 'cause ye wanted t' steal agen—steal the last thin' ye'd left me—my part o' him—no, the hull o' him—ye saw he looked like me—ye knowed he was all mine—an' ye couldn't b'ar it—I know ye! Ye killed him fur bein' mine! (*All this has driven him almost insane. He makes a rush past her for the door—then turns—shaking both fists at her, violently.*) But I'll take vengeance now! I'll git the Sheriff! I'll tell him everythin'! Then I'll sing "I'm off to Californi-a!" an' go—gold—Golden Gate—gold sun—fields o' gold in the West! (*This last he half shouts, half croons, incoherently, suddenly breaking off passionately.*) I'm a-goin' fur the Sheriff t' come an' git ye! I want ye tuk away, locked up from me! I can't stand t' luk at ye! Murderer an' thief 'r not, ye still tempt me! I'll give ye up t' the Sheriff! (*He turns and runs out, around the corner of the house panting and sobbing, and breaks into a swerving sprint down the road.*)

ABBIE (*struggling to her feet, runs to the door, calling after him*): I love ye, Eben! I love ye! (*She stops at the door weakly, swaying, about to fall.*) I don't care what ye do—if ye'll on'y love me agen— (*She falls limply to the floor in a faint.*)

SCENE IV

(*About an hour later. Same as Scene III. Shows the kitchen and* CABOT'S *bedroom. It is after dawn. The sky is brilliant with the sunrise. In the kitchen,* ABBIE *sits at the table, her body limp and exhausted, her head bowed down over her arms, her face hidden. Upstairs,* CABOT *is still asleep but awakens with a start. He looks toward the window and gives a snort of surprise and irritation—throws back the covers and begins hurriedly pulling on his clothes. Without looking behind him, he begins talking to* ABBIE *whom he supposes beside him.*)

CABOT: Thunder 'n' lightnin', Abbie! I hain't slept this late in fifty years! Looks 's if the sun was full riz a'most. Must've been the dancin' an' likker. Must be gittin' old. I hope Eben's t' wuk. Ye might've tuk the trouble t' rouse me, Abbie. (*He turns—sees no one there—surprised.*) Waal—whar air she? Gittin' vittles, I calc'late. (*He tiptoes to the cradle and peers down—proudly*) Mornin', sonny. Purty's a picter! Sleepin' sound. He don't beller all night like most o' em. (*He goes quietly out the door in rear—a few moments later enters kitchen—sees* ABBIE*—with satisfaction*) So thar ye be. Ye got any vittles cooked?

ABBIE (*without moving*): No.

CABOT (*coming to her, almost sympathetically*): Ye feelin' sick?

ABBIE: No.

CABOT (*pats her on shoulder. She shudders*): Ye'd best lie down a spell. (*Half jocularly*) Yer son'll be needin' ye soon. He'd ought t' wake up with a gnashin' appetite, the sound way he's sleepin'.

ABBIE (*shudders—then in a dead voice*): He ain't never goin' to wake up.

CABOT (*jokingly*): Takes after me this mornin'. I ain't slept so late in . . .

ABBIE: He's dead.

CABOT (*stares at her—bewilderedly*): What . . .

ABBIE: I killed him.

CABOT (*stepping back from her—aghast*): Air ye drunk—'r crazy—'r . . . !

ABBIE (*suddenly lifts her head and turns on him—wildly*): I killed him, I tell ye! I smothered him. Go up an' see if ye don't b'lieve me! (CABOT *stares at her a second, then bolts out the rear door, can be heard bounding up the stairs, and rushes into the bedroom and over to the cradle.* ABBIE *has sunk back life-*

lessly into her former position. CABOT *puts his hand down on the body in the crib. An expression of fear and horror comes over his face.*)

CABOT (*shrinking away—tremblingly*): God A'mighty! God A'mighty. (*He stumbles out the door—in a short while returns to the kitchen—comes to* ABBIE, *the stunned expression still on his face—hoarsely*) Why did ye do it? Why? (*As she doesn't answer, he grabs her violently by the shoulder and shakes her.*) I ax ye why ye done it! Ye'd better tell me 'r . . . !

ABBIE (*gives him a furious push which sends him staggering back and springs to her feet—with wild rage and hatred*): Don't ye dare tech me! What right hev ye t' question me 'bout him? He wa'n't yewr son! Think I'd have a son by yew! I'd die fust! I hate the sight o' ye an' allus did! It's yew I should've murdered, if I'd had good sense! I hate ye! I love Eben. I did from the fust. An' he was Eben's son—mine an' Eben's—not your'n!

CABOT (*stands looking at her dazedly—a pause—finding his words with an effort—dully*): That was it—what I felt—pokin' round the corners—while ye lied—holdin' yerself from me—sayin' ye'd a'ready conceived— (*he lapses into crushed silence—then with a strange emotion*) He's dead, sart'n. I felt his heart. Pore little critter! (*He blinks back one tear, wiping his sleeve across his nose.*)

ABBIE (*hysterically*): Don't ye! Don't ye! (*She sobs unrestrainedly.*)

CABOT (*with a concentrated effort that stiffens his body into a rigid line and hardens his face into a stony mask—through his teeth to himself*): I got t' be—like a stone—a rock o' jedgment! (*A pause. He gets complete control over himself—harshly*) If he was Eben's, I be glad he air gone! An' mebbe I suspicioned it all along. I felt they was somethin' onnateral—somewhars—the house got so lonesome—an' cold—drivin' me down t' the barn —t' the beasts o' the field. . . . Ay-eh. I must've suspicioned—somethin'. Ye didn't fool me—not altogether, leastways—I'm too old a bird—growin' ripe on the bough. . . . (*He becomes aware he is wandering, straightens again, looks at* ABBIE *with a cruel grin*) So ye'd liked t' hev murdered me 'stead o' him, would ye? Waal, I'll live to a hundred! I'll live t' see ye hung! I'll deliver ye up t' the jedgment o' God an' the law! I'll git the Sheriff now. (*Starts for the door.*)

ABBIE (*dully*): Ye needn't. Eben's gone fur him.

CABOT (*amazed*): Eben—gone fur the Sheriff?

ABBIE: Ay-eh.

CABOT: T' inform agen ye?

ABBIE: Ay-eh.

CABOT (*considers this—a pause—then in a hard voice*): Waal, I'm thankful fur him savin' me the trouble. I'll git t' wuk. (*He goes to the door—then turns—in a voice full of strange emotion*) He'd ought t' been my son, Abbie. Ye'd ought t' loved me. I'm a man. If ye'd loved me, I'd never told no Sheriff on ye no matter what ye did, if they was t' brile me alive!

ABBIE (*defensively*): They's more to it nor yew know, makes him tell.

CABOT (*dryly*): Fur yewr sake, I hope they be. (*He goes out—comes around to the gate—stares up at the sky. His control relaxes. For a moment he is old and weary. He murmurs despairingly:*) God A'mighty, I be lonesomer'n ever! (*He hears running footsteps from the left, immediately is himself again.* EBEN *runs in, panting exhaustedly, wild-eyed and mad looking. He lurches through the gate.* CABOT *grabs him by the shoulder.* EBEN *stares at him dumbly.*) Did ye tell the Sheriff?

EBEN (*nodding stupidly*): Ay-eh.

CABOT (*gives him a push away that sends him sprawling—laughing with withering contempt*): Good fur ye! A prime chip o' yer Maw ye be! (*He goes toward the barn, laughing harshly.* EBEN *scrambles to his feet. Suddenly* CABOT *turns—grimly threatening*) Git off this farm when the Sheriff takes her—or, by God, he'll have t' come back an' git me fur murder, too! (*He stalks off.* EBEN *does not appear to have heard him. He runs to the door and comes into the kitchen.* ABBIE *looks up with a cry of anguished joy.* EBEN *stumbles over and throws himself on his knees beside her—sobbing brokenly.*)

EBEN: Fergive me!

ABBIE (*happily*): Eben! (*She kisses him and pulls his head over against her breast.*)

EBEN: I love ye! Fergive me!

ABBIE (*ecstatically*): I'd fergive ye all the sins in hell fur sayin' that! (*She kisses his head, pressing it to her with a fierce passion of possession.*)

EBEN (*brokenly*): But I told the Sheriff. He's comin' fur ye!

ABBIE: I kin b'ar what happens t' me—now!

EBEN: I woke him up. I told him. He says, wait 'til I get dressed. I was waiting. I got to thinkin' o' yew. I got to thinkin' how I'd loved ye. It hurt like somethin' was bustin' in my chest an' head. I got t' cryin'. I knowed suddenly I loved ye yet, an' allus would love ye!

ABBIE (*caressing his hair—tenderly*): My boy, hain't ye?

EBEN: I begun t' run back. I cut across the fields an' through the woods. I thought ye might have time t' run away—with me—an' . . .

ABBIE (*shaking her head*): I got t' take my punishment—t' pay fur my sin.

EBEN: Then I want t' share it with ye.

ABBIE: Ye didn't do nothin'.

EBEN: I put it in yer head. I wisht he was dead! I as much as urged ye t' do it!

ABBIE: No. It was me alone!

EBEN: I'm as guilty as yew be! He was the child o' our sin.

ABBIE (*lifting her head as if defying God*): I don't repent that sin! I hain't askin' God t' fergive that!

EBEN: Nor me—but it led up t' the other—an' the murder ye did, ye did 'count o' me—an' it's my murder, too, I'll tell the Sheriff—an' if ye deny it, I'll say we planned it t'gether—an' they'll all b'lieve me, fur they suspicion everythin' we've done, an' it'll seem likely an' true to 'em. An' it is true—way down. I did help ye—somehow.

ABBIE (*laying her head on his—sobbing*): No! I don't want yew t' suffer!

EBEN: I got t' pay fur my part o' the sin! An' I'd suffer wuss leavin' ye, goin' West, thinkin' o' ye day an' night, bein' out when yew was in—(*lowering his voice*)—'r bein' alive when yew was dead. (*A pause.*) I want t' share with ye, Abbie—prison 'r death 'r hell 'r anythin'! (*He looks into her eyes and forces a trembling smile.*) If I'm sharin' with ye, I won't feel lonesome leastways.

ABBIE (*weakly*): Eben! I won't let ye! I can't let ye!

EBEN (*kissing her—tenderly*): Ye can't he'p yerself. I got ye beat fur once!

ABBIE (*forcing a smile—adoringly*): I hain't beat—s'long's I got ye!

EBEN (*hears the sound of feet outside*): Ssshh! Listen! They've come t' take us!

ABBIE: No, it's him. Don't give him no chance to fight ye, Eben. Don't say nothin'—no matter what he says. An' I won't neither. (*It is* CABOT. *He comes up from the barn in a great state of excitement and strides into the house and then into the kitchen.* EBEN *is kneeling beside* ABBIE, *his arms around her, hers around him. They stare straight ahead.*)

CABOT (*stares at them, his face hard. A long pause—vindictively*): Ye make a slick pair o' murderin' turtle doves! Ye'd ought t' be both hung on the same limb an' left thar t' swing in the breeze an' rot—a warnin' t' old fools like me t' b'ar their lonesomeness alone—an' fur young fools like ye t' hobble their lust. (*A pause. The excitement returns to his face, his eyes snap, he looks a bit crazy.*) I couldn't work today. I couldn't take no interest. T' hell with the farm! I'm leavin' it! I've turned the cows an' other stock loose! I've druv 'em into the woods whar they kin be free! By freein' 'em, I'm freein' myself! I'm quittin' here today! I'll set fire t' house an' barn an' watch 'em burn, an' I'll leave yer Maw t' haunt the ashes, an' I'll will the fields back t' God, so that nothin' human kin never touch 'em! I'll be a-goin' to Californi-a—t' jine Simeon an' Peter—true sons o' mine if they be dumb fools—an' the Cabots'll find Solomon's Mines t'gether! (*He suddenly cuts a mad caper*) Whoop! What was the song they sung? "Oh, Californi-a! That's the land fur me." (*He sings this—then gets on his knees by the floorboard under which the money was hid.*) An' I'll sail thar on one o' the finest clippers I kin find! I've got the money! Pity ye didn't know whar this was hidden so's ye could steal . . . (*He has pulled up the board. He stares—feels—stares again. A pause of dead silence. He slowly turns, slumping into a sitting position on the floor, his eyes like those of a dead fish, his face the sickly green of an attack of nausea. He swallows painfully several times—forces a weak smile at last.*) So—ye did steal it!

EBEN (*emotionlessly*): I swapped it t' Sim an' Peter fur their share o' the farm—t' pay their passages t' Californi-a.

CABOT (*with one sardonic*) Ha! (*He begins to recover. Gets slowly to his feet—strangely*): I calc'late God give it to 'em—not yew! God's hard, not easy! Mebbe they's easy gold in the West but it hain't God's gold. It hain't fur me. I kin hear His voice warnin' me agen t' be hard an' stay on my farm. I kin see his hand usin' Eben t' steal t' keep me from weakness. I kin feel I be in the palm o' His hand, His fingers guidin' me. (*A pause—then he mutters sadly:*) It's a-goin' t' be lonesomer now than ever it war afore—an' I'm gittin' old, Lord—ripe on the bough. . . . (*then stiffening*) Waal—what d'ye want? God's lonesome hain't He? God's hard an' lonesome! (*A pause. The* SHERIFF *with two men comes up the road from the left. They move cautiously to the door. The* SHERIFF *knocks on it with the butt of his pistol.*)

SHERIFF: Open in the name o' the law! (*They start.*)

CABOT: They've come fur ye. (*He goes to the rear door.*) Come in, Jim! (*The three men enter.* CABOT *meets them in doorway.*) Jest a minit, Jim. I got 'em safe here. (*The* SHERIFF *nods. He and his companions remain in the doorway.*)

EBEN (*suddenly calls*): I lied this mornin', Jim. I helped her to do it. Ye kin take me, too.

ABBIE (*brokenly*): No!

CABOT: Take 'em both. (*He comes forward—stares at* EBEN *with a trace of grudging admiration*) Purty good—fur yew! Waal, I got t' round up the stock. Good-by.

EBEN: Good-by.

ABBIE: Good-by. (CABOT *turns and strides past the men—comes out and around the corner of the house, his shoulders squared, his face stony, and stalks grimly toward the barn. In the meantime the* SHERIFF *and men have come into the room.*)

SHERIFF (*embarrassedly*): Waal—we'd best start.

ABBIE: Wait. (*Turns to* EBEN.) I love ye, Eben.

EBEN: I love ye, Abbie. (*They kiss. The three men grin and shuffle embarrassedly.* EBEN *takes* ABBIE'S *hand. They go out the door in rear, the men following, and come from the house, walking hand in hand to the gate.* EBEN *stops there and points to the sunrise sky.*) Sun's a-rizin'. Purty, hain't it?

ABBIE: Ay-eh. (*They both stand for a moment looking up raptly in attitudes strangely aloof and devout.*)

SHERIFF (*looking around at the farm enviously—to his companion*): It's a jim-dandy farm, no denyin'. Wished I owned it!

PART TWO
THE ESSAYS

Aristotle:
From *THE POETICS*
Translated by L. J. Potts

[*Art Is Imitation*] Let us talk of the art of poetry as a whole, and its different species with the particular force of each of them; how the fables must be put together if the poetry is to be well formed; also what are its elements and their different qualities; and all other matters pertaining to the subject.

To begin in the proper order, at the beginning. The making of epics and of tragedies, and also comedy, and the art of the dithyramb, and most flute and lyre art, all have this in common, that they are imitations. But they differ from one another in three respects: the different kinds of medium in which they imitate, the different objects they imitate, and the different manner in which they imitate (when it does differ). . . . When the imitators imitate the doings of people, the people in the imitation must be either high or low; the characters almost always follow this line exclusively, for all men differ in character according to their degree of goodness or badness. They must therefore be either above our norm, or below it, or normal; as, in painting, Polygnōtus depicted superior, Pauson inferior, and Dionysius normal, types. It is clear that each variant of imitation that I have mentioned will have these differences, and as the object imitated varies in this way so the works will differ. Even in the ballet, and in flute and lyre music, these dissimilarities can occur; and in the art that uses prose, or verse without music. . . . This is the difference that marks tragedy out from comedy; comedy is inclined to imitate persons below the level of our world, tragedy persons above it.

[*Origins of Poetry*] There seem to be two causes that gave rise to poetry in general, and they are natural. The impulse to imitate is inherent in man from his childhood; he is distinguished among the animals by being the most imitative of them, and he takes the first steps of his education by imitating. Everyone's enjoyment of imitation is also inborn. What happens with works of art demonstrates this: though a thing itself is disagreeable to look at, we enjoy contemplating the most accurate representations of it—for instance, figures of the most despicable animals, or of human corpses. The reason for this lies in another fact: learning is a great pleasure, not only to philosophers but likewise to everyone else, however limited his gift for it may be. He enjoys looking at these representations, because in the act of studying them he is learning—identifying the object by an inference (for instance, recognizing who is the original of a portrait); since, if he happens not to have already seen the object depicted, it will not be the imitation as such that is giving him pleasure, but the finish of the workmanship, or the colouring, or some such other cause.

And just as imitation is natural to us, so also are music and rhythm (metres, clearly, are constituent parts of rhythms). Thus, from spontaneous beginnings, mankind developed poetry by a series of mostly minute changes out of these improvisations.

[*The Elements of Tragedy*] Let us now discuss tragedy, having first picked up from what has been said the definition of its essence that has so far emerged. Tragedy, then, is an imitation of an action of high importance, complete and of some amplitude; in language enhanced by distinct and varying beauties; acted not narrated; by means of pity and fear effecting its purgation of these emotions. By the beauties enhancing the language I mean rhythm and melody; by "distinct and varying" I mean that some are produced by metre alone, and others at another time by melody.

Now since the imitating is done by actors, it would follow of necessity that one element in a tragedy must be the *Mise en scène*. Others are Melody and Language, for these are the media in which the imitating is done. By Language, I mean the component parts of the verse, whereas Melody has an entirely sensuous effect. Again, since the object imitated is an action, and doings are done by persons, whose individuality will be determined by their Character and their Thought (for these are the factors we have in mind when we define the quality of their doings), it follows that there are two natural causes of these doings, Thought and Character; and these causes determine the good or ill fortune of everyone. But the Fable is the imitation of the action; and by the Fable I mean the whole structure of the incidents. By Character I mean the factor that enables us to define the particular quality of the people involved in the doings; and Thought is shown in everything they say when they are demonstrating a fact or disclosing an opinion. There are therefore necessarily six elements in every tragedy, which give it its quality; and they are the Fable, Character, Language, Thought, the *Mise en scène,* and Melody. Two of these are the media in which the imitating is done, one is the manner of imitation, and three are its objects; there is no other element besides these. Numerous poets have turned these essential components to account; all of them are always present—the *Mise en scène,* Character, the Fable, Language, Melody, and Thought.

The chief of these is the plotting of the incidents; for tragedy is an imitation not of men but of doings, life, happiness; unhappiness is located in doings, and our end is a certain kind of doing, not a personal quality; it is their characters that give men their quality, but their doings that make them happy or the opposite. So it is not the purpose of the actors to imitate character, but they include character as a factor in the doings. Thus it is the incidents (that is to say the Fable) that are the end for which tragedy exists; and the end is more important than anything else. Also, without an action there could not be a tragedy, but without Character there could. (In fact, the tragedies of most of the moderns are non-moral, and there are many non-moral poets of all periods; this also applies to the paintings of Zeuxis, if he is compared with Polygnōtus, for whereas Polygnōtus is a good portrayer of character the painting of Zeuxis leaves it out.) Again, if any one strings together moral speeches with the language and thought well worked out, he will be doing what is the business of tragedy; but it will be done much better by a tragedy that handles these elements more weakly, but has a fable with the incidents connected by a plot. Further, the chief means by which tragedy moves us, Irony of events and Disclosure, are elements in the Fable. A pointer in the same direction is that beginners in the art of poetry are able to get the language and characterization right before they can plot their incidents, and so were almost all the earliest poets.

So the source and as it were soul of tragedy is the Fable; and Character comes next. For, to instance a parallel from the art of painting, the most beautiful colours splashed on anyhow would not be as pleasing as a recognizable picture in black and white. Tragedy is an imitation of an action, and it is chiefly for this reason that it imitates the persons involved.

Third comes Thought: that is, the ability to say what circumstances allow and what is appropriate to them. It is the part played by social morality and rhetoric in making the dialogue: the old poets made their characters talk like men of the world, whereas our contemporaries make them talk like public speakers. Character is what shows a man's disposition—the kind of things he chooses or rejects when his choice is not obvious. Accordingly those speeches where the speaker shows no preferences or aversions whatever are non-moral. Thought, on the other hand, is shown in demonstrating a matter of fact or disclosing a significant opinion.

Fourth comes the Language. By Language I mean, as has already been said, words used semantically. It has the same force in verse as in prose.

Of the remaining elements, Melody is the chief of the enhancing beauties. The *Mise en scène* can excite emotion, but it is the crudest element and least akin to the art of poetry; for the force of tragedy exists even without stage and actors; besides, the fitting out of a *Mise en scène* belongs more to the wardrobe-master's art than to the poet's.

[*The Tragic Fable*] So much for analysis. Now let us discuss in what sort of way the incidents should be plotted, since that is the first and chief consideration in tragedy. Our data are that tragedy is an imitation of a whole and complete action of some amplitude (a thing can be whole and yet quite lacking in amplitude). Now a whole is that which has a beginning, a middle, and an end. A beginning is that which does not itself necessarily follow anything else, but which leads naturally to another event or development; an end is the opposite, that which itself naturally (either of necessity or most commonly) follows something else, but nothing else comes after it; and a middle is that which itself follows something else and is followed by another thing. So, well-plotted fables must not begin or end casually, but must follow the pattern here described.

But, besides this, a picture, or any other composite object, if it is to be beautiful, must not only have its parts properly arranged, but be of an appropriate size; for beauty depends on size and structure. Accordingly, a minute picture cannot be beautiful (for when our vision has almost lost its sense of time it becomes confused); nor can an immense one (for we cannot take it all in together, and so our vision loses its unity and wholeness)—imagine a picture a thousand miles long! So, just as there is a proper size for bodies and pictures (a size that can be well surveyed), there is also a proper amplitude for fables (what can be kept well in one's mind). The length of the performance on the stage has nothing to do with art; if a hundred tragedies had to be produced, the length of the production would be settled by the clock, as the story goes that another kind of performance once was. But as to amplitude, the invariable rule dictated by the nature of the action is the fuller the more beautiful so long as the outline remains clear; and for a simple rule of size, the number of happenings that will make a chain of probability (or necessity) to change a given situation from misfortune to good fortune or from good fortune to misfortune is the minimum.

[*Unity*] Unity in a fable does not mean, as some think, that it has one man for its subject. To any one man many things happen—an infinite number—and some of them do not make any sort of unity; and in the same way one man has many doings which cannot be made into a unit of action. . . . Accordingly, just as in the other imitative arts the object of each imitation is a unit, so, since the fable is an imitation of an action, that action must be a complete unit, and the events of which it is made up must be so plotted that if any of these elements is moved or removed the whole is altered and upset. For when a thing can be included or not included without making any noticeable difference, that thing is no part of the whole.

[*Probability*] From what has been said it is also clear that it is not the poet's business to tell what has happened, but the kind of things that would happen—what is possible according to probability or necessity. The difference between the historian and the poet is not the difference between writing in verse or prose; the work of Herodotus could be put into verse, and it would be just as much a history in verse as it is in prose. The difference is that the one tells what has happened, and the other the kind of things that would happen. It follows therefore that poetry is more philosophical and of higher value than history; for poetry unifies more, whereas history aggregates. To unify is to make a man of a certain description say or do the things that suit him, probably or necessarily, in the circumstances (this is the point of the descriptive proper names in poetry); what Alcibiades did or what happened to him is an aggregation. In comedy this has now become clear. They first plot the fable on a base of probabilities, and then find imaginary names for the people—unlike the lampooners, whose work was an aggregation of personalities. But in tragedy they keep to the names of real people. This is because possibility depends on conviction; if a thing has not happened we are not yet convinced that it is possible, but if it has happened it is clearly possible, for it would not have happened if it were impossible. Even tragedies, however, sometimes have all their persons fictitious except for one or two known names; and sometimes they have not a single known name, as in the *Anthos* of Agathon, in which both the events and the names are equally fictitious, without in the least reducing the delight it gives. It is not, therefore, requisite at all costs to keep to the traditional fables from which our tragedies draw their subject-matter. It would be absurd to insist on that, since even the known legends are known only to a few, and yet the delight is shared by every one. . . .

[*Simple and Complex Fables*] The action imitated must contain incidents that evoke fear and pity, besides being a complete action; but this effect is accentuated when these incidents occur logically as well as unexpectedly, which will be more sensational than if they happen arbitrarily, by chance. Even when events are accidental the sensation is greater if they appear to have a purpose, as when the statue of Mitys at Argos killed the man who had caused his death, by falling on him at a public entertainment. Such things appear not to have happened blindly. Inevitably, therefore, plots of this sort are finer.

Some fables are simple, others complex: for the obvious reason that the original actions imitated by the fables are the one or the other. By a simple action I mean one that leads to the catastrophe in the way we have laid down, directly and singly, without Irony of events or Disclosure.

An action is complex when the catastrophe involves Disclosure, or Irony, or both. But these complications should develop out of the very structure of the fable, so that they fit what has gone before, either necessarily or probably. To happen after something is by no means the same as to happen because of it.

[*Irony*] Irony is a reversal in the course of events, of the kind specified, and, as I say, in accordance with probability or necessity. Thus in the *Oedipus* the arrival of the messenger, which was expected to cheer Oedipus up by releasing him from his fear about his mother, did the opposite by showing him who he was; and in the *Lynceus* (Abas), who was awaiting sentence of death, was acquitted, whereas his prosecutor

Dănaüs was killed, and all this arose out of what had happened previously.

A Disclosure, as the term indicates, is a change from ignorance to knowledge; if the people are marked out for good fortune it leads to affection, if for misfortune, to enmity. Disclosure produces its finest effect when it is connected with Irony, as the disclosure in the *Oedipus* is. There are indeed other sorts of Disclosure: the process I have described can even apply to inanimate objects of no significance, and mistakes about what a man has done or not done can be cleared up. But the sort I have specified is more a part of the fable and of the action than any other sort; for this coupling of Irony and Disclosure will carry with it pity or fear, which we have assumed to be the nature of the doings tragedy imitates; and further, such doings will constitute good or ill fortune. Assuming then that it is a disclosure of the identity of persons, it may be of one person only, to the other, when the former knows who the latter is; or sometimes both have to be disclosed—for instance, the sending of the letter led Orestes to the discovery of Iphigeneia, and there had to be another disclosure to make him known to her.

This then is the subject-matter of two elements in the Fable, Irony and Disclosure. A third element is the Crisis of feeling. Irony and Disclosure have been defined; the Crisis of feeling is a harmful or painful experience, such as deaths in public, violent pain, physical injuries, and everything of that sort.

[*The Tragic Pattern*] Following the proper order, the next subject to discuss after this would be: What one should aim at and beware of in plotting fables; that is to say, What will produce the tragic effect. Since, then, tragedy, to be at its finest, requires a complex, not a simple, structure, and its structure should also imitate fearful and pitiful events (for that is the peculiarity of this sort of imitation), it is clear: first, that decent people must not be shown passing from good fortune to misfortune (for that is not fearful or pitiful but disgusting); again, vicious people must not be shown passing from misfortune to good fortune (for that is the most untragic situation possible—it has none of the requisites, it is neither humane, nor pitiful, nor fearful); nor again should an utterly evil man fall from good fortune into misfortune (for though a plot of that kind would be humane, it would not induce pity or fear—pity is induced by undeserved misfortune, and fear by the misfortunes of normal people, so that this situation will be neither pitiful nor fearful). So we are left with the man between these extremes: that is to say, the kind of man who neither is distinguished for excellence and virtue, nor comes to grief on account of baseness and vice, but on account of some error; a man of great reputation and prosperity, like Oedipus and Thyestes and conspicuous people of such families as theirs. So, to be well informed, a fable must be single rather than (as some say) double—there must be no change from misfortune to good fortune, but only the opposite, from good fortune to misfortune; the cause must not be vice, but a great error; and the man must be either of the type specified or better, rather than worse. This is borne out by the practice of poets; at first they picked a fable at random and made an inventory of its contents, but now the finest tragedies are plotted, and concern a few families—for example, the tragedies about Alcmeon, Oedipus, Orestes, Mĕlĕāger, Thyestes, Tēlĕphus, and any others whose lives were attended by terrible experiences or doings.

This is the plot that will produce the technically finest tragedy. Those critics are therefore wrong who censure Euripides on this very ground—because he does this in his tragedies, and many of them end in misfortune; for it is, as I have said, the right thing to do. This is clearly demonstrated on the stage in the competitions, where such plays, if they succeed, are the most tragic, and Euripides, even if he is inefficient in every other respect, still shows himself the most tragic of our poets. The next best plot, which is said by some people to be the best, is the tragedy with a double plot, like the *Odyssey,* ending in one way for the better people and in the opposite way for the worse. But it is the weakness of theatrical performances that gives priority to this kind; when poets write what the audience would like to happen, they are in leading strings. This is not the pleasure proper to tragedy, but rather to comedy, where the greatest enemies in the fable, say Orestes and Aegisthus, make friends and go off at the end, and nobody is killed by anybody.

[*The Tragic Emotions*] The pity and fear can be brought about by the *Mise en scène;* but they can also come from the mere plotting of the incidents, which is preferable, and better poetry. For, without seeing anything, the fable ought to have been so plotted that if one heard the bare facts, the chain of circumstances would make one shudder and pity. That would happen to anyone who heard the fable of the *Oedipus.* To produce this effect by the *Mise en scène* is less artistic and puts one at the mercy of the technician; and those who use it not to frighten but merely to startle have lost touch with tragedy altogether.

We should not try to get all sorts of pleasure from tragedy, but the particular tragic pleasure. And clearly, since this pleasure coming from pity and fear has to be produced by imitation, it is by his handling of the incidents that the poet must create it.

Let us, then, take next the kind of circumstances that seem terrible or lamentable. Now, doings of that kind must be between friends, or enemies, or neither. If an enemy injures an enemy, there is no pity either beforehand or at the time, except on account of the bare fact; nor is there if they are neutral; but when sufferings are engendered among the affections—for example, if murder is done or planned, or some similar outrage is committed, by brother on brother, or son on father, or mother on son, or son on mother—that is the thing to aim at.

Though it is not permissible to ruin the traditional fables—I mean, such as the killing of Clytemnestra by Orestes, or Erĭphȳle by Alcmeon—the poet should use his own invention to refine on what has been handed down to him. Let me explain more clearly what I mean by "refine." The action may take place, as the old poets used to make it, with the knowledge and understanding of the participants; this was how Euripides made Medea kill her children. Or they may do it, but in ignorance of the horror of the deed, and then afterwards discover the tie of affection, like the Oedipus of Sophocles; his act was outside the play, but there are examples where it is inside the tragedy itself—Alcmeon in the play by Astydămas, or Tēlĕgōnus in *The Wounded Odysseus.* Besides these, there is a third possibility: when a man is about to do some fatal act in ignorance, but is enlightened before he does it. These are the only possible alternatives. One must either act or not act, and either know or not know. Of these alternatives, to know, and to be about to act, and then not to act, is thoroughly bad—it is disgusting without being tragic, for there is no emotional crisis; accordingly poets only rarely create such situations, as in the *Antigone,* when Haemon fails to kill Creon. Next in order is to act; and if the deed is done in ignorance and its nature is disclosed afterwards, so much the better—there is no bad taste in it, and the revelation is overpowering. But the last is best; I mean, like Mĕrŏpe in the *Cresphontes,* intending to kill her son, but recognizing him and not killing him; and the brother and sister in the *Iphigeneia;* and in the *Helle,* the son recognizing his mother just as he was going to betray her.—This is the reason for what was mentioned earlier: that the subject-matter of our tragedies is drawn from a few families. In their search for matter they discovered this recipe in the fables, not by cunning but by luck. So they are driven to have recourse to those families where such emotional crises have occurred. . . .

[*Character*] And in the characterization, as in the plotting of the incidents, the aim should always be either necessity or probability: so that they say or do such things as it is necessary or probable that they would, being what they are; and that for this to follow that is either necessary or probable. . . . As for extravagant incidents, there should be none in the story, or if there are they should be kept outside the tragedy, as is the one in the *Oedipus* of Sophocles.

Since tragedy is an imitation of people above the normal, we must be like good portrait-painters, who follow the original model closely, but refine on it; in the same way the poet, in imitating people whose character is choleric or phlegmatic, and so forth, must keep them as they are and at the same time make them attractive. So Homer made Achilles noble, as well as a pattern of obstinacy. . . .

[*Chorus*] Treat the chorus as though it were one of the actors; it should be an organic part of the play and reinforce it, not as it is in Euripides, but as in Sophocles. In their successors the songs belong no more to the fable than to that of any other tragedy. This has led to the insertion of borrowed lyrics, an innovation for which Agathon was responsible.

David Hume:
OF TRAGEDY

It seems an unaccountable pleasure which the spectators of a well-written tragedy receive from sorrow, terror, anxiety, and other passions that are in themselves disagreeable and uneasy. The more they are touched and affected, the more are they delighted with the spectacle; and as soon as the uneasy passions cease to operate, the piece is at an end. One scene of full joy and contentment and security is the utmost that any composition of this kind can bear; and it is sure always to be the concluding one. If in the texture of the piece there be interwoven any scenes of satisfaction, they afford only faint gleams of pleasure, which are thrown in by way of variety, and in order to plunge the actors into deeper distress by means of that contrast and disappointment. The whole art of the poet is employed in rousing and supporting the compassion and indignation, the anxiety and resentment, of his audience. They are pleased in proportion as they are afflicted, and never are so happy as when they employ tears, sobs, and cries, to give vent to their sorrow, and relieve their heart, swollen with the tenderest sympathy and compassion.

The few critics who have had some tincture of philosophy have remarked this singular phenomenon, and have endeavored to account for it.

L'Abbé Dubos, in his *Reflections on Poetry and Painting* [1719], asserts, that nothing is in general so disagreeable to the mind as the languid, listless state of indolence into which it falls upon the removal of all passion and occupation. To get rid of this painful situation, it seeks every amusement and pursuit: business, gaming, shows, executions; whatever will rouse the passions and take its attention from itself. No matter what the passion is: let it be disagreeable, afflicting, melancholy, disordered; it is still better than that insipid languor which arises from perfect tranquillity and repose.

It is impossible not to admit this account as being, at least in part, satisfactory. You may observe, when there are several tables of gaming, that all the company run to those where the deepest play is, even though they find not there the best players. The view, or, at least, imagination of high passions, arising from great loss or gain, affects the spectator by sympathy, gives him some touches of the same passions, and serves him for a momentary entertainment. It makes the time pass the easier with him, and is some relief to that oppression under which men commonly labor when left entirely to their own thoughts and meditations.

We find that common liars always magnify, in their narrations, all kinds of danger, pain, distress, sickness, deaths, murders, and cruelties, as well as joy, beauty, mirth, and magnificence. It is an absurd secret which they have for pleasing their company, fixing their attention, and attaching them to such marvellous relations by the passions and emotions which they excite.

There is, however, a difficulty in applying to the present subject, in its full extent, this solution, however ingenious and satisfactory it may appear. It is certain that the same object of distress which pleases in a tragedy, were it really set before us, would give the most unfeigned uneasiness; though it be then the most effectual cure to languor and indolence. Monsieur Fontenelle [in *Réflexions sur la Poétique* (1691)] seems to have been sensible of this difficulty, and accordingly attempts another solution of the phenomenon, or at least makes some addition to the theory above mentioned.

"Pleasure and pain," says he, "which are two sentiments so different in themselves, differ not so much in their cause. From the instance of tickling it appears, that the movement of pleasure pushed a little too far, becomes pain, and that the movement of pain, a little moderated, becomes pleasure. Hence it proceeds, that there is such a thing as a sorrow, soft and agreeable: It is a pain weakened and diminished. The heart likes naturally to be moved and affected. Melancholy objects suit it, and even disastrous and sorrowful, provided they are softened by some circumstance. It is certain, that, on the theater, the representation has almost the effect of reality; yet it has not altogether that effect. However we may be hurried away by the spectacle, whatever dominion the senses and imagination may usurp over the reason, there still lurks at the bottom a certain idea of falsehood in the whole of what we see. This idea, though weak and disguised, suffices to diminish the pain which we suffer from the misfortunes of those whom we love, and to reduce that affliction to such a pitch as converts it into a pleasure. We weep for the misfortune of a hero to whom we are attached. In the same instant we comfort ourselves by reflecting, that it is nothing but a fiction. And it is precisely that mixture of sentiments which composes an agreeable sorrow, and tears that delight us. But as that affliction which is caused by exterior and sensible objects is stronger than the consolation which arises from an internal reflection, they are the effects and symptoms of sorrow that ought to predominate in the composition."

This solution seems just and convincing; but perhaps it wants still some new addition, in order to make it answer fully the phenomenon which we here examine. All the passions, excited by eloquence, are agreeable in the highest degree, as well as those which are moved by painting and the theater. The epilogues of Cicero are, on this account chiefly, the delight of every reader of taste; and it is difficult to read some of them without the deepest sympathy and sorrow. His merit as an orator, no doubt, depends much on his success in this particular. When he had raised tears in his judges and all his audience, they were then the most highly delighted, and expressed the greatest satisfaction with the pleader. The pathetic description of the butchery made by Verres of the Sicilian captains, is a masterpiece of this kind. But I believe none will affirm, that the being present at a melancholy scene of that nature would afford any entertainment. Neither is the sorrow here softened by fiction. For the audience were convinced of the reality of every circumstance. What is it then which in this case raises a pleasure from the bosom of uneasiness, so to speak, and a pleasure which still retains all the features and outward symptoms of distress and sorrow?

I answer: this extraordinary effect proceeds from that very eloquence with which the melancholy scene is represented. The genius required to paint objects in a lively manner, the art employed in collecting all the pathetic circumstances, the judgment displayed in disposing them; the exercise, I say, of these noble talents, together with the force of expression, and beauty of oratorial numbers, diffuse the highest satisfaction on the audience, and excite the most delightful movements. By this means, the uneasiness of the melancholy passions is not only overpowered and effaced by something stronger of an opposite kind, but the whole impulse of those passions is converted into pleasure and swells the delight which the eloquence raises in us. The same force of oratory, employed on an uninteresting subject, would not please half so much, or rather would appear altogether ridiculous; and the mind, being left in absolute calmness and indifference, would relish none of those beauties of imagination or expression, which, if joined to passion, give it such exquisite entertainment. The impulse or vehemence arising from sorrow, compassion, indignation, receives a new direction from the sentiments of beauty. The latter, being the predominant emotion, seize the whole mind, and convert the former into themselves, at least tincture them so strongly as totally to alter their nature. And the soul being at the same time roused by passion and charmed by eloquence, feels on the whole a strong movement, which is altogether delightful.

The same principle takes place in tragedy; with this addition, that tragedy is an imitation, and imitation is always of itself agreeable. This circumstance serves still further to smooth the motions of passion, and convert the whole feeling into one uniform and strong enjoyment. Objects of the greatest terror and distress please in painting, and please more than the most beautiful objects that appear calm and indifferent.[1] The affection, rousing the mind, excites a large stock of spirit and vehemence; which is all transformed into pleasure by the force of the prevailing movement. It is thus the fiction of tragedy softens the passion, by an infusion of a new feeling, not merely by weakening or diminishing the sorrow. You may by degrees weaken a real sorrow, till it totally disappears; yet in none of its gradations will it ever give pleasure; except, perhaps, by accident, to a man sunk under lethargic indolence, whom it rouses from that languid state.

To confirm this theory, it will be sufficient to produce other instances, where the subordinate movement is converted into the predominant, and gives force to it, though of a different, and even sometimes though of a contrary nature.

Novelty naturally rouses the mind, and attracts our attention; and the movements which it causes are always converted into any passion belonging to the object, and join their force to it. Whether an event excites joy or sorrow, pride or shame, anger or good-will, it is sure to produce a stronger affection, when new or unusual. And though novelty of itself be agreeable, it fortifies the painful, as well as agreeable passions.

[1]Painters make no scruple of representing distress and sorrow, as well as any other passion. But they seem not to dwell so much on these melancholy affections as the poets, who, though they copy every emotion of the human breast, yet pass quickly over the agreeable sentiments. A painter represents only one instant; and if that be passionate enough, it is sure to affect and delight the spectator: But nothing can furnish to the poet a variety of scenes, and incidents, and sentiments, except distress, terror, or anxiety. Complete joy and satisfaction is attended with security and leaves no further room for action. *(Hume's note.)*

Had you any intention to move a person extremely by the narration of any event, the best method of increasing its effect would be artfully to delay informing him of it, and first excite his curiosity and impatience before you let him into the secret. This is the artifice practised by Iago in the famous scene of Shakespeare; and every spectator is sensible that Othello's jealousy acquires additional force from his preceding impatience, and that the subordinate passion is here readily transformed into the predominant one.

Difficulties increase passions of every kind; and by rousing our attention, and exciting our active powers, they produce an emotion which nourishes the prevailing affection.

Parents commonly love that child most whose sickly infirm frame of body has occasioned them the greatest pains, trouble, and anxiety, in rearing him. The agreeable sentiment of affection here acquires force from sentiments of uneasiness.

Nothing endears so much a friend as sorrow for his death. The pleasure of his company has not so powerful an influence.

Jealousy is a painful passion; yet without some share of it, the agreeable affection of love has difficulty to subsist in its full force and violence. Absence is also a great source of complaint among lovers, and gives them the greatest uneasiness; yet nothing is more favorable to their mutual passion than short intervals of that kind. And if long intervals often prove fatal, it is only because, through time, men are accustomed to them, and they cease to give uneasiness. Jealousy and absence in love compose the *dolce peccante* [sweet sinning] of the Italians, which they suppose so essential to all pleasure.

There is a fine observation of the elder Pliny, which illustrates the principle here insisted on. "It is very remarkable," says he [*Natural History,* Book XXXV], "that the last works of celebrated artists, which they left imperfect, are always the most prized, such as the *Iris* of Aristides, the *Tyndarides* of Nicomachus, the *Medea* of Timomachus, and the *Venus* of Apelles. These are valued even above their finished productions. The broken lineaments of the piece, and the half-formed idea of the painter, are carefully studied; and our very grief for that curious hand, which had been stopped by death, is an additional increase to our pleasure."

These instances (and many more might be collected) are sufficient to afford us some insight into the analogy of nature, and to show us, that the pleasure which poets, orators, and musicians give us, by exciting grief, sorrow, indignation, compassion, is not so extraordinary or paradoxical as it may at first sight appear. The force of imagination, the energy of expression, the power of numbers, the charms of imitation; all these are naturally, of themselves, delightful to the mind. And when the object presented lays hold also of some affection, the pleasure still rises upon us, by the conversion of this subordinate movement into that which is predominant. The passion, though perhaps naturally, and when excited by the simple appearance of a real object, it may be painful; yet is so smoothed, and softened, and mollified, when raised by the finer arts, that it affords the highest entertainment.

To confirm this reasoning, we may observe, that if the movements of the imagination be not predominant above those of the passion, a contrary effect follows; and the former, being now subordinate, is converted into the latter, and still further increases the pain and affliction of the sufferer.

Who could ever think of it as a good expedient for comforting an afflicted parent, to exaggerate, with all the force of elocution, the irreparable loss which he has met with by the death of a favorite child? The more power of imagination and expression you here employ, the more you increase his despair and affliction.

The shame, confusion, and terror of Verres, no doubt, rose in proportion to the noble eloquence and vehemence of Cicero: So also did his pain and uneasiness. These former passions were too strong for the pleasure arising from the beauties of elocution; and operated, though from the same principle, yet in a contrary manner, to the sympathy, compassion, and indignation of the audience.

Lord Clarendon, when he approaches towards the catastrophe of the royal party [in his *History of the Rebellion*], supposes that his narration must then become infinitely disagreeable; and he hurries over the king's death without giving us one circumstance of it. He considers it as too horrid a scene to be contemplated with any satisfaction, or even without the utmost pain and aversion. He himself, as well as the readers of that age, were too deeply concerned in the events, and felt a pain from subjects which an historian and a reader of another age would regard as the most pathetic and most interesting, and, by consequence, the most agreeable.

An action, represented in tragedy, may be too bloody and atrocious. It may excite such movements of horror as will not soften into pleasure; and the greatest energy of expression, bestowed on descriptions of that nature, serves only to augment our uneasiness. Such is that action represented in the *Ambitious Step-mother* [by Nicholas Rowe (1700)], where a venerable old man, raised to the height of fury and despair, rushes against a pillar, and, striking his head upon it, besmears it all over with mingled brains and gore. The English theater abounds too much with such shocking images.

Even the common sentiments of compassion require to be softened by some agreeable affection, in order to give a thorough satisfaction to the audience. The mere suffering of plaintive virtue, under the triumphant tyranny and oppression of vice, forms a disagreeable spectacle, and is carefully avoided by all masters of the drama. In order to dismiss the audience with entire satisfaction and contentment, the virtue must either convert itself into a noble courageous despair, or the vice receive its proper punishment.

Most painters appear in this light to have been very unhappy in their subjects. As they wrought much for churches and convents, they have chiefly represented such horrible subjects as crucifixions and martyrdoms, where nothing appears but tortures, wounds, executions, and passive suffering, without any action or affection. When they turned their pencil from this ghastly mythology, they had commonly recourse to Ovid, whose fictions, though passionate and agreeable, are scarcely natural or probably enough for painting.

The same inversion of that principle which is here insisted on, displays itself in common life, as in the effects of oratory and poetry. Raise so the subordinate passion that it becomes the predominant, it swallows up that affection which it before nourished and increased. Too much jealousy extinguishes love; too much difficulty renders us indifferent; too much sickness and infirmity disgusts a selfish and unkind parent.

What so disagreeable as the dismal, gloomy, disastrous stories, with which melancholy people entertain their companions? The uneasy passion being there raised alone, unaccompanied with any spirit, genius, or eloquence, conveys a pure uneasiness, and is attended with nothing that can soften it into pleasure or satisfaction.

Ralph Waldo Emerson:
THE TRAGIC

He has seen but half the universe who never has been shown the house of Pain. As the salt sea covers more than two thirds of the surface of the globe, so sorrow encroaches in man on felicity. The conversation of men is a mixture of regrets and apprehensions. I do not know but the prevalent hue of things to the eye of leisure is melancholy. In the dark hours, our existence seems to be a defensive war, a struggle against the encroaching All, which threatens surely to engulf us soon, and is impatient of our short reprieve. How slender the possession that yet remains to us; how faint the animation! how the spirit seems already to contract its domain, retiring within narrower walls by the loss of memory, leaving its planted fields to erasure and annihilation. Already our thoughts and words have an alien sound. There is a simultaneous diminution of memory and hope. Projects that once we laughed and leapt to execute find us now sleepy and preparing to lie down in the snow. And in the serene hours we have no courage to spare. We cannot afford to let go any advantages. The riches of body or of mind which we do not need to-day are the reserved fund against the calamity that may arrive to-morrow. It is usually agreed that some nations have a more sombre temperament, and one would say that history gave no record of any society in which despondency came so readily to heart as we see it and feel it in ours. Melancholy cleaves to the English mind in both hemispheres as closely as to the strings of an Æolian harp. Men and women at thirty years, and even earlier, have lost all spring and vivacity, and if they fail in their first enterprises, they throw up the game. But whether we and those who are next to us are more or less vulnerable, no theory of life can have any right which leaves out of account the values of vice, pain, disease, poverty, insecurity, disunion, fear and death.

What are the conspicuous tragic elements in human nature? The bitterest tragic element in life to be derived from an intellectual source is the belief in a brute Fate or Destiny; the belief that the order of Nature and events is controlled by a law not adapted to man, nor man to that, but which holds on its way to the end, serving him if his wishes chance to lie in the same course, crushing him if his wishes lie contrary to it, and heedless whether it serves or crushes him. This is the terrible meaning that lies at the foundation of the old Greek tragedy, and makes the Œdipus and Antigone and Orestes objects of such hopeless commiseration. They must perish, and there is no overgod to stop or mollify this hideous enginery that grinds or thunders, and snatches them up into its terrific system. The same idea makes the paralyzing terror with which the East Indian mythology haunts the imagination. The same thought is the predestination of the Turk. And universally, in uneducated and unreflecting persons on whom too the religious sentiment exerts little force, we discover traits of the same superstition: "If you balk water you will be drowned the next time;" "if you count ten stars you will fall down dead;" "if you spill the salt;" "if your fork sticks upright in the floor!" "if you say the Lord's prayer backwards;"—and so on, a several penalty, nowise grounded in the nature of the thing, but on an arbitrary will. But this terror of contravening an unascertained and unascertainable will cannot co-exist with reflection: it disappears with civilization, and can no more be reproduced than the fear of ghosts after childhood. It is discriminated from the doctrine of Philosophical Necessity herein: that the last is an Optimism, and therefore the suffering individual finds his good consulted in the good of all, of which he is a part. But in destiny, it is not the good of the whole or the *best will* that is enacted, but only *one particular will*. Destiny properly is not a will at all, but an immense whim; and this the only ground of terror and despair in the rational mind, and of tragedy in literature. Hence the antique tragedy, which was founded on this faith, can never be reproduced.

After reason and faith have introduced a better public and private tradition, the tragic element is somewhat circumscribed. There must always remain, however, the hindrance of our private satisfaction by the laws of the world. The law which establishes nature and the human race, continually thwarts the will of ignorant individuals, and this in the particulars of disease, want, insecurity and disunion.

But the essence of tragedy does not seem to me to lie in any list of particular evils. After we have enumerated famine, fever, inaptitude, mutilation, rack, madness and loss of friends, we have not yet included the proper tragic element, which is Terror, and which does not respect definite evils but indefinite;

an ominous spirit which haunts the afternoon and the night, idleness and solitude.

A low, haggard sprite sits by our side, "casting the fashion of uncertain evils"—a sinister presentiment, a power of the imagination to dislocate things orderly and cheerful and show them in startling array. Hark! what sounds on the night wind, the cry of Murder in that friendly house; see these marks of stamping feet, of hidden riot. The whisper overheard, the detected glance, the glare of malignity, ungrounded fears, suspicions, half-knowledge and mistakes, darken the brow and chill the heart of men. And accordingly it is natures not clear, not of quick and steady perceptions, but imperfect characters from which somewhat is hidden that all others see, who suffer most from these causes. In those persons who move the profoundest pity, tragedy seems to consist in temperament, not in events. There are people who have an appetite for grief, pleasure is not strong enough and they crave pain, mithridatic stomachs which must be fed on poisoned bread, natures so doomed that no prosperity can soothe their ragged and dishevelled desolation. They mis-hear and mis-behold, they suspect and dread. They handle every nettle and ivy in the hedge, and tread on every snake in the meadow.

> "Come bad chance,
> And we add it to our strength,
> And we teach it art and length,
> Itself o'er us to advance."

Frankly, then, it is necessary to say that all sorrow dwells in a low region. It is superficial; for the most part fantastic, or in the appearance and not in things. Tragedy is in the eye of the observer, and not in the heart of the sufferer. It looks like an insupportable load under which earth moans aloud. But analyze it; it is not I, it is not you, it is always another person who is tormented. If a man says, Lo! I suffer—it is apparent that he suffers not, for grief is dumb. It is so distributed as not to destroy. That which would rend you falls on tougher textures. That which seems intolerable reproach or bereavement does not take from the accused or bereaved man or woman appetite or sleep. Some men are above grief, and some below it. Few are capable of love. In phlegmatic natures calamity is unaffecting, in shallow natures it is rhetorical. Tragedy must be somewhat which I can respect. A querulous habit is not tragedy. A panic such as frequently in ancient or savage nations put a troop or an army to flight without an enemy; a fear of ghosts;

a terror of freezing to death that seizes a man in a winter midnight on the moors; a fright at uncertain sounds heard by a family at night in the cellar or on the stairs,—are terrors that make the knees knock and the teeth clatter, but are no tragedy, any more than seasickness, which may also destroy life. It is full of illusion. As it comes, it has its support. The most exposed classes, soldiers, sailors, paupers, are nowise destitute of animal spirits. The spirit is true to itself, and finds its own support in any condition, learns to live in what is called calamity as easily as in what is called felicity; as the frailest glass bell will support a weight of a thousand pounds of water at the bottom of a river or sea, if filled with the same.

A man should not commit his tranquillity to things, but should keep as much as possible the reins in his own hands, rarely giving way to extreme emotion of joy or grief. It is observed that the earliest works of the art of sculpture are countenances of sublime tranquillity. The Egyptian sphinxes, which sit to-day as they sat when the Greek came and saw them and departed, and when the Roman came and saw them and departed, and as they will still sit when the Turk, the Frenchman and the Englishman, who visit them now, shall have passed by,—"with their stony eyes fixed on the East and on the Nile," have countenances expressive of complacency and repose, an expression of health, deserving their longevity, and verifying the primeval sentence of history on the permanency of that people, "Their strength is to sit still." To this architectural stability of the human form, the Greek genius added an ideal beauty, without disturbing the seals of serenity; permitting no violence of mirth, or wrath, or suffering. This was true to human nature. For in life, actions are few, opinions even few, prayers few; loves, hatreds, or any emissions of the soul. All that life demands of us through the greater part of the day is an equilibrium, a readiness, open eyes and ears, and free hands. Society asks this, and truth, and love, and the genius of our life. There is a fire in some men which demands an outlet in some rude action; they betray their impatience of quiet by an irregular Catilinarian gait; by irregular, faltering, disturbed speech, too emphatic for the occasion. They treat trifles with a tragic air. This is not beautiful. Could they not lay a rod or two of stone wall, and work off this superabundant irritability? When two strangers meet in the highway, what each demands of the other is that the aspect should show a firm mind, ready for any event of good or ill, prepared alike to give death or to give life, as the emergency of the next moment may require. We must walk as guests in Nature; not impassioned, but cool and disengaged. A man should try Time, and his face should wear the expression of a just judge, who has nowise made up his opinion, who fears nothing, and even hopes nothing, but who puts Nature and fortune on their merits: he will hear the case out, and then decide. For all melancholy, as all passion, belongs to the exterior life. Whilst a man is not grounded in the divine life by his proper roots, he clings by some tendrils of affection to society—mayhap to what is best and greatest in it, and in calm times it will not appear that he is adrift and not moored; but let any shock take place in society, any revolution of custom, of law, or opinion, and at once his type of permanence is shaken. The disorder of his neighbors appears to him universal disorder; chaos is come again. But in truth he was already a driving wreck before the wind arose, which only revealed to him his vagabond state. If a man is centred, men and events appear to him a fair image or reflection of that which he knoweth beforehand in himself. If any perversity or profligacy break out in society, he will join with others to avert the mischief, but it will not arouse resentment or fear, because he discerns its impassable limits. He sees already in the ebullition of sin the simultaneous redress.

Particular reliefs, also, fit themselves to human calamities; for the world will be in equilibrium, and hates all manner of exaggeration.

Time the consoler, Time the rich carrier of all changes, dries the freshest tears by obtruding new figures, new costumes, new roads, on our eye, new voices on our ear. As the west wind lifts up again the heads of the wheat which were bent down and lodged in the storm, and combs out the matted and dishevelled grass as it lay in night-locks on the ground, so we let in Time as a drying wind into the seed-field of thoughts which are dark and wet and low bent. Time restores to them temper and elasticity. How fast we forget the blow that threatened to cripple us. Nature will not sit still; the faculties will do somewhat; new hopes spring, new affections twine, and the broken is whole again.

Time consoles, but Temperament resists the impression of pain. Nature proportions her defence to the assault. Our human being is wonderfully plastic; if it cannot win this satisfaction here, it makes itself amends by running out there and winning that. It is like a stream of water, which, if dammed up on one bank, overruns the other, and flows equally at its own convenience over sand, or mud, or marble. Most suffering is only apparent. We fancy it is torture; the patient has his own compensations. A tender American girl doubts of Divine Providence whilst she reads the horrors of "the middle passage;" and they are bad enough at the mildest; but to such as she these crucifixions do not come; they come to the obtuse and barbarous, to whom they are not horrid, but only a little worse than the old sufferings. They exchange a cannibal war for the stench of the hold. They have gratifications which would be none to the civilized girl. The market-man never damned the lady because she had not paid her bill, but the stout Irishwoman has to take that once a month. She, however, never feels weakness in her back because of the slave-trade. This self-adapting strength is especially seen in disease. "It is my duty," says Sir Charles Bell, "to visit certain wards of the hospital where there is no patient admitted but with that complaint which most fills the imagination with the idea of insupportable pain and certain death. Yet these wards are not the least remarkable for the composure and cheerfulness of their inmates. The individual who suffers has a mysterious counterbalance to that condition, which, to us who look upon her, appears to be attended with no alleviating circumstance." Analogous supplies are made to those individuals whose character leads them to vast exertions of body and mind. Napoleon said to one of his friends at St. Helena, "Nature seems to have calculated that I should have great reverses to endure, for she has given me a temperament like a block of marble. Thunder cannot move it; the shaft merely glides along. The great events of my life have slipped over me without making any demand on my moral or physical nature."

The intellect is a consoler, which delights in detaching or putting an interval between a man and his fortune, and so converts the sufferer into a spectator and his pain into poetry. It yields the joys of conversation, of letters and of science. Hence also the torments of life become tuneful tragedy. solemn and soft with music, and garnished with rich dark pictures. But higher still than the activities of art, the intellect in its purity and the moral sense in its purity are not distinguished from each other, and both ravish us into a region whereunto these passionate clouds of sorrow cannot rise.

E. M. W. Tillyard: From *SHAKESPEARE'S PROBLEM PLAYS*

No single formula will cover all those works we agree to call tragic: at least three types of feeling or situation are included in the word. The first and simplest is that of mere suffering; and it has been very well set forth by J. S. Smart.[1] Suffering becomes tragic when it befalls a strong (even a momentarily strong) nature, who is not merely passive but reacts against calamity. Then "There is a sense of wonder," and the tragic victim

> contrasts the present, weighed as it is with unforeseen disaster and sorrow, with the past which has been torn from him: it seems as if the past alone had a right to exist, and the present were in some way unreal. The stricken individual marvels why his lot should be so different from that of others, what is his position among men; and what is the position of man in the universe.

This simple conception is needed because it includes certain things which we recognize as tragic but which elude any conception more rigid or more complicated. The *Trojan Women* and the *Duchess of Malfi* are tragedies of simple suffering, where the sufferers are not greatly to blame. In fact the conception resembles the simple medieval one, with the addition that the sufferer's quality of mind causes him to protest and to reflect. *Hamlet* is certainly, among other things, a tragedy of this kind. Terrible things do befall its protagonist; while as a tragic hero Hamlet lacks a complication and an enrichment common in much tragedy: that of being to some extent, even a tiny extent, responsible for his misfortunes. Othello and Samson were part responsible for theirs. Even with Desde-

[1] *Essays and Studies of the English Association,* VIII. 26.

mona and her loss of the handkerchief we think faintly that perhaps she was the kind of person who might have been so careless. No one could accuse Hamlet of being the kind of person whose mother was bound to enter into a hasty and incestuous re-marriage, of being such a prig that his mother *must* give him a shock at any cost. If you read the play with a main eye to the soliloquies, you can easily persuade yourself that *Hamlet* is principally a tragedy of this first simple kind.

The second type of tragic feeling has to do with sacrificial purgation and it is rooted in religion. The necessary parties in a sacrifice are a god, a victim, a killer, and an audience; and the aim is to rid the social organism of a taint. The audience will be most moved as the victim is or represents one of themselves. The victim may be good or bad. Shakespeare's Richard III is a perfect example of a sacrificial victim carrying the burden of his country's sins; and he is bad. Once again, *Hamlet* is tragic, and in this second way. There is something rotten in the state of Denmark, and one of its citizens, blameless hitherto and a distinguished member of society, is mysteriously called upon to be the victim by whose agency the rottenness is cut away. And when Hamlet curses the spite by which he was born to be the victim and the cure, we thrill because it might be any of us. Like the first we can make this second tragic feeling the principal thing, if we narrow our vision sufficiently. But we should be wrong, for in actual fact our sense of Denmark's rottenness is much weaker than our sense of what a lot happens there. Denmark is not at all like Macbeth's Scotland, for instance, where the social and political theme is dominant. We have the liveliest sense of Malcolm destined to rule a purged body politic; no one gives a thought to Denmark as ruled by Fortinbras.

A third kind of tragic feeling has to do with renewal consequent on destruction.[1] It occurs when there is an enlightenment and through this the assurance of a new state of being. This kind penetrates deep into our nature because it expresses not merely the tragedy of abnormal suffering but a fundamental tragic fact of all human life: namely that a good state cannot stay such but must be changed, even partially destroyed, if a succeeding good is to be engendered. This paradox of the human condition, however plain and unescapable, is hard to accept; nevertheless tragedy gives us pleasure in setting it forth and making us accept it. The usual dramatic means of fulfilling

[1]See M. Bodkin, *Archetypal Patterns in Poetry* (London, 1934), sections I and II, for this topic, psychologically elaborated.

this tragic function is through a change in the mind of the hero. His normal world has been upset, but some enlightenment has dawned, and through it, however faintly, a new order of things. Milton's Samson is for a second time reconciled to God, and this second reconciliation is other than the earlier state of friendship with God, which was destroyed. Othello is more than the stoical victim of great misfortune. He has been enlightened and though he cannot live it is a different man who dies. Those tragedies which we feel most centrally tragic contain, with other tragic conceptions, this third one.

I. A. Richards:

From *PRINCIPLES OF LITERARY CRITICISM*

What clearer instance of the "balance or reconciliation of opposite and discordant qualities" can be found than Tragedy. Pity, the impulse to approach, and Terror, the impulse to retreat, are brought in Tragedy to a reconciliation which they find nowhere else, and with them who knows what other allied groups of equally discordant impulses. Their union in an ordered single response is the *catharsis* by which Tragedy is recognized, whether Aristotle meant anything of this kind or not. This is the explanation of that sense of release, of repose in the midst of stress, of balance and composure, given by Tragedy, for there is no other way in which such impulses, once awakened, can be set at rest without suppression.

It is essential to recognize that in the full tragic experience there is no suppression. The mind does not shy away from anything, it does not protect itself with any illusion, it stands uncomforted, unintimidated, alone and self-reliant. The test of its success is whether it can face what is before it and respond to it without any of the innumerable subterfuges by which it ordinarily dodges the full development of experience. Suppressions and sublimations alike are devices by which we endeavor to avoid issues which might bewilder us. The essence of Tragedy is that it forces us to live for a moment without them. When we succeed we find, as usual, that there is no difficulty; the difficulty came from the suppressions and sublimations. The joy which is so strangely the heart of the experience is not an indication that "all's right with the world" or that "somewhere, somehow, there is Justice"; it is an indication that all is right here and now in the nervous system. Because Tragedy is the experience which most invites these subterfuges, it is the greatest and the rarest thing in literature, for the vast majority of works which pass by that name are of a different order.

Tragedy is only possible to a mind which is for the moment agnostic or Manichean. The least touch of any theology which has a compensating Heaven to offer the tragic hero is fatal. That is why *Romeo and Juliet* is not a Tragedy in the sense in which *King Lear* is.

But there is more in Tragedy than unmitigated experience. Besides Terror there is Pity, and if there is substituted for either something a little different—Horror or Dread, say, for Terror; Regret or Shame for Pity; or that kind of Pity which yields the adjective "Pitiable" in place of that which yields "Piteous"—the whole effect is altered. It is the relation between the two sets of impulses, Pity and Terror, which gives its specific character to Tragedy, and from that relation the peculiar poise of the Tragic experience springs.

The metaphor of a balance or poise will bear consideration. For Pity and Terror are opposites in a sense in which Pity and Dread are not. Dread or Horror are nearer than Terror to Pity, for they contain attraction as well as repulsion. As in color, tones just not in harmonic relation are peculiarly unmanageable and jarring, so it is with these more easily describable responses. The extraordinarily stable experience of Tragedy, which is capable of admitting almost any other impulses so long as the relation of the main components is exactly right, changes at once if these are altered. Even if it keeps its coherence it becomes at once a far narrower, more limited, and exclusive thing, a much more partial, restricted and specialized response. Tragedy is perhaps the most general, all-accepting, all-ordering experience known. It can take anything into its organization, modifying it so that it finds a place. It is invulnerable; there is nothing which does not present to the tragic attitude *when fully developed* a fitting aspect and only a fitting aspect. Its sole rivals in this respect are the attitudes of Falstaff and of the Voltaire of *Candide*. But pseudo-tragedy—the greater part of Greek Tragedy as well as almost all Elizabethan Tragedy outside Shakespeare's six masterpieces comes under this head—is one of the most fragile and precarious of attitudes. Parody easily overthrows it, the ironic addition paralyzes it; even a mediocre joke may make it look lopsided and extravagant.

Joseph Wood Krutch:

From *THE TRAGIC FALLACY*

Tragedy, said Aristotle, is the "imitation of noble actions," and though it is some twenty-five hundred years since the dictum was uttered there is only one respect in which we are inclined to modify it. To us "imitation" seems a rather naïve word to apply to that process by which observation is turned into art, and we seek one which would define or at least imply the nature of that interposition of the personality of the artist between the object and the beholder which constitutes his function and by means of which he transmits a modified version, rather than a mere imitation, of the thing which he has contemplated.

In the search for this word the estheticians of romanticism invented the term "expression" to describe the artistic purpose to which apparent imitation was subservient. Psychologists, on the other hand, feeling that the artistic process was primarily one by which reality is modified in such a way as to render it more acceptable to the desires of the artist, employed various terms in the effort to describe that distortion which the wish may produce in vision. And though many of the newer critics reject both romanticism and psychology, even they insist upon the fundamental fact that in art we are concerned, not with mere imitation, but with the imposition of some form upon the material which it would not have if it were merely copied as a camera copies.

Tragedy is not, then, as Aristotle said, the *imitation* of noble actions, for, indeed, no one knows what a *noble* action is or whether or not such a thing as nobility exists in nature apart from the mind of man. Certainly the action of Achilles in dragging the dead body of Hector around the walls of Troy and under the eyes of Andromache, who had begged to be allowed to give it decent burial, is not to us a noble action, though it was such to Homer, who made it the subject of a noble passage in a noble poem. Certainly, too, the same action might conceivably be made the subject of a tragedy and the subject of a farce, depending upon the way in which it was treated; so that to say that tragedy is the *imitation* of a *noble* action is to be guilty of assuming, first, that art and photography are the same, and, second, that there may be something inherently noble in an act as distinguished from the motives which prompted it or from the point of view from which it is regarded.

And yet, nevertheless, the idea of nobility is inseparable from the idea of tragedy, which cannot exist without it. If tragedy is not the imitation or even the modified representation of noble actions it is certainly a representation of actions *considered* as noble, and herein lies its essential nature, since no man can conceive it unless he is capable of believing in the greatness and importance of man. Its action is usually, if not always, calamitous, because it is only in calamity that the human spirit has the opportunity to reveal itself triumphant over the outward universe which fails to conquer it; but this calamity in tragedy is only a means to an end, and the essential thing which distinguishes real tragedy from those distressing modern works sometimes called by its name is the fact that it is in the former alone that the artist has found himself capable of considering and of making us consider that his people and his actions have that amplitude and importance which make them noble. Tragedy arises then when, as in Periclean Greece or Elizabethan England, a people fully aware of the calamities of life is nevertheless serenely confident of the greatness of man, whose mighty passions and supreme fortitude are revealed when one of these calamities overtakes him.

To those who mistakenly think of it as something gloomy or depressing, who are incapable of recognizing the elation which its celebration of human greatness inspires, and who, therefore, confuse it with things merely miserable or pathetic, it must be a paradox that the happiest, most vigorous, and most confident ages which the world has ever known—the Periclean and the Elizabethan—should be exactly those which created and which most relished the mightiest tragedies; but the paradox is, of course, resolved by the fact that tragedy is essentially an expression, not of despair, but of the triumph over despair and of confidence in the value of human life. If Shakespeare himself ever had that "dark period" which his critics and biographers have imagined for him, it was at least no darkness like that bleak and arid despair which sometimes settles over modern spirits. In the midst of it he created both the elemental grandeur of Othello and the pensive majesty of Hamlet and, holding them up to his contemporaries, he said in the words of his own Miranda, "Oh, brave new world that has *such* creatures in't."

All works of art which deserve their name have a happy end. This is indeed the thing which constitutes them art and through which they perform their function. Whatever the character of the events, fortunate or unfortunate, which they recount, they so mold or arrange or interpret them that we accept gladly the conclusion which they reach and would not have it otherwise. They may conduct us into the realm of pure fancy where wish and fact are identical and the world is remade exactly after the fashion of the heart's desire or they may yield some greater or less allegiance to fact; but they must always reconcile us in one way or another to the representation which they make and the distinctions between the genres are simply the distinctions between the means by which this reconciliation is effected. Comedy laughs the minor mishaps of its characters away; drama solves all the difficulties which it allows to arise; and melodrama, separating good from evil by simple lines, distributes its rewards and punishments in accordance with the principles of a naïve justice which satisfies the simple souls of its audience, which are neither philosophical enough to question its primitive ethics nor critical enough to object to the way in which its neat events violate the laws of probability. Tragedy, the greatest and the most difficult of the arts, can adopt none of these methods; and yet it must reach its own happy end in its own way. Though its conclusion must be, by its premise, outwardly calamitous, though it must speak to those who know that the good man is cut off and that the fairest things are the first to perish, yet it must leave them, as *Othello* does, content that this is so. We must be and we are glad that Juliet dies and glad that Lear is turned out into the storm.

Milton set out, he said, to justify the ways of God to man, and his phrase, if it be interpreted broadly enough, may be taken as describing the function of all art, which must, in some way or other, make the life which it seems to represent satisfactory to those who see its reflection in the magic mirror, and it must gratify or at least reconcile the desires of the beholder, not necessarily, as the naïver exponents of Freudian psychology maintain, by gratifying individual and often eccentric wishes, but at least by satisfying the universally human desire to find in the world some justice, some meaning, or, at the very least, some recognizable order. Hence it is that every real tragedy, however tremendous it may be, is an affirmation of faith in life, a declaration that even if God is not in his Heaven, then at least Man is in his world.

We accept gladly the outward defeats which it describes for the sake of the inward victories which it reveals. Juliet died, but not before she had shown how great and resplendent a thing love could be; Othello plunged the dagger into his own breast, but not before he had revealed the greatness of soul which makes his death seem unimportant. Had he died in the instant when he struck the blow, had he perished still believing that the world was as completely black as he saw it before the innocence of Desdemona was revealed to him, then, for him at least, the world would have been merely damnable, but Shakespeare kept him alive long enough to allow him to learn his error and hence to die, not in despair, but in the full acceptance of the tragic reconciliation to life. Perhaps it would be pleasanter if men could believe what the child is taught—that the good are happy and that things turn out as they should—but it is far more important to be able to believe, as Shakespeare did, that however much things in the outward world may go awry, man has, nevertheless, splendors of his own and that, in a word, Love and Honor and Glory are not words but realities.

Thus for the great ages tragedy is not an expression of despair but the means by which they saved themselves from it. It is a profession of faith, and a sort of religion; a way of looking at life by virtue of which it is robbed of its pain. The sturdy soul of the tragic author seizes upon suffering and uses it only as a means by which joy may be wrung out of existence, but it is not to be forgotten that he is enabled to do so only because of his belief in the greatness of human nature and because, though he has lost the child's faith in life, he has not lost his far more important faith in human nature. A tragic writer does not have to believe in God, but he must believe in man.

And if, then, the Tragic Spirit is in reality the product of a religious faith in which, sometimes at least, faith in the greatness of God is replaced by faith in the greatness of man, it serves, of course, to perform the function of religion, to make life tolerable for those who participate in its beneficent illusion. It purges the souls of those who might otherwise despair and it makes endurable the realization that the events of the outward world do not correspond with the desires of the heart, and, thus, in its own particular way, it does what all religions do, for it gives a rationality, a meaning, and a justification to the universe. But if it has the strength it has also the weakness of all faiths, since it may—nay, it must—be ultimately lost as reality, encroaching further and further into the realm of imagination, leaves less and less room in which that imagination can build its refuge.

A NOTE ON THE GREEK THEATER

The Greek drama developed from Greek religion and was never completely separated from it. Its origins are obscure, but, according to Aristotle, it evolved from the choral lyric or early dithyramb, which was sung and danced in honor of Dionysus, a Greek nature god associated with spring, fertility, regeneration, and especially wine. This early hymn was sung by a chorus dressed as satyrs, creatures half human and half animal. Aristotle suggests that tragedy evolved from this satyr dithyramb, and though the two seem to be dissimilar, no more convincing explanation accounts for the origin of tragedy. In the satyric dithyramb the chorus presumably engaged in dialogue with the chorus leader, and perhaps at some point in history the leader, instead of narrating events, impersonated some traditional hero. With such impersonation drama begins.

The sixth-century B.C. playwright, Thespis, none of whose dramas survive, is said to have introduced into the framework of chorus and leader the first actor, and Aeschylus, probably Greece's first great dramatist, introduced, in the following century, the second actor. Sophocles added a third, but it should be noted that one actor could play several succeeding roles; thus, in an early Aeschylean drama there are only two speakers (apart from the chorus and its leader) on stage at any given time, but the list of characters may be as many as three or four. Furthermore, "mutes"—non-speaking actors—were employed, so a drama with only two speaking actors might represent, with the aid of a mute, a scene calling for three figures. The leader of the chorus sometimes engaged in dialogue with the actors, thereby making the limited number of speaking actors more flexible than, at first sight, it might seem.

The dramatic chorus, an outgrowth of the original dithyramb, was reduced from fifty to twelve by Aeschylus, and then increased to fifteen by Sophocles. Although in some plays it seems to be an encumbrance, it often performs several important dramatic functions. For example, it sometimes (through its leader) adds an actor to the scene; often (notably when it admires and yet pities the hero) it represents the emotions of the average spectator, thus supplying a link between audience and actors. And it can also be used to inform the audience of the antecedent action, to comment on the present action, or to supply lyric interludes.

By the time of Thespis, presumably, the stories dramatized were not necessarily connected with the legends of Dionysus, but attendance at the theater was still a kind of religious observance, and not until much later did the drama lose contact with life and become something for books. As Ivor Brown, a contemporary English dramatic critic, has noted, the history of the Greek theater is a movement from riot to rite to writing.

By 534 B.C. Athens held a formal dramatic festival wherein playwrights competed for prizes. Drama in Athens, being connected with religion, was not a daily event but was confined to two holidays, the *Lenaea* (Festival of the Wine Press), and, more important, the *Greater* or *City Dionysia*. The Lenaea occurred in January or February, the City Dionysia occurred in March or April. The latter festival lasted five or six days, and on each of the last three mornings a tragic dramatist presented three tragedies and one satyr-play. These three dramatists were selected well in advance by a magistrate who probably scrutinized drafts of numerous plays, and their works were financed partly by the state and partly by wealthy citizens whom the state honored by ordering them to assist in the subsidy. The playwright also wrote the music, supervised the production, and sometimes acted. Since the three competing poets had already been screened, each was awarded a prize, but the first prize (money and a garland) was of course most esteemed, and to win a third prize was at times a dubious honor.

Some Greek theaters were enormous, holding as many as 16,000 spectators. Built along the side of a hill, the theater was an open-air semicircle, with the actors performing at the foot and the spectators sitting in tiers ascending the hillside. In the center of the first row a throne was reserved for the priest of Dionysus, and facing him on the level ground was an altar—which sometimes served as a theatrical prop. Behind the actors was the *skene,* or scene-building, which probably served as a dressing room before the performance and as a background during the performance. This building would suggest to the audience who saw the actors against it a palace or temple, and movable panels with landscape paintings were sometimes placed between the columns if another set was needed. Equally important, this wall helped to provide good acoustics, for speech travels well if there is a solid barrier behind the speaker and a hard, smooth surface in front of him, and if the audience sits in tiers. The wall of the scene-building provided the barrier; surrounding the altar a smooth place for choral dancing, called the orchestra, provided the surface in front of the actors; and the seats on the hill fulfilled the third demand. Furthermore, the acoustics were somewhat improved by slightly elevating the actors above the orchestra, but it is not known exactly when this platform was constructed in front of the scene-building.

The actors were masked, perhaps to suggest their essential character to the most distant spectator. Thus, a performer might wear a mask whose bold outlines suggested a king, or an old man, or a servant. Costumes were colorful and the actors may have worn thick-soled shoes to elevate them, though this special boot seems to have postdated the great dramas of Aeschylus, Sophocles, and Euripides in the fifth century B.C. Two pieces of stage equipment are worth mentioning: the "machine" and the *eccyclema*. The former was a derrick or crane which could suspend an actor impersonating a deity. Because the god was sometimes introduced to resolve a plot arbitrarily, the phrase *deus ex machina* (a god from a machine) has come to mean an unsatisfactory resolution, especially through some contraption—perhaps a long-lost letter, or the discovery of a gold mine. The *eccyclema* seems to have been a wheeled platform which was thrust out from the scene-building and conventionally indicated to the audience that the scene acted upon it was to be understood as occurring indoors.

Finally we should note the structure of a Greek play. Generally a Greek tragedy begins with a speech by an actor or a piece of dialogue, known as a "prologue"; then the chorus enters singing and dancing (the *parodos*); this is followed by four or five dialogues between the actors, called "episodes," which alternate with choral odes. Each ode is a *stasimon,* and the chorus' final departure is the *exodos*. The total result of combining speech with singing and dancing would be a sort of music-drama roughly akin to opera with some spoken words, such as Mozart's *Magic Flute*. It is a tribute to the greatness of the poetic dramatists that although we can no longer hear their plays with the appropriate music, or witness the graceful dancing and colorful costumes, we nevertheless derive from the texts an insight into some of the greatest achievements of antiquity.

BIBLIOGRAPHY

The following books represent a highly readable fraction of the enormous literature on the subject.

GENERAL

Banham, Martin. *The Cambridge Guide to Theatre* (1995)
Bennett, Susan. *Theatre Audiences: A Theory of Production and Reception* (1990)
Brooks, Cleanth, ed. *Tragic Themes in Western Literature* (1955)
Clark, Barrett H., ed. *European Theories of the Drama*, rev. ed. (1947)
Fergusson, Francis. *The Idea of a Theater: A Study of Ten Plays* (1949)
Henn, Thomas R. *The Harvest of Tragedy* (1956)
Jaspers, Karl. *Tragedy Is Not Enough*, trans. by Harold A. T. Reiche (1952)
Langer, Susanne K. *Feeling and Form* (1953)
Lucas, Frank L. *Tragedy: Serious Drama in Relation to Aristotle's Poetics*, rev. and enl. ed. (1957)
Muller, Herbert J. *The Spirit of Tragedy* (1956)
Nicoll, Allardyce. *The Theory of the Drama* (1931)
Pottle, Frederick A. "Catharsis," *Yale Review*, 40 (Summer 1951): 621–41
Thompson, Alan Reynolds. *The Dry Mock: A Study of Irony in Drama* (1948)
Weisinger, Herbert. *Tragedy and the Paradox of the Fortunate Fall* (1953)

THE GREEKS

Dodds, E. R. "Euripides the Irrationalist," *Classical Review*, 43 (1929): 97–104
Else, Gerald. *The Origin and Early Form of Greek Tragedy* (1965)
Fergusson, Francis. *The Idea of a Theater: A Study of Ten Plays* (1949)
Gagarin, Michael. *Aeschylean Drama* (1976)
Greene, William Chase. *Moira* (1944)
Grube, G. M. A. *The Drama of Euripides* (1941)
Hamilton, Edith. *The Greek Way* (1949)
Jaeger, Werner, *Paideia: the Ideals of Greek Culture*, 2nd ed., trans. by Gilbert Highet. Vol. I (1945)
Kitto, H. D. F. *Greek Tragedy*, 2nd rev. ed. (1950)
Knox, Bernard M. *Oedipus at Thebes* (1957)
Michelini, Ann N. *Euripides and the Tragic Tradition* (1987)
Rosenmeyer, Thomas G. *The Art of Aeschylus* (1982)
Segal, Erich, ed. *Greek Tragedy: Modern Essays in Criticism* (1983)
Thomson, George. *Aeschylus and Athens* (1941)
Waldock, A. J. A. *Sophocles the Dramatist* (1951)
Whitman, Cedric H. *Sophocles* (1951)

SHAKESPEARE

Bradley, A. C. *Shakespearean Tragedy* (1949)
Danby, John F. *Shakespeare's Doctrine of Nature: A Study of King Lear* (1949)
Danson, Lawrence, ed. *On King Lear* (1981)
Empson, William. *The Structure of Complex Words* (1951)
Granville-Barker, Harley. *Prefaces to Shakespeare*, Vol. I (1947)
Heilman, Robert Bechtold. *This Great Stage: Image and Structure in King Lear* (1948)

Lusardi, James P., and June Schlueter. *Reading Shakespeare in Performance: King Lear* (1991)
Mack, Maynard. *King Lear in Our Time* (1965)
Rosenberg, Marvin. *The Masks of King Lear* (1972)

IBSEN

Bentley, Eric. *In Search of Theater* (1953)
———, *The Playwright as Thinker* (1946)
Bradbrook, M. C. *Ibsen: The Norwegian* (1947)
Fergusson, Francis. *The Idea of Theater: A Study of Ten Plays* (1949)
Hardwick, Elizabeth. *Seduction and Betrayal: Women and Literature* (1974)
Marker, Frederick J., and Lise-Lone Marker. *Ibsen's Lively Art: A Performance Study of the Major Plays* (1989)
Northam, John. *Ibsen's Dramatic Method: A Study of the Prose Dramas* (1953)
Shaw, George Bernard. *The Quintessence of Ibsenism* (1913)

STRINDBERG

Cargill, Oscar. *Intellectual America: Ideas on the March* (1942)
Carlson, Harry G. *Strindberg and the Poetry of Myth* (1982)
McGill, Vivian J. *August Strindberg, the Bedevilled Viking* (1930)
Mortensen, Brita, and Brian W. Downs. *Strindberg: An Introduction to His Life and Work* (1949)
Sprigge, Elizabeth. *The Strange Life of August Strindberg* (1949)
Sprinchorn, Evert. *Strindberg as Dramatist* (1982)

YEATS

Bentley, Eric. *In Search of Theater* (1953)
Bjersby, Birgit. *The Interpretation of the Cuchulain Legend in the Works of W. B. Yeats* (1950)
Ellis-Fermor, Una M. *The Irish Dramatic Movement*, 2nd ed. (1954)
Ellmann, Richard. *Yeats: The Man and the Masks* (1948)
Flannery, James W. *W. B. Yeats and the Idea of a Theatre* (1976)
Jeffares, A. Norman, and A. S. Knowland. *A Commentary on the Collected Plays of W. B. Yeats* (1975)
Miller, Liam. *The Noble Drama of W. B. Yeats* (1977)
Peacock, Ronald. *The Poet in the Theatre* (1946)

O'NEILL

Bogard, Travis. *Contour in Time: The Plays of Eugene O'Neill*, rev. ed. (1988)
Cargill, Oscar. *Intellectual America: Ideas on the March* (1942)
Engel, Edwin. *The Haunted Heroes of Eugene O'Neill* (1953)
Gelb, Arthur, and Barbara Gelb. *O'Neill*, enlarged ed. (1987)